SURVEY OF WORLD CULTURES

Donald N. Wilber

Pakistan

its people   its society   its culture

in collaboration with

DONALD ATWELL   LELAH DUSHKIN   HENRY GOODNOW
RUTH HORINE   MUHAMMAD HUSSAIN   MARY JEAN KENNEDY
ALICE TYRNER   STANLEY MARON   THOMAS WISE

HRAF PRESS
NEW HAVEN

Already Published in This Series

PUBLISHER'S NOTE

A NONPROFIT CORPORATION founded in 1949 to collect, organize, and distribute information of significance to the natural and social sciences and humanities, the Human Relations Area Files is today supported by twenty-three member universities and research organizations here and abroad. The research program is centered on the continuing development and expansion of a unique system for codification of basic source materials to facilitate cross-cultural research. Corollary programs have included the compilation of bibliographies, the translation of foreign sources, and the preparation of comprehensive country handbooks. To implement the policy of making important research materials more readily available, a publication program was initiated. As the demand for the first small editions of translations, monographs, and bibliographies grew, publishing activities were extended and given a separate identity as the Human Relations Area Files Press.

HRAF Press publishes seven different series of books at present, including this series of new country studies. The purpose of the *Survey of World Cultures*, of which *Pakistan* is the thirteenth in the series, is to bring together in one comprehensive volume all those aspects of a country and culture—geography, history, government, politics, economics, sociology, art—usually scattered among a variety of sources. Each book represents a collation and synthesis of the best and most authoritative materials available on the country, including foreign and unpublished information. It is hoped that this series will in some measure help to meet the need for better understanding of other peoples in an increasingly interdependent world community.

PREFACE

PAKISTAN is a new nation, faced with the difficult problem of establishing and maintaining national unity. Favoring such effort are the facts that the great majority of its population is of the Moslem faith and that these people take pride in the history and cultural traditions of the centuries in which Moslems dominated the Indian subcontinent. Serious obstacles to such effort include the regional rivalries resulting from gross discrepancies in language, ethnic stock, and way of life between the peoples of West Pakistan and East Pakistan, and a decade of strife and contention inspired by rival politicians and religious leaders. In this first decade of the country's history, political and social institutions modeled on those of the West, more specifically those of British India, failed to mature. Since President Muhammad Ayub Khan came to power at the end of October 1958, efforts have been made to make such institutions more reflective of public needs and aspirations and to encourage public participation, while protecting this same public against exploitation by individuals, groups, and special interests. However, a stable democracy is not yet assured and the goal of creating a social welfare state remains a distant one.

Plagued, as is India, by problems of overpopulation and under-production, Pakistan has made remarkable progress in implementing sound economic planning, especially in the development of industry. In the field of foreign relations, an initial inclination toward neutrality was replaced by a policy of alignment with the Western powers as sources of military aid and financial assistance. Currently there is a shift toward a more independent policy, expressed in a cultivation of friendly relations with the Communist bloc.

This volume represents an extensive revision of the *Area Handbook on Pakistan,* issued by HRAF in June 1958 in a very limited number of copies as a reference work, and it differs in a number of respects from the earlier study. In view of the emphasis in the present series on producing comprehensive, reliable works for the general reader, the present text is considerably shorter and contains less specialized material than its predecessor. It has been extensively rewritten and reorganized, while the material on such subjects as the financial and economic situation, internal political and social developments, and foreign relations has been brought up to date through 1962 and into 1963.

In the course of a trip to Pakistan in late 1962 I received invaluable assistance and support in the collection of source material from the Press Information Department and from the Department of Films and Publications. Professor Aftab Ahmad Khan, Chief Economist, Planning Commission, offered helpful advice with regard to the chapters on the economics and finances of Pakistan. The task of updating these same chapters was entrusted to Muhammad Hussain, Research Officer, Planning Commission, with eminently satisfactory results. In addition, officers of the Embassy of Pakistan in Washington displayed a continuing interest in supplying statistical and topical information.

DONALD N. WILBER

December 1963
Princeton, New Jersey

A NOTE ON NOMENCLATURE

THE TRANSLITERATION of place names, personal names, and descriptive terms from languages written in the Arabic script, such as Urdu and Persian, offered serious problems. For the sake of consistency, all place names follow the usage of the United States Board on Geographic Names Gazetteer No. 67 (1962). In the transliteration of personal names an effort was made to approach uniformity within a system based on that employed by the Library of Congress. However, the fact that the English language has so long played a prominent role in the subcontinent works against any solution of this problem. On the one hand, names of rulers and of dynasties are familiar in transliterations employed by historians in forms which are not standardized. On the other hand, political and intellectual leaders often made purely personal choices in transliterating their own names into English. In a number of cases such forms have been retained, for example, Mahomed 'Ali Jinnah rather than Muhammad 'Ali Jinnah.

The fact that family names are not in general use in Pakistan gives rise to problems in the indexing of personal names. In general, names are indexed as they are said, or read, but some exceptions have been made in cases where the final element of the name has acquired the significance of a family name.

CONTENTS

Contents (*continued*)

LIST OF PLATES

LIST OF TABLES

List of Tables (*continued*)

Pakistan

CHAPTER *1*

The Culture and the Society

WHEN THE BRITISH SURRENDERED CONTROL of the Indian subcontinent in 1947, the non-Moslem-majority areas became the independent nation of India, while most of the Moslem-majority areas successfully pressed for a separate sovereignty. The new nation of Pakistan consisted of two widely separated areas on opposite sides of India. Many differences characterize the two, but the people had in common the religion of Islam, the traditions and institutions of British government in India, and a desire not to remain a minority in an independent India.

Although many political and economic factors were involved in the movement leading to the creation of the Republic of Pakistan, the uniqueness of Islam and its adherents was the rallying point for mass support. As expressed by the "Father of Pakistan," Mahomed 'Ali Jinnah, the Moslems of India constituted a nation by virtue of their religion and as such were entitled to a separate sovereign state. What Jinnah contemplated was a state in which Moslems could rule themselves and follow their own way of life. It is this justification for the existence of Pakistan that is found most often in the statements of the educated leaders of the country and to a degree is reflected in the sentiment of the masses.

The ideal Moslem society is one in which religious and temporal authority are united so that the state is the instrument of the religious law revealed in the Qur'an. A devout Moslem follows certain customs and practices which have been set forth in codes handed down from the earliest followers of Muhammad. Religion is a pervasive influence in most aspects of life in Pakistan. It influences diet, marriage customs, education, and the celebration of festivals and holidays and is an important consideration in the country's foreign relations and internal politics.

In spite of the emphasis in the teachings of Islam on the brotherhood of believers, the effect of the religion has not always been a unifying one. Islam has no priestly hierarchy which can settle religious disputes. There are several different sects and some of the most violent riots in Pakistan's short history resulted from the attempt of the majority sect to brand the members of another sect as infidels to be excluded from public office. Nor has the bond of a common religion been sufficient to ensure good relations between East and West Pakistan. Indeed, it has had little effect in reducing the antagonisms even among the various linguistic groups in West Pakistan. Since there is a sizable Hindu minority in East Pakistan, the politicians there do not emphasize religion to the same extent as in West Pakistan, where ambitious politicians presented their followers as representing the true party of Islam.

The emphasis in Islamic doctrine and practice on the community of all Moslems has produced both a sense of identity with Moslem countries in the rest of the world and the drive for national expression in the state of Pakistan. These crosscurrents are reflected in the country's relations with the nations of the Middle East. Its large size and Islamic origins suggest a role of leadership among the nations of the Moslem world, but in this Pakistan has been rebuffed. National self-interest among these states has on more than one occasion in recent years clashed with pan-Islamic sentiment.

The crosscurrents of nationalism and Islam have also been responsible for internal tensions. This is well illustrated by the fact that more than eight years were required to frame a constitution that was satisfactory to the majority of the country's legislators. Many economic and political problems also faced the constituent assembly, but the question of the role of Islam in the newly created state was a fundamental issue. As finally accepted, the 1956 constitution did not resolve the issue. Basically it represented a compromise, leaving many of the controversial points to be settled at a later date, and the 1962 constitution also avoided the fundamental issue.

Land and Cultivation

West Pakistan, like most of Southwest Asia, consists of semiarid plains and rugged mountains. Viewed from the air it is brown and barren; one-fifth of the land is cultivated and more than three-quarters of this is irrigated. The distribution of its population, which is overwhelmingly Moslem, is determined primarily by the availability of water.

East Pakistan is one-sixth the size of West Pakistan but much more densely and evenly populated. In topography, climate, and area it is roughly comparable to the State of Louisiana. As in the rest of Southeast Asia the land is green and the rainfall abundant.

Both in area and population Pakistan exceeds in size any European country except Russia and is the seventh most populous country in the world.

Despite the recent emphasis on industrial development, the economy of the country is primarily agricultural. The methods of cultivation, judged in terms of output, are extremely inefficient. Oxen are generally the only source of power available to the cultivator. Little or no fertilizer or improved seed is used. The fields are fragmented into tiny plots, frequently smaller than a quarter of an acre, and are separated by low earthen ridges which help to channel the irrigation water during the dry season. On most of the land in East Pakistan, jute and rice are under cultivation; in West Pakistan, where agriculture is primarily limited to the irrigated areas near the Indus river and its tributaries, the principal crops are wheat, cotton, and sugar cane.

Although the pattern varies, about half of the cultivated land is tilled by those who have some rights in the land, while the rest belongs to the large landowners. The intensive pressure on the arable land grows even greater as the population steadily increases by more than a million persons each year. In both West and East Pakistan, land reform legislation of recent date has sharply curtailed the influence of the landlords.

Village and City

Most of East Pakistan is lush and green and covered by a network of streams and canals. Much of the land is flat and is flooded annually during the period of heavy monsoon rainfall. Families generally live in bamboo huts on some slight rise in the ground near the land they till, with related families similarly situated nearby. Although most of East Pakistan is densely settled there are relatively few towns with any substantial concentration of population. Communication is poor and during the rainy season a boat is the feasible method of local transportation in much of the province.

3

In normal times the people lead a self-sufficient and isolated existence. Regional differences exist but are less pronounced than in West Pakistan because Bengali is spoken throughout East Pakistan.

In West Pakistan villages are larger and more clearly demarcated —except in the Sind area where the sharecroppers move periodically in accordance with the practice of cultivating different areas in different years. Along the western borders there are militant tribes who have long regarded any constituted authority with suspicion. Allegiance is felt only to their own tribe and tribal chief. Villages in this area retain the walls formerly constructed for defense purposes and look more like a series of forts than dwelling places.

In 1961 only 5.2 per cent of the people in East Pakistan lived in urban areas containing more than 5,000 population, and only four cities had a population of more than 100,000 persons; in West Pakistan there were twelve such urban centers. The institutions of higher learning, the intellectual and professional classes, and the bulk of the commercial and industrial enterprises are concentrated in these urban areas. This is where the villager comes in search of employment and where the twentieth century has its greatest impact—creating a ferment of dislocations, anxieties, and change. The more turbulent political demonstrations have occurred in the cities, with the students invariably playing an active role. Each city has its congested areas, its commercial center where handmade native articles are sold in open stalls alongside rather cheaply made mass production goods, its movie houses and tearooms, its overloaded buses, and a variety of other forms of transportation which may include donkey carts and camel wagons, bicycle rickshaws, horse-drawn tongas, and trucks and automobiles. By contrast the rural villages seem to live in the quiet atmosphere of the previous centuries; the women fill their pots at the village well or pond; the older men weave, or smoke a hookah; the younger men work in the fields.

Status and Security

The importance placed on one's rank in society may well be directly related to the question of security. Most of Pakistan's population is engaged in a virtual struggle for survival. When the harvests are poor, there is not enough food to go around. There are many applicants for every unskilled job. Pakistan was born amidst turmoil and loss of life and property. Under such conditions, the main object in life is to achieve security for oneself and one's family. Initiative is dangerous—it may offend a superior and endanger one's career. Caution and conformity are the rule.

The Moslems of Pakistan adhere to the religious teaching that all believers are equal in the sight of Allah, but in ordinary social matters they are highly conscious of difference in rank and prestige. All menial tasks or manual labor is performed by servants or by people with a very low rank in society. A cook is not willing to do the work of a "sweeper" lest he lose "face." A professional man avoids clerical work lest others misjudge his true position. Similarly it is very difficult to rise above one's accepted station in life. The higher civil services are virtually closed to those who are in clerical services. The difference in status between the professionally trained person and the manual worker or mechanic is so great that communication between them is difficult—a situation that raises many problems of an administrative nature in the numerous development projects where the training of unskilled workers to perform new tasks is an essential part of the professional worker's job.

For most Pakistanis the family is the only real source of security. It is the fundamental social and economic unit. A family is usually a fairly large group that includes the families of sons, widowed sisters, and other relatives. In time of sickness or other misfortune, the home is the place of refuge and comfort. Its reputation and status are important especially when the time comes to arrange a marriage, and loyalty to and identity with the family is very intense.

As the undisputed head of the family, the father is responsible for earning a living, protecting the family, and arranging the marriage of his daughters. In general he is the one who must make the many outside contacts, as the women are expected to remain in seclusion as much as possible. His children are trained to give respect and implicit obedience. A person brought up under this rather rigid system with its overtones of authoritarianism generally lacks any training in responsibility. In adult life this early pattern contributes to acceptance of authority to the detriment of individual initiative and belief in the effectiveness of collective effort.

The Elite and the Masses

In form, Pakistan is a democracy; in practice, it is an oligarchy. The ruling groups—civil servants, politicians, lawyers, and a few

5

industrialists, educators, and military officers—have much in common. All can speak English and are familiar with English law, history, and customs; most have been educated in England. Members of this ruling class tend to have a secular rather than a religious or parochial approach to most important problems and are characterized by a vested interest in the success, stability, and permanence of Pakistan. Most live well, travel widely, and have several servants. Perhaps one person in ten thousand will be a member of this influential group.

There is another educated class in Pakistan, considerably larger in size, that does not live so well. The majority are clerks who work in the cities and whose low income barely suffices to pay the costs of an urban existence in a period of slowly rising prices. Petty officials, school teachers, and small shopkeepers also belong to this class, which comprises between 1 and 2 per cent of the working population.

The overwhelming proportion of Pakistan's citizens are in a third category. They strive merely to exist. They till the soil, perform menial and manual tasks of all kinds, live in an isolated village or an urban slum, visit the mosque and the bazaar, and pass their days in the customary pattern of family and village existence. They accept guidance from those more fortunate but except in times of illness or famine rarely seek such guidance. Their way of life has not changed appreciably through the centuries, nor is it likely to change in the immediate future. Their primary concern is obtaining food, water, a small quantity of cloth, and shelter from the weather.

Both the first and the third groups are conservative, for different reasons: the first group has a vested interest in things as they are; the third group is too concerned with survival and too ignorant and isolated to press for change. Any radical political movements would probably get the most sympathetic hearing from those in the second category, which is restive and dissatisfied but not yet politically powerful.

To raise the living standards of the masses requires the greatest diligence and patience on the part of those who direct and operate the government, industry, and educational institutions. The country's resources are marginal at best. There is a shortage of skilled personnel of all types, yet those who are skilled often fail to find suitable jobs. There are signs that too few fully understand the importance of acting in "the public interest." Pakistan's future status as a nation may largely depend on the ability of those in positions of influence to place the public interest first even though it may conflict with their immediate personal interests and security.

Role of the Government

For nearly a century the area which is now Pakistan was governed by a corps of British civil servants. The essence of British administration in the Indian subcontinent was firm control exercised by a small number of well-qualified persons placed in key positions throughout the country. In the decades immediately preceding partition a considerable number of Indians were taken into the higher civil services. Except for the withdrawal of most of the British personnel, the system of administration in Pakistan after independence changed very little. The most important positions of administrative control are still held by a few hundred officers in the higher civil services who are normally recruited by a competitive examination of university graduates. These civil servants are assigned to all parts of the country and are made directly responsible for law and order in their area of jurisdiction. In emergencies they can call on the police and even the armed forces for assistance in maintaining the peace.

Although Pakistan has a democratic federal constitution of the parliamentary type with a president, the political forces themselves are unstable. In the absence of either a majority political party or a cohesive coalition of parties, the president and the bureaucracy control the country.

Pakistan is endeavoring to establish an economic system based on private enterprise, but the government takes the initiative in matters of industrial development and through many controls, especially on imports and exports, can exert a decisive influence. The five-year plans and the constitution both commit Pakistan to "welfare state" policies. Nevertheless the society as a whole appears to be essentially conservative and noncompetitive, with active concern for the country's many problems a new development among government personnel and the small educated minority.

The country's leaders are, in general, internationally minded and since 1947 Pakistan has been extremely active in the field of diplomacy. To some extent this was forced by the conflict with India over Kashmir—which tended to make Pakistan well aware of the importance of having friendly nations to support its position. Receipt of large amounts of foreign aid, both economic and military, have had a similar effect.

National Attitudes

In the light of the comparatively brief history of Pakistan, it is not surprising that basic national attitudes have developed slowly. The natural order of identification for Pakistanis still begins with the family, and this primary loyalty is stronger there than in most Western countries. From his family, a man's loyalty extends, in diminishing degree, to his lineage, his ethnic group, and perhaps to the worldwide community of Islam. Similarly, there is usually a strong sense of loyalty to the home village—a loyalty that extends to the district and thence, at times, to the linguistic region. Loyalty to the state of Pakistan is a totally new concept which would logically fall somewhere between the ethnic and pan-Islamic loyalties. It is a strange, new, Western kind of loyalty which Pakistanis, especially the older generation, find difficult to understand. In this connection partition and the great hardships that had to be overcome in order to keep Pakistan intact have worked as an educative process providing a common experience and a body of legend in which Pakistanis feel fierce pride. Accomplishments in the form of new industries established since partition, the status of Pakistan's armed forces, and even Pakistani successes in international sports events have provided another source of inspiration for this new kind of nationalism. With constant reiteration in schools and on national holidays of the necessity for loyalty to Pakistan, the new generation may in time develop a deeper loyalty to Pakistan, in addition to the traditional loyalties.

National symbols are expected to aid in the strengthening of public loyalty to the state. During the years of the struggle for independence members of the All-India Moslem League displayed green flags with crescents and stars of various sizes, often in different places on the field. From these prototypes came the present flag of the country: a white crescent and star on a green ground alongside a white stripe.

The color green has long been associated with Islam and appears in the flags of most Moslem countries. The green in the Pakistani flag is, therefore, symbolic of the Moslem population. The white crescent and star in the green are also ancient Islamic symbols and have been given a place on the flag because of their appeal to the Moslem people. The white portion of the flag represents all the religious minority groups. The reason for selecting white was that it contains all the different colors of the spectrum and could not therefore be associated with any one single group.

The emblem of the Republic of Pakistan consists of a wreath which embraces a shield divided into four sections. Each of the sections shows one of Pakistan's four principal products: cotton, jute, wheat, and rice. A crescent moon and star, symbol of Islam, are set above the shield between the open ends of the wreath. A scroll bearing the motto, "*Iman, Ittihad, Nazm* [Faith, Unity, Discipline]" constitutes the base of the emblem.

The words and music of the national anthem of Pakistan derive from a contest held among leading composers and poets of the country. In English translation, its verses are as follows:

> Blessed be the sacred land
> Happy be the bounteous realm
> Symbol of high resolve
> Land of Pakistan
> Blessed be thou citadel of faith.
>
> The order of this sacred land
> Is the might of the brotherhood of the people
> May the nation, the country, and the State
> Shine in glory everlasting
> Blessed be the goal of our ambition.
>
> This flag of the Crescent and the Star
> Leads the way to progress and perfection
> Interpreter of our past, glory of our present
> Inspiration of our future
> Symbol of Almighty's protection.

The loftiness of the text very clearly symbolizes the idealistic aspiration, expounded by the intelligentsia, that the life of society in Pakistan should be ordered according to the ideals of Islam.

9

CHAPTER 2

Historical Setting

ALTHOUGH A NEW STATE the Republic of Pakistan has ancient origins. The coming of Islam in the eighth century—Islam that bore the seeds of latter-day nationalism—seems a relatively recent event when compared to the total span of history in this area. Though perhaps not the earliest hearth of civilized man, the Indus valley contains some of the very early indications of his development. The origins of the peoples of the Indus and of the lower Ganges and Brahmaputra valleys remain indistinct and it is safe to say only that they are the product of a mingling of successive waves of migrants from Central Asia and the Iranian plateau with the indigenous population.

Migrations and Empires

What is known of the history of the area of West Pakistan goes back some five thousand years. The civilization which flourished in the Indus valley then was already highly developed—excavations have revealed cities of a size and content paralleled only in Mesopotamia and Egypt. Little is known of this civilization's origins or of the area it controlled. Even the script on the beautifully carved seals found in the two main cities of Mohenjodero and Harappa has not been deciphered. About 1500 B.C. the Indus civilization declined, whether because of internal pressures is a matter of conjecture.

Tribes speaking Indo-European languages began their migration to the Indian subcontinent from Central Asia at about this time, settling first in the Indus valley, then moving further to the east. The newcomers seemingly assimilated much of what they found; the Hinduism which emerged among them in the next millennium had definite links with the earlier civilization. The records of the period are incomplete and depend primarily on the oral traditions of the classic Vedic Sanskrit literature consisting of the Rig-Veda and later Hindu epics. Limited evidence of the slaughter of their inhabitants and of burning suggests that the sites of Mohenjodero and Harappa were destroyed by the new arrivals about 1500 B.C. The first recorded of many foreign political and military influences was the extension of the Persian empire to the Indus valley in the sixth century B.C. To the north and east the mountain borders of the subcontinent effectively isolated the area from the rest of Asia; cultural influences, migrants, and invading armies came mainly through the passes of the northwest frontier.

Alexander the Great appeared on the scene briefly in the fourth century B.C., leading his troops as far east as the Indus, but the political impact of this invasion was minimal since a new empire under the Mauryas was beginning to expand its control over North India. The invasion served primarily to establish links with Hellenic culture and tradition, an influence which was to linger on in minor kingdoms such as Bactria and Gandhara after Greek power receded.

By the middle of the third century B.C. the Mauryan empire had reached its zenith under the emperor Asoka, whose rule extended from Afghanistan to Bengal and included all the lands south of the Himalayas except the southern tip of the peninsula. The center of the empire was at Bihar, just to the west of Bengal, where three centuries earlier a new tradition had grown up around the teachings and the person of the Buddha. The acceptance of Buddhism by Asoka caused the spread of the new religion to all parts of the empire.

After Asoka's death this first and most famous Indian empire disintegrated, and five and a half centuries intervened before the rise of the next major indigenous power under the Guptas. In the interval, successive waves of peoples crossed the northwest frontier, beginning with the Greeks from the kingdom of Bactria north of the Hindu Kush in the valley of the Oxus river, who ruled briefly in the Punjab and Sind. But the Greeks were soon driven out of Bactria by Central Asian peoples—first the Sakkas, then the Parthians, ultimately the Kushans.

The Kushans pressed on into the subcontinent and for almost a century controlled a large area of Central Asia, Afghanistan, and the upper reaches of both the Ganges and the Indus valleys.

Kaneshka, best known of the Kushan rulers, accepted Buddhism, and under his patronage the famous art and culture of the Gandharan school, representing a blend of Greco-Roman tradition, flourished in the vale of Peshawar and in neighboring valleys. The spread of Buddhism by way of land routes of Central Asia to China and the Far East occurred in this period.

In the fourth and fifth centuries A.D. another empire rose in North India—that of the Guptas. From their capital in Bihar they ruled from the Indus to the Brahmaputra river in Bengal, north of a line drawn from the Rann of Kutch to the Bay of Bengal. Pressure from Central Asian nomads—this time a group called the White Huns, believed to be related to the hordes that devastated Europe in the fifth century—again contributed to the empire's decline. Like their predecessors the Sakkas and Kushans, they were in time absorbed in the general population.

Among the many kingdoms and principalities which marked the following centuries, one dynasty of particular note came to power in Bengal and Bihar—that of the Buddhist Palas, who inaugurated a period of unusual prosperity. The three centuries of their rule are regarded in Bengal as the classic period of Bengali history. In the century between the decline of Pala power and the coming of the first Moslem invaders, the Brahmanical Sena dynasty held sway over parts of Bengal, Bihar, and Assam.

The Advent of Islam

Arab sailors and traders following the ancient trade routes in the Indian Ocean and the Persian Gulf first carried Islam to the subcontinent. Toward the end of the seventh century the Arabs established themselves on the Makran coast of Baluchistan and early in the next century, under Muhammad bin Qasim, successfully invaded the lower Indus valley. For various reasons they did not penetrate far beyond the first tributaries of the Indus in the north or into Rajasthan in the east. At first they acknowledged the suzerainty of the Caliph of Baghdad but later they became independent.

The effective introduction of Islam into India came in the eleventh century with successive Turkish invasions, the first series led by Mahmud of Ghazni. By the end of the twelfth century Turkish control had been carried to the Ganges-Brahmaputra delta by Muhammad Baktiar Khilji. As in the case of western India, there had been Arab Moslems on the Arakan and Chittagong coasts from the eighth century, but their influence had remained localized and it was left to the later overland invaders to introduce Islam on a wide scale in the wake of military conquest.

Turkish Dynasties

The five centuries between Mahmud of Ghazni and the appearance of Portuguese sea power witnessed a series of Turkish dynasties, whose sultanates, wielding their power largely from Delhi, expanded and contracted in response to pressure from Mongol and Afghan raiders from the northwest, independent Hindu rulers to the south, and internal wars of dynastic succession. Their sporadic control in the east generally extended to the eastern edge of the Ganges-Brahmaputra delta. In the fourteenth century under Muhammad bin Tughluq, the Delhi sultanate reached, briefly, its greatest extent.

During the years of Turko-Afghan rule the heads of state acknowledged only ceremonial allegiance to the caliphs of Baghdad and Egypt. As the numbers of the invaders were never large, considerable dependence was placed on local support. The gulf which separated the monotheism of Islam from the polytheism of Hinduism was undoubtedly a major deterrent to extensive contact between adherents of the two religions, although there was intermarriage between the invaders and native women. In this period there also began a synthesis of art, language, and architecture. The number of converts to Islam and the emergence of religious customs not found elsewhere in the Islamic world are further evidence of contact.

In the centuries after the reign of Mahmud of Ghazni, Islam spread rapidly, largely by conversion of the conquered. The number of adherents to Islam continued to grow in the following period of the Moghul empire, slackening off only as the expansion of British control marked the end of Moslem ascendancy. The question of whether conversion was by force or by persuasion is often disputed by Hindu and Moslem historians, but available evidence suggests that forceful conversion was relatively unimportant. Certainly the irregular geographic distribution of Moslems and their relative numbers (24 per cent) in prepartition India would be difficult to explain if forceful conversion had been the rule. For example, all of north India, where successive Moslem rulers exerted their greatest influence and control, would have been predominantly Moslem if forceful conversion had been widely practiced.

Unfortunately, little satisfactory documentation exists to explain the distribution of Moslems which in the twentieth century was to make possible the state of Pakistan. The high proportion of Moslems in the population of the Indus and the trans-Indus region can be partially explained by proximity to the lands from which the Moslem invaders came. Elsewhere in the subcontinent convincing explanations are missing. In the Ganges valley the relative strength of Moslems decreases, though for many centuries this was the seat of Moslem power and the most continuously occupied territory. South of the Indo-Gangetic plain the proportion is even less. In the entire region there is only one small area, on the southwest coast, where the number of Moslems exceeds one in four of the population. The distance from the center of power in Delhi, the difficulty of communication, and the sporadic nature of Turko-Afghan control are explanations for this distribution. Yet with similar conditions prevailing in Bengal more than half the population accepted Islam. The singular success of Islam in the eastern marchlands has been attributed to conflict between a declining Buddhism and an aggressive Hinduism. This set the stage for a number of saints and dervishes, renowned for their spiritual powers, who followed the Moslem conquerors and won large numbers of converts to Islam.

The Moghuls

Turko-Afghan control was undermined in the sixteenth century by the rise of the powerful Moghul empire and the arrival of the Europeans. First of the Moghul line, Babur, was a Turk from Chinese Turkestan who could claim direct descent from the Mongol "Lords of the Earth," Genghis Khan and Tamerlane. Kabul fell to him, then after initially unsuccessful thrusts to the north and east he established himself in Delhi by defeating the Turko-Afghan Lodis. Except for a brief period during which the Afghans reasserted their power under Sher Shah, Babur and five successive generations of Moghul emperors ruled over an empire which at its height included the major portion of the subcontinent and Afghanistan.

The reign of Babur's grandson, Akbar (1556-1605), was in many ways the golden age of the Moghuls. His rule was marked by exceptional military and administrative skill combined with a remarkable degree of religious tolerance. Akbar promulgated policies which secured the loyalty of his Hindu subjects and, in the matter of religious customs, made a particular effort to limit those practices of each group which were most offensive to the others. During his reign no allegiance was given to the caliph and to all intents and purposes the empire was a secular one.

Aurangzeb, the last of the great Moghuls, came to power in the mid-seventeenth century. At his death in 1707, the empire, which had extended from Kabul to Chittagong and from Kashmir to the Cauvery river, was disintegrating. Wars of succession, the rise of Rajput and Maratha power, European encroachment—these all but completed its dismemberment by the middle of the seventeenth century. The reasons for this decline are complex but to a major degree must be directly attributed to Aurangzeb. He was a devout Moslem who would not compromise. In the intensity of his zeal he reversed Akbar's policy of toleration of non-Moslems and aroused powerful hostile forces. An able military leader and a shrewd politician, he lacked the statesmanship of Babur and Akbar.

The Europeans, who swiftly capitalized on the ensuing disorganization, had been a part of the Indian scene since the Portuguese rounded the Cape of Good Hope in the last quarter of the fifteenth century. They came seeking trade and remained to wield economic and political power. The British role, best known to the present generation, was but the final act of a drama which lasted four and a half centuries and included Portuguese, Dutch, French, and Danes in its cast.

Vasco da Gama anchored off Calicut on the west coast six years after Columbus arrived in the New World. A number of Portuguese settlements were established soon afterwards. Under the Portuguese admiral, Albuquerque (1453-1515), Arab sea power and influence in the Indian Ocean was challenged and defeated. For the next hundred years the trade and control of the Indian Ocean remained a Portuguese monopoly.

The Dutch East India Company, founded in the first decade of the seventeenth century, grew in influence and gradually began to erode Portuguese control of the Indian coast and the East Indies in the course of establishing factories along the coast and in the interior on the lower Ganges river. The English East India Company, founded in the same period, was slower to expand its trade in the area but, as the Portuguese influence waned, rivalry between the British and the Dutch mercantile establishments in-creased. The contest continued into the middle of the eighteenth century, when Dutch influence declined rapidly.

The French were the last of the European powers to arrive on the scene, establishing their first factory near Madras in 1670. Following the initial settlement they set up factories on the south-west and east coasts and moved their main base to Pondichery. In Bengal they established themselves on the Hooghly river at Chandernagore, north of present-day Calcutta.

British Conquest and Rule

The first British settlement on the west coast was followed by factories in Madras, Bombay, and the lower Ganges valley. In Bengal the British were forced to withdraw, as had the Portuguese before them, but were able to re-establish at the present site of Calcutta by 1690. Due to a local rebellion they were permitted to fortify the place and eight years later were granted rent collection rights over three adjacent villages.

This digression of the company from trade and concomitant protective military activity to the acquisition of rent-producing land and consequent administrative activities marked the begin-ning of British rule in India. Aurangzeb's power had declined to the extent that anarchy was spreading on the frontiers of his empire. To maintain peaceful conditions which would favor trade, the British extended their control and indirectly embarked on the course of empire.

Imperialism in India had to wait upon the establishment of supremacy over the French in wars fought in Europe and North America as well as India. Not until Napoleon was finally defeated at Waterloo was French power completely eliminated. The struggle for ascendancy on land was largely carried on by warring frag-ments of the Moghul empire aided and abetted by the French and British. Factories, which were often fortified villages serving as col-lecting and transshipping points for trade, grew into large terri-torial holdings.

A side issue of the fighting between the French in Chandernagore and the British in Calcutta involved the Indian viceroy of Bengal. After the initial loss of Calcutta the British returned under Clive, captured Chandernagore, and decisively defeated the viceroy's forces at Plassey in 1757. In the following hundred years the

British company expanded its area of control from footholds in Bengal, Madras, and Bombay. By 1805 British administration extended to the borders of the Punjab beyond Delhi. Eastward expansion was slower until success in the First Anglo-Burmese War in 1826 added parts of Assam and Arakan. By 1870 the remainder of Assam, with the exception of the tribal areas lying east of Bhutan and north of the Brahmaputra river, was annexed outright or attached by treaty. In the west, Sind, Punjab, and Kashmir were added following the Afghan and Sikh wars. In the south, annexation or treaties with various rulers consolidated the company's position. On the eve of the Mutiny the territories controlled by the English East India Company were, with the exception of Baluchistan and Upper Assam, essentially those held by the British in 1947.

The end of a century of territorial expansion and consolidation following Clive's victory at Plassey was marked by the Mutiny of Indian Sepoy forces. Changes in administration concomitant with the rapid expansion of the company's power, Hindu objection to the abolition of certain religious practices, the spread of Western education, and the activities of the Wahabi sect of Islam were among the contributing factors—in addition to the rumored greasing of cartridges with pork fat.

The Mutiny of 1857 marked a turning point in Indian history. Justly or unjustly British feeling was hardened against the Moslems, to whom at least at the time they ascribed a major share of the blame. This stigma, added to the effects of a measure which twenty years earlier had replaced Persian with English as the language of higher education and administration, marked a final stage in Moslem decline from the high position Islam had enjoyed under the Moghul empire less than a century before.

The Mutiny also marked the end of company rule in India. From then on the Crown was to rule directly in British India and exercise decisive control over the remainder of the territories in the subcontinent. The internal boundaries of the subcontinent were to remain largely unchanged for the next ninety years, until independence and partition.

The recovery of Moslem India from its low estate was a gradual process which was still going on a century later. In education, commerce, and government service the Moslems lagged behind the Hindus, who were quicker to adapt themselves to the rapidly changing socioeconomic conditions. By standing aloof from the Western-oriented education system the Moslems cut themselves off from the many new avenues opening up for the emerging middle class. These shortcomings led to an intensification of awareness of their minority role. Toward the end of the nineteenth century they even opposed the extension of representative government, hoping thereby to re-establish rapport with the British, who by that time were casting about for support against rising Hindu nationalism.

In the last quarter of the nineteenth century under the leadership of Sir Sayyid Ahmed Khan a beginning was made toward reconciliation between the traditional views of Indian Moslems and the new ideas and education system being introduced by the British. Sir Sayyid was responsible for the founding in 1875 of the Mohammeddan Anglo-Oriental College at Aligarh (later Aligarh University), at which Islamic orientation and religious instruction were combined with an English university system. Graduates of the school not only came to fill important posts in the government but provided leadership in the nationalist movement of the twentieth century. In the field of politics Sir Sayyid was one of the first Moslems to recognize the problem facing his community under a government ruled by the majority, insisting that the Moslems must be loyal to the British since British rule provided stability and protection.

The Rise of Nationalism

Britain's conquest of India had been made relatively easy by the absence of unity and nationalism, but by the first decade of this century the nationalist movement had gathered sufficient force to be a factor influencing government policy. Under its aegis it united the most diverse political, social, and economic elements—elements which could not agree on what was to replace the existing order. As the hour of freedom drew near, this negative unity proved unequal to the task of holding the Hindu and Moslem communities of India together.

Despite evidence of nationalist awakenings earlier, the division of Bengal in 1905 into West Bengal and East Bengal was the first major issue to occasion widespread public reaction. The hostile reaction, which began among Hindu Bengalis, spread until a state of unrest prevailed in much of India. Moslems generally favored the division, but their voices were lost in the more articulate outcry of the economically powerful Hindus. Out of the furor, two things emerged. First, there was an awareness that regional sympathies were so strong that they verged on the antinational except as they might unite in opposition to British rule. Second, there was need for a political party which would serve the interests of the Moslem community.

Seven years later the partition of Bengal was voided in recognition of the grievances of the Hindu Bengalis, who found themselves outnumbered in the legislatures in the provinces of West Bengal and East Bengal. This action, which recognized the existence of the growing estrangement between Moslems and Hindus in many parts of the country, was followed by removal of the capital of India from the highly charged atmosphere of Calcutta to Delhi.

During the years of the partition of Bengal, nationalism had asserted itself in the formation of the Moslem League, which met in Dacca for the first time in 1906 to support the partition of Bengal. These years also saw the Moslem request for separate electorates incorporated in the governmental reforms of 1909. But the Moslem League was not the first Indian national party. The Indian National Congress had been founded twenty years before the first partition of Bengal. From its inception the Congress claimed to represent Indian national aspirations regardless of religious community. Some leaders in the Moslem community opposed Moslem participation in its meetings on the grounds that it was Hindu-dominated; other Moslems joined, participated in its deliberations, and on occasion provided active leadership. The Moslem League on the other hand never claimed to represent any interests other than those of the Moslem community. Both parties, composed of intellectuals and the middle class, lacked mass following until after 1930. Both demanded self-government, with the stipulation in the case of the Moslem League of safeguards for its minority community.

During and after World War I, the League and the Congress did make common cause in desiring independence. Mahomed 'Ali Jinnah was both a member of the Congress and president of the Moslem League when the Lucknow Pact of 1916 between the two parties expressed agreement on communal representation and national independence.

In the early years of the twentieth century there had been growing concern among Indian Moslems over the fate of Turkey. The Balkan Wars, the Italo-Turkish War, and the struggles of World War I were portrayed by Moslem writers in India as Islam confronted by Western imperialism. The sultan of Turkey was recognized by most Moslems as the caliph, that is, the spiritual ruler of the Moslems. When the British government reneged on its wartime promises and turned a deaf ear to pleas for the preservation of Turkey's territorial integrity, Moslems in India issued the Khilafat Manifesto. Soon the Khilafat movement was taken up by the Congress and appeared as a strange combination of nationalism and pan-Islamic sentiment with strong anti-British overtones.

For several years the Khilafat movement replaced the Moslem League as the major focus of Moslem interest. An agreement between the leaders of the movement and Gandhi, the leading figure in the Congress, resulted in the joint advocacy of home rule for India on the one hand and agitation for the protection of Moslem holy places and the restoration of the caliph of Turkey on the other.

In 1922 the Hindu-Moslem accord suffered a double blow when the noncooperation movement miscarried and the Khilafat movement foundered. The outbreak of rioting with communal aspects in a number of places had caused Gandhi to call off the joint noncooperation movement, and the Khilafat movement lost its purpose when the Young Turks under the leadership of Mustafa Kemal exiled the caliph and shortly thereafter proclaimed Turkey a secular state.

Working unity was never re-established. The Congress insisted that there was no religious or communal problem and took an uncompromising stand, seriously underestimating the intensity of Moslem minority fears that were to strengthen the influence and power of the League. In 1935 the British enacted the Government of India Act, which widened the franchise and provided the basic administrative machinery for self-government but did not make the viceroy or provincial governors responsible to the local electorate. Elections in 1937 for the new provincial assemblies gave Congress candidates majorities in seven of the eleven provinces. Moslem premiers headed coalition parties in the Punjab and Bengal, but by the application of uncompromising parliamentary procedures the League was excluded from participation in any of the seven provincial governments formed by the Congress.

This marked the real parting of the ways. Many prominent Moslems who had supported the national noncommunal approach now saw in the League the only alternative to political submergence in the Hindu-dominated Congress. For the first time many came to feel that power in the hands of a Hindu majority might be used to exclude Moslems from all power once the British had departed. Mahomed 'Ali Jinnah, who had returned from practicing law in England in 1934 and had earlier advocated Hindu-Moslem unity, now worked for the cause of Moslem autonomy. He again became the League's spokesman and leader, this time without Congress affiliations. To members of the League the main issue became one of finding an alternative to replacing British with Congress (that is, Hindu) rule.

The Concept of "Pakistan"

One of the first public statements to contain the idea of a Moslem state was made by the poet, Muhammad Iqbal, who in delivering the presidential address at a meeting of the League in 1930 spoke of the consolidation of a North-West Indian Moslem state to include the Sind, Baluchistan, the North-West Frontier province, and the Punjab. A year later he wrote of the need "to redistribute the country and to provide one or more Moslem states with absolute majorities." A more specific proposal for partition came in 1933 from a group of Moslem students at Cambridge University. They not only demanded a national state but gave it the name PAKISTAN—from (P)unjab, (A)fghan province; (K)ashmir; (S)ind; and Baluchis(TAN).

These concepts came to the fore in 1940 when the Moslem League, meeting in Lahore, resolved "that the areas in which the Moslems are numerically in a majority, as in the North-Western and Eastern zones of India, should be grouped to constitute 'Independent States' in which the constituent units shall be autonomous and sovereign." The Lahore resolution was the first declaration of a major group for the partition of India along communal lines. At the same session Mahomed 'Ali Jinnah was elected president of the League for life. All that remained was for the Moslem League to prove that it represented a majority of India's Moslems and, to win over the community, its leaders held up the vision of a Moslem state in which the believers would be free from oppression, injustice, and poverty.

By 1944 Jinnah was advocating a state made from six provinces. Five of them, Sind, Baluchistan, the North-West Frontier province, the Punjab, and Bengal had Moslem majorities. Assam did not have a Moslem majority but was included because of its location and the large number of non-Hindu tribes. According to this plan, India, with a Moslem minority of 24 per cent in 1941, was to be divided into Pakistan with a non-Moslem minority of 44 per cent and India with a Moslem minority reduced to 12 per cent.

The Congress, of course, did not agree to the proposal. To many, the creation of a sovereign state based on a common religion seemed a historical anachronism. Certainly the federation of two areas separated from each other by over a thousand miles could be viewed as a geographical absurdity with no modern precedent.

India in World War II

During the war years (1939-45) the League and the Congress adopted different attitudes toward the British government. The Congress showed its displeasure over the declaration of war for India without the assent of the Indian people by resigning from the ministries in eight out of the eleven provinces. Failing to obtain a promise of complete independence, the Congress launched a civil disobedience campaign. The League, following a course of limited cooperation, gained British favor and won time to consolidate its claim that it represented the majority of India's Moslems.

Under the spur of the Japanese advance into Malaya and Burma in 1942 the British government sent out a mission under Sir Stafford Cripps that hoped to secure Indian help in the war effort in exchange for a promise of Indian independence after the war and the right of self-determination for each province. The mission failed, as both the Congress and the League rejected the proposals. The Congress called for open rebellion against British rule, but the League abstained from this action.

In June 1945 Lord Wavell, the new viceroy, called Indian leaders to a conference at Simla and proposed an interim form of government for the country. Jinnah rejected the proposal because it failed to recognize the Moslem League as the sole spokesman for the Moslem community and, to prove his point, insisted on new elections for the central and provincial assemblies. The voting in 1946 resulted in the election of Congress candidates for the majority of the general seats and a sweep of 90 per cent of the Moslem seats by League candidates. From winning a mere 4.5 per cent of the Moslem electorate votes in the 1937 elections the League had made great progress toward proving its claim that it represented all the Moslems of India.

There were, however, a number of influential Moslems who clung to their membership in the Congress or in small non-League Moslem parties. These contended that regional nationalism was incompatible with Islam, which stood for a single community of all the faithful. Though these Moslems desired safeguards for the minority community, they did not seek it in a separate sovereign state.

In March 1946, before the elections had been held, a British cabinet mission arrived in India to discuss independence. Its purpose was to explore with Indian leaders the means for the transfer of power, including the machinery through which the Indians could decide their political future. Initially, the League and the Congress accepted the Cabinet Mission Statement, but both began to make reservations on controversial points. Jinnah called for a "direct action" campaign for the attainment of a sovereign state of Pakistan, which contributed materially to an outbreak of communal rioting at Calcutta, Bombay, and elsewhere on a scale heretofore unknown in India. In October, League members did join the interim government, established a month earlier with Hindu participation, but reiterated Moslem determination not to attend the constituent assembly until a fixed program had been established.

The Partition of India

In February 1947 Prime Minister Clement Attlee announced that His Majesty's government would transfer authority to Indian hands not later than June 1948, hopefully to a local government operating under its own constitution, or else to existing provincial governments. At the same time he appointed Lord Mountbatten viceroy of India to arrange the transfer of power.

Communal rioting broke out with renewed vigor, especially in the Punjab where Hindus and Sikhs opposed the Moslems. Mountbatten arrived late in March to begin lengthy talks with Indian political leaders, representatives of the various religious communities, and the rulers of the princely states. By April it was certain that the separate states of Pakistan and Hindustan would emerge from divided India.

On June 3 Mountbatten released the British plan for partition of India on the basis of a separation of contiguous Moslem-majority districts together with the Punjab, Bengal, and Assam if the inhabitants so desired. Also, the people of the North-West Frontier

23

province would decide which state they wished to join. Special boundary commissions would have final say in the actual lines of partition.

Members of the League and the Congress were appointed to a partition committee which worked with a steering committee and several experts committees to put into effect all the details of the plan. So much progress was made that Mountbatten proposed that the transfer of power take place three months later, on August 15, 1947. As was expected, West Punjab, East Bengal, Sylhet in Assam, and the North-West Frontier province voted to join Pakistan. Meanwhile, in London the Parliament was debating the text of the Indian Independence Act, enacting the bill on July 18, 1947 and creating the independent dominions of India and Pakistan.

The Indian Independence Act provided for a governor general of each dominion, who might be the same person during the period of transition. The Congress agreed to accept Lord Mountbatten as governor general of India, but in the last weeks Jinnah felt he must follow the League mandate and himself become Pakistan's first governor general.

The division of the assets of the existing central government of India, such as the armed forces, the railways, the civil service, and fixed assets prior to August 15, proceeded remarkably well considering the thorny nature of the problem. According to the agreement, Pakistan was to receive 17.5 per cent of the joint assets. When an item could not be divided, compensation would be made in cash. The civil servants were given the choice of opting for Pakistan or remaining in India. In the case of the British, they could retire with compensation if they did not wish to continue or had not been invited to do so by either of the dominions. Many of them stayed on, particularly in Pakistan where the need for trained administrative personnel was greater. Early in August the vanguard of the new government had begun to arrive in Karachi and Dacca to establish themselves wherever space could be found.

At first it appeared as if the military services, largely composed of mixed Hindu-Moslem units, would disintegrate before a process of reconstitution could be worked out on the basis of place of birth and community. Therefore the two armies were placed under a Joint Defense Council until reorganization could be completed after partition. British officers serving in the Indian army were urged to stay on and many of them did. For a while after partition the senior army, air force, and navy officers in both dominions were British.

In 1946 Winston Churchill, speaking in the House of Commons, stated that the British could quit India regardless of what happened or could frankly face up to partition and be prepared to prevent anarchy and massacres. Violence did break out. The first serious incident occurred in Bengal in August 1946: Hindus and Moslems suffered equally in four days of madness in which the dead may have exceeded four thousand. Reverberations spread among both communities. In the district of Noakhali in East Bengal an estimated two hundred Hindus died and five thousand were made homeless in November. Bihar and the United Provinces were infected shortly afterwards; perhaps five thousand died here, most of them Moslem. March 1947 saw violence flare in the Punjab where an estimated two thousand died. Sporadic incidents continued across northern India until August 1947. It is against this background of fear and distrust that the events leading up to independence must be viewed.

Following decisions in the Punjab and Bengal legislatures to opt for Pakistan, boundary commissions were established. Four high court judges were appointed to each commission: two Moslems, a Sikh, and a Hindu in the Punjab; and two Hindus and two Moslems in Bengal. Sir Cyril Radcliffe came out from England to act as chairman of both commissions. The terms of reference for the commissions that included "ascertaining the contiguous majority areas of Moslems and non-Moslems . . . also taking into account other factors" seem to have been accepted by each of the parties with the hope of gaining a more favorable settlement. It was further agreed that in the event of a tie in the voting of the four judges the chairman's decision was to be accepted as final. Both the Congress and the League jointly pledged to abide by the boundary commissions' awards.

The deliberations of the judges failed to produce agreement on the issues. As a result the award, published three days after independence, represented the decisions of the chairman. Inevitably it pleased neither group. As communal distributions were not necessarily in accord with economics or geography the boundaries suffered similar defects. To Pakistan the award in the Punjab seemed most unjust. Apparently in concession to the Sikh community, the boundary divided canal colonies so as to give to India parts of the Moslem-majority district of Gurdaspura. The latter area gave

India a land link with Kashmir and made it possible at a later date to supply her forces in Kashmir by road rather than only by air.

Independence Day was acclaimed enthusiastically in the new dominions on August 15, 1947. (Independence was officially declared on midnight of August 14 and has subsequently been celebrated in Pakistan on the 14th and in India on the 15th.) For Jinnah and the League it marked the end of a long struggle not only to be free of British rule but to establish a state where Moslems would not be in a minority. To Mahomed 'Ali Jinnah's determination and leadership must be ascribed a major share of the credit. Whether the Moslem community was actually a nation or not became an academic question.

In the divided provinces, communal reactions came swiftly on the heels of independence. Bengal, quiet for the first time since the "Great Calcutta Killing," remained calm until news of rioting in the Punjab began to have its effect. Gandhi's presence in Calcutta helped to halt an outbreak of rioting and killing which broke out early in September.

Trouble had been anticipated in the Punjab where law and order had broken down over large areas in which communal rioting had been the cause of more than a thousand deaths in the first weeks of August. The landowning, close-knit, militant Sikh minority community, which had cast its lot with the Congress, saw its traditional homeland bisected by the boundary award and apparently decided to concentrate their numbers in the East Punjab, driving all Moslems out of the area.

Much of the blame for the Punjab disaster has been ascribed to the Sikhs, though none, including the British, can be considered blameless. Moslems were not loath to retaliate and through August and September, Moslems, Hindus, and Sikhs fought each other. Those who survived fled toward Pakistan or India. Estimates suggest that twelve million fled their homes and over a million died. So violent was the struggle that today there are virtually no Sikhs in West Pakistan and very few Moslems in East Punjab.

The memory of the violence and death in 1947 lingered on to poison relations between the two new dominions, and new differences were soon in the making. The most serious of these arose over the accession of the Princely State of Jammu and Kashmir to India. The act of accession by the Hindu ruler of a predominantly Moslem state was a violation of the principle of partition on the basis of contiguous Moslem-majority areas. At the time the

26

Maharaja's accession was accepted, Lord Mountbatten stated that as soon as law and order had been restored the question of accession should be settled by popular referendum. The developments in Kashmir very nearly led to general war between India and Pakistan. But for the intervention of Lord Mountbatten, and the action of the British commanders of the military forces in both countries, it is quite probable that the local conflict would have expanded into a general war.

CHAPTER 3

Geography and Transportation

PAKISTAN CLAIMS THE UNIQUE DISTINCTION among the countries of the world of being divided into two major parts separated from each other by a thousand miles of foreign territory. These two wings of the country have a combined area and population greater than the area or population of any country in Western Europe but their contributions to this total contrast sharply. West Pakistan has a much greater area—comparable to the aggregate area in Utah, Arizona, and New Mexico—but the smaller population; East Pakistan, with a larger population than France has, is only a little bigger than Louisiana.

Geography

Occupying a central position on the southern rim of the Eurasian land mass, the extensive area of the subcontinent is to a large degree isolated from the rest of Asia by mountain barriers. Extension southward into the Indian Ocean gives the subcontinent a relatively straight and long coastline but an unprotected one that is poorly adapted to important maritime activity.

On the basis of its physiography the subcontinent is divisible into three regions: the mountain borderlands which form a great arc of folded mountains; the peninsular extension southward into the Indian Ocean; and the Indo-Gangetic plains which reach from the Arabian Sea to the Bay of Bengal between the mountains and the peninsula. West Pakistan includes nearly all of the plain drained by the Indus river and its tributaries as well as the mountains that flank it on the west and north. At the eastern end of the great alluvial arc, East Pakistan includes the delta and the lower reaches of the Ganges, Brahmaputra, and the Meghna rivers and minor portions of the hilly borderland to the east.

Representing one of the four major population aggregations of the world, the subcontinent lies between two other major centers, Europe and the Far East. Access to the subcontinent from these centers has been important historically and continues to be a significant factor in economic, political, and cultural development. The fact of its dual location on the western and eastern borders of the subcontinent makes Pakistan adjacent to and, to a considerable degree, part of the Moslem world of Southwest Asia (the western wing) and also adjacent to Burma and Southeast Asia (the eastern wing). The country's territorial dualism has other unusual aspects of relative location. By air Baghdad and the oilfields of the Persian Gulf are closer to Karachi than Dacca, the provincial center of East Pakistan. From Dacca, Hong Kong and Ceylon are closer by air than Karachi.

The relative accessibility of Pakistan by air is an important consideration, but the bulk of interregional traffic in people and commodities moves by sea. The distance from either of Pakistan's coasts to Europe and the Far East by sea is considerably longer than the air distances: the great peninsular outliers of the Asian continent are responsible for this increase. Land mobility across the frontiers of the subcontinent is limited to trails except on the northwest frontier where three roads cross the mountain heights. No railroads cross the frontiers of the subcontinent except in the west where one line extends a few miles into Iranian territory.

In addition to relative location, the two wings of Pakistan differ greatly in size and in the patterns of population density. The western wing with an area of 310,378 square miles is nearly six times as large as the eastern wing with 55,126 square miles. These figures illustrate the extent of the territory which the government must administer and control, while East Pakistan's population of 50.8 million versus the 42.8 million in West Pakistan point up the importance of other factors such as climate and arable land.

Contrast and variety are the most striking features of Pakistan's physical geography. The western wing, as its size would suggest, exhibits considerably more variety than the eastern wing, and the two wings offer the contrasts which differentiate the desert and semiarid world of Southwest Asia from the humid, rice-producing areas of Southeast Asia.

More than half of West Pakistan is included in the mountains and interior basins which border the subcontinent on the west and north. The western ranges are young, folded, and faulted mountains supporting little vegetation, averaging between 4,000 and 8,000 feet in elevation, with peaks over 10,000 feet. Access to the Indus valley from the Iranian plateau or Soviet Central Asia across the Hindu Kush is possible through a number of passes of which the Khyber is the most famous. North of the Khyber, elevations increase as the ranges merge with the Hindu Kush and continue east and southeast in the mighty Himalayas backed by the Karakorams. Here passes ranging from 10,000 to 18,000 feet are overshadowed by giant peaks. It has been reported that there are no less than 92 peaks in these two ranges exceeding 24,000 feet. The balance of the western province is an alluvial plain exhibiting little relative relief, in which the flood plains of the Indus and its tributaries are only slightly intrenched. The slope of this surface to the south is less than one foot in a mile. To the east the alluvium merges indistinctly with the peninsular block which lies outside the borders of the province.

East Pakistan is situated astride the delta of the Ganges-Brahmaputra rivers and includes only minor portions of the flanking Assam-Burma hills. Structurally similar to its western counterpart, elevations in this portion of the mountain rim are somewhat lower. On the Pakistan-Burma border the hills are little more than 1,500 feet high, although they rise to more than 6,000 feet further east in Burma and along the India-Burma frontier to the north. Covered by tropical forests, the ranges have proved a more formidable barrier than the higher ones on the northwest frontier. No roads or railroads traverse them and in historic times few invaders of the subcontinent successfully crossed them. The Ledo Road of World War II fame, which connected Assam and upper Burma, has already been reclaimed by the jungle.

The alluvial plain, which makes up more than 80 per cent of East Pakistan, is a smaller area than its western counterpart. It is intricately dissected by the three major rivers and their distributaries. Immediately to the northeast of the provincial border an outlier of the peninsular block, the Shillong plateau, rises abruptly to elevations between 2,000 and 4,000 feet. To the north of the frontier, across a corridor averaging fifty miles in width, the Indo-Gangetic plain is bordered by the Himalayas.

Climate

Distinct climatic patterns characterize the two wings of Pakistan and are of major significance in an economy primarily dependent on agriculture. Where food production is marginal even in the best years, deviation from normal climatic conditions always means hardship and occasionally disaster and famine. In both wings the monsoon rhythm of winds dominates climatic patterns and dictates two distinct seasons based on the amount of rainfall rather than on temperature. Variations in temperature and rainfall are primarily influenced by relation to the summer monsoon in the Bay of Bengal and distances from the coast.

A winter dry season and a wide range in the amount of annual precipitation are the essence of the country's rainfall regimes. The western districts of East Pakistan receive 50 to 60 inches annually which increase in the north, east, and southeast to 100 inches and to more than 200 inches south of the Shillong plateau in Sylhet district. As significant as the amount of rainfall is its seasonal concentration from June through September. In this period, 60 to 70 per cent of the total is received. The four winter months from November through February are relatively dry, with precipitation less than 4 inches in most of the province.

Proceeding westward across India to the Indus valley precipitation decreases steadily. Except in the northern mountains, annual rainfall in West Pakistan averages less than 20 inches. Such low rainfall combined with high temperatures results in arid or semiarid conditions in the Indus plain and the western mountain rim. At least 80 per cent of the cultivated acreage in the province depends on some form of irrigation during the year. Actual rainfall figures vary from 8 inches at Karachi to 18 inches at Lahore, 600 miles inland, and 15 inches at Peshawar. The variability of this precipitation is high and includes the factor of risk from long dry periods or from flooding after torrential rains.

Temperature variations within the country exhibit considerable variety but are a much less critical factor than rainfall. Protection afforded by the Himalayas in the north and exposure to the Indian Ocean in the south result in tropical conditions except in the northwest where lower winter temperatures and a greater annual range prevail. In the eastern wing, the annual temperature range is approximately 20° F. The average temperature in January is 60°.

31

Colder winters and hotter summers in West Pakistan, inland from the coast, result in an annual range of 40°. At Peshawar and Lahore the average January temperature is 50°. Occasional frosts impose some limitation on agricultural activity in the winter though the growing season is actually year round except at higher elevations. Summers are hot. At Lahore and Karachi the average temperature in the hottest month is 93° and 87° respectively.

River Systems

The rivers of Pakistan play a major role in the life of the country but with very different emphases in the two wings. Common to all is a wide variance in rates of discharge in response to the seasonality of rainfall. At one extreme are the rivers of Baluchistan which carry water only after the infrequent rains, and many of these watercourses end in interior basins, never reaching the sea. At the other extreme are the large rivers of the eastern province which are fed by the snow and ice fields of the northern mountain rim as well as by the torrential rains of the summer monsoon. Discharge during the summer rainy season is ten times the dry season flow, which is still quite substantial.

The major river of West Pakistan is the Indus. It rises in the Himalayas and flows through deep gorges before reaching the plains. Unlike the Ganges or the Brahmaputra it traverses nearly 800 miles of country with low rainfall before reaching the sea. A major portion of its basin lies in West Pakistan, although its headwaters rise beyond the northeastern frontier in Tibet and Kashmir. Summer floods in the Indus plain still cause considerable damage, though a major portion of the river's discharge is spread over the plain through the irrigation system, which is one of the most extensive in the world. About 24 million acres—65 per cent of the cultivated area—are irrigated by canals.

A serious limitation on the effectiveness of irrigation works is salinity and waterlogging caused by poor subsurface drainage. Accumulation of alkali salts in the surface soil as the subsurface level of the water table rises is already so acute a problem, with some 70,000 acres going out of production annually, that only continuing effort on a vast scale can correct these conditions. During the Second Five Year Plan the completion of new barrages and canal systems will bring more than 9.5 million additional acres under perennial irrigation. Even these developments will not exhaust

32

the potential of the Indus basin if additional water can be made available, present canal seepage reduced, and drainage improved.

The creation of storage reservoirs on the Indus river and its tributaries offers multipurpose development by using the stream head to generate hydroelectricity. In 1955 West Pakistan's generating capacity was 268,200 kilowatts and in 1960 it was 730,300 kilowatts with the use of water power primarily responsible for the increase. Because of the presence of five major barrages and the diversion of water for irrigation, the Indus is not navigable except for small craft over short reaches.

The rivers in East Pakistan differ greatly from those of the western wing in the smaller percentage of the various river basins lying within the province, the size of the rivers, and their economic significance. The Ganges and the Brahmaputra each have a discharge approximately three times that of the Indus. The two major streams that rise in the eastern hill margins, the Surma-Meghna and the Karnaphuli, in aggregate have a greater flow than the Indus. During the summer months the flood plains of the rivers, which comprise 20 to 25 per cent of the province, are inundated to varying depths. Large quantities of silt deposited at this time greatly enrich the land, making possible double and in some cases triple cropping. During the winter dry period stream flow is reduced but is still adequate for transportation requirements and possible irrigation schemes. At low water 2,500 miles of waterways remain navigable for steamers of five and six foot draft; another 1,500 miles are added to this system in the rainy season.

The network of navigable waterways extends beyond the borders of the province into India. The Ganges system includes access to Calcutta and the interior of Bihar, but the most heavily traveled route continues up the Brahmaputra for 350 miles into Assam and carries much of the important Indian transit traffic between Assam and Calcutta. On the Surma-Meghna, steamer services continue beyond the eastern border only for a few miles. This navigational aspect of the rivers is a commentary on both their size and the obstacle they offer to land communications. Within the province, the Ganges and the Meghna are bridged only once and the Brahmaputra not at all.

As the rivers are not deeply entrenched in valleys, except in the eastern hill margins, possibilities of flood control or hydroelectric development are limited. A reservoir on the Karnaphuli river produces 120,000 kilowatts.

Coasts

The sea margins of Pakistan are contrasts in extremes, though each serves the basic requirements of its hinterland and contributes an additional source of food and income from the fisheries of the offshore waters. Except for its southeast coast, East Pakistan's seaface at the head of the Bay of Bengal is typical of many deltaic regions. It is low lying land cut by estuaries and tidal creeks in such profusion that land and sea appear to merge over a wide zone. Tidal forests dominate the western portion of the coast, giving way in the east and southeast to paddy cultivation which reaches almost to the edge of the bay. Neither of the two ports that handle the province's seaborne trade are ideally situated, since communications with the interior are restricted. Much of this difficulty stems from the fact that there are really two hinterlands—one to the west of the Brahmaputra-Meghna, the other to the east of it. The smaller of the two ports, Chalna, is an anchorage sixty miles up the Pusur river serving the western hinterland. Goods are moved by lighter to Khulna several miles upstream, where there is access to the western broad-gauge rail net and the steamers of the inland waterways. Chittagong, the main port, lies on the Karnaphuli river ten miles upstream from the coast. River silting and coastal sand bars limit the effectiveness of the port. Access to the eastern meter-gauge railroad is available at dockside, although the port's location in the southeast corner of the province entails long rail hauls. To reach the inland waterways from Chittagong it is necessary to cross forty miles of open water in the bay, which involves the use of special craft and an additional trans-shipment of goods.

West Pakistan's seaface is a long exposed coast on the Arabian Sea offering little shelter and hampered by difficult communications with the arid interior. Only at Karachi, west of the Indus delta, does one find a good harbor, adequate supplies of fresh water, and easy access to the interior. The port serves the hinterland of West Pakistan and Afghanistan by road and rail.

Boundaries

Not the least of many unusual aspects presented by Pakistan's territorial duality are the recent origin of many of the boundaries, the religious basis of their delimitation, and the manner in which delimitation was made. Their effectiveness as limits of political control and lines of contact with adjacent states, though conditioned by patterns of human and physical geography, depend on the sometimes precarious relations between the government of Pakistan and those of the contiguous states.

When the new state of Pakistan was created out of the Moslem-majority areas of northwest and northeast India, the political units thus formed were not based on economic considerations or strategic possibilities, or even on a division of resources proportional to the relative strength of the Moslem community in the total population. It is not surprising, therefore, that the new borders with India have been the cause of some friction. What is remarkable is that they have not been the cause of greater dispute.

Pakistan's dominant position in the lower Ganges and Brahmaputra valleys leads to concern with economic and strategic developments in the northeast frontier area though only a short section of the frontier became a part of its border. Added to these involvements with the frontiers of the subcontinent is the influence of direct contact with India along almost 3,500 miles of common boundaries. In terms of length the 1,400-mile border with Afghanistan is next in importance after India followed by those with Iran and Burma. No common frontier exists with Nepal or the Soviet Union though both are separated from Pakistan by narrow strips of land. An important corridor between Assam and the rest of India separates Pakistan from Nepal. The panhandle of Afghan territory separating Pakistan and the Soviet Union is mountainous country where the main pass is at an elevation above 14,000 feet. None of these former boundaries of the Indian empire are very old: the Burmese frontier was established in the first quarter of the nineteenth century, those of the northwest frontier in the last two decades of that century.

Along the entire length of the land boundary there are few continuous sections of the frontier which coincide with prominent topographical features. From the Hindu Kush to the Arabian Sea the frontier follows the mountain borderlands of the subcontinent in an historic marchland undistinguished by any continuous range or valley. The only sharp physical divide is the western edge of the Indus valley and this is not a religious or linguistic divide. To the east of the Indus the frontier with India borders the Rann of Kutch, a distinct physical divide, and the Thar desert, a zone of transition. In the eastern wing the border parallels the edge of the alluvial plain south of the Shillong plateau and west of the Indian state of Tripura, but this represents only a small part of the land boundary which for the rest of its length wanders across the country, occasionally following rivers or valleys and water divides in the eastern hill margins.

The creation of international frontiers around Moslem-majority areas in the subcontinent divided regions which had economic, linguistic, historical, and geographic unity—particularly in the case of the former provinces of Bengal and the Punjab. The new boundaries in eastern India also cut across the transportation routes connecting Assam with the rest of India. In the Punjab, partition destroyed the natural unity of the irrigation canal system. As the result of mass migration following partition, the border area in the Punjab changed from a broad religious transition zone to a sharp line of demarcation between Moslem and non-Moslem.

Numerous disputes have grown out of the location of Pakistan's boundaries and the question of jurisdiction over areas adjacent to the border, most serious being the dispute over Kashmir and Jammu. The de facto boundary here is the cease-fire line which neither India nor Pakistan accepts as the final delimitation; at the present time this frontier is a military no man's land. On the northwestern frontier, claims by Afghanistan, purportedly on behalf of the Pushtu-speaking tribal groups seeking autonomy, have strained the relations with Pakistan. In this dispute the presence of Pushtu-speaking groups on both sides of the border has been an important consideration. Minor disputes with India over the location of East Pakistan's boundaries have been settled by arbitration, and similar progress has been achieved on the delineation of the western province's Indian border. West Pakistan's area of intensive settlement and economic development is represented by a narrow corridor reaching from Karachi on the coast up the Indus valley to the fertile Multan-Peshawar-Lahore triangle. Except for the impediment offered by the Thar desert, it is exposed along its entire eastern flank. In the north a second side of the triangle is flanked by the Kashmir border which skirts the foothills of the Himalayas. Backed by a barren mountainous interior the coast for most of its length offers little shelter and difficult access to the interior. Only the short stretch from Karachi eastward to the Indus delta provides easy access to the Indus valley.

Geography and the State

Pakistan offers no exception to the generalization that popular views differ from geographic realities in most countries of the world. Economic discussion in journals and newspapers is almost invariably infused with optimism about the country's resource base. While a less favorable position than India's in this respect is acknowledged, the limitations of present resources are not always recognized. There is certainly very little recognition in the eastern wing of the country that present differences in availability of fuels and minerals in the two wings must inevitably favor more rapid industrial development in West Pakistan.

As would be expected, where regional differences are so great local preferences are very strong. The agriculturalist of the Indus plain may know something of the landscapes and the way of life of the mountain borderlands but he is essentially provincial, confined to his own narrow horizons. The Bengali too has strong regional preferences and, if transplanted to the western wing, finds the geographic and cultural environment very different and unsatisfactory.

Transportation System of East Pakistan

The economic development of East Pakistan is held in check both by the subsistence nature of the economy and by the very bad transport facilities (see the map, Transportation System of East Pakistan). But construction of railways and roads is a difficult and costly undertaking in a region of so extensive a river system. Indeed, the embankments built up in road and railway construction stop natural drainage and can lead to disastrous floods. The railway system is rudimentary, and good roads are practically nonexistent outside the main towns and the Sylhet tea-growing area.

With few exceptions the roads that do exist are fair weather roads—unusable during the monsoon season from June to September and for varying periods after every downpour. The First Five Year Plan estimated that about three-quarters of the nonlocal freight movement is by inland waterways, of which about 4,000 miles are estimated to be navigable by river steamers in the monsoon season, one-quarter on the 1,700 miles of railway, and a negligible proportion on the roads. However, about 740 miles of new roads are under construction and an additional 130 miles will be added during the

TRANSPORTATION SYSTEM OF EAST PAKISTAN

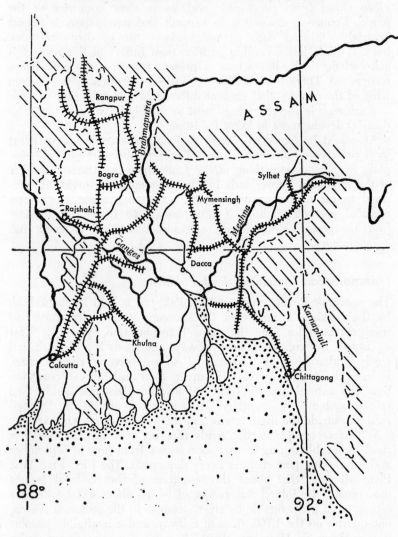

Second Five Year Plan. Bus traffic in Dacca and Chittagong will be augmented by new services effected by state-owned corporations. In the private sector provisions are made for the introduction of 1,000 buses and 2,400 trucks. In addition, the sum of Rs. 310 million has been allotted for the rehabilitation of the railway system of East Pakistan.

Rivers, the backbone of the province's transport system, do provide cheap transportation for goods and passengers but movement is slow. Although East Pakistan is much smaller than West Pakistan, the absence of cheap and available air travel means that most journeys involve both rail and water transport. Of four distinct groups of boat operators, by far the most numerous are the owner-operators of hundreds of thousands of small craft, normally called country boats, propelled by manpower. Country boats vary in size from the *dinghies* (the word is of Bengali origin) used as runabouts by every family that can afford one, through the sampan-like *pulwars*, to the larger *putelees*. The putelees carry up to 35 tons of jute to the baling presses, their hulls barely visible under the weight of the piles of jute, a sail perched on top. Practically all local rural traffic and an estimated 75 to 90 per cent of the total traffic is handled by these boats, which are still being built to centuries-old designs.

Competing with the country boats, however, and likely to supersede them eventually, are a growing number of small motorized craft which provide local passenger and freight traffic, comparable in a way to the local bus and truck services in West Pakistan. Somewhat larger in size are the ships of the government-owned East Pakistan Railway flotilla and about half a dozen Pakistani companies. These are mostly concerned with the transport of baled jute to factories and especially to Chalna port. Close to two-thirds of longer distance traffic, both passenger and freight, is still carried by two British-owned and managed inland shipping companies, the Rivers Steam Navigation Company, Ltd. and the India General Navigation and Railway Company, Ltd. Even excluding several hundred "flats" used as landing stages and transit sheds, these two companies are believed to have a combined fleet of more than five hundred craft, including passenger and freight steamers for operation on both main routes and feeder services, barges of varying types and sizes, and tugs and launches.

While water transport in East Pakistan potentially offers a very cheap and efficient transport system, at present it falls far short of doing so, due largely to poor coordination of necessary services. There is growing recognition of the need for an agency to direct river surveys, the provision of navigational aids, maintenance of water channels through dredging and river training, eradication of water hyacinth (a weed which fouls waterways), provision of pilotage and salvage facilities, enforcement of navigation rules, survey of vessels, and maintenance of inland ports. A step in this direction was the establishment in October 1958 of the Inland Water Transport Authority in East Pakistan with functions analogous to those recommended earlier by the Planning Commission. This authority initiated schemes for the improvement of navigational aids, the development of inland ports, and the provision of other facilities. During the term of the Second Five Year Plan attention will be focused on the development of major and secondary inland ports, the dredging of navigational channels, and provision of such facilities as landing stages, research centers, and navigational aids. In the private sector the program includes modernization and replacement of the existing fleet, development of shipyards, and a pilot yard for the construction of tugs and other small craft. In summary, the Second Plan provides Rs. 80 million in the semipublic sector and Rs. 95 million in the private sector for the development of inland water transport in East Pakistan. Since 1957, shipyards have been active at Khulna and Narayanganj for the construction of large and small vessels respectively.

At the time of partition, Chittagong was a very small and somewhat dilapidated port, concerned mainly with the export of tea and the import of tea plantation stores. It had only four berths and could handle about a half million tons of cargo a year. Suddenly it was required to handle the main traffic of East Pakistan, and works were rushed forward that brought the capacity to about three million tons a year. There are now seventeen berths, nine of which have improved facilities such as modern cranes, three moorings, and the necessary storage warehouses. Chittagong suffers from being on a heavily silted river, with a bar at the mouth which limits the size of ships using it to some 8,000 tons.

To take the place of Calcutta, particularly for the western area of the province, an anchorage first at Chalna, now moved eight miles downstream to Mungla, is in process of being developed into a major port. All shore installations are at Khulna, some twenty-five miles upstream from Mungla, which also serves as a railhead, but this distance does not matter too much as the port mainly serves as a transshipment point for jute exports from inland water transport, and the river ships and barges can and do lie alongside the deep-sea vessels. The channel at Mungla is wide, straight, and deep, and considerably bigger ships can enter the Pusur river to reach Mungla than can cross the bar at the mouth of the Karnaphuli to reach Chittagong. In the Second Five Year Plan the sum of Rs. 29 million has been allocated for the construction of a jetty and of housing for port personnel at Khulna, for supplying fresh water to Mungla, for the purchase of tugs, launches, and barges, and for the provision of other navigational facilities for Mungla. No major works are to be undertaken until the hydraulic investigation of the Pusur river to determine the permanent site for the port has been completed and studied.

At partition, East Pakistan inherited from undivided India two distinct railway systems. East of the Brahmaputra was the meter-gauge (3′ 3¼″) of the old Bengal and Assam Railway, built originally to serve the tea plantations of Assam but with connections to Dacca-Mymensingh in the northeastern half of the province. West of the Brahmaputra were two segments of broad-gauge (5′ 6″) track now joined in Pakistan by the construction of a 43-mile link from Jessore to Darsana so as to make a broad-gauge main line from the northern border just short of Silguri in India to Khulna, the railhead for the port of Chalna. This broad-gauge main line crosses the Ganges at the Hardinge bridge. There is also a meter-gauge network north of the Ganges.

Both the railway networks were in a very poor condition at partition, having been very much overused in the war on the Burmese frontier. The bridges and track are still in a condition that compels slow running over much of the main line. The rolling stock is also overage and, with very few replacements having been made, the biggest problem has been the creation of effective repair facilities, especially for the lines west of the Brahmaputra. Railway operations in East Pakistan are made extremely difficult by the riverine conditions: most track is laid on high embankments and there are very many bridges. Both the embankments and the bridges are liable to heavy damage in the annual floods. A change in the rail situation is likely under the Second Five Year Plan, which includes Rs. 427.7 million for new rolling stock, track and repair facilities, and the construction of new railway lines for the Pakistan Eastern Railway system.

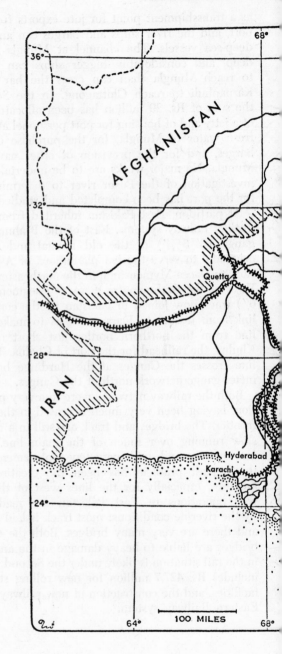

36°

JAMMU
AND
KASHMIR

Peshawar

Rawalpindi

Jhelum

Chenab

Ravi R.

32°

Lahore

Sutlej

Multan

Bahawalpur

Indus

28°

Sukkur

I N D I A

24°

72°   76°

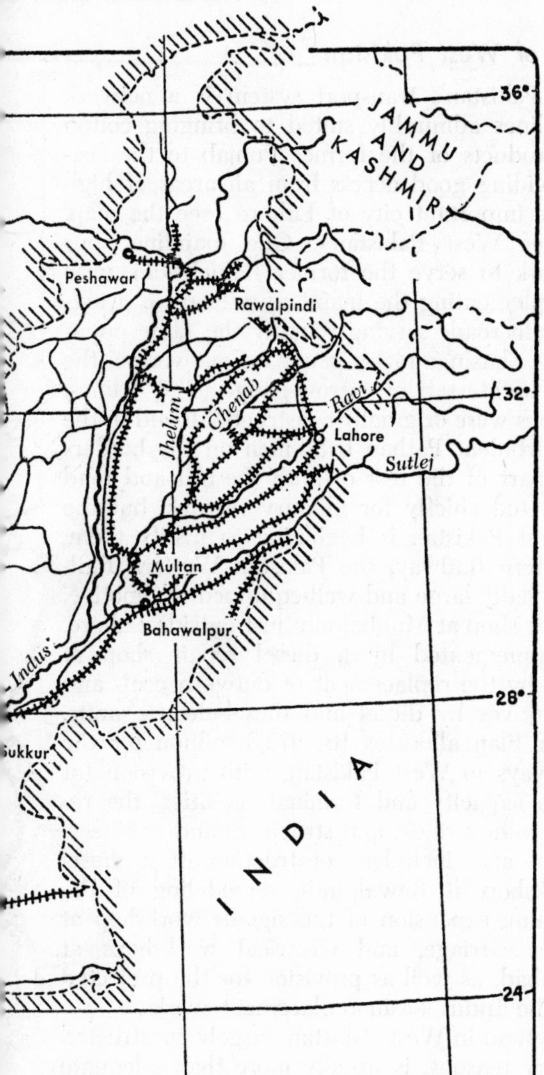

Transportation System of West Pakistan

The backbone of West Pakistan's transport system is a network of broad-gauge railway lines admirably suited to bringing cotton and other agricultural products of the former Punjab to the seaport at Karachi and providing good access from all areas of high population density to the important city of Lahore (see the map, Transportation System of West Pakistan). One mainline spur leaves this central network to serve the former Baluchistan, with Quetta as its center. Supplementing the mainline railways is a network of hard-surfaced main roads serving roughly the same populous areas of the Indus river basin, a meter-gauge rail network in the former Sind, and three separate sets of narrow-gauge (2′ 6″) lines.

These narrow-gauge lines were originally constructed to aid in the military control of the turbulent Pathan tribesmen on the borders of Afghanistan. A large part of the rest of both the rail and road systems was also constructed chiefly for military reasons, but the growing economy of West Pakistan is beginning to justify them. Unlike the Pakistan Eastern Railway, the Pakistan Western Railway inherited an exceptionally large and well-equipped locomotive, carriage, and wagon repair shop at Mughalpura just outside Lahore. This has now been supplemented by a diesel repair shop at Karachi, made necessary by the replacement of outworn coal- and oil-burning steam locomotives by diesel and diesel-electric units.

The Second Five Year Plan allocates Rs. 972.3 million for the development of the railways in West Pakistan, with provision for the improvement of line capacity and terminal facilities, the rehabilitation of track and rolling stock, and structural and engineering works. The program also includes construction of a diesel electric locomotive workshop at Rawalpindi, remodeling of the bridge workshop at Jhelum, expansion of the signals workshop at Lahore, and locomotive, carriage, and electrical workshops at Mughalpura and Hyderabad, as well as provision for the projected traffic requirements of the Indus basin replacement works.

While the main road system in West Pakistan, largely constructed by the British for military reasons, is usually more than adequate to the present traffic, many villages are connected to the system by the roughest of trails. Villagers have to bring themselves and their produce to the nearest main road in oxcarts or horse-drawn, two-wheeled tongas or, in areas where the trails are too bad even for these wheeled vehicles, on the backs of donkeys, camels, or huge lumbering water buffaloes. It is not surprising that the few miles' trip to the nearest road or railway station is often more expensive than the rest of the journey to cities such as Lahore or Karachi.

But whenever the roads are in any way passable, there is a local truck or bus service. Often this will take the form of a truck with a wooden bus body put together by the local carpenter. Despite an almost complete dearth of factory-made spare parts, these makeshift vehicles manage to provide a much cheaper, faster, and more comfortable mode of transport than the animal-drawn transport they replace.

On the main roads the West Pakistan Road Transport Board now runs a fleet of more than 850 well-maintained buses. Fares are relatively higher but these buses have a monopoly of the longer routes. There are also a growing number of private truckers on the roads, particularly for the haulage of rural produce to nearby towns. Among the most enterprising independent truckers are the Shinwari tribesmen of the Khyber Pass, who appear to have found little difficulty in converting from camels to trucks and have even developed a system of hire-purchase for selling trucks to the younger generation. The Shinwari control almost all trade to Afghanistan and also own and drive a large percentage of the trucks as far south as Lahore.

The Second Five Year Plan has provided Rs. 319 million for roads and bridges in West Pakistan (including special and frontier areas and Azad Kashmir). To serve the vast land mass of the province and to open up the less accessible areas, about 2,875 miles of new roads are to be built. Also planned are new bridges over the Indus near Thalta, the Sutlej near Bahawalpur, the Ravi near Lahore, and the Jhelum near Jhelum city. Some 900 vehicles are to be replaced and 500 buses added to the fleet of the West Pakistan Road Transport Board; an additional 700 buses will be bought for the Karachi Road Transport Corporation. In the private sector, provision has been made for 3,000 new buses and 10,000 new trucks.

Air services too are to be expanded under the Second Five Year Plan. Runways and other facilities at Multan, Mianwali, Lyallpur, and Sukkur are scheduled for improvement; some airports will be equipped to handle jet traffic; and Rs. 200 million has been set aside, apart from the PIA development expenditure, its own resources, and loans from government and private sources, for the civil aviation development program.

CHAPTER 4

Population and Ethnic Groups

WITH A POPULATION OF 93,691,000 according to the 1961 census (see Table 1), Pakistan ranks seventh among the world's most populous countries after China, India, the USSR, the United States, Japan, and Indonesia. The distinctiveness of the regional divisions in Pakistan produces several unusual demographic features, beginning with the marked differences between and within the two wings. But because the population is part of a larger subcontinental aggregation many underlying similarities are to be found too.

Given the primarily rural and agricultural nature of the country, the pattern of population density and distribution reflects the location and productivity of arable land. Average population density for the country in 1961 was 256 persons per square mile, but this figure derives from an average 922 persons per square mile in the eastern wing compared to 138 in the western wing. Behind this discrepancy is the fact that East Pakistan, with more than half the national population, has substantially less area under cultivation than West Pakistan despite a higher ratio—64 per cent—of arable land to total area. The highest densities within East Pakistan are found in the fertile flood plains of the major rivers, where there are an average 1,000 persons per square mile. In the districts of Dacca, Comilla, and Noakhali the figure is over 1,200. Only in one district—a district in the southeastern hill margins entirely outside the Ganges-Brahmaputra plain—does the density go below 100 persons per square mile.

West Pakistan, with an average population density of 138, presents a remarkable contrast to East Pakistan. Unlike the eastern wing, where the area of intensive settlement closely approximates the area of the political unit, intensive settlement in the western wing occupies but a minor part of total area, being confined to a northern triangle between Lahore, Peshawar, and Multan and a narrow corridor to the coast oriented along the irrigation canal system of the Indus valley.

Population densities of less than 100 per square mile prevail in more than half of West Pakistan. Indeed, Baluchistan is the most extensive "empty" land in the subcontinent, having population densities as low as 7 persons per square mile over vast areas. As in East Pakistan the distribution and productivity of arable land is the primary determinant of intensive settlement, e.g. more than half of West Pakistan's population is concentrated in the former province of the Punjab where the first large-scale irrigation projects were undertaken by the British.

The low ratio of urban to rural population is another demographic characteristic of the country. By the census definition, urban includes those persons living in cities and towns with more than 5,000 inhabitants. Some 12,295,000 people or 13.1 per cent of the population are classified in this category. The balance of the population, classified as rural, live in some sort of nucleated settlement. An exception to this is found in East Pakistan where the cultivators are more likely to live in dispersed homesteads on the land they till. The relatively small urban element in the population points up the importance of agriculture in the economy and the lack of industrialization. Yet the national average for the urban percentage of the population conceals considerable differences between the two wings. The urban element amounts to 22.5 per cent in West Pakistan against 5.2 per cent in East Pakistan and only three of twelve cities with more than 100,000 population are located in the eastern wing (see Table 2).

In the 1951-61 decade the most remarkable urban growth occurred in Karachi, whose population went from 1,068,000 to 1,916,000, due largely to the temporary establishment of the new national capital there and a rapid expansion in the volume of traffic handled by the port. According to the results of the census of 1961, Pakistan's population is currently increasing at the rate of 2.16 per cent a year—a rate of growth bound to affect the efforts being made to improve the general standard of living. Should growth continue at this rate, by 1970 there will be another 18 million inhabitants in the country.

Obviously many questions are raised by such demographic trends, but few answers are forthcoming as to the probable duration or magnitude of the present growth. Some answers are to be found in an examination of the factors of fertility, mortality, and population mobility, but the weakness of the statistical information in these areas renders any conclusions liable to serious error. One of the factors affecting fertility as well as contributing to variations in sociocultural patterns is the sex ratio. In the rural population of Pakistan this ratio—defined as the number of males per 100 females—is recorded at the high figure of 109 and jumps to 129 in the urban population. While evidence from other parts of the world indicates that a higher urban ratio is normal, such a preponderance of males in the population is unusual. A probable explanation in Pakistan is the underenumeration of women in the census due to the custom of purdah among Moslems.

The sex ratio takes on particular significance as a factor in differential rates of fertility when related to the age structure of the population. In Pakistan, because of high fertility and mortality, the population is relatively young. A standard graph of the age structure showing the number of people by sex in each of the age groups would resemble a broad-based pyramid rising rapidly to a point. Fifty-three per cent of the population is under twenty years of age, 41 per cent is between twenty and fifty-nine, and only 4.97 per cent is from age sixty up. The comparable figures for the United States are 34 per cent for the under-twenty group, 54 per cent for the middle-age group, and 12 per cent for the old-age group. This means that the degree of dependency in a young population like Pakistan's is high. A large number of the male population below the age twenty are at least partially employed, but it is the twenty to fifty-nine age group which makes up the bulk of the labor force and which must provide support for the others. The age structure has added ramifications in terms of the growth of the population. The present trends in birth and death rates suggest that the sides of the age structure pyramid are becoming less steep and that there is a growing number in the childbearing ages.

Birth and death rates are highly speculative because the registration of vital statistics in Pakistan is incomplete. But on the basis of information from the 1951 and 1961 censuses, it is possible to indicate the general magnitude of the figures, their trends, and the factors responsible for them. On the basis of this data, it has been estimated that death rates have been declining more rapidly than birth rates since the turn of the century. This differential decline is the primary factor in the substantial population growth during the period.

Between the 1920s and the 1930s the death rate in India is estimated to have fallen from 36 to 31 per thousand. The estimated life expectancy at birth of the average Indian rose from 23 to 31 years during the same period. In 1961 the life expectancy of the West Pakistani was 36.2 years and that of the East Pakistani was 31.1 years. The reasons for this high mortality rate are exceedingly complex. Uncertainty of the monsoon rains, a predominantly agrarian society, high population densities per unit of arable land, a limited variety of food crops and low yields related not only to soils and climate but to socioeconomic factors, and in general poorly developed human and natural resources are the main contributors to such high mortality. Until recently, famine and disease were the chief causes of death, but widespread mortality due to actual starvation has declined in importance despite evidence of increasing food shortage. The most recent famine was in 1943 in Bengal where 1.5 million deaths in excess of normal mortality were estimated. Though the accounts of its devastation are appalling, it was but a shadow of earlier ones which ravaged the subcontinent. Malnutrition currently contributes to debilitation and heightens susceptibility to disease, but for the moment famine has left the stage to disease and natural causes.

Of the reported deaths—a figure quite unrelated to the actual number of deaths—at least 85 per cent are from unknown causes. Most of the population die without having seen a doctor in their lifetime. Authorities seem to concur, however, in the opinion that malaria is the chief cause of death, followed by tuberculosis and then by cholera, smallpox, and enteritis. The fact that malaria causes more sickness and loss of working-power than any other disease is the more remarkable when one considers the presence of many debilitating fevers and unnumbered intestinal disorders which are endemic among the population.

Infant mortality as estimated for 1961 is 206 per thousand in West Pakistan and 237 per thousand in East Pakistan. These rates, among the highest in the world, are paralleled by a high maternal mortality rate estimated to be five times the figure in western European countries. In fact the subcontinent is one of the few areas in the world where the life expectancy of women is less than that of men.

Migration as a factor in population trends has many facets in

49

Pakistan. An unusual one, arising from the sharp contrast in population densities between the two wings, is the probability as conditions become favorable of interwing movement to equalize
population pressures. There were of course large-scale movements
of people across the frontiers with India at the time of partition.
Less apparent but of considerable social and economic significance
is a rural-urban movement which has been accelerated by increasing industrialization.

Prior to 1947 the population of the Indo-Pakistan subcontinent
was relatively immobile. The absolute number of internal and
external migrants was large, but relative to the total population,
movement was a minor factor. In the first four decades of the
century the per cent of the population living outside the province
or state of birth was low. Predominance of agriculture, the caste
system and its various modifications among the Moslems, early
marriage, the joint family system, and diversity of languages and
customs all contributed to this immobility. The largest sustained
internal migration was in the northeast. Between 1931 and 1951,
more than 15 million acres were brought under cultivation in
Assam by migrants from Bengal. There was also a flow of people
into the new lands opened up by the extension of irrigation in the
Indus valley. This movement was particularly apparent in the
province of Punjab and state of Bahawalpur where the rate of
population increase was consistently higher than the national
average. In Bengal, the number of migrants was never large enough
relative to the total population to affect the rate of growth.

Between East and West Pakistan, despite the greater population
pressure in the eastern wing, migration has been negligible. This
situation is not likely to change in the near future. Provincialism is
so strongly developed and economic opportunity so limited that
a long time will pass before the national labor force moves freely
from one wing to the other. Were provincialism not so strongly
developed, the lower per capita income and greater density per
unit of arable land in East Pakistan would tend to encourage
migration to the western wing.

The extent of internal migration in the two wings is difficult
to assess. There is seasonal migration of labor with the demands of
agriculture in both wings and there is movement of nomadic groups
in the western mountain borders to winter grazing in the Indus
plain. Seasonal migration formerly took place across the border
of West Pakistan, with large groups of Afghan tribespeople moving

their flocks to winter along the Indus plains, but stricter control measures at the Pakistan frontier have almost eliminated this movement. Rural-urban migration, which has been going on since the turn of the century, apparently accelerated in the years following partition. In the decade 1941-51 the population living in urban places increased by 41.9 per cent compared to an increase of 5 per cent in the rural areas; in the period 1951-61 these figures became 56.4 per cent and 19.8 per cent.

The migrations involving the greatest number of people are those that began with the increasing emphasis on communalism in 1946. After independence in 1947 this migration became an external movement, with the bulk of the exchange of Moslem and non-Moslem communalists occurring in the two divided provinces of Bengal and the Punjab. By 1951 an estimated sixteen million persons had been exchanged between India and Pakistan and in the period 1951-61 an additional 800,000 people migrated from India to Pakistan. Migration stemming from the partition of Bengal amounted to approximately five million persons by 1951. Non-Moslem emigrants from East Pakistan were approximately three million versus two million Moslem immigrants. Since that date Hindu emigration from East Pakistan has continued but has not been balanced by similar numbers of Moslems migrating from India. Net migration therefore represents a decrease of at least one million and probably more in the eastern wing. The opposite situation prevailed in West Pakistan where a net increase in population resulted from communal migrations. The number of refugees probably exceeded eleven million, most of whom had moved in the twelve months following August 1947. Indian sources cite 4.7 million refugees from West Pakistan while the census of Pakistan lists 6.5 million refugees from India.

As a result of these large-scale communal migrations the religious composition of the population has altered. In addition, minor alterations in the relative size of the linguistic groups occurred and the traditional immobility of the population underwent considerable change. In West Pakistan the percentage of Moslems in the population rose from 78 per cent in 1941 to 97 per cent a decade later and to 97.2 per cent in 1961. The change in East Pakistan was less pronounced. From 70.4 per cent in 1941 it rose to 70.6 per cent in 1951 and to 80.4 per cent in 1961. Changes in linguistic patterns were less significant, as most of the refugees came from the Indian portions of the Punjab and Bengal. The only overall

51

effect was an increase in the number of Urdu speakers in both wings.

The most apparent impact of the refugees occurred in the urban areas. By 1951, 45 per cent of the urban population of West Pakistan was made up of refugees. The census figure for the eastern wing was a much lower 12 per cent but there enumeration of refugees was admittedly incomplete. The sum effect of communal migration was not so much a rapid increase in the urban population as a marked change in the religious composition of the towns and cities.

One important question which should be examined is the prospect of continuing communal migration. In 1951 there were thirty-five million Moslems in India and ten million Hindus in Pakistan and the figure for Hindus in Pakistan was the same in 1961. Some migration can therefore be expected to continue, but in numbers determined by the policies of the two governments. The availability of passports and visas and the financial or other kinds of aid offered to the migrants in the country of resettlement are major determinants of the number of migrants. Neither country appears interested in accepting any large-scale net increase in population from communal migration now that the initial dislocations are over.

In Pakistan there has been official recognition of the special problems of the refugees. Efforts have been made to provide low-cost housing in a number of satellite towns. The First Five Year Plan included $41.9 million for essential needs in housing, water supply, drainage, and sanitation, and the Second Five Year Plan provides an additional $28.7 million. Much of these funds go to improving the condition of the refugees.

The critical long-range problem of population growth received considerable notice in government and private circles, but for some years resulted in few concrete proposals. The First Five Year Plan, while taking cognizance of the controversial aspects of family planning, noted that all attempts to improve the standard of living may fail unless population growth can be kept at a low rate. Private groups made modest efforts to disseminate information on family planning, and the central government made provisions in the budget for 1957-58 of 500,000 rupees ($105,000) to commence a program of education in family planning. The Second Five Year Plan allocates $1.4 million for family planning. In 1962 some 800 family planning centers were in operation, and plans had been made to increase the total to 3,000.

Ethnic Groups and Traditional Groups

One of the major features of Pakistan is the existence of a wide racial, linguistic, and cultural diversity in the population and of a large number of distinctive traditional groups with strong group identity. In so far as the term "ethnic groups" has meaning in Pakistan it does not refer to large national minorities distinguished by a combination of race, language, and culture. It refers, instead, to fairly small hereditary social groups defined in a variety of ways. A distinguishing feature of the traditional social group may be its religion or sect, its language or dialect, its occupation, caste, tribe, home territory, or any combination of these, but nearly always there is more than one. Its members may also accentuate their identity by distinctive forms of dress and deportment, and by these signs the members of other groups will know, in part, how to behave toward them.

Of all the defining features, language and dialect are probably the most important. The traditional groups usually have linguistic as well as social boundaries and will therefore often function and have meaning within the context of the linguistic region rather than the nation as a whole. The five main regions generally correspond with the former provincial boundaries. Baluchi is the most important language in the former Baluchistan Province and States Union; Pushtu prevails in the former North-West Frontier Province and Tribal Agencies; Punjabi is spoken in the Punjab and the former Bahawalpur State; the Sindhi-speaking region includes Sind, the former Khairpur State, and the area of Karachi; and Bengali is the language of East Bengal. The first four regions now form the single province of West Pakistan and the fifth is called East Pakistan, but the former names will be used here. Language and dialect are also important defining factors within some of the regions but not in others. Since there is no single set of criteria by which all the important groups can be included, it is necessary to adopt shifting principles of definition.

The categories by which an individual is identified also shift, of course, depending on the circumstances. He may be labeled according to traditional social group in one case, to family, profession, religion, or political party in others, or according to home district or province if he is outside it. It is impossible to determine always which category is the most significant, but the geographical is increasing in importance. And certain stereotypes

53

about the members of each linguistic province bear on the conduct of national affairs.

The Significance of Ethnic Groups

The great majority of the people of India and Pakistan belong racially to various branches of the Caucasoid stock, but virtually every racial type may be seen in Pakistan: the tall, fair-skinned, blue-eyed man of the extreme northwest; the olive-skinned, fine-boned, hawk-nosed "Iranian" type; the smaller, dark-skinned peoples of "Dravidian" and "Australoid" origin; some peoples with Negroid features; the wheaten-skinned, dark-eyed "Indo-Aryan" types; and short- and long-headed Mongoloid peoples. There are innumerable permutations and combinations of all of these strains.

In consequence, the social significance of particular racial features is extremely variable. No ideal racial type is accepted by all Pakistanis, or even by a large majority of them. In Baluchistan, for example, the short Iranian head is admired, so much so that the three major tribes sometimes bind their daughters' heads. In other areas long-headedness is valued; in still others the shape of the head is a matter of complete indifference. In the North-West Frontier the people pride themselves on their height and fair skin; in Bengal, where the people are shorter and darker, other qualities are valued. In so far as skin color is given any consideration in Pakistan, fair skin is generally preferred to dark skin.

While race may have little and varying social significance, foreign origin (from Islamic rather than European countries) has definite and widespread prestige. The traditional social groups of Pakistan are popularly classified in two groups: the *ashraf* or *sherif* class (the "high-born") and the *ajlaf* or *atraf* (the "low-born"). Technically, the ashraf groups are those descended from the Moslems who invaded and ruled the subcontinent and are of Arab, Turkish, or Afghan ancestry. The ajlaf, the great majority, are descended from indigenous peoples converted to Islam. Thus, in the traditional ranking system of Pakistan, groups establishing a claim to origin outside the country in Moslem lands to the west have the highest prestige.

Baluchis

The traditional social groups of Baluchistan are tribes which are classified primarily by language and dialect but may also be

54

distinguished by dress and customs. Tribal organization was so developed that the British could administer the area through negotiations with the tribal chiefs, who were generally strong enough to exact obedience from the tribesmen. At independence this system was in large part retained by the Pakistan government. Because of the administrative importance of having statistics on the tribes, the 1951 census of Baluchistan retained the "race and tribe" enumeration of previous censuses, though Baluchistan is the only former province in which this was done. The 1961 census merely recorded that there were 1,161,011 people in the area.

The "indigenous" or permanent resident population accounts for 91 per cent of the total for the province and can be divided into several groups, of which the most important are the Baluchi, Brahui, and Pathan. In 1951 the 301,000 Baluchis, after whom the province was named, accounted for 26 per cent of its population. About the same number live in adjacent Iran; many have settled in southeastern Punjab; others are scattered about West Pakistan and northwestern India. There are more than a dozen main tribes in Baluchistan, each with a number of clan subdivisions. The Baluchi dialects are of the Iranian branch of the Indo-European language family and the tribes are divided into two groups, eastern and western, largely on the basis of dialect. The 189,000 eastern Baluchis include seven main tribes, the largest being the Rind, Mari, and Bugti. The 112,000 western Baluchis include nine main tribes, of which the Rind and Rakhshani are by far the largest.

The Baluchis are of medium to tall stature and slender, muscular build, with round heads, squarish faces, straight or convex noses, and dark eyes and hair. Living in arid and inhospitable terrain, they are basically pastoral nomads, though many have become farmers, soldiers, policemen, and rent collectors for big landlords. It has been said that the Baluchis make good soldiers and policemen but, still close to banditry and nomadism, hate to farm.

Brahuis

In 1951 there were 262,000 Brahuis in Baluchistan, forming 23 per cent of the population. Their language, Brahui, is a Dravidian tongue allied to those spoken in southern India. In other respects, however, the Brahuis have little in common with the Dravidians of South India. All of them are Sunni Moslems. Their height ranges from medium to over six feet; their eyes and skin are light to dark brown; their heads are large with heavy brow ridges and often snub noses. They were probably long-headed originally but have absorbed much Baluchi blood and so admire the short Iranian head that they mold their children's skulls. They are said to be bold, talkative, dependable, suspicious of outside authority, quick to anger, quick to forgive and forget.

The Brahuis claim both an origin in Aleppo and descent from the peoples of the Mohenjodero civilization of the third millennium B.C. As these conflicting accounts suggest, the Brahuis are composed of extremely heterogeneous elements which have in common only their language and the unity of a tribal confederation formed for political and military purposes. The confederation is headed by the ruler of the former Kalat State. There are twenty-nine Brahui tribes grouped into four branches. The small original nucleus of eight "true Brahui" tribes supplied the ruling house of Kalat. The Sarawan branch lives in northern Kalat, while the Jhalawan branch, which includes more than half the Brahuis, lives in southern Kalat. The fourth branch contains miscellaneous small tribes.

The Brahuis are nomadic farmers and herdsmen. From March to October they grow cereals, fruits, and vegetables; in November they move south to sell cattle and handicrafts and work as seasonal laborers; and they return to the north in the spring. In the past, increasing numbers of them remained in Sind to settle on land opened up by irrigation.

Other Groups in Baluchistan

The 244,000 Pathans make up 21 per cent of the population of Baluchistan. Of the six main Pathan tribes in the area, the Kakar is by far the largest, followed by the Tarin and Pani. These Pushtu-speaking tribes live primarily in the northern areas near the North-West Frontier province, the Pathan homeland in Pakistan.

Other sizable indigenous groups include the Jatts, Lassis, and some distinctive tribes of Makran. The Jatts (88,522) are cultivators in north-central Baluchistan and have their own dialect, Jattki, a variant of Sindhi; they are unrelated to the Jats of Punjab. The Lassis (39,465) live in the former Las Bela State; their tongue, Lassi, is also a variant of Sindhi and there has been a steady flow of Lassis into Karachi and Sind for employment. The tribes of Makran such as the Darzada, Nakib, and Lori are often called simply "Makranis" by outsiders. Some of them, traditionally gypsies, tinkers, and minstrels, display marked Negroid features and have moved into Karachi to become stevedores and unskilled laborers.

Pathans

The Pathans are the major ethnic group of the former North-West Frontier Province and Tribal Agencies and are found in sizable numbers in some other parts of Pakistan. The term "Pathan" is an Anglicization of Pakhtun or Pashtun, the pronunciation of one letter of the name varying in the two dialects of the Pakhto or Pashto language. Sometimes "Pathan" refers loosely to all persons whose home is the North-West Frontier province, but a distinction should be made between the "true" Pathans and others. The "true" Pathans or Pakhtuns belong to recognized tribes. In Afghanistan they have supplied the ruling families for two centuries and are sometimes referred to as the "true Afghans." There is no agreement as to their original ethnic strain, but they may reflect Aryan origins with later mixtures of Turkish stock. Generally speaking, they are tall and well-built, with long heads, large hawk noses, and sharp angular features; they have dark hair, rather fair skin, and many have blue or gray eyes. The census of 1961 gave a total of some seven million inhabitants of the areas in which Pathans are found, and it may be suggested that the Pathans number about five million.

In the tribal areas (see the map, Tribes of the North-West Frontier) there are numerous Pathan tribes and lineages, each of which has a more or less clearly defined home territory and may have special forms of dress, speech, and manners that distinguish it from its neighbors. The Pathan tribes have never been united. By tradition, they have a fierce spirit of independence, both personal and tribal. Their code of honor, *pakhtunwali,* calls for blood vengeance regardless of cost; asylum to all fugitives and acceptance of truce offers; and generous hospitality to all guests. Arrogant and unruly, the Pathans are known for their fighting prowess, their endless feuds, and their pride in their independent way of life.

These stereotypes apply more to the Pathans in the Malakand, Mohmand, Khyber, Kurram, and Waziristan Agencies than to the settled Pathans in the districts of the former North-West Frontier province. Whereas the Pathans in the Agencies are still governed to a large extent by their own codes and institutions, the tribes to which the settled Pathans belong have long since ceased to be

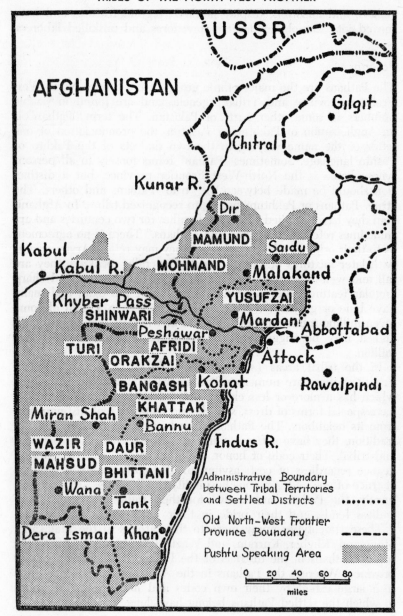

tribes in the political sense of the term. In the districts, the Pathans are generally law-abiding, less distinctive, and more prosperous. Besides being farmers and landlords, many have taken to business, trade, the professions, and government service. The Khattaks, once the fiercest opponents of the Moghul rulers, are now nearly all settled in the districts and have won a reputation as hard-working cultivators and craftsmen. Similarly, the Yusufzai bitterly fought the British during the last century but have now moved into Mardan district and farm some of the best land in the province.

. The current "problem tribes" of the region—Wazirs, Mahsuds, Mohmands, and Afridis—inhabit the most isolated and barren hill country, but even they are not as wild as they once were. The Afridis, experts in gun manufacture, operate a profitable trucking business in the Khyber Pass and are skilled mechanics and drivers. They, and the other tribes like them, increasingly favor the introduction of schools, welfare services, and economic development, but on their own terms, so that they will not sacrifice their independence for economic advantage.

Historically, the hill tribes lived by raiding the more fertile lowlands and by making the most of their only asset, control of the passes to the subcontinent. They continually made trouble for the British, who considered control of the passes essential to the safety of the Indian empire. British policy toward the tribes alternated between punitive military expeditions and the calculated payment of subsidies. At independence, the tribesmen voted overwhelmingly for accession to Pakistan. The government withdrew its military forces while continuing the subsidies and increasing welfare services and economic aid where these were wanted. As a government of fellow Moslems with able civil servants in the Agencies, Pakistan has had much less difficulty in handling the tribes and there are now very few raids into the settled valleys. The Pathans continue to be very proud of their martial exploits, including their participation in the 1947 Kashmir *lashkar* (war party).

The government of Afghanistan has attempted to exploit the fact that the political boundary between the two nations is not an ethnic one by demanding the creation of an autonomous state called Pushtunistan. Pushtunistan would include the former North-West Frontier province, the region of the Agencies, and a part of Baluchistan, but no Afghan tribal territory. This campaign, financed from Kabul, gained support among some tribal factions and has caused much bad feeling between the two governments. Among the settled Pathans, there is some dissatisfaction over the incorporation of the districts of the North-West Frontier province into West Pakistan because the one-unit government is more remote from the governed and might be dominated by Punjabis.

Other Groups in the Pathan Areas

The approximately three million people in the settled districts can be divided about equally between the Pathans and a large number of functional and agricultural groups of mixed origin. One of the latter, the Sayyids, has a special religious status and, though generally dependent on the patronage of the Pathan landlords, is only slightly inferior socially. The rest of the groups make up the lower class.

The two most important lower class groups, each more numerous than the Sayyids, are the agriculturist Awans and Gujars, who work for the landowning Pathans as laborers and servants. Their status is definitely inferior and intermarriage with the Pathans very rare. The group names among the lower class and often the dialects too are similar to those of corresponding groups in the Punjab and, like their Punjabi neighbors, these people have softer features and somewhat darker skin than the Pathans.

Until recently as many as 70,000 Pashtuns from the highlands of Afghanistan moved across the frontier every year to spend the winter in Pakistan while their sheep and goats grazed on familiar pastures. Known as *powindehs,* or purveyors of merchandise, the nomadic Pashtuns brought skins, wool, and rugs to exchange for sugar, tea, and textiles. But as a result of the dispute over Pushtunistan, the government of Pakistan instituted measures of control along the frontier, e.g. demanding certificates of health and identity papers, which have inhibited the movement of these tribes.

In the remote mountain valleys of the Malakand Agency in the northern frontier region—particularly Chitral, the northernmost state of West Pakistan—are a number of small communities of Moslems distinguished by language, custom, dress, and physical type. The bulk of these people or about ninety thousand are Khos, whose features are slightly darker, a little broader, and more Mongoloid than the Pathans. Their language, Khowar, is Indo-European, but of the Dardic rather than the Iranian branch—and quite different from Pushtu.

60

In Chitral too are the so-called Kafirs ("unbelievers") who live in remote villages. There are an estimated three thousand in Pakistan compared to about sixty thousand in Afghanistan. The Kafirs in Pakistan are divided into two sections, Black and Red, which speak different dialects. The Kafir tongues, classified as Dardic in the census, are related to early forms of Sanskrit and the people—medium to tall, fair-skinned, long-headed, and many with light hair and eyes—may represent the remnants of the original Indo-European invaders of India in the second millennium B.C. Though most have been at least nominally converted to Islam, the Kafirs continue to follow some of their own peculiar customs, notably, their unusual burial customs and rites for the dead and their vigorous forms of dancing.

The Groups of the Punjab and Bahawalpur

The twenty-five million people of the Punjab and Bahawalpur belong to a large number of traditional groups. Language, race, and tribal organization play a less important part in differentiating groups here than in Baluchistan or the North-West Frontier. In general these people, most of whom speak Punjabi, are racially of the Indo-Aryan type, with wheaten or light brown complexions, medium to tall stature, and dark hair and brown eyes.

Except for a few minorities distinguished by religion, the major distinguishing feature is caste, defined as an endogamous group with either a common traditional occupation or a tradition of descent from a common ancestor or both, but without the Hindu connotations of religious (as distinct from social) hierarchy and hereditary ritual purity or pollution. Used in this sense, the term caste is as applicable to Moslems as to Hindus. Most of the traditional social groups of the Punjab constitute such castes, with customs and rites that differ from those of castes elsewhere in Pakistan only in matters of detail.

In the prepartition Indian censuses the Punjabi castes were usually described either as functional castes or as "agricultural tribes." Tribal groups typically claim descent from a single ancestor and functional groups tend to have traditional occupations. The actual occupational situation may be different. In a number of the functional castes, both Hindu and Moslem, the majority of the members no longer follow the traditional caste occupation even though their name and general social status still derive from the occupation. The agricultural tribes are occupational castes too but differ in tracing their origins to common mythological ancestors rather than to nonagricultural specializations. The largest Moslem castes in the Punjab are agricultural, the groups described below all having 300,000 or more members as of 1931, with endogamous subsections in many cases.

Moslem Castes of the Punjab

According to the census of 1931, the last to enumerate "race, tribe, and caste," there were three castes with over a million Moslem members in this area: the Jats, Rajputs, and Arains.

In terms of social precedence, the Rajputs come first. The name "Rajput" means "prince" (literally "raja's son") and the Rajputs are by tradition warriors, rulers, landowners, and cultivators. They are believed to be descended largely from Central Asian peoples who entered India before the coming of Islam. Divided into numerous lineages, the Rajputs are known for their quasi-feudal tribal system, their romantic character, chivalrous valor, and punctilious regard for personal honor. The Moslem Rajputs are believed to stem from local aristocrats who were converted to Islam during the Moghul period and who held positions of honor in the army and administration. The Rajputs contributed large numbers of excellent soldiers to the British Indian army and today remain the most important element in the army of Pakistan.

The Jats, with nearly three million Moslems according to the 1931 census, are the largest caste in the Punjab. Sharing with the Rajputs a resemblance to the Spaniard or Italian in physical type, the Jats enjoy a social position only slightly lower than that of the Rajputs, the line between the two sometimes becoming indistinct. The Jat is the Punjabi peasant par excellence and has on occasion contributed substantially to the fighting forces of the country. Though respected as a landowning cultivator and a superb, hardworking farmer, the Jat is also characterized by some as stolid or even taciturn, unimaginative, and perhaps somewhat dim-witted. The Arains, like the Jats an agricultural tribe of good social standing, moved into the colony districts in large numbers when land was first being opened by irrigation and, bearing out a reputation for enterprise, have also taken up several new occupations.

There are five other castes which in 1931 had just over a half million Moslems each. The Bilochs, derived largely from the tribes of Baluchistan, constitute one and are to be found in the southwest Punjab engaged largely in agriculture and animal husbandry. Their fame as camel drivers is so widespread that in some areas all camel drivers, whatever their origin, are called Bilochs. Two other of the smaller castes are the Awans and Gujars, agricultural tribes living mostly in the northwest Punjab. These tribes are related to the Awans and Gujars of the North-West Frontier province but have a higher social status in the Punjab, ranking just below the Jats, who are apparently better cultivators. Of the remaining two groups, the Lohars and the Tarkhans together constitute a functional caste whose members have traditionally been blacksmiths, carpenters, and artisans. The Julahas are a functional caste of weavers with a status only slightly higher than that of the Untouchables. In the folklore of some areas the Julahas are cast as cowards by nature. At least two-thirds of the workers in both these castes engage in the traditional occupations.

Five other functional castes had between 340,000 and 460,000 Moslem members in 1931. Four of these—the shoemakers and cobblers; the oil pressers; the potters; and the water carriers, boatmen, and fishermen—have a status roughly comparable to the Julahas. The Chuhras and Mussallis, the fifth caste, who are traditionally sweepers and scavengers or, often, landless agricultural laborers and menials have the lowest status. The Chuhras, the parent group, are believed to have been originally a dark-skinned Dravidian tribe, but although they retain some of their own practices and beliefs they are not now racially distinct from most of the rest of the population. Hindu Chuhras are Untouchables, now called Scheduled Castes. Moslem Chuhras are usually called Mussallis and retain much of their stigma upon conversion, but occupational figures indicate that, especially in urban areas, the Mussalli is given odd jobs denied to a Hindu Chuhra.

It is difficult to determine the extent to which the Moslem castes and subcastes have or at present observe rules of endogamy for there is only scattered information on the subject. Many lower castes converted from Hinduism retain their Hindu customs and marriage practices to some degree, and the upper classes tend to be endogamous owing to their pride in purity of blood. Yet Islamic values generally operate against caste exclusiveness and the influx of millions of refugees has further weakened traditional stratification.

Available evidence indicates that there is a great deal of variation between individuals, groups, villages, and districts in this respect.

The same can be said of the importance of group identity in taking up new occupations after partition. In many villages and towns a number of important occupational gaps were caused by the departure of Hindus and Sikhs. Sometimes such a gap was filled by members of one caste, sometimes it was filled by individuals from several castes, and it has not been possible to determine any specific trends.

Another intangible element is the degree of identity and loyalty to traditional social groups reflected in political behavior. Some of the local elections are known to have been contested largely on a tribe or caste basis. However, the extent to which political parties and factions coincide with or cut across traditional social groupings seems to vary greatly with the time, place, personalities, and issues involved.

Christians in the Punjab

The Christians are the most important religious minority in the Punjab and Bahawalpur and far outnumber the Hindus. As a result of partition, the Hindu population was reduced to a mere 42,000 persons in 1961, of whom 37,500 were Scheduled Caste Hindus. The Christians, by contrast, numbered 524,700 in 1961— 71 per cent of the entire Christian community of Pakistan.

The Christians are a heterogeneous group but can be divided roughly into two classes. The upper class consists of Caste Hindu converts and persons of mixed descent, formerly known as "Anglo-Indians" and "Goans." The Anglo-Indians, who now prefer to call themselves simply "Christians," are of mixed British and Indian blood; the Goans are of mixed Portuguese and Indian stock. Many of the Catholics with Goan names, however, are descended not from Eurasians but from Indians who took Portuguese names in honor of the men who converted them. It is generally believed that the great majority of the upper-class Christians are of purely indigenous stock. They are prominent in medicine, education, law, trade, and the railways.

The lower-class Christians are converts from Scheduled Castes such as the Chuhras. Although many have been able to improve their position through the education provided by the missions, most of them continue to be sweepers and menials.

The Groups of Sind

The Sindhi-speaking region, to be referred to here as Sind, includes the former Sind Province and Khairpur State and the former
Federal Capital Area of Karachi. The ethnic history and traditional
social grouping of Sind are exceedingly confusing. Past attempts at
classification have had to be only tentative in nature because of the
lack of adequate research. The confusion has been compounded
by the changes in the composition of the population at partition
and the absence of a "race, tribe, and caste" enquiry in the current
census. Initially, the most meaningful classification is by religion.
Although Moslems now account for more than 90 per cent of the
population, some of the minority communities are quite distinctive
and important.

Of the 8.5 million Moslems in 1961, about one million were refugees and more than half of them had moved into Karachi. Apart
from the refugees, the Moslems of Sind may be divided into two
categories: the *pukka*, or "true" Sindhis, and others derived largely
from peoples of Baluchistan.

The pukka Sindhis, who are in the great majority, are of medium
height, stocky, and well built. They have narrow faces, black hair
and eyes, long straight noses, and skins ranging from fair to very
dark. Victims of an environment conducive to indolence, they are
often called lazy but have become more optimistic and energetic
since independence. They are amiable and hospitable and less
warlike, less doctrinaire than their northern neighbors.

The pukka Sindhis are divided into an extraordinary number of
rather small occupational, geographical, tribal, lineage, and caste
groups which appear to be generally endogamous. Sometimes coin-
ciding with such groups and sometimes cutting across them are
the followings of particular saints (pirs), who abound in Sind.
In a few cases the followers of a saint form a distinctive social
group, the most notorious example being the Hurs, the followers
of Pir Pagaro who were once listed as a "criminal tribe." More
often, however, allegiance to a saint does not involve any social
features which mark the group as a whole.

In 1931 the two largest traditional social groups in Sind were
the Baluchis and the Brahuis (called "Brohis" in Sindhi). They are
not pukka Sindhis although they may have been living in Sind for
generations. The Baluchis ruled much of Sind in the past and it was
from them that the British acquired control of the province. The

descendants of these ruling houses continue to have rather high social prestige and family connections are evidently given much weight. The most prominent example is the Talpur family or clan, which provided the rulers of Khairpur until the state's abolition and which continues to be influential in Sindhi politics.

The Moslems of the Shi'ah sect do not fall under either the pukka or non-pukka category as they include members from both, together with a number of refugees. Many are descended from Hindu trading castes converted to Islam and today have prominent roles in trade, industry, and law. Sind was a part of Bombay Presidency until 1935 and before partition the centers of the Shi'ah sect were Gujrat and Bombay City; at partition many of the Shi'ah traders and lawyers migrated to Pakistan and their center is now Karachi. To a greater extent than any other Moslem group, the Shi'ahs, especially those from Bombay, have moved in to fill the economic gaps caused by the departure of the Hindu and Sikh traders and bankers.

Partition brought not only a drastic reduction in the number of Hindus but a marked change in the character of the Hindu community. Before partition four out of five Hindus were Caste Hindus, usually active as traders, moneylenders, and white-collar workers. Primarily urban dwellers, the Caste Hindus made up the largest community in Karachi and were the Hindus who left the country in 1947, causing severe economic dislocation in some fields. By 1961 there were only 189,700 Caste Hindus in the area compared to 195,000 members of Scheduled Castes. In the cities the members of the Scheduled Castes are generally sweepers and unskilled laborers who perform the meanest jobs; in rural areas their role becomes that of the landless agricultural laborer or village menial.

Of the two other religious minorities in Sind, the Christians and the Parsis, the Christians are the larger group and are similar to the Christian community of Punjab. The Parsis are Zoroastrian by faith and Persian by extraction. Their ancestors left Persia to escape persecution after the Moslem conquest in the eighth century and settled on the west coast of India. The great bulk of the Parsis live in India and the center of the community continues to be the city of Bombay.

Most of the Parsis of Pakistan live in Karachi. There are only 5,200 of them and their importance in commerce and industry is out of all proportion to their number. Their prominence stems partly from the fact that during the nineteenth century they were quick to avail themselves of the new economic opportunities introduced by British rule and to gain a Western education. The Parsis have a very high literacy rate, a high standard of living, and are known as shrewd, hardheaded businessmen. A people with strong group cohesion and an ethical code which emphasizes moderation and service to the community, the Parsis were prominent in the development of Karachi under British rule and since partition have been leaders in Pakistan's industrial development.

The Groups of East Pakistan

The ethnic composition of East Pakistan is even more confusing than that of Sind. The Chittagong Hill tribes are quite distinct in terms of language, race, religion, and customs (see the map, Tribes of the Chittagong Hill Tracts), but within the Bengali-speaking population there are no clear-cut ethnic divisions.

Racial classifications made of the Bengali population are exceedingly complex because there are innumerable mixtures of the dark Australoid stock resembling the Australian aborigines, the Aryan and other strains similar to those of West Pakistan, and the short-headed Mongoloid elements akin to the Burman or Khmer peoples. The great majority are Caucasoids, belonging generally to subtypes which are shorter and darker-skinned than the subtypes which prevail in West Pakistan or Europe. According to popular stereotype, they are nonaggressive and unwarlike, possessed of a dreamy and emotional temperament, and prone to mysticism, art, music, erotic poetry, and radical politics.

In regard to religion, over one-fourth of the Bengalis in East Pakistan are Hindus, most of whom are lower-class cultivators, laborers, and artisans. Prior to 1947 most of the Bengali traders, white-collar workers, and professional men were upper-class Hindus. A number of them moved to India a few years after partition, but many, particularly those in trade and banking, have remained in Pakistan. Apart from such occupational distinctions, the Hindus are not very different from their Moslem counterparts. The two religions have borrowed much from each other and both partake of local traditions and customs indigenous to Bengal.

The traditional social grouping of Bengal appears to be roughly similar to that of Punjab, except that the castes tend to be larger and less clearly defined and the social distance between them is less marked. This is true of Hindus as well as Moslems, but the

67

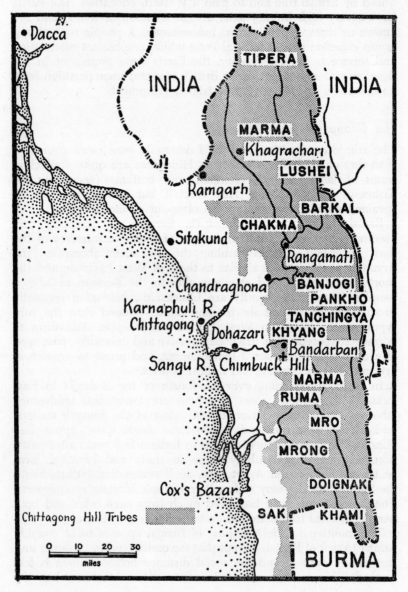

TRIBES OF THE CHITTAGONG HILL TRACTS

• Dacca

INDIA   INDIA

TIPERA

MARMA
• Khagrachari

LUSHEI

Ramgarh   BARKAL

CHAKMA

• Sitakund   Rangamati

Chandraghona   BANJOGI
                      PANKHO
Karnaphuli R.   TANCHINGYA
Chittagong   KHYANG
        Dohazari
                • Bandarban
Sangu R. Chimbuck Hill

                MARMA
                RUMA
                MRO
                MRONG
        Cox's Bazar   DOIGNAK

Chittagong Hill Tribes   SAK   KHAMI

0   10   20   30
        miles   BURMA

68

Moslems are generally less strict in observing caste distinctions. The four largest Hindu castes are the Brahmans, who are priests, teachers, lawyers, and businessmen, many of whom appear to have moved to India; the Kayasthas, a mercantile caste also prominent in the professions; the Rajbanshis, a caste of cultivators largely in the northern districts; and the Namashudras, largest of all, a Scheduled Caste of peasants, fishermen, and laborers living mostly in the southern districts. The Namashudras are believed to be the original inhabitants of the southern delta, and many of the Moslems living in the region are of Namashudra extraction. No reasonably comprehensive information has been gathered on the different Moslem castes since the turn of the century.

Throughout Pakistan there is an increasing tendency to identify a man not by his traditional social group but by his home district or town, especially if he is outside it. This is particularly true of Bengal, where the dialects spoken in the various districts are sometimes quite different from each other. A man from Noakhali district, for example, is much more likely to be identified as a Noakhali than as a member of a particular social group. Persons from Chittagong, Noakhali, and Sylhet districts account for a large proportion of Pakistan's merchant seamen and travel about the world over water routes. Although Sylhet is not a coastal district, the Sylhetis are especially known for this sort of mobility, and there are significant numbers of them in the United Kingdom.

The Chittagong Hill Tracts form a special administrative area roughly analogous to the North-West Frontier region. The people generally inhabit forested hills and are considerably more peaceful than the Pathan tribes. As a rule, they practice a form of shifting cultivation known as *jhum* in which patches of forest are burned off and seeds scattered over the cleared ground. Trade is entirely in the hands of outsiders.

According to the 1961 census, the twelve hill tribes have a total population of 385,000. They are racially and culturally more akin to the peoples of Burma than to the Bengalis, although some of them reflect increasing Bengali influence. They speak Tibeto-Burman, rather than Indo-European languages and, although every tribe contains adherents of more than one religion, they are predominantly Buddhists. Several thousand are Hindus, only a handful are Moslems, and many have animistic beliefs. Baptist and Adventist missions have made converts in all the tribes but only two small ones are predominantly Christian.

The largest tribes are the Chakma, Marma (Magh), Tipera, and Mro (Morang); the rest are quite small. The tribes have tended to intermingle to some extent and are distinguished from each other more by their peculiarities of dialect, dress, and custom than by their tribal cohesiveness. Only the Chakmas and Marmas display any formal tribal organization, although all groups contain definitely recognized clans.

The Chakma, with a population of 125,000, is by far the largest tribe. Nearly all of them are officially Buddhists, but Hinduism and animism are popular among them. They are of mixed and obscure origin, resemble Bengalis in appearance, and their language is largely a corrupted form of Bengali.

"Marma" means "Burmese" and the members of the tribe dislike the more popularly used "Magh," a term which has come to be synonymous with pirates. There are 66,000 of them. They are of Thai origin and are believed to have come to the Hill Tracts by way of Arakan. They are short and sturdy, with broad, rather Mongoloid faces and sallow brown complexions. Although several religions are represented among them, nearly all of them are zealous Buddhists. They continue to regard Burma as the center of their cultural life but have no hostility toward Pakistan and live on good terms with the local authorities.

The Tiperas, some 37,246, are nearly all Hindus and account for virtually the entire Hindu population of the Tracts. They migrated slowly from the Tipera hills in the north, and the northern Tiperas are partly Bengalized. A small southern section known as Mrungs show considerably less Bengali influence.

The Mros (population 16,121) are considered to be the original inhabitants of the Tracts. Of medium height and light build, they display almost no Mongoloid traits. They live on the hilltops and often fortify their villages. They have no written language of their own, but some of them can read the Burmese and Bengali scripts. Most of them claim to be Buddhists but their religious practice is largely animistic. They are said to be fond of music and dancing, and excel in hunting.

CHAPTER 5

Languages

THIRTY-TWO DISTINCT LANGUAGES ARE SPOKEN in Pakistan, not counting a number of dialects, but no single language is commonly spoken or understood in all parts of the country. Many of the languages are spoken by a relatively small proportion of the population and some are not even commonly written, but sentiment and association among the speakers is almost invariably opposed to absorption into one of the larger units. Only two of the country's languages are not regionally limited, yet neither is spoken by any significant proportion of the population. With minor exceptions all the languages are also spoken outside the country—often by more people than claim them within Pakistan. Whereas one wing of the country very closely approximates a linguistic unit, the other presents a complex polyglot.

Within this array of languages are five which together constitute the mother tongues of 97 per cent of the population—Bengali, Punjabi, Urdu, Pushtu, and Sindhi—the first two accounting for slightly over 80 per cent (see Table 3). Unfortunately for the cause of linguistic unity, rarely is either Bengali or Punjabi learned as a second language (somewhat less true of Punjabi than Bengali) which considerably reduces their chances as a national language. Furthermore, their regional distribution leaves the two wings of the country without a common popular language. Probably the variety of Urdu spoken in the bazaars (Hindustani) comes closest to a lingua franca, but even for this limited purpose Hindustani is far from satisfactory.

The many languages of Pakistan can be divided into four major linguistic families—the Indo-European, Austric, Dravidian, and Sino-Tibetan. Numerically the most important are those of the Indo-European family, brought to the subcontinent in their primitive

71

forms by migrating tribes after 1500 B.C. Fewer than one per cent of the population speak languages of the other three, which are of interest primarily for their historical and ethnic associations.

The languages of the Austric family, which include Santhali and Khashi of East Pakistan, are claimed by the smallest number of speakers and are believed to be derived from very ancient tongues of the subcontinent. Sometime in the fourth millennium B.C. Dravidian speakers came to India only to be displaced by later migrants; though the majority of south Indian languages belong to this family, an isolated fragment of Brahui speakers in Baluchistan is all that remains of the Dravidian language family in Pakistan. Sino-Tibetan languages were brought to the subcontinent beginning in the first millennium B.C. but have never represented a large number of speakers; Arakanese and Burmese of East Pakistan are the most important languages of the family followed by a large number of more or less distinct languages collectively referred to as Assam-Burman tongues.

With these exceptions all the languages of Pakistan belong to the Indo-European family. Of the four branches of the large family recognized in Pakistan the Dardic claims the fewest speakers, totaling less than even the Brahui of Baluchistan. Only in the northern and northwestern mountain borderlands of West Pakistan do the Dardic languages survive as a mother tongue. The sole language of the European branch of the family spoken in the country by more than a few persons is English. The mother tongue of a few thousand at most, English is important as a widely spoken and understood second language among the middle and upper classes.

Two other languages which, though inextricably bound to religious and cultural traditions, might be classed as foreign are Arabic and Persian. Arabic is the mother tongue of only 1,200 persons in the country and is commonly spoken by no more than 65,000, but because the Holy Qu'ran is written in Arabic 6.6 million people can "read" the Arabic in it and are familiar with its pronunciation and script. Persian, an important cultural language, is claimed as a mother tongue by 25,000 but its literature is familiar to a much greater number.

In the two wings of the country there is some difference in views on the subject of foreign languages. The use of Arabic is roughly the same in East and West Pakistan. Persian is much more important in the western wing, but even in East Pakistan its cultural associations are strong. The minor languages of Baluchi or Brahui could hardly be more foreign to a Bengali villager. Similarly the Arakanese of the Chittagonian is much more foreign to a West Pakistani than English.

This linguistic diversity has presented many problems to the new nation, the most obvious being the choice of a national language. The constitution designates Urdu and Bengali as the national languages of Pakistan and states that in 1976 the president will appoint a commission to examine and report on the question of the replacement of the English language for official purposes. English may be expected to remain the language of government at the provincial as well as the national level for some years and probably until such a time as one of the vernacular tongues is widely enough spoken to be acceptable in both East and West Pakistan. Of these three languages, two—Urdu and English—can appropriately be called national languages on the basis of geographical distribution. Bengali, although spoken by almost everyone in East Pakistan, is of no consequence in West Pakistan, whereas some speakers of Urdu can be found in both provinces.

Bengali and Other Languages of East Pakistan

Numerically, Bengali is the most important of the eastern group of the Indo-Aryan languages and in prepartition India was second only to Hindi-Urdu in number of speakers. There are 41 million speakers in East Pakistan in addition to 25 million in the adjacent provinces of India, notably West Bengal. The linguistic unity of the Bengali-speaking area was not strong enough to prevail against the divisive force of Moslem nationalism, but the common language remains as a tangible bond between Bengalis whether they live in East Pakistan (formerly East Bengal) or in India (West Bengal).

There are actually two distinct styles of Bengali, literary and vernacular, and included in the latter are many dialects and local variants. The speech of a villager in the northern part of East Pakistan differs markedly from one in the southwestern district of Khulna or in the eastern districts of Sylhet, Noakhali, and Chittagong. The eastern dialects in fact are quite distinct. It is claimed that standard Bengali is closer to Assamese than these eastern dialects. Assamese belongs to the eastern group of Indo-Aryan languages and is closely related to Bengali but is still considered a separate language. The dialectical differences in Bengali are therefore considerable. Even within the eastern dialects there are significant variants. A person from Sylhet will find it difficult to understand the speech of a person from Chittagong partly because of his different use of idioms and vocabulary but primarily because of differences in accent.

Bengali unity comes from the literary form which is the same for all who are literate in Bengali. The difference between the standard Bengali, which is the spoken form most closely related to literary Bengali, and local dialects is not only due to wide variance in accent but to vocabulary differences. Some of the dialects use more words borrowed from Persian and Arabic than appear in the literary form, which itself has many words of Persian and Arabic origin. In this way, also, a distinction can be made between Moslem Bengali and Hindu Bengali.

The script employed in writing Bengali is derived from the same fifth-century Gupta script to which the Devanagari of Hindi owes its origins. The two have developed independently and to one not familiar with either their appearance is similar. A person who learns to read Bengali, however, does not thereby acquire the ability to read Devanagari. The script, which is written from left to right, is alphabetical in concept but syllabic in use; a unit in a written word is a whole syllable made up of consonant and vowel combinations. Because of its syllabic construction Bengali requires a large number of types for printing—approximately fifty letters and many more combinations even in its most simplified form. Typewriters have been produced and are used but the necessity of combining strokes to produce one symbol makes it impossible to achieve any speed in turning out finished copy.

Bengali claims the distinction of having been in the vanguard of the literary renaissance in modern India. With important exceptions, this rich literary tradition is largely Hindu in origin but the feeling for the language and the regional traditions expressed in it are no less strong among Bengali Moslems. The best measure of the strength of this sentiment regarding the language was the forceful reaction of the East Pakistanis to the proposal for the gradual introduction of Urdu in the province as the official language.

Considering the importance of Bengali it might have been chosen as the national language of Pakistan. Rich literature, however, is not sufficient recommendation. More important is a language associated with the traditions that led to the founding of the state or a language with the backing of a powerful group of political leaders. Urdu had this in the leaders of the Moslem League and in its association with Islamic culture and the period of Moslem ascendancy in the subcontinent, while there was no similar drive or association connected with Bengali.

These differences between the two languages are reflected in the linguistic traditions of the two wings of the country. A well-educated Moslem Bengali would learn Urdu because of its historic associations. The absence of similar Moslem traditions associated with Bengali has meant that a well-educated person in West Pakistan would only in exceptional instances learn Bengali. He would be much more likely to learn Persian if the question of an additional language arose. The literary traditions of the two languages have also contributed to this situation. Whereas the literature in Bengali is varied and extensive enough to occupy one fully, Urdu literature is limited in quantity and in appeal.

The Bengali traditions were so strong that all attempts by the leaders of the Moslem League to carry out their plans for the use of Urdu as the sole language of Pakistan were destined for failure. For nine years recognition of Bengali as one of the national languages was denied. In the course of the controversy much bitterness developed in East Pakistan, bitterness that was to contribute to increasing demands for political autonomy and to prejudice many against the use of Urdu even as a second language.

Among the languages spoken in East Pakistan other than Bengali, English is the most important, followed closely by Urdu-Hindi. Each is claimed by approximately half a million speakers. Persian is spoken by only 25,000 persons though this is more than the total number who speak Pushtu, Sindhi, or Punjabi. In only one district are non-Bengali languages important and even there more than half the population speak Bengali. Approximately 47 per cent of the people of the Chittagong Hill Tracts speak Arakanese, Burmese, and an assortment of Assam-Burman tongues. The district with the next largest linguistic minority is Dinajpur in the northwest. Here a combination of refugees speaking Urdu and Hindi and tribal groups speaking Santhali and Khashi account for 6 per cent of the district population.

Just as unity is the keynote of the linguistic pattern in East Pakistan, variety is the hallmark of the western wing. Even the unity which appears to exist in the preponderance of Punjabi speakers is largely illusory. Only Urdu and Pushtu have literary traditions of some note. All of the languages with the exception of Urdu have very definite regional concentrations within the western wing.

Urdu

Urdu in its spoken form is very similar to Hindi and Hindustani and is mutually intelligible to speakers of all three. In India there are 140 million persons claiming Hindi (and Urdu) as their mother tongue. It is estimated that nearly twice as many understand Hindustani. In Pakistan 5.4 million persons speak Urdu-Hindi and probably more than twice as many understand Hindustani. Hindustani, in at least one of its many meanings, does not refer to a third language but to a bazaar Hindi-Urdu which has no written form, possesses a very simplified grammar and vocabulary, and is the most widely used lingua franca in the subcontinent.

Hindi and Urdu are differentiated from each other by differences in script and higher vocabulary. The latter is written in an Arabic script while Hindi is written in a locally derived script called Devanagari. Hindi draws heavily on Sanskrit for its higher vocabulary and Urdu on Persian.

Although Urdu is the mother tongue of no more than 2.5 million persons it is commonly spoken by an additional 3 million persons. Any estimate of the number who understand it in its bazaar form (Hindustani) is purely a matter of conjecture, though it must exceed 15 million persons. Its greatest concentration is in the former province of the Punjab and Bahawalpur State where approximately 60 per cent of the total Urdu speakers are located. Many of the Hindi-Urdu speakers are refugees from North India and Hyderabad in the Deccan. Also in this group of speakers are the educated Moslems, most of whom in West Pakistan are literate in Urdu.

It is difficult to equate the importance of Urdu in Pakistan with the relatively small number who speak it unless the element of literacy is considered, Urdu being the most important language of literacy in the country. In East Pakistan it is taught as a second language in the middle schools along with English though according to the 1951 census fewer than half a million persons commonly speak it; in West Pakistan it is the normal medium of instruction in primary and secondary schools and even where English or one of the vernacular languages is used it is learned as a second language. With the spread of education the number of persons able to understand and speak Urdu will inevitably increase.

The origins of Urdu can be traced to the Moslem invaders who came to the subcontinent speaking first Turki and later Persian. These languages became intermixed with the local dialect spoken in the area of Delhi, which was most often the seat of Moslem power. When the Moghul armies carried out their campaigns from Delhi their speech came to be called *zaban-i-urdu-i-mo'alla* or the language of the exalted camp or court. The name was shortened eventually to Urdu. From its earliest use in the subcontinent it was written in the Arabic script. Its vocabulary came from vernacular Hindi, Punjabi, and Sanskrit to which were gradually added Persian and Turkish words. From the time of the Moghuls it was used as the Moslem form of a Western Hindi speech that preferred a Persianized vocabulary and sought inspiration from Persian literature and the atmosphere of Islamic faith and culture. In general, when the Hindus of the north used the language it retained more of the Hindi and Sanskrit words and in writing employed the native Devanagari script. In modern times members of the two communities living side by side in a North Indian town might learn to read and write in different scripts. A Moslem would learn the Arabic script and his neighbor, speaking the same tongue, might learn the Devanagari form.

The Arabic-Urdu script is not well suited for modern printing as each letter has various forms depending on its position in a word or its relation to other vowels or consonants. Urdu typewriters have been produced but, because a letter may have as many as three different forms, typing is not a very rapid process. The real advantage of the Urdu typewriter of course is that it assures a standard of legibility. A number of other languages spoken in West Pakistan generally use the Arabic-Urdu script—notably Punjabi, Pushtu, and Kashmiri—and Sindhi is written in an Arabic-derived script similar to Urdu but distinct enough to be considered a separate script.

In addition to printing difficulties resulting from a complex alphabet, and the strong traditions of the vernacular language, Urdu faces the handicap of a limited technical vocabulary. At present the military forces of the country rely heavily on English, in part because of the still strong British traditions but in part because of the large number of technical terms for which there are no Urdu equivalents. The army down to the company level uses English

77

for most of its commands and administrative procedure. At the lower levels when Urdu is used in written form it employs a romanized rather than the standard Urdu form. The air force and the navy use English almost exclusively. Much of the military "hardware" is of British or American manufacture with training and operational manuals in English.

The substitution of Urdu for English as the medium of instruction at the university level is confronted by the same vocabulary limitations. The translation of texts in the natural sciences would require much borrowing and adaptation of words. This is equally true of many of the social sciences. Much of their terminology has been developed in the West and has no counterpart in Urdu.

Some confusion has also been created by persons seeking to purify the language of its Hindi- and Sanskrit-derived words by substituting words of Persian or Arabic origin. A similar program has been advocated by some in India to eliminate the words of Persian and Arabic derivation in Hindi with the substitution of Sanskrit words. The end result of these attempts in Pakistan has on occasion resulted in a language so "pure" as to be unintelligible to the average speaker of Urdu. Needless to say this effort has not contributed to the standardization of Urdu or an increase in the numbers who can understand it.

Other Languages of West Pakistan

The second language of Pakistan in terms of the numbers who speak it is Punjabi, found in an area that includes all of the former province of the Punjab, two of the adjacent districts of the former North-West Frontier province, and Bahawalpur. Punjabi is spoken by approximately 12 million persons in India and 20.8 million in West Pakistan. In Pakistan, the language is not commonly written and its many dialects differ from each other to an even greater extent than those of Bengali, with the consequence that the linguistic unity of the Punjabi-speaking area is not nearly as pronounced as that of Bengal.

A Punjabi proverb holds that "the language changes every fifteen miles." This variety and diversity of dialects is confirmed by the linguistic classification of Punjabi. It is one of the Indo-Aryan languages though some of its dialects are classed as Western Punjabi (or Hindi or Lahnda) in the northwestern group that also includes Sindhi. The eastern dialects are classified as Eastern

Punjabi with the central group of the Indo-Aryan branch which also includes Hindi-Urdu and the various Rajasthani-Gujarati tongues. The degree of mutual intelligibility among these dialects varies considerably. The differences are perhaps greatest between Lahore and the district of Multan in the south or the northwestern districts on the Indus river. The largest numbers who speak Urdu are found in the Punjab. Punjabi and Urdu have a large common vocabulary, and a person equipped with Urdu would not have any difficulty with simple communication in the area of the former province of the Punjab.

Punjabi can be written in Urdu, Devanagari, or Gurumukhi scripts. The latter is widely used by the Sikh community but since the violence and migrations following the partition of the Punjab there are few Sikhs in West Pakistan and a marked lack of interest in anything associated with that community. Generally, Pakistanis who speak Punjabi learn to read and write in Urdu. Some efforts have been made to increase the use of Punjabi with the Urdu script. Though the written literature is negligible, the oral traditions are strong and there are many verses and songs composed in the various dialects of Punjabi.

Sindhi is spoken by a relatively small percentage of the population of West Pakistan. It is divided into fewer dialects than Punjabi and has a small but important literary tradition of its own. The four million persons who claim it as a mother tongue are concentrated in the former province of Sind and Khairpur State as well as in the area of Karachi and in Baluchistan. The Sindhi script is similar to Urdu script but different enough not to be easily read by a person who had learned to read in Urdu. Because Sindhi has a separate script and distinct literary traditions, opposition to the use of Urdu has been particularly strong in the Sindhi-speaking areas. The strength of local sentiment favoring Sindhi is reflected in the fact that 300,000 persons are literate in it. In the former province of Sind and Khairpur State three times as many persons claim to be literate in Sindhi as in Urdu, making this the only area in West Pakistan where literacy in a vernacular language exceeds that in Urdu. A certain dispersion or mixture of other groups with Sindhis, which has been taking place in recent years, may affect this linguistic unity. For example, the completion of new irrigation projects in the Indus valley has attracted non-Sindhi-speaking people into the area with a consequent decrease in the concentration of persons claiming Sindhi as their mother tongue.

Pushtu, the one important language of West Pakistan that does not belong to the Indo-Aryan branch of languages, is part of the Iranian branch together with Persian and Baluchi, though the degree of mutual intelligibility among these tongues is not great. An estimated five million persons in Pakistan claim Pushtu as a mother tongue. The linguistic unity of these speakers is open to some discussion as there is no written literary tradition associated with Pushtu, except in Afghanistan. Two major dialects can be differentiated and these in turn can be subdivided into local variants. Differences between the northern and southern dialects are best characterized by the hard and soft pronunciations of certain consonants. The northern, or Peshawar variety, might be called Pakhtu in contrast to Pushtu in the south. Distribution of speakers is concentrated in an area that straddles the Pakistan-Afghanistan border. Pushtu is spoken by 80 per cent of the population in the former North-West Frontier Province and Tribal Agencies, and the percentage would be considerably higher but for the two eastern districts of the former North-West Frontier province where the majority speak Punjabi. In Baluchistan nearly 300,000 persons claim Pushtu as a mother tongue. Across the Durand Line in Afghanistan there are estimated to be at least five million persons who also speak Pushtu.

Like Punjabi, Pushtu is not normally written. A person from the area who learns to read and write does so in Urdu. In recent years efforts to increase the literary usage of Pushtu have grown—for example, some sections of newspapers published in Peshawar appear in Pushtu—but the Pushtu vocabulary is so limited that many words must be borrowed from Persian or Urdu. Like Persian it is written in an Arabic script using additional letters: four more as in Persian plus eight distinctly Pushtu.

The heightened interest in developing a script and increasing the usage of Pushtu rather than accepting Urdu as the language of literacy is a reflection of the strong regional sentiment in Pakistan. Its most serious consequences are seen in the education system. With the present hierarchy of languages, a child from the frontier area receives his primary schooling in Urdu, and later in middle school is introduced to English, which becomes the medium of instruction on the college level. If he goes to the University of Peshawar he will be encouraged to study Pushtu and become literate in his mother tongue. His exposure to the three languages results in some ability to use all of them but no real proficiency in any one of them. The remark is made, only half facetiously, that instead of becoming literate in one language he becomes illiterate in three.

The area of Karachi and the former province of Baluchistan and States Union have vastly different areas but very similar populations with a variety of languages spoken in each of them. Neither of these former political divisions can be said to represent a linguistic unit though they may include parts or all of a number of linguistic units. Baluchi is more widely spoken than any other language in Baluchistan (34 per cent) though there are actually more persons who claim it as a mother tongue in the adjacent area of the former province of Sind. Pushtu is spoken by 23 per cent of the population and, as previously noted, is part of a larger block of Pushtu speakers to the north. Persons claiming Brahui as their mother tongue (17 per cent) represent the only linguistic unit which is complete within the region. Brahui speakers are few in number but quite distinct from their neighbors as they speak the only remnant of the Dravidian family of languages remaining in Pakistan. Sindhi is spoken by some 16 per cent of the population, most of whom are concentrated along the eastern borders. They are part of a larger block of speakers in the adjacent former province of Sind. In all of these groups there is surprisingly little mixture of languages. This is not to say that the linguistic units are sharply defined but that they do not broadly overlap each other. This is equally true of the other linguistic units of West Pakistan.

The area of Karachi includes speakers of practically all the languages of Pakistan though one language predominates: it is the one part of the country where Urdu is locally the most important language. Half of the population claim Urdu or Urdu-Hindi as their mother tongue and nearly 70 per cent commonly speak it. The mother tongues of the other half of the population include Sindhi (14 per cent), Gujarati (11 per cent), and Punjabi and Baluchi (9 per cent).

English and the Problem of a National Language

The only language other than Urdu spoken to some extent in all parts of the country is English. A mere 12,000 persons claim it as the language of their homes but 1.4 million commonly speak it and some 2.4 million claim to be able to read it. Under the British rule it was the language of government, higher education, and business and this status changed very little with independence in 1947. Anglo-Indians make up the bulk of the people who speak English in their homes. Those who know it as a second language include all the members of the most powerful groups in the country.

As noted previously, the official use of English was confirmed by the constitution and the documents, records, and communications of the federal government are always issued in English. A similar situation prevails in the provincial governments, though with somewhat greater use of Urdu and Bengali in West and East Pakistan respectively. In keeping with the official use of English, some of the leading newspapers in Karachi, Lahore, and Dacca are printed in English and Radio Pakistan broadcasts in English as well as the vernacular languages. But despite its obviously important role in the life of the country, English is almost exclusively confined to urban centers and would be of little or no value as a lingua franca for someone wishing to travel through the rural areas of East or West Pakistan.

Yet English, though foreign to Pakistan and emotionally regarded as a remnant of the colonial period, enjoys a number of advantages over Urdu or any of the vernacular tongues as a national language. Perhaps the most important of these is that it can be learned and used in both wings of the country without a regional stigma. Urdu is not popular in East Pakistan and Bengali is virtually unknown in West Pakistan. Similar problems in India relating to strong preferences for regional languages over the national language of Hindi have resulted in demands that English be retained for higher education and official uses of the federal government. In Pakistan the lack of agreement between exponents of the various indigenous languages has resulted in increasing acceptance of English as a national compromise. Certainly if the controversy on the issue of a national language continues with the same intensity displayed during the first decade of independence, English may well be retained not because of its popularity but because it represents the only feasible alternative.

Another advantage enjoyed by English is a fairly simple script which facilitates printing. As yet this is not as critical a factor as it will become with the spread of literacy. There is, also, a large body of literature available in English providing an important contact with Western technical knowledge. Such contact is doubly important for a country which has embarked on an ambitious program of economic development. English is also one of the important languages of international communication. None of these factors, however, outweighs the fact that English is a foreign language to the great mass of Pakistanis, and its retention will only come as the result of a need for compromise.

This may turn out to be the case. Education is spreading literacy more slowly than anticipated by the nation's founders and it does not appear likely to bring about a single language in the country in this generation or, in fact, the next. The use of Urdu is steadily increasing in West Pakistan but for the reasons mentioned above is unlikely to achieve any popularity in East Pakistan. Rather than decreasing, the preference for the regional languages is evidently increasing.

On the assumption that Urdu will eventually achieve widespread use in the western wing and based on the present predominance of Bengali in the eastern wing, the country seems most likely to become bilingual. Such a situation need not present insurmountable difficulties to the continuation of national unity. Bilingual and trilingual states exist in Europe and manage to function without undue expense or internal stress. Whether English is retained or not will have to be determined by future developments.

CHAPTER 6

Religion

RELIGION IS A FAR MORE PERVASIVE INFLUENCE in Pakistan than in most Western countries. To their adherents, Islam or Hinduism is apt to be a total way of life, but for all Pakistanis there is also the towering fact that a religion, Islam, provided the basis for the creation of the country itself. The application of Islamic law today, its relationship to secular affairs, and its correspondence to modern conditions are all live issues in the nation, making some knowledge of the religious background of Moslem law essential to an appreciation of the political problems posed by the Islamic clauses of the Pakistan constitution.

The way in which Islam came to the subcontinent has had a profound effect on the nature of the religion in modern Pakistan. The great majority of Pakistani Moslems are descended from Indian converts whose conversion on a significant scale began about the time the first Moslem kingdom was established at Delhi in 1206. This was several centuries after the Arabs first conquered Sind, but during the period between the conquest of Sind and the establishment of the Delhi kingdom a tradition of Islamic mysticism known as Sufism had grown up outside the subcontinent so that the missionaries who accompanied the political conquerors and won converts from among the Indian masses were predominantly men inspired by Sufism. Though both main branches of Islam, i.e. Sunni and Shi'a, were represented, the overwhelming majority of the Sufi missionaries were Sunnis and today most Pakistani Moslems are Sunnis. Their message was new but the missionaries themselves were of a type long familiar to the indigenous peoples and there is some evidence that these men won converts fully as much by their personal spiritual achievements as by their message. Conversion to their form of Islam may not initially have been the radical change it is sometimes held to be. In 1943 it was estimated that at least two-thirds of the

Moslems of prepartition India were to some extent under the influence of one of the Sufi religious orders.

Although the Sufis may be less important in what is now Pakistan, any discussion of religious leadership in the country must include Sufism and its saints. Yet along with the introduction of Islam came the spread of the Bhakti tradition of Hinduism, and Islamic religion in Pakistan, not immune to such influences, can perhaps best be described as a two-sided phenomenon. Because popular Islam is a mixture of the imported creed and indigenous elements, the actual religious beliefs and practices of many ordinary Moslems are often similar to those of the local non-Moslems. Just as real is the fact that Moslems continue to regard themselves as very different from non-Moslems—different enough in any case to have brought Pakistan into existence.

Tenets of Islam

The word "Islam" means "submission" to the will of Allah and the person who so submits is a "Moslem." Moslems honor Muhammad as an apostle of Allah and as the last and greatest of the prophets. The revelation from Allah as dictated to Muhammad is the Qur'an. When a Moslem repeats the familiar phrase, "Muhammad is the Prophet of Allah," he accepts the validity of the message of Muhammad and thereby the Qur'an. This record of the revelation is supplemented by the body of traditions, or Hadith.

The unity and supremacy of Allah are affirmed in the recitation of the *shahad'a*, the confession of faith: "There is no God but Allah, and Muhammad is the Prophet of Allah." The unity of Allah finds expression in a variety of beliefs and doctrines, an important one being the abhorrence of all forms of idolatry. The supremacy of Allah is strongly reflected in Moslem speech and writing. The constitution of Pakistan, for example, begins:

> In the name of Allah, the Beneficent, the
> Merciful. WHEREAS sovereignty over the
> entire Universe belongs to Almighty Allah
> alone, and the authority exercisable by
> the people is a sacred trust . . .

As the Word of Allah, the Qur'an is fixed and immutable. Its verses are popularly believed to have supernatural powers and are used to ward off or cure all kinds of sickness and distress.

In rural East Pakistan it is common in times of need to obtain water that has had a Qur'an verse blown or recited into it by a local religious leader; allegedly the power of the Qur'an enters into the man who drinks such water and cures him of his affliction. Water so treated may be sprinkled on the fields to ensure a good crop. Other common charms are amulets or arm bands containing a Qur'anic verse.

The Qur'an names four main angels: Israfil, who will sound the trumpet on the Last Day; Azrail, the angel of death; Michael, who presides over nature; and, most important, Gabriel, Allah's messenger who revealed the Qur'an to Muhammad. There are also two angels who record the good and evil deeds of men, another who guards Heaven, and one who guards Hell. Along with the doctrine of angels goes a belief in the spirits and devils called jinn, who, like men, are created, but of mist or flame rather than earth. The jinn can be good or bad, believers or infidels, and will be judged along with men on the Last Day. The evil jinn are led by Shaitan, or Iblis, a fallen angel. Neither the angels nor the jinn play a major role in the established creed, but the villages of Pakistan seem to contain an extraordinary number of evil jinn who are present to lead men astray, to plague a man who has been cursed by another, and to cause sickness and distress. But jinn are frightened away by righteousness and, especially, by the recitation of the Qur'an. Since disease is believed to be caused by jinn, the most effective cures employ the power of the Qur'an.

On the Day of Judgment and Resurrection, also called the Last Day, all men and jinn will be called to answer for their deeds. Apart from monotheism, it was the doctrine of the Last Judgment which most distinguished the Qur'an from pre-Islamic Arab beliefs. Moslem theology and ethics are based on the view that Allah is the omnipotent master and man is always in danger of incurring his wrath. Forgiveness cannot be won by merit; it comes only by the grace of Allah. The characteristic sign of the believer is his ever present fear of Allah. Yet Muhammad's message was not simply one of fear and awe but also of hope. Man can make himself worthy of divine forgiveness by undeviating service to Allah. Allah is not only terrible and majestic but "the Compassionate One, the Merciful," the terms by which he is named in the formula prefixed to every verse in the Qur'an.

Similarly the destiny of man is presented as both predetermined by the will of Allah and subject to human choice. Certain verses of the Qur'an are cited to support belief in predestination as a fundamental tenet of Islam, making the "submission" to the will of Allah a fatalistic acceptance of whatever happens. This belief is very widespread among ordinary Moslems. At the same time, there are verses which present a conception of free will. Here the "submission" is not simply an acceptance of what is beyond one's control but a commitment to the moral law, a continual striving by individuals and the community as a whole to choose the actions that will most closely conform to the divine pleasure as revealed in the Qur'an. Some modern Moslem writers, notably Muhammad Iqbal, have laid great stress on this aspect of Islam.

A number of prophets other than Muhammad are recognized by Islam and Moslems are required to believe in them all without distinction. In fact, next to the unity of Allah, the doctrine of apostles is the central doctrine of the Qur'an. At many times and to all men Allah has sent messengers or prophets to preach his unity and transmit his Word. Since men are by their nature prone to error, the followers of one prophet would allow the revelation to become corrupted and forgotten and an ever merciful Allah would choose a new messenger. Notable among these have been Adam, Noah, Abraham, Moses, Jesus, and Muhammad, all of whom preached the same doctrine, though in matters of detail there was a gradual evolution in their messages toward the final and perfect revelation transmitted by Muhammad.

The Moslem Community

The temporal Moslem community, referred to as *millet* or *umma*, has a special religious meaning which has played a profound part in the very existence of Pakistan. Muhammad delivered, interpreted, and lived the law of Allah and launched a community that implemented the law politically and socially as well as spiritually, thus initiating its rapid spread to all mankind.

In the year of the Hegira, 622 A.D., the year of the flight or migration, Muhammad and his followers moved from Mecca to Medina, came into political power, and established themselves as an independent community. During the remaining ten years of Muhammad's life and the succeeding twenty-eight-year period, religious and temporal authority were united in the persons of Muhammad and his first four caliphs or "successors," the representatives of the Prophet on earth. Under the dynastic caliphates which succeeded the first four caliphs, religious and temporal authority were partly, but never completely, separated. In theory, the ideal Moslem society is one in which the two are again united and the state is the instrument of religious law.

It was this sense of the religious importance of the community, along with the social and political importance of religion, that was the basis for the "two-nation theory" and the founding of Pakistan. The source of mass support for the Pakistan movement lay less in a commitment to the abstract doctrine of the unity of church and state than in the strong emphasis placed on the social practice of Islam and on the solidarity of the community.

With the exception of the core beliefs in Allah, his law, and his Apostle, matters of practice are more important in Islam than articles of doctrine. Moslem thought has been less concerned with truth than with righteousness, less with theology than with history and law. The good Moslem is one whose religious commitment is expressed not so much in a belief that conforms to a given doctrine as in a practice that conforms to an accepted code.

The constitution of Pakistan speaks of the Holy Qur'an and Islamiat. The Islamiat includes the Sunna, defined as custom or regulation and as the system of legal and social usages developed historically as a supplement to the Qur'an, but its main component is the Hadith, the body of traditions recording examples of the Prophet's life and sayings.

Islam is traditionally divided into two major sects, Sunnis and Shi'as. The split stemmed from a political dispute over the succession to the caliphate after Muhammad's death and subsequently involved some divergence of doctrine and practice. The Sunnis, a term derived from Sunna, accept the first four caliphs and the subsequent dynasties as legitimate and follow the Sunna developed during their rule. Only one out of every twelve or fifteen Pakistani Moslems is a Shi'a. The Shi'as are the "partisans" of the family of 'Ali, the fourth caliph and son-in-law of the Prophet, and they reject those caliphs not of the line of 'Ali in favor of the line of twelve descendants called Imams.

The Practice of Islam

The five fundamental obligations of a Moslem include the profession of faith, prayer, almsgiving, fasting during the month of Ramazan, and observance of the hajj or pilgrimage to Mecca.

All Moslems are required to pray in a prescribed manner five times a day. The formal ritual consists of a series of obeisances in the direction of Mecca made from standing, kneeling, and prostrate positions and accompanied by the intonement of set prayers, most of which are brief Qur'anic verses in Arabic. When Moslems pray together the movements are led by an imam who stands in front of the rest. Ablutions are required before prayer. No music is allowed during prayer. Hindu religious processions, by contrast, are usually accompanied by music. Prior to independence the passage of such a procession near a mosque, particularly during prayer, was considered an insult to Islam and was one of the most common causes of communal clashes.

Men are free to pray by themselves in any appropriate spot; women pray in the seclusion of the home. Whenever possible, the men should pray together in a mosque (masjid, literally "place of prostration"). The mosque is not a consecrated church; it is a structure for private and congregational prayer. It may be used on occasion as a meeting place for the community when there are common problems to discuss and may also have a primary school, *maktab*, connected with it.

On Fridays males are expected to attend the mosque at noon to take part in communal prayer and hear the weekly sermon (*khutbah*). However, Friday is not considered the equivalent of the Sabbath and the ordinary business holiday for government offices, banks, and the larger stores in Pakistan is Sunday. In practice, many places are also closed on Friday afternoons; the less Westernized shops in the bazaars and some of the universities are closed all day Friday and open for all or part of Sunday.

The Qur'an lays great insistence on the giving of alms and in early Islamic times payment of a tax or tithe called *zakat* was obligatory. Nowadays few Moslems pay the zakat but *sadaqat*, or freewill offerings, are ordinarily given by the more prosperous to the poor, the needy, and orphans. Such offerings are customarily given especially at the time of the Ids, or commemorative feasts.

For centuries it has been the custom for Moslem rulers, high officials, and wealthy individuals to establish religious trusts or endowments (*vaqf*). The properties placed in these trusts were exempt from taxation and the annual income in many cases was assigned to charitable purposes such as the upkeep of hospitals, schools, and mosques. In addition, hundreds of the shrines and tombs in the areas that became Pakistan were maintained by the income from endowments or from gifts in the form of new trusts. To ensure that the incomes were used strictly for the purposes stated in the deeds of endowment, the Pakistan government in 1961 issued a decree putting all such endowments under the control of the provincial governments.

The fast of Ramazan, in the ninth month of the Moslem year, provides the severest test of a Moslem's ability to carry out the dictates of his faith. From daybreak until the last ray of light has disappeared from the sky, he is required to abstain from all food, drink, tobacco, and indulgence in worldly pleasure. Exceptions are made for the sick, the aged, young children, pregnant or nursing women, soldiers on duty, and travelers. Ramazan is widely observed in Pakistan, though perhaps not as rigorously as in some Arab countries.

Since Moslem observances follow a lunar calendar, Ramazan occurs at a different time each year. When it comes during the hot season the ordeal is particularly severe. Business in many instances comes almost to a standstill; laborers and household servants perform only a minimum of work. The psychological impact of the fast is marked: as the month progresses, tension increases, tempers become frayed, and personal violence may rise sharply. Prior to independence, Ramazan was often a time of communal tensions, especially if it came during the hot season or coincided with an important Hindu religious festival.

The pilgrimage, hajj, to the holy city of Mecca, usually made during the last month of the Moslem year, is regarded as the culmination of the Moslem's religious experience. Mecca contains the Kaaba, a rectangular structure of gray stone, at which the pilgrim performs various rituals culminating his visits to other holy places in the vicinity of Mecca. The insistence of the Qur'an on the true holiness of Mecca has made the hajj something which must be performed at least once in a lifetime if humanly possible. The hajj is also a source of social prestige in Pakistan, giving the returned pilgrim the right to dye his beard red and wear a distinctive cap; his title, hajji, is one of respect. Most Pakistanis cannot make the hajj but it is common to go to the shrines of saints and other sites not as far away as Mecca, with religious merit accruing in proportion to the distance covered.

In theory jihad (literally "exertion") is a permanent struggle to make the Word of Allah supreme. It is presented to Moslems as part of their collective duty to Allah and is thus sometimes called the sixth pillar of the faith. The notion that jihad is strictly a "holy war" which follows naturally from the division of the world into the Dar al-Islam, or House of Islam, and the Dar al-Harb, or House of War, is erroneous. The Qur'an emphasizes peaceful jihad: the "people of the book" (Christians and Jews) are not to be Islamized by force, and the sword is to be used on other religions only as a last resort. Yet, although many appropriate political compromises were made, the concept of jihad was often invoked in the past by Moslem leaders wishing for political reasons to wage war on non-Moslem states.

A conspicuous feature of Moslem religious discipline is the emphasis placed on the oneness of the community of believers. The sentiment that this engenders is psychologically more important than the rather abstract concept of the equality of all believers in the eyes of Allah. Although the Brotherhood of Islam is sometimes conspicuous by its absence, the communal aspect of the religion makes it possible to evoke a strong sentiment of Moslem solidarity in the face of challenge. It is this rather than the official use of jihad for military purposes that has been important on the subcontinent. Thus the cry of "Islam in Danger" during the height of communal friction would often bring forth a call for jihad resulting in physical violence. A recent example of the use of the jihad concept occurred toward the end of 1947 when the Pathans called their invasion of Kashmir a jihad for the purpose of rescuing their Moslem brothers from the tyrannies of the Hindu ruler.

The most important religious events other than Ramazan are the commemorative feasts known as Ids. The Bakr-i-Id, also called the Id al-Azha, or Great Feast, is a four-day commemoration of Abraham's readiness to obey God to the point of sacrificing his son and coincides with the end of the ceremonies of the pilgrimage. It is customary for every person who can afford the expense to sacrifice an animal—in most Moslem countries a sheep, goat, or camel. In Pakistan a goat is sacrificed, or seven persons may join together to sacrifice a cow. In practice, only a few families in a village can afford the sacrifice, but Moslems have insisted on their right to sacrifice animals, especially cows, as essential to their religion. Cow slaughter is as offensive to Hindu religious feeling as music before a mosque is to the Moslems and, like the latter, it was a common cause of communal rioting in the days before partition.

The Id al-Fitr is a festival of rejoicing and charity marking the end of the ordeal of Ramazan. At both of the Ids it is usual for the

91

whole community to gather for prayer and a sermon in a large field at the edge of town or in an area known as the Idgah. Those who can afford it put on new clothes, presents and visits are exchanged with friends and relatives, and alms are given to the poor.

A third feast observed in Pakistan is the Id-i-Milad, the festival marking the birthday of the Prophet. In East Pakistan, Milad, a ceremony in which aspects of the life of the Prophet and his teachings are narrated and the assembled persons send blessings to him, occurs not only on this holiday but on all important religious and social occasions.

Other important religious commemorations occur during Muharram. As it is the first month of the Moslem year the first day is an official holiday in Pakistan. The first ten days of the first month are observed by Shi'as as a period of mourning for Husayn, the Prophet's grandson, who was killed at Karbala. On Ashura, the tenth day, large processions wind through the streets sometimes accompanied by frenzied dancing and swordplay in symbolic enactment of the death scene. In the past this was occasionally a time of Sunni-Shi'a clashes, and when it coincided with the joyful Hindu festival of Holi there were sometimes Hindu-Moslem disorders. However, in recent years this mourning festival has become a more solemn and less popular occasion.

A final religious event widely observed in Pakistan is the Shab-i-Barat, which comes on the fourteenth evening of the eighth month. It is given a variety of meanings and is customarily a night on which people flock to the graveyards and offer prayers for dead relatives.

The commemorations mentioned above are all official holidays in Pakistan. There are also three other Moslem holidays officially recognized in parts of the country and numerous unofficial festivals associated with the anniversaries of saints which are sometimes more important to the local populations than the official observances.

A number of other practices stem from or are supported by religious injunctions in Pakistan. The only important one not mentioned in the Qur'an is circumcision, a custom universal in the Islamic world. When a man becomes converted to Islam he is expected not only to recite the profession of faith but to be circumcised. In East Pakistan a boy is usually circumcised between the ages of five and seven. The ceremony is particularly important in his life because it signifies initiation into full membership in the community. Thereafter he is expected to obey all the injunctions of Islam, especially the daily prayers, and he begins observing the Ramazan fast. Elsewhere in Pakistan he may be circumcised as a baby.

The Qur'anic injunction against idolatry has been extended to proscribe the representation of any human or animal creatures in art, especially in connection with religion. With great ingenuity and artistic refinement Moslems have, instead, adorned their mosques with Qur'anic verses in the Arabic script and with floral designs. The art of painting has been highly developed in the Moslem world but in portraying humans it has been usually confined to secular subjects.

The Qur'an prohibits the eating of carrion, blood, and swine flesh; the consumption of alcohol; adultery; gambling; and usury. Moslems not only refuse to eat pork but the aversion to pigs is extended to dogs. It was sometimes difficult in the past to determine whether some of the borderline castes were Hindus or Moslems by religious criteria alone, but observance of the customs of circumcision, eating meat but not eating pork, and burial rather than cremation of the dead was sufficient to put such castes in the Moslem column.

These injunctions have not necessarily prevented Moslems from consuming alcohol or lending money on interest, but socially they operate to give liquor sellers and moneylenders a low status. Prior to partition these occupations were not ordinarily engaged in by Moslems, at least in Moslem-majority areas. Of the two, the ban on usury is certainly the more challenging and was the subject of considerable debate in the constituent assemblies. Numerous formalities have been adopted to get around it in ordinary practice, particularly since partition, and although it does not affect the financial operations of the government, the subject still has social and economic repercussions. The Pathans of the northwest, for example, are often moneylenders in other parts of the subcontinent, particularly among non-Moslems, but they seldom engage in moneylending in their home districts because they would not be considered "good Moslems" if they did.

Marriage, divorce, inheritance, purdah, and naming are all affected or regulated by the Qur'an, by the Sunna, and by local custom. In regard to the seclusion of women the Qur'an enjoins the modesty of women and makes reference to concealing their features. Thus purdah is considered essential, on religious grounds, in most of Pakistan. The Qur'an says that Moslems should be given an honorable name. In practice this means that all boys are given religious names: one finds Abdullahs and Abdur Rahmans (both mean "servant of Allah") throughout the Moslem world and Muhammad outranks numerically all other given names in the world.

Moslem Sects

The Moslems of Pakistan are sometimes divided into three categories: the Sunnis, the Shi'as, and the Ahmadiyas. These headings are used here for convenience rather than accuracy, because the three-way division is misleading. Only Sunni and Shi'a are comparable terms. A much smaller group, the Ahmadiyas are the followers of one of the late nineteenth-century reformers and, though originating within the Sunni fold, are now considered a separate, distinctive sect.

As noted earlier, the Sunnis form the majority and are so called for their adherence to the Sunna developed and interpreted by the historic leaders and jurists of the community. The Hadith and Sunna were further developed into four schools of law, all equally orthodox. A Sunni usually follows only one and as a rule only one prevails in a given country. Pakistanis generally follow the Hanafite school. There are of course numerous groups, divisions, and movements within the Sunni fold, but no sects as such. Some Moslems characterize themselves as Ahl-i-Qur'an ("followers, or people, of the Qur'an"), some as Ahl-i-Hadith ("followers of the Hadith"), and some by the name of a past leader or saint whose teachings they follow. Others, descended from particular Hindu castes, retain their group identity, revere the man who converted their ancestors, and have certain peculiarities of doctrine. The Memons, who constitute an influential business community, are an example of this kind of group. Finally, some Sunnis follow one of the several reform movements of the recent past. These reform movements were of all kinds, ranging from progressive to purist or fundamentalist. Whereas the Ahmadiya movement now has a sectarian character, most of them were much more loosely organized. The best organized and most active fundamentalist group today is the Jama'at-i-Islami, founded (1941) and led by Maulana Abul 'Ala Maudoodi.

The origin of the Sunni-Shi'a division in Islam has already been indicated. Partisanship for 'Ali was not only political but also involved loyalty to the line of 'Ali's descendants. Imams in this line were regarded as the only rightful leaders of the Moslem community and as sole interpreters of religious doctrine, some Shi'a sects even attributing various forms of mystical or divine authority to them. Shi'a doctrines and practices greatly influenced the early Sufis of Islam but dogmatic Shi'ism has generally been hostile to the formation of Sufi brotherhoods.

The Shi'as hold that there were twelve Imams, beginning with 'Ali. The twelfth having disappeared without posterity, it is believed that at some time in the future this "Mahdi" will reappear. One sect in Pakistan came into being directly as a result of a dispute over the succession of the seventh Imam. Those who advocated the succession of his brother, Ismail, became known as Ismailis: most of them are followers of the Agha Khan. One Agha Khan was an important liberal in Indian politics early in the twentieth century; his son, the late 'Ali Khan, was Pakistan's chief delegate to the United Nations. The present Agha Khan, installed in October 1957, is a son of 'Ali Khan. Of an estimated 200,000 Ismailis in Pakistan, the two best known groups are the Khojas and the Bohoras. Most of the Khojas, a Hindu trading caste converted in the fourteenth century by a famous saint, follow the Agha Khan, whereas the Bohoras, who are merchants, do not. Both are castelike commercial groups which have extended their business activities to East and South Africa, Southeast Asia, and other parts of the world. Their importance in Pakistani banking, industry, and trade is far in excess of their numbers.

The doctrinal differences between the Sunnis and Shi'as are no longer of any real significance and no longer lead to communal riots, as they sometimes did in the past. The Shi'as have contributed not only commercial enterprise but several prominent political leaders, such as Mahomed 'Ali Jinnah (a Khoja); Iskandar Mirza, formerly president of Pakistan; and Ismail I. Chundrigar, prime minister in 1957.

Numbering about 250,000 the Ahmadiyas, although fairly important in secular affairs, have today a significantly smaller religious importance. But in 1953 agitation directed against them by other Moslems became so violent that it shook the very foundations of the new state. Their beliefs are summarized below in order to provide the religious background of the 1953 riots.

The Ahmadiya movement was founded by Mirza Ghulam Ahmad, who was born to an important family in Qadian, a village of the Punjab, in 1835 and died in 1908. He claimed to have received a series of divine revelations beginning in 1882 and in 1901 founded the Ahmadiya Society (Jama'at-i-Ahmadiya), which he had listed as a separate sect in the census. His adherents are known for their vigorous and able proselytizing both in Pakistan and abroad, where they have several missionary centers. His movement combined a purifying spirit of orthodox reform, a tinge of Sir Sayyid Ahmad Khan's modern liberalism, a mystic irrationalism, the infallible authority of a new revelation, and the enthusiasm of a small and self-conscious group.

Some of the revelations proclaimed by Ghulam Ahmad met with intense opposition from Moslem theologians, who issued *fatwas* (judgments) against him. The one given greatest prominence in recent years was his claim to be a prophet. He also claimed to be the Shi'a Mahdi and the Messiah who would appear with the attributes of Christ. Apart from these doctrines, however, there was nothing in Ghulam Ahmad's religious message that was not in orthodox Islam. The ideas of the liberal wing, which seceded in 1914 and repudiated the prophethood of Ghulam Ahmad, have come to be virtually the same as those of ordinary Sunnis of a moderately liberal bent. The section that remained in Qadian (now in India) elected Maulavi Nur ud-Din as the first successor of Ghulam Ahmad, and then, in 1914, Ghulam Ahmad's son Mirza Bashir ud-Din Mahmud Ahmad succeeded to the leadership of the sect. They are sometimes called Qadianis, although they have set up a new center in Pakistan. It was against the Qadianis that the recent agitation was directed.

Even in the case of the Qadianis, however, the hostility toward the Ahmadiya movement did not stem primarily from its theology but from its social aspects. It has a strong and closely knit organization. With high corporate enthusiasm its members devote themselves to the service of the community. They strictly enforce purdah; encourage polygamy; have an ascetic morality that disapproves of all worldly indulgence; collect alms from their rich for their poor; have a very high literacy rate; find jobs for their members; and run their own mosques, courts, schools, and welfare institutions, for which they impose heavy taxes. In 1947 they were the best educated Moslem group native to the area which became West Pakistan.

As a result, they were drawn upon to fill many posts in the foreign ministry and other departments of the new government.

The widespread belief that Ahmadiyas find all their members government jobs, give scholarships to all their university students, and care only about other Ahmadiyas is certainly an exaggeration. Yet the strong internal cohesion of the group did involve external aloofness and it was this social exclusiveness that brought about the antagonism between themselves and the rest of the Moslems. Submerged for a while during the height of Hindu-Moslem communalism, this social animosity was strong enough that after 1947 a semipolitical group, the Ahrars, could fan it into violence by focusing attention on the doctrinal differences mentioned above. Indeed, Sunni groups continue to claim that the movement is a heretical one and that the Ahmadiyas must be considered non-Moslems.

Moslem Institutions

The Moslem's relationship with Allah is a personal and direct one. The Qur'an recognizes no communion of saints to intercede for sinners, no holy orders, and no priesthood. The religious commemorations in the Moslem calendar are not analogous to the high days and holy days of the Christian ecclesiastical year. Despite a sometimes sacred atmosphere, mosques and tombs are not hallowed or consecrated places.

Although there is no institutionalized hierarchy of ordained priests in Islam there are two groups of men in Pakistan who provide religious leadership and often function, in effect, as priests. One is the body of men known collectively as the "ulama," who are learned in Islamic law and have traditionally provided what might be called the orthodox leadership of the community. The other is the collection of men often called "pirs," who are associated with the mystical or devotional side of Islam known as Sufism. Both traditions and kinds of leadership—the law and the ulama, Sufism and the pirs—are important in popular Islam.

The leadership of the ulama is the leadership of a community which follows the law of Allah as revealed through the Prophet and interpreted by him. The authority of the ulama is thus based on their knowledge of the shari'a, the religious law. The science of law is usually defined as "the knowledge of the rights and duties whereby man may fitly conduct his life in this world and prepare himself for the future life." There was never a full separation made between law in the sense of the limits on human freedom and law in the sense of duty. Since the basis of the law is the Word of Allah, to violate or neglect it is not simply to infringe a rule of social order, it is an act of religious disobedience and involves a religious penalty. Because the shari'a, or "highway" of divine command, never became a formal code, it is sometimes construed simply as the essential principles, or spirit, of Islam. More often, it is construed as the injunctions embodied in the Qur'an and Hadith, interpreted and developed historically in response to the needs of the rapidly expanding Moslem community.

The development and preservation of this law came to require a high degree of scholarship. If a matter was not explicitly covered in the Qur'an, the early Moslems turned to the oral Hadith for guidance and methods were devised to separate the large number of spurious traditions from the genuine traditions and to rank the latter in order of authenticity. To the Qur'an and Hadith were applied various forms of analogical reasoning (kiyas) to derive further interpretations. Some time in the second century of the Islamic era the principle was secured that the consensus of the community (ijma) had binding force. In practice, this meant the consensus of the ulama since only they possessed the required knowledge (ilm).

Once ijma was exercised the decision was regarded as irrevocable. The right of individual interpretation (ijtihad) was confined to points on which no agreement was yet reached. These diminished in time and the majority of the ulama held that after the first three or four centuries of Islam the "gate of ijtihad" was closed. Adjustment, elaboration, and refinement continued and the four schools of law were developed, but the basic canon law has remained essentially the same. Thus the function of the ulama became that of expounding and preserving a system of law and practice that was already formulated. Their conservatism has had its virtues, for historically they have acted as the sheet anchor of Islam, maintaining the unity of the Moslem world and withstanding successive challenges from Hellenism, mysticism, and indigenous popular cults.

The combined total of the great effort of traditionalism and reasoned interpretation makes up the corpus of Moslem law known as the fiqh (understanding). In effect, the shari'a thus finds itself contained in a mass of books, documents, and legal decisions (*fatwas*), the methodical knowledge of which constitutes the fiqh. Sometimes the fiqh is defined as positive law, in contrast with the shari'a, or moral law.

In Pakistan today, many of the law books and past decisions are not available; there are no shari'at courts; and it is the British legal system which is operative. In matters of personal law, however, the British attempted to apply the shari'a as they understood it and there are local judges or lawyers known as *qadis* who continue to adjudicate it. Apart from this, the ulama in Pakistan do not perform the official juridical functions that they perform in some other Moslem countries. Their function, as they conceive it, is still that of teaching and preserving the Islamic way of life in the face of outside challenge. Today the challenge comes from modern sociopolitical ideas stemming from Christian morality. The problem of adjustment involves deep religious issues, for if one starts compromising and throwing out portions of the fiqh and Sunna it is exceedingly difficult to establish, on logical Islamic grounds, the point at which the revision should stop.

The members of the ulama are called *maulvis, maulanas, imams,* and *mullahs.* The first two are titles accorded to those who have completed special training in Moslem theology and law: the maulvi has pursued higher studies in the madrasa, equivalent to a religious seminary, while additional study on the graduate level leads to the title of maulana. However, either title may be accorded to any distinguished Moslem. The term, imam, has a number of meanings. In a general sense, it refers to the leader of the group prayers but in ordinary usage it is a functional term which refers to the paid official in charge of a mosque. His income is not secure: he may be paid out of voluntary contributions or funds from trust property, or he may receive a conventional share of village produce at harvest time. In addition to looking after the mosque, collecting its revenues, leading the prayer, and delivering the weekly sermon, he acts as a consultant on points of Moslem law and is usually called upon to preside at birth ceremonies, marriages, circumcisions, and funerals. When the village mosque is also used as a school, the imam is the teacher. The office of imam is accorded by the consensus of the community and in practice is hereditary.

In the larger mosques of the towns the imam is ordinarily a maulvi or maulana and may be highly respected as a person of some learning and distinction, but few village imams have received any higher training. The village imam may know the Arabic script well enough to read the Qur'anic verses and is familiar with all the obligatory prayers and the accompanying ritual. His authority often stems less from his learning than from the magical powers he is believed to possess by virtue of his familiarity with the Qur'an. In the villages the imams are called mullahs, as distinguished from the learned ulama. As the recognized religious leader of the community the mullah may be very influential and possess considerable authority in some villages; in other villages he may be regarded with friendliness and indulgence but little respect.

The villagers call upon the mullah for the socioreligious functions mentioned above and may also consult him to determine whether a particular kind of behavior is permissible, though in important matters of this sort they may travel some distance to consult someone of higher reputation. More commonly (in East Pakistan at least) they come to him for holy water, amulets, and charms to cure sickness, snakebite, and sexual impotence; to ward off evil jinn; to bring good luck in projected undertakings; to ensure the birth of sons; and so on.

Sufism

The tradition of Islamic mysticism known as Sufism is common throughout the Moslem world and is especially prevalent, in a bewildering variety of forms, in Pakistan and India. It first appeared in Iraq in the eighth century A.D. and has grown up almost entirely within the Sunni fold. As it spread it became essentially a popular movement emphasizing love rather than fear of Allah and a direct, personal devotion to Allah rather than the often mechanical outward observance of the communal discipline. While the ulama claimed that truth could be found only through detailed knowledge of the arduously developed science of law, the Sufis sought truth through the living experience of Allah culminating in momentary union with Him. Sufism gave an emotional release to the people's religious instincts, which were all too often starved by the dry scholasticism of the ulama.

In the first four or five centuries of its existence, more and more non-Islamic popular elements, such as celibacy and saint worship, became a part of sufism, and the ulama countered with increasing pedantry and repression. However, at the end of the eleventh century the philosopher and mystic theologian, al-Ghazali, brought Sufism within the bounds of orthodox Moslem belief.

As a result, men were led back from scholasticism to living contact with the Qur'an and Hadith, which were brought within the range of the ordinary mind, and a new vigor and warmth were infused into the orthodox religious discipline. Many gifted poets and orthodox legal scholars of both Sunni and Shi'a persuasions have been inspired by the higher Sufi ideas without formally becoming Sufis themselves. Refreshed and strengthened, Islam was brought to large new areas, including the Indian subcontinent, where the men most active in winning converts were the Sufis or those inspired by Sufism.

On the other hand, the emotional side of religion and the "way" of the mystics became an integral part of Islam, and this had some unforeseen consequences. Within the ranks of the Sufis there were wide gradations ranging from men of great intellect and character, whose mysticism strengthened and enriched their understanding of Islamic doctrine, down to those who found mystical cults emotionally satisfying and were ready to admit non-Islamic ideas and practices if they produced results. Some of the Hindu elements that were retained after the people's conversion to Islam have consequently disappeared over the years, but many others have been only modified rather than eliminated. In addition, there are numerous purely local indigenous cults, not necessarily Hindu or Moslem, which are still fully observed by Hindus and Moslems alike.

Among the followers of Sufism it is believed that a man cannot pursue the path to spiritual salvation or communion with Allah without the help of a preceptor, or *murshid*, who has amassed sufficient spiritual power and merit to help his disciple, or *murid*. From the time Sufism swelled into a popular movement to the present day, pious men of outstanding personality, reputed to have the gift of miraculous powers, have found followers crowding to them. The murid can be a kind of lay associate, earning his living in secular occupations, consulting the murshid at times, participating in the ceremonies (*dhikr*), and making offerings contributing to the murshid's support. Or he may be initiated into a brotherhood which pledges its devotion to the murshid, lives in close association with him, and spends its time in pious exercises to bring about mystical enlightenment.

These brotherhoods of "poor men" or "mendicants," called dervishes (from Persian) or fakirs (from Arabic), grew out of loose, voluntary associations and developed into organized monastic orders somewhat similar to those of Christianity and Buddhism. The center of the dervish community would be the residence of the murshid, and monasteries would be established by supporters. When the murshid died he was, of course, venerated as a saint, his tomb functioned as a shrine, and his place could be taken by his son or, if celibacy was a rule, by a disciple elected to leadership. The pursuit of mystical experience came to involve successive stages of discipline and enlightenment. When a dervish had reached the higher stages of initiation he might go out to preach his master's *tariqa*, or way, gain new disciples at another center, and found a new monastery. In this way, from about the twelfth century on, networks of Sufi orders were spread throughout the Islamic world.

There are four major Sufi orders on the Indo-Pakistan subcontinent and a large number of small, irregular orders. There is no way of knowing the geographical distribution or size of their respective followings. The orders and their many subsections vary widely according to whether they were initially urban or "rustic," the nature and degree of organization, the extent to which their beliefs and practices conform to those of the ulama, their litany, and their practices for inducing the mystic state. The four main ones are the Qadiri, Naqshbandi, Suhrawardi, and Chisti orders. The beliefs and practices of the first two are quite close to those of orthodox Islam. The third, also quite orthodox, has given rise to a particularly large number of irregular orders. The fourth, founded in Ajmer, India, is peculiar to the subcontinent and has a number of unorthodox practices such as the use of music in its litany. It has included many musicians and poets in its ranks.

It has already been noted that possibly as many as two-thirds of the Moslems of India and Pakistan are under the influence of one of the Sufi orders. This influence often involves only occasional consultation or celebration rather than formal affiliation. According to one scholar, a large proportion of such people are under the influence of the irregular orders, which display a wide variety of beliefs, rituals, and customs.

While the Sufi orders are a part of the orthodox life of Moslems, the worship of *pirs*, or saints, is not always so regarded. A pir may be the living descendant of a saintly man or he may pass through discipleship and then gain his own following. A number of the most notable pirs in the past, many of whom were the Sufi missionaries who won converts to Islam, founded what have aptly been called "dynasties" of saints. Along with his sainthood a pir might inherit property contributed over the years by his ancestor's followers, whom he would visit periodically to receive offerings and grant spiritual merit. A pir is therefore quite apt to be a landed aristocrat at the head of a sizable establishment. This dynastic sainthood appears to be characteristic of Sind, although it occurs throughout Pakistan. The birthright pir usually resides, along with his subordinates and murids, near the tomb of the original saint, which serves as a holy shrine for the community.

There are innumerable tombs of the saints which function as chapels or shrines in the subcontinent. An incomplete list of the more important ones in India compiled in 1938 names over 500, most of which are now in Pakistan (particularly West Pakistan). At some, a descendant of the pir functions as the living saint; at others there is no living pir descended from the original one but there is an hereditary official who looks after the tomb and administers its property and revenues. Many other tombs are simply wayside shrines visited in times of need. Persons may make pilgrimages to the shrines to make personal prayers, give offerings of food or money, make vows, burn oil lamps, and engage in similar forms of veneration.

Behind this worship at the tombs of saints lies the belief that owing to their spiritual power the saints are able to intercede for the devout with Allah. The annual observance of the pir's death anniversary is held to be an especially propitiatory time for seeking his intercession. Large numbers of devotees take part in these ceremonies, known as *urs,* in their best and gayest attire and often with more enthusiasm and faith than they display in observing the official commemorations. The urs often appear to be quite similar, in form, content, and timing, to the local Hindu festivals of the agricultural year. The fairs, dancing girls, and general festivities are attended and enjoyed by Hindus and Moslems alike.

Just as there are many kinds of pirs, so there are many ways in which the living pirs are regarded. A few are worshiped as the deity incarnate. Many more are venerated as persons who have attained special spiritual or magical powers but are not worshiped. Many well-educated professional men will visit a particularly wise and dignified pir for spiritual solace and personal advice. The villagers rely upon the pir, even more than the mullah, for magical cures and charms.

At times the functions of the pirs and the ulama overlap and merge—an important pir may be the leader of his community in every way, or the local mullah may combine the functions of pir and imam—but it is possible to make a rather general distinction between the kinds of religious leadership provided by the two. The qualifications are different: the maulvi undergoes formal training in the law while the pir gains his powers through various mystical experiences and may have no formal education at all. The maulvis and maulanas may carry on an independent profession in addition to their services as imams, while the pir usually spends all of his time in religious devotion. The maulvis are ordinarily proponents of one of the four Sunni schools of law or that of the Shi'as, while the message of the pir transcends such divisions. The maulvis or mullahs are usually the most orthodox Moslems in the village, whereas the pirs may not observe all of the ordinary rules of the community because, by virtue of their special relationship with Allah, such rules do not apply to them.

The office of imam may, in practice, be hereditary, but it is formally conferred by the consensus of the community as a whole, whereas no such consensus is necessary for a pir and he may be highly venerated by some members of the village and ignored or scoffed at by others. The religious leadership of the mullah is the leadership of the community as a community; the guidance of the pir is the guidance of people more as individuals. A Moslem may go to the pir for personal inspiration and advice and be terribly impressed by his magical prowess but he would not want or expect the pir to lead the communal prayers or deliver the weekly sermon.

In many areas the mullahs and the pirs, while they may not be personal friends, have an easy relationship because each ministers to different religious needs. There are, however, a number of exceptions to this situation. Although Sufism was finally recognized as an integral part of the Sunni doctrine, many aspects of it have remained suspect to the ulama. In villages where a pir has come in and taken over some of the mullah's functions and following it is understandable that the mullah would regard him with disfavor or hostility, especially if he preached a message and followed customs that a purist would consider un-Islamic.

That the messages and practices often were un-Islamic by such standards should be obvious: no sainthood is recognized in the Qur'an but there are saints; Muhammad proclaimed that there would be "no monkery in Islam" but there are, in effect, monks;

a doctrine of divine attributes of human beings and intercession with Allah violates the unity of Allah, but such beliefs are widely held; and so on. Some of these attitudes and beliefs are closely akin to those of Hinduism and the many purely local cults that go under the name of Hinduism. In the past there was sometimes little to distinguish the Moslem pir from the Hindu guru or the itinerant fakir from the wandering sadhu and the practitioners themselves might have been unaware of such distinctions.

The first object of attack in the purist Moslem reform movements of the last century was saint worship and what went with it. The matter has not been adequately studied but it appears that the mullahs were especially active in spreading these movements in the villages. The forms which Sufism took in India, and mysticism itself, were regarded by the purists as corruptions produced by the Hindu environment. The movements for internal purification tended to become movements for the external preservation of Islam from Hindu encroachment, with increasingly political overtones. Under the leadership of the ulama they made a significant contribution to the growth of the communal sentiments which led ultimately to the creation of Pakistan.

The tendency for Hindus and Moslems to attend each other's festivals and have common local cults certainly diminished under the influence of the reform movements and communalism but is by no means absent today. The influence of the pirs does not seem to have declined significantly in comparison with that of the mullahs, although this varies from one area to another. It is reported that in some districts the authority of both men has declined to some extent owing to the spread of education and in some cases they have discredited themselves by readily issuing fatwas during the election campaigns. Other cases are on record, however, of pirs whose control over the votes of their followers was so great that they determined the outcome of the elections, or got elected themselves.

Among the urban educated classes, particularly the younger generation, a good deal of disillusionment set in after the first wave of enthusiasm for the new Islamic nation. It is now being doubted in some quarters whether Moslem solidarity alone will provide the basis for future national unity and overcome the growing provincial consciousness between the two wings and the different linguistic regions. To say that disillusionment with their Islamic state is directed at the concept itself, however, would probably be an exaggeration. Discontent and disgust are directed more at the "corrupt" quality of political leadership, the "narrow-mindedness" of poorly educated religious leaders, and the hypocritical use of the Islamic state concept for un-Islamic political purposes. There is still rather wide support for the ideal, however vague, of the Islamic state among both the educated and uneducated classes. Yet there is some evidence that the educated people with progressive ideas are tending more and more to express their views in secular terms rather than to attempt to evolve a distinctively Islamic liberalism as they did in the past.

Hinduism

Of the 10,002,000 Hindus enumerated in the 1961 census of Pakistan, 93.7 per cent live in East Pakistan, where they form almost a fifth of the total population. Four-fifths of the 622,000 Hindus in West Pakistan live in the former province of Sind. In its statistics on religion, the Pakistan government gives separate figures for the lowest caste Hindus, formerly known as "untouchables" and now called Scheduled Caste, and the upper caste Hindus, called Caste Hindus. In Pakistan today, 54.1 per cent of the Hindus are Scheduled Caste as compared with 16 per cent in the Union of India. This stems largely from the fact that most of the Caste Hindus left Pakistan at partition.

"Hinduism" is a name applied to a large number of extraordinarily diverse creeds and practices. As practiced by the great majority of its adherents, the religion can only be understood in a regional context. Although there are some common elements, the caste systems, beliefs, rituals, and festivals of the Hindus in Pakistan are distinctively Bengali or Punjabi or Sindhi, as the case may be. The great majority of Pakistani Hindus are Bengalis; consequently, after a very general sketch of the major levels and some of the fairly common features of Hinduism, the discussion here will be of the main religious traditions and festivals in East Pakistan.

Varied and complex as it is, Islam is simplicity itself when compared to Hinduism. Both are distinctive religions, but Islam is known by its attributes, Hinduism by its atmosphere; you can define Islam, you must feel Hinduism. Hindus are characterized by broad intellectual and religious tolerance and freedom and close social exclusiveness and conformity; Moslems tend to be the other way around. Islam is proselytizing, Hinduism assimilative; one is converted to Islam, one's social group is absorbed into Hinduism. The history of the community is of great importance in Islam and the religion soon developed a high level of historical scholarship. Traditional Hinduism developed virtually no historical sense of scholarship because the temporal history of society and of individual lives had no religious significance whatever.

Whereas one can distinguish a concept of orthodoxy in Islam—in the sense of a belief in One God, His Book, His Apostle, and a code of righteous behavior—there is no such concept in Hinduism. One cannot say that certain beliefs and practices are essential to Hinduism, but one can point to certain values and attitudes which are rather common within it. There is also, in a sense, a ranking of values and customs as well as of the groups which hold or practice them, so that the lower groups will often emulate the socioreligious practices of the higher ones.

In a slightly different sense, a distinction has sometimes been made between the "higher" religion and the "lower" or popular religion. The latter, which may be engaged in by all classes, is sometimes called the "lesser" or "local" tradition and varies widely with the caste, the village, and the linguistic region. The former is called the Sanskritic or "great" tradition and is, by comparison, more uniform in the subcontinent. Sometimes called Brahmanism, the great tradition was developed under the leadership of Hinduism's highest class, the Brahmans, who, as the custodians of sacred lore, are the traditional priests, teachers, and astrologers and enjoy marked social privileges.

In any particular region the great and local traditions merge into one another; one cannot say where one stops and the other begins. The Sanskritic tradition also contains or merges into a third, more refined and abstract philosophical tradition which. while it may vary widely from one individual thinker to another, exhibits the least degree of regional variation. The three levels are more or less harmonized by an emphasis on the concept of unity in diversity and a pervasive attitude of relativism.

On its highest level Hinduism recognizes the Absolute (Atman or Brahma) as eternal, unbound by time, space, and causality, consisting of pure existence, consciousness, and bliss. The highest end is the union of one's own soul with the absolute Atman and consequent attainment of *moksha*, release from the cycle of birth and rebirth. To attain it, one may follow one of several methods of

107

"yoking" (yoga) depending on one's own temperament or capacity. They are regarded as several paths up the same mountain and represent not simply methods of enlightenment but operative values in Hindu society.

The five major types of yoga are as follows: (1) The Raja or "kingly" path is that of consciousness in which union is achieved by will: it is a combination of the other types in their advanced stages. (2) Jnana yoga stresses union by knowledge. (3) Karma is the yoga of disinterested right-action: the performance of one's duty (the function of one's caste or sex, service to others, and so on) from the highest motives and without personal involvement in the consequences of the act. (4) Bhakti is the yoga of devotion and union by love; its essence is complete, sometimes passionate, faith in a personal deity, "a faith which closely corresponds to what Christians understand by the term," and it is often regarded as the best way to begin one's spiritual evolution. (5) Hatha yoga is the method of physical control, involving successive exercises to gain such complete mastery of mind over body that all physical processes become a voluntary system.

Each form partakes of the others to some extent, and especially of Hatha yoga. In the West, yoga and its practitioners, the yogis, are usually known only by the forms of Hatha yoga. The different forms of yoga, particularly spiritual knowledge, disinterested action, and devotion, are major values or ideals of human conduct in Hindu society. Renunciation is also given a high place in the Hindu value system, less for its own sake than as a means to a spiritual end. It is generally felt that if a person wishes to attain the highest spiritual levels he must devote his whole time to it; he must renounce society, all its attachments, desires, and obligations, and devote himself to the rigorous disciplines of gaining self-mastery and self-knowledge.

At its middle level, for the great majority of men, Hinduism operates as a variety of religions and sects which center around one or more of the great gods and are expressed at least partly in a regional context. The great tradition recognizes a trinity of gods or forms of Brahman, the supreme godhead: Brahma, the Creator; Vishnu, the Sustainer; and Shiva, the Destroyer. Brahma is the demiurge at the beginning of each huge cycle of the universe but is otherwise unimportant. Creative powers are attributed to both Vishnu and Shiva. The major Hindu traditions are the

Vaishnava and Shaiva traditions centered on Vishnu or Shiva, who are known by a variety of names, as are their respective consorts.

On its lowest levels Hinduism admits worship of spirits and godlings of rivers, mountains, vegetation, animals, stones, disease, and much else. It fosters many holy men and ascetics conspicuous for their bodily mortifications. Ritual bathing, vows, and pilgrimages are important in its practice, taking devotees to the sacred rivers, mountains, shrines, and cities where they gain an auspicious view, if only by the eye of faith, of the great beings honored there. An ordinary Hindu will often worship at any holy place, including the shrines of Moslem pirs, without being concerned with the religion to which that place is supposed to be affiliated. People who can only so much as see the bodily form of a great holy man or political leader (called taking his *dharshan*) also believe themselves to be benefited.

On all but the most refined philosophical levels Hinduism makes wide use of images, which the sophisticated may recognize as symbols and many others may take for the deity itself. Highly imaginative, it is a faith which has inspired a rich art. Its ethics generally center around the principle of *ahimsa*, noninjury to living creatures —especially the cow, which is held sacred. The principle is expressed in the dietary rule against the eating of beef, which is almost universally observed. By no means are all Hindus vegetarians, but abstinence from meat is regarded as a "higher" practice. Bengali Hindus, however, unlike higher castes elsewhere, will ordinarily eat fish.

Religious rituals, which vary widely from caste to caste and region to region, permeate the lives of the great majority of Hindus. Most observances occur in the home, which usually contains some sort of shrine or alcove housing the god. The women, as might be expected, are more devout, meticulous, and conservative about such matters than the men. There is little about their lives that has not been invested with religious meaning by some group at some time or place. Many other observances are caste-wide affairs. There is little or no emphasis placed on common, community-wide observances. Hindus generally go to their temples individually or in small groups, the distance to which they can approach the central shrine being determined, in theory, by the status of their caste. If a whole village takes part in a festival the roles of the different castes are prescribed more or less clearly by custom.

In East Pakistan, where most people live in poverty and where the many rivers can be placid and life-giving one day and horrible torrents of destruction the next, participation in the rituals of the daily, yearly, and life cycles and the group ceremonial feasts, dancing, and singing of religious literature, gives a sense of continuity and enjoyment to a life that would otherwise be unendurably hard.

There are no beliefs that are essential to Hinduism but there are two that are fairly universal. One is the acceptance of the Sanskrit texts known as the Veda, of the Upanishads, and of later epics. The two great epics, the Mahabharata and the Ramayana, are especially popular. Their ballads, legends, and teachings are woven into the fabric of the ordinary Hindu's life.

The other common element is the acceptance of the caste system as the structure of society. For virtually all Hindus, even those in revolt against some aspects of the system, caste is taken for granted as the way of life. A group which is to be considered Hindu at all is a group which identifies itself in some way as a unit in the caste hierarchy, unless it is a group which has renounced society altogether. One cannot join a caste; one is born into it, lives, marries, and dies in it. Similarly, an individual cannot join Hinduism by conversion; but the group into which he is born can be absorbed into it, and such a group is absorbed as a caste.

The kind of conformity expected of castes in the Hindu system in turn is outward rather than inward, a matter of social practices, such as the rules concerning the acceptance of food and water, conventions of speech and deportment toward other castes, and so on, rather than a matter of orthodox beliefs and observances. Thus the broad religious tolerance and diversity and the narrow social group—conformity and exclusiveness of Hinduism are but two sides of the same coin. Although this caste relativism is very important the social and religious aspects of Hinduism cannot be fully separated. The caste rules are not simply social restrictions but expressions of positive religious duty (dharma); it should be remembered too that certain religious customs are considered higher or more desirable. The most common procedure adopted by low castes attempting to establish their claim to a higher status is to adopt the socioreligious practices of the higher castes, such as abstinence from certain foods, drinks, and marriage customs and relatively greater seclusion of women, thus making themselves "better" Hindus and more worthy of respect.

The religious sanction or rationale of the caste system is the joint doctrine of rebirth and karma (act). Unless he is one of the rare individuals who realizes ultimate truth and identity with the Absolute Soul and succeeds in saving himself from rebirth, a person who dies passes on to another life in this world. In his new life his status and some of the things that happen to him are determined by the acts and desires of his previous life (or lives) and his future condition will be determined by what he does now. Thus he deserves to be where he is. Theoretically, if he is to stay there or to rise to a better state in his next life he must live righteously, endure his hardships and disabilities with equanimity, unquestioningly fulfill the occupation and duty (dharma) of his particular caste, and adhere to the caste conventions for respect toward higher castes and freedom from contamination by lower ones.

The doctrine of karma, the concept of ceremonial pollution, and the attitude of relativism are, among other things, expressions of the sense of religious hierarchy which permeates the Hindu social system and differentiates it from that of Pakistan's Moslems. At the same time, it should be noted that the Hindu social order, while immutable in theory, has always been flexible in practice and is especially so today. While an individual must ordinarily be born again to raise his caste status, castes and subcastes can gradually rise in the hierarchy, for their rank is fixed not by law but by social convention. Often the observance of the commensal and connubial restrictions is construed more in terms of the social prestige of the group than in terms of providing conditions for the rapid evolution of individual souls. Then too, in East Pakistan the caste system has fewer small discrete units, there is less hierarchical ranking of castes, and the social distance between them is smaller and less clearly expressed than in many other parts of the subcontinent. And the application of the doctrine of karma to justify the imposition of exaggerated disabilities on the lowest castes has been condemned on religious grounds by leading Hindus for many years.

The history of Hinduism in Bengal is quite unlike that of any other region in the subcontinent and accounts in large part for the forms of the religion in East Pakistan today. Buddhist rule over the region was not overthrown by a Hindu dynasty until about 1100 A.D. and the Moslem armies and missionaries entered only a century later. One of the Hindu rulers, Ballal Sen, made a

111

vigorous attempt to impose Brahmanical supremacy and control, but in the areas which now form East Pakistan his efforts were impeded by the general lack of communications and the backwardness of the local inhabitants. The limited Brahmanical teachings which managed to infiltrate soon succumbed to the influence of an indigenous sexo-yogic tradition known as Tantrism, which appears to be neither Hindu nor Buddhist in origin.

Out of the teachings of the Buddha had emerged the notion that reality consists of two main principles, vacuity and compassion; under Tantric influence these were transformed into consciousness and activity and were identified with the male and female principles respectively. By this interpretation reality was construed as a drama in which these two principles interact. Under Hinduism the basic dualism of the male and female principles gave rise to the Shaiva and Vaishnava traditions which predominate today. In Vaishnavism, devotion became oriented toward the divine element in man and away from theism. Human love became the vehicle for the attainment of the divine mystical bond, a notion which has influenced a considerable portion of Bengali poems and songs.

The major festival centered on Vishnu is Holi, a festival of fun and rejoicing in the middle of March. As with spring festivals the world over, the element of fertility rites is not absent. The most conspicuous feature of Holi is its happily uninhibited behavior, in which colored water and powder are thrown over everyone in sight.

Buddhism

According to the 1961 census there are 376,312 Buddhists in Pakistan, of whom only 2,445 live in West Pakistan. Buddhism, in various forms, appears to have been the prevailing religion of East Bengal at the time of the Moslem conquest in 1197. The invading armies apparently found numerous monasteries which they destroyed, thinking them to be fortresses, and with the destruction of its centers of learning, Buddhism rapidly disintegrated.

The only significant concentration of Buddhists today is in the easternmost region, in the Chittagong Hill Tracts, where Buddhist tribes form the majority of the population. Their religion has become a mixture of tribal animist cults and Buddhist doctrines. There is almost no information available as to which Buddhist schools or doctrines prevail in the Chittagong region, but there is some evidence that Buddhism may have come to the area from Burma rather than from Bengal. The essentially ethical teachings of the Buddha included the recommendation that one should renounce society and live a simple life of self-discipline. The men who renounced society became organized into the many monastic orders common in the Buddhist world today. There are several monasteries in the Chittagong region, some of which have been given grants by the government, and in most Buddhist villages there is a school (*kyong*) in which the boys live and are taught to read Burmese and some scriptures in Pali by the monks. It is common for men who have finished their schooling to return for periods of residence in the kyong at regular intervals. The local Buddhist temple is often an important center of village life.

Apart from the general moral law and the importance of contributing to the support of the monasteries and temples, early Buddhism appears not to have concerned itself with the religious beliefs and worship of the lay members who did not withdraw from society. Essentially tolerant, Buddhism outside the monastic retreats thus absorbed and adapted the indigenous popular creeds and cults of the regions to which it spread. Although its earliest form has been characterized as a religion without a god, popular Buddhism contains a whole galaxy of gods and godlings, of whom the chief deity is the Buddha himself. In most areas religious ritual centers around the image of the Buddha, and the major festivals observed by Buddhists in Pakistan commemorate the important events of the legends of his life.

Christianity

Christianity, the third largest religion in Pakistan, is professed by 732,787 persons, according to the 1961 census. Of these, 583,884 live in West Pakistan, most of them in the former Punjab. A slight majority of the Christians are Roman Catholics.

The first contact of Christianity with the subcontinent is attributed to the Apostle St. Thomas who is said to have preached in southern India. Although Jesuit priests were active at the Moghul courts in the sixteenth and seventeenth centuries, the first Christian settlements in what is now Pakistan appear to have been established by Portuguese.

When the Portuguese established themselves at Goa in the sixteenth century they made vigorous efforts to win converts to Roman Catholicism and had a policy of intermarrying freely with the local population. In the same century they settled in the vicinity of Chittagong port, which for some time was their base of operations in Bengal for piracy and slave-trading. In the seventeenth century some of them moved to Dacca, and in West Pakistan most of them are located today in the Karachi area. Many Catholics in Pakistan, including non-Eurasians, have Portuguese names because it was customary for a convert to adopt the name of the man responsible for his conversion. Other Roman Catholics, especially in West Pakistan, stem from the missionary activities of Irishmen after the British came to power. In Karachi, one of the largest schools and the largest church were originally the garrison school and church for the Irish soldiers stationed there.

Protestant missionary efforts began seriously only in the first half of the nineteenth century. In East Pakistan the Baptist Mission, active since 1816, the Oxford Mission, and others have been largely successful among the tribal peoples of the Garo hills in the northern part of Mymensingh and Sylhet districts. The center of Protestant missionary organizations in West Pakistan is the city of Lahore, which contains several distinguished Christian schools and colleges. The American Presbyterian Mission, established in the Punjab in 1834, and subsequently several other groups, found a favorable atmosphere in the Punjab and there are now more than a half dozen major missions active there. Many of the Christian churches, schools, and hospitals were initially set up to serve the European community and only later became centers of conversion activities, with particular success among the Scheduled Caste Hindus. Since partition the missions have been especially busy in welfare projects.

The most important contributions of the Christian community have been, and remain, in the fields of medicine and education and Pakistan could ill afford to do without the facilities provided by the missions. Many of the best hospitals are Christian-run, and most nurses are Christian because the nursing profession is still considered improper for respectable Moslem girls. Many of the best schools are also run by Christians and because of their ability to maintain high standards admission to them has consistently been at a premium. Christian schools, as might be expected, have been pioneers in the education of girls. Other fields in which upper-class Christians are especially prominent are in the railroads, law, and public administration. A large number of the low-class Christians, converted from the Scheduled Castes, continue in their traditional occupations as sweepers, scavengers, leatherworkers, and so forth.

Although many Christians are Eurasians, most are converts or their descendants, who differ in no way from their countrymen. During the British period it used to be fashionable to affect European ways, at least among the urban Christians, but since independence there has been a noticeable trend toward assimilation in manners and customs. Politically, the Christian leaders gave their support to the Islamic clauses of the constitution and have in other ways attempted to gain the reputation of a loyal, indigenous community rather than that of a group of foreign imports or dependents. The primary objective of the local Christians now is to establish their community on a self-sustaining basis with their own ministers and priests.

Zoroastrianism

Zoroastrianism is the religion of the Parsis, a small urban community of Iranian extraction and modern commercial prominence far in excess of their number. According to the 1961 census there are only 5,412 Parsis in Pakistan, nearly all at Karachi, a city in whose development the Parsis have been very prominent.

The monotheistic religion of the Parsis was founded by the prophet Zoroaster, who lived in about the sixth century B.C. The supreme deity is called Ormazd, or Ahura-Mazda. Ormazd is all-pervasive—the spirit of spirits, synonymous with truth, light, and life. In order to explain the existence of evil in the world the Parsi scriptures postulate a lesser power, Ahriman, the origin and principle of evil, who is independent of and coexists with Ormazd and is synonymous with falsehood, darkness, and death. Parsis believe that ultimately and inevitably Ormazd will triumph but in the meantime the world is torn by ceaseless conflict in which Ahriman obstructs the complete realization of good on earth.

The Parsi scripture is the Avesta, a collection of sacred writings of which the most important are the *gathas* (divine songs), composed by Zoroaster, which mingle practical advice with ecstatic songs of praise and communion with God. Ormazd is not invested with any anthropomorphic character; the most beautiful form of this intangible spirit of light is the sun and its earthly symbol is fire, which forms the center of Parsi ritual worship. The Parsis have a

115

priesthood, and priests preside at all important ceremonies. Their most unusual religious custom is their treatment of the dead. Parsis do not cremate their dead like the Hindus or bury them like the Moslems and Christians. Instead, the bodies are exposed in the Towers of Silence, where the bones are picked clean by the vultures, purified by the sun, and eventually interred.

The Parsi's feet are planted squarely on the ground, and his religion does not advocate asceticism, celibacy, or withdrawal from the world in any form. Contemplation is recommended only if accompanied by practical achievement; life is to be enjoyed, consistent with virtue; Parsis are conspicuous for their business acumen. Thus, for example, alcohol is not prohibited, but the good Parsi is moderate in his enjoyment of it; temperate themselves, the Parsis have virtually monopolized the liquor trade.

The choice of the good involves not only the obligation to be truthful and to hold to the practical virtues mentioned above but to be of service to others. The Parsis are conspicuous for their sense of group welfare and the services which they provide for each other. As a matter of course a rich Parsi will devote some, often a large part, of his wealth to the betterment of his community. But they do not limit their services to their own community. The Parsis have provided leaders in commerce, industry, and the urban development of Karachi, and have also set up sizable trust funds and institutions for the benefit of society as a whole.

CHAPTER 7

Social Structure

CONSCIOUSNESS OF THE POWERFUL COMMON BOND of being Moslem was the basis on which millions of people dissociated themselves from Hindu India and established a separate nation in 1947, and its intellectual leaders continue to assert that Pakistani society is democratic and egalitarian. Such spokesmen point out to their fellow citizens that they have escaped from the rigidly stratified society of old India and from a system of inherited social exclusiveness and inequality in which they felt themselves underprivileged and relatively powerless with respect to the Hindu majority. As Moslems they believe in the Islamic ideal of a classless society devoid of inherited rank and privilege.

This egalitarian ideal, however strongly it is believed in by its proponents, is far from being practiced or accepted at all levels of the society. In village and town, in government and the army, in business and education, it is evident that the society still bears the stamp of prepartition India and that, while Moslems are no longer second-class citizens, much remains of class and caste and of inherited differences in rank and privilege.

The cultural diversity within Pakistan permits only approximate description of the total social structure. There is not one system of social organization and ranking but several, and the ranking of the self and the social group depend upon the frame of reference and values of the individual.

Moslem Society

As noted earlier, the Moslem society of India was long divided into two main groups: the Ashraf (or Sherif), which was highborn, and the Ajlaf (or Atraf), the lowborn. Technically the four elements that make up the Ashraf—Sayyid, Shaikh, Moghul, and Pathan—are of foreign origin. Sayyids claimed descent from 'Ali, son-in-law of the Prophet Muhammad, while Moghuls and Pathans claimed descent from the Turkic and Afghan military conquerors of northern India. The Shaikhs were descendants of the Qureshi tribe to which the Prophet belonged and included some tribal leaders and converts from Hinduism as well. It has been observed that the social organization of Moslem India was of a military character and persons who rendered military service to the Moslem rulers were rewarded by the assignment of land revenue. Over the generations these gifts were consolidated by the families into hereditary landholdings. While the small Moslem ruling elite was primarily of foreign origin, it was augmented to some extent by members of the princely Hindu castes who had been converted to Islam.

The census of India taken in 1911 seems to have been the last occasion on which the Moslems were asked to identify themselves according to group and subdivision. Some 56 per cent belonged to the Ashraf, and of this total about 85 per cent were Shaikhs and less than 1 per cent Moghuls. In the 1921 census of Bengal (the last to enumerate Moslem castes and tribes) the great majority of the Moslems listed themselves as shaikhs. In addition, "shaikh" used to be a term of respect given to Moslem teachers, saints, and missionaries, and it was common for converts to take the name in honor of the man responsible for their conversion. Nowadays it is well known that claims to belong to a higher class have little basis in fact. The point is well illustrated by a proverb common throughout northern India and Pakistan: "Last year I was a *julaha* [weaver]. This year I am a shaikh. Next year, if the crops are good, I shall be a sayyid." The claim to sayyid status, however, should be supported by a detailed genealogy, so sayyids have gained by accretion less than the other groups.

The Ajlaf, by contrast, is largely descended from indigenous peoples who were converted to Islam from Hinduism and, to a lesser extent, from Buddhism. As might be expected, these people retained many of their old customs and caste practices after conversion.

A caste in the Hindu social system is probably best defined as an endogamous group with its own customs governing the selection of marriage partners within the caste. Identification of a caste may be by descent from a common ancestor or by a common traditional

IMP

118

occupation or by both. Nearly always both descent and occupation are involved and the caste is often further distinguished by peculiarities of diet, ritual, and family custom. Although caste members may and often do engage in other callings, social rank is ascribed largely on the basis of the traditional occupation. Since the status of the individual depends on his birth, i.e. his caste, social mobility is traditionally possible only on a group basis and is gradual.

Castes generally have their own governing institutions, which are quite informal among the upper castes but usually take the form of caste councils (*panchayats*) among the lesser castes. The panchayats may meet only when the occasion requires it or at regular intervals, the primary purpose in either case being to govern the conduct of caste members. A final element of the Hindu system is that each caste has a more or less definite rank in the religious hierarchy. With this rank are associated varying degrees of religious purity or pollution which are in turn expressed socially by a number of rules pertaining to the acceptance of food and water, interdining, and degree of deference or privilege.

Some, but not all, of these elements of the indigenous caste system appear throughout the Moslem society of Pakistan. For example, in describing Moslem society Muhammad Iqbal wrote that "there are castes and sub-castes like the Hindus," adding: "Surely we have out-Hindued the Hindu himself; we are suffering from a double caste system, sectarianism, and the social caste system which we either learned or inherited from the Hindus." One item which is emphatically rejected is the concept of a religious hierarchy of human souls. It is anathema to the Moslems, for all believers are equal in the eyes of Allah and all pray together in the mosque.

Islamic opposition to a social as distinct from a religious hierarchy is less pronounced, the Moslems generally being more flexible in this respect than their Hindu counterparts; changes in the practices of castes converted to Islam have been matters of degree more than kind. Some castes initially retained the customs and attitudes most closely associated with the religious hierarchy, such as those pertaining to food, drink, and dining or smoking together, but these distinctions based on religious rank have disappeared to a large extent. With regard to occupations, however, the Moslem castes generally follow the traditional calling—or at least have shown less tendency to take up new trades than have the equivalent

Hindu castes. Social rank is generally on the basis of profession: those practicing learned or traditional Moslem occupations are socially higher than those engaging in manual labor. A certain amount of prejudice is directed against castes whose work is considered defiling by Hindu belief, such as the cobblers, tanners, sweepers, and latrine cleaners. However, if Moslems from such castes change to cleaner occupations their chance for social advancement improves.

The intermediate and lower Moslem castes, especially the occupational castes, have tended to retain their caste government to some extent. In such cases the caste panchayat is less concerned than its Hindu counterpart with socioreligious and family matters and more with trade practices, thus becoming a sort of guild council.

Marriage practices form the most important element of caste cohesiveness and identity, for a caste which is not endogamous, that is, does not have definite rules for the arrangement of marriages with certain other castes, soon ceases to be a caste. Moslem groups of all classes are generally endogamous in Pakistan since it is both natural and customary for parents to marry children into families "of their own kind." Castes converted from Hinduism retain a number of their old marriage customs but, whereas marriage outside the caste is a contradiction in terms for most Hindus, it is quite permissible, but unusual, for Moslems. Ashraf elements also tend to be endogamous, not because they have inherited caste practices but because they observe the Islamic preference for cousin marriage and have inherited an emphasis on purity of blood and other attitudes from ancestors. Here, as with the lower groups, marriage outside the group is uncommon but permissible.

During the period of Moslem rule, high social status and economic power lay with the families that could claim foreign descent and were associated with the feudal land system by inheritance or marriage. The coming of the British affected this stratum of society differently in the two areas of predominately Moslem populations.

In Bengal the Moslem aristocracy found its control and its land revenue reduced by the various economic and legal changes introduced by the British. By the end of the nineteenth century, economic power had shifted to the Hindus, who had bought up much of the land. In the late nineteenth and early twentieth centuries, the new leaders of Moslem society were not the ancient nobility but the emerging middle class, which had improved its status by going through the British educational system and securing administrative posts. This group tried to consolidate its improved social position by citing relationship with the Ashraf, and frequently by marriages with Ashraf families.

In the area which is now West Pakistan, in contrast, the great landowners were and continue to be Moslem, the old nobility being augmented by some who had given loyal service to the British and had been given *jagirs*, land revenue holdings, as rewards. The area of West Pakistan has retained its hereditary noble landed families, and until very recently this group was the most powerful social and economic class in Pakistan. To this group were added the families of those occupying high posts in the government, many of whom are members of refugee families of high status from India. To a considerable extent, these families and the hereditary Ashraf are the same, since the avenues to education, and therefore to position and power, are open to very few. In a country which is 84 per cent illiterate the few educated and privileged persons play a disproportionate part in the national life, and these constitute the national elite. Membership in the elite is on the basis of family rather than the individual, as the achievement of power is ordinarily possible only through family position.

In the cities, power and wealth combined with concepts of ancestry, are the bases for social status and prestige. As the social system protects the educated and privileged, it is extremely difficult for an individual without family or of low social position to contemplate any considerable upward mobility. Yet for those who have educational qualifications and the capacity and influence for maneuvering, there are possibilities for great advancement on a regional or national level. For example, it is possible for such persons to gain recognition of their advanced status through marriage with the "good families."

The exodus of the entire Hindu and Sikh community from West Pakistan, and of the professional class of Hindus from East Pakistan, considerably increased the number of business and professional posts open to Moslems. The exchange of populations between India and Pakistan led to considerable change in the rural areas, but most dramatically in the government and in varied facets of urban life. In West Pakistan, the movement of Moslems of the area and from India into government, business, banking, and professional fields resulted in the creation of new social groups.

121

The Role of the Family

Pakistani society has as its fundamental unit the family, which provides the individual with models for later interpersonal relationships, teaches him the duties and privileges associated with his social status, instills the values and behavior patterns which make him a predictable member of society, gives religious training, and prepares him for his life trade or profession. The extended family is the most common Moslem family unit. Reinforced by religion and custom, the Moslem family system has certain characteristics which transcend regional, linguistic, and cultural boundaries, while the family systems of the Hindu, Buddhist, and Christian minorities represent variations from this predominant type.

In a society presently lacking in social security or old-age pensions (except for government employees), family membership is the primary source of security. Today, modern development and Westernization, which reward the capable individual at the expense of group security, are threatening the unity of the extended family. In rural areas, the opinion of village elders and religious leaders is against any behavior that changes customary family relationships, and there has been little change in the traditional pattern. In urban areas, however, certain changes are taking place, with those occurring in the middle-class families being the most pronounced.

Moslem Family Structure

In all major areas—descent and residence, authority and succession, ownership and inheritance of property—the structure of the Moslem family in Pakistan is strongly male-oriented. The family, urban or rural, is invariably organized around related males, and descent is reckoned through the male line. The two main kin groups, in which membership is determined by the blood relationship of the males, are the extended family and the lineage.

The typical family household contains an extended kin group: husband and wife, their married and unmarried sons, unmarried daughters, and married sons' wives and children. There may also be a widowed sister or aunt, distant kinsmen, and servants. A man may have more than one wife living in the same house, but men who can afford additional wives usually prefer to maintain them and their children in separate households. In all families where social

122

and economic position permits, and particularly in urban areas, domestic servants are part of the household. They work very long hours and ordinarily receive maintenance and clothing but little in cash payment. Servants are traditional among the nobility and gentry and their availability and low wages have also enabled many low-income families to hire them and thus to observe purdah. Servants of both sexes have a position of confidence in the household; very warm, loyal relationships exist despite differences in social position, especially between servants and those they tended in childhood.

The lineage group is known by a variety of names in different areas, the most common being *baradari,* or brotherhood. Its size and exact composition vary, but in general it includes all persons related by blood through the male line for about five or six generations back. The group composed of the living members of a man's lineage is of much greater socioeconomic significance to him in Pakistan than it is in Western countries. In rural areas especially, the lineage is important for the support and security it provides for its members. The Pakistani is not only more conscious than the Westerner of his family tree, he also knows just what relationship each kind of cousin or in-law bears to him. The Pakistani languages contain different terms for each kind of relative on both sides of the family for about three or four generations. Relationships other than those of kin are also commonly phrased in kinship terms; the terms are used to express various kinds of respect toward persons with whom the individual has social contact, regardless of actual kin relationship. In addition, baradari is also used to designate, in general terms, class groupings.

Authority in the Moslem family is vested in the men and is organized hierarchically by respect relationships. Males are considered inherently superior to females and, under Islamic law, the legal rights granted women, while numerous, are inferior to those granted men. In Pakistan, as elsewhere, the women often have their way but ultimately it is the men who are responsible for direction and discipline.

The characteristic of family life which is paramount in its effect on personality formation is the absolute authoritarian control of the eldest male. He directs the affairs of the family, protects its interests, and exacts complete obedience from its members as a religious and ethical obligation. Complete submission is expected from children and it is unthinkable for them to question his decisions. Paternal authority is most extreme in the Pathan tribal areas of the north-west frontier, where the father holds the power of life and death over all family members and has been known to use that power.

The submission of younger to older and female to male in the family sets the pattern for all later relationships between the individual and authority. The individual submits to authority until he assumes it himself, at which time he presses his power as far as possible. Not to make use of authority is interpreted as weakness.

Upon the death of the head of the household, authority customarily passes to his eldest son. The eldest son also inherits the better pieces of family property, although in theory all sons receive equal shares. The rule, however, is not inflexible and problems connected with succession may generate a certain amount of tension or conflict between brothers. The elder son may have an outside job and prefer not to take on the full responsibility of management, or a younger son may be more able and aggressive and succeed in winning leadership for himself.

The laws regulating ownership and inheritance of property and other family matters stem from three sources. First of course is Islamic law. Second is the British legal system, applied in matters pertaining to the family in conformity with Islamic law, and third, the customary usage of particular Moslem groups.

The main features of Moslem property and inheritance law are as follows: first, a man during his lifetime has absolute right of disposal over his own property but none whatever over that of his wife, who remains mistress of her own estate; second, at his death his property is divided among his family in fixed shares, after his debts and certain expenses have been met; third, women inherit some of the property. The females in each category of relationship to him (children, parents, siblings) receive half the portion of the males unless the shares are too small to allow of further reduction. His widow inherits one-fourth of his property if there are no children, one-eighth if there are children. If he had more than one wife the widow's share is divided among them.

The actual regulations in effect differ considerably from some, but not all, of these provisions. Automatic division of the property upon the decease of the head of the family is widely observed in principle. In practice, it is often impossible to divide all of the property or, if divided, to allot equal shares to all sons. In general, although some groups have customs or laws restricting the division of property, it is usually the practical difficulties of division rather

124

than customary law which serves to keep some or all of the property undivided.

The property and inheritance rights of women, however, have been greatly modified by customary law. In keeping with his position of dominance, the husband has *de facto*, if not *de jure*, power over his wife's property. Among the Pathans, land can be inherited only by males; in the Punjab until recently Hindu customary law, which denies the right of women to inherit property and grants widows only the right of maintenance, took precedence over Islamic law among most Moslems; and similar changes have been in effect in other parts of Pakistan. Thus, just as kinship is reckoned through the male and control over the family is accorded to him, so the family property is generally inherited by males only. In regard to other matters as well it is the provisions of Islamic law relating to the rights of women that have been subject to the greatest modification or change by the application of customary usage in the Indo-Pakistan subcontinent. At the same time, these customs are themselves justified in popular opinion by Islamic traditions and values.

Within the traditional family the axial relationship is that between father and sons, especially the eldest son, who is due to inherit the prestige and responsibilities of his father. The father is charged with disciplining the child to make him God-fearing and obedient, proud of family name and status, and aggressive in defending the rights and honor of the family. Waywardness is immediately punished by physical chastisement as it is regarded as a threat to the father's authority. Punishment is often harshly administered by the father, the father's brothers, or an older brother and is considered essential in shaping the boy's character. Because of the respect due to the father as the head of the family or household, the relationship to the male parent is ceremonious and formal in its expression.

Children have a closer, more affectionate relationship with their mother than with their father and experience greater participation in the women's activities. A mother intercedes for her children with their father and identifies herself with their interests. Both sons and daughters owe respect to their mother, and this is usually given. It is generally believed that ties with the mother's people are more affectionate, and persons will use kinship terms of the mother's family such as *mamu* (mother's brother) when they wish to establish a close and warm tie with a man of the next older generation, rather than the more general *baba* (father's elder brother).

125

Because of the general view that women are weaker and do not need training in self-reliance, daughters are usually treated more indulgently than sons and their discipline is entrusted to the mother. Normally the relationship between a woman and her daughters is very close, and a married daughter returns to the parental household for the birth of a child and to share in family festivities. As a child she is often a favorite of the father and may have a less formal relationship with him than do her brothers. As she reaches puberty, however, greater restrictions are placed on her behavior, and many orthodox families observe the custom that a father and his daughter above the age of puberty may not be in a room alone together.

Probably the warmest relationship within the family during childhood is that between brother and sister. At best, the brother is protective and confidential with his sister, sharing with her some of his experiences outside the household, while she for her part tells him the gossip of the other women, ministers to his food preferences, and intercedes in his behalf with their parents. A sister may undertake inquiries concerning a possible bride for her brother or his sons, and her views are thought to be disinterested and have much influence. In the event a woman's marriage ends unhappily by death or divorce, she counts on acceptance in the household of her brother. Normally, the brother makes gifts to his sister's children upon the occasion of their marriage, and a woman will visit her paternal household often with her children.

The relationship between brothers is subject to considerable tension and represents a weak point in the extended family system. The ceremonious respect due to the eldest brother and the father's preference for him cause jealousy on the part of younger brothers, which can produce serious disputes over property rights. The situation is exacerbated in polygamous households, where the wives live in attitudes of rivalry for the husband's attention and each wife promotes the interests of her own children at the expense of those of other wives.

Sisters participate a good deal in each other's lives both before and after marriage, yet there is a covert rivalry comparable to that which exists between brothers. The younger sisters are placed in a respect relationship to the older sister, to whom the respect term of *apa* is given. After marriage, each sister assumes the status of her husband, and comparisons are made of the jewelry and other possessions which indicate her position. If the position of one is markedly superior, the relationship often becomes strained.

The relationship between husband and wife depends upon traditional behavior patterns and certain situational factors. A wife must always defer to her husband and accept his authority. Where the couple lives with the husband's parents, as is usual, the wife is under the control of the ranking woman of the household, and with the separation of the sexes in daily activities and at mealtimes, the husband and wife have at first only a sexual relationship. The compartmentalization of activities minimizes the effect the newcomer has in the family. Until she has borne a child, especially a son, she has no real acceptance in the family, for her participation in the family is through her children. A childless wife is likely to suffer the disgrace of a co-wife in a few years, and the mother of daughters faces the same possibility.

A wife's relationship with her brothers-in-law depends on whether they are older or younger than her husband. She enjoys a friendly joking relationship with her husband's younger brothers but shows deference and respect to his older brothers by covering her head in their presence. The relationship with her mother-in-law is the source of more friction than any other, as popular stories bear out. When the birth of sons insures her position in the family and she becomes a mother-in-law in turn, a woman may come to wield considerable influence in family matters. The mother of the head of the family has the highest prestige and, often, no small degree of power.

Sexual Behavior

In the male-oriented society of Pakistan, sex is the primary category for defining the role of the individual. Emphasis is placed on the mutually exclusive but complementary roles of men and women both in the family and in society at large. Distinctions are made on the basis of sex from the moment of birth and increase in number and emphasis as the child grows into adulthood.

Within the family, a son is conditioned to be dominant, protective, and defensive of family interests and its good name. His training exacts unqualified obedience in childhood, respect for elders and religious leaders, and a sensitivity to concepts of honor which may, and frequently does, lead to aggressive behavior or acts of violence. He is regarded as an asset and a permanent part of the family who will reinforce the family power and status. His sister, on the other hand, is not regarded as an asset, although she may be fondly treated. Since she will ultimately move into another family, her behavior is a matter of concern, and her marriage, traditionally an occasion for gaining prestige for the family, may entail heavy expenditure. She is encouraged to be docile, modest, obedient, and above all, unassertive. She is always supposed to defer to male family members and is protected from situations that would require her to be self-reliant.

Small children of both sexes play together freely in or near the family compound and are pampered by all. As they grow older, their activities are gradually affected by an increasing number of distinctions on the basis of sex. At the age of seven or eight the great majority of children in village and city begin to learn the trade or occupation of their parents. The little girls assist their mothers in cooking or cleaning utensils or act as nursemaids for younger children; the boys begin to assist their fathers in the field or shop and gradually emerge from the compound to participate in a male world.

Children of the same age from more privileged families begin learning to read and write. The boys go to school, learning the alphabet in Urdu or Bengali and the reading of the Qur'an in Arabic. A Moslem rite marks the first step of learning the alphabet, just as ritual is observed for naming, the first tonsure, and circumcision for boys. Circumcision may be performed at infancy, at the age of starting school, or not later than the age of twelve. Girls in some areas are attending primary schools with boys or separate girls' schools, but more commonly and acceptably they are instructed in reading the Qur'an in Arabic by the wife of the local imam at her dwelling or by tutors in their own homes.

Beginning at about the age of puberty, children of both sexes are expected to observe the Ramazan fast and other Islamic rituals as adults, the girls praying at home with the women and the boys joining the men for daily prayer and Friday services in the mosque. In other fields also, puberty marks the time when boys and girls are expected to conform fully to the separate sex roles for adults.

In economic affairs, it is the role of the man to provide the family livelihood, and a man who allows his womenfolk to take jobs outside the home is reproached. Women often contribute to the family economy but generally do so by performing ancillary work in the family compound. Though custom permits women to go out

128

to shop in the bazaars, often much of the family marketing is done by the men. Socially, it is the men who move about freely, gossiping in the bazaars and coffeehouses, attending professional gatherings, and taking part in public life. The women's life is essentially private.

A woman's participation in public life, such as it is, is vicarious participation through her husband and other male kin. The social fabric of most women's lives is made up of household activities, personal grooming, calls on female relatives, gossip at the village well or tank (if they belong to the lower agricultural classes), religious observances, and visits to the shrines of saints, to whom they are especially devoted. In the feminine society in which she moves, a woman's status is determined by that of her husband, and she is ordinarily zealous in maintaining the exact precedence to which she believes her husband's rank entitles her. As the wife of the headman of a Punjabi village expects deference from the women of the village, so the wives of senior civil servants assume as their right the offices in the All-Pakistan Women's Association equivalent to the status position of their husbands.

The role of women is to care for the children, cook, manage the household, and discharge reciprocal family obligations at the time of marriages, deaths, and similar occasions. It is also to serve as symbols of family honor and prestige by their chaste and exemplary behavior, their jewelry, and, if possible, their seclusion.

Ideal feminine behavior is exemplified in the institution of purdah, which involves the seclusion of women from males unrelated to them and their nonparticipation in mixed society. Inside the household a purdah-observing woman does not wear a veil and may adorn herself elegantly if she can afford it. If she leaves the household for visits or shopping she must obtain the permission of the head of the family, and when she goes outside she wears a *borqa'*, a plain tentlike garment which covers her completely.

Observance of purdah is considered positive evidence that a family is orthodox, conservative, respectable, and God-fearing. For the woman, it is a sign of her piety, her dignity, and her good reputation in marriage. Purdah is generally observed in middle-class families in East Pakistan and, to a greater or lesser extent, by families of substance in West Pakistan: landowners, business and bazaar people, and the middle and lower-middle classes in urban areas. The Pathans, especially in the Peshawar valley, keep their women nearly invisible, for it has become the hallmark of family

129

prestige to do so. In many Pathan areas it is both impolite and risky to ask a man any questions about the women in his home, even for purposes of census enumeration.

Although purdah generally confers prestige, it cannot be fully observed where women engage in agricultural or menial pursuits. Village women in Punjab do not observe purdah as much as they might elsewhere and at harvest time often work with their men or bring them food. Poor rural families in East Pakistan find it economically impossible to seclude their women completely. The male labor force is usually in ample supply in the fields so that women labor in the compound, but in many families they wash the clothing in public places, carry water, and perform other outside tasks. They cover their heads and maintain a reserve toward strangers when they are unveiled and engaged in tasks outside the home. Among Pathan and Baluchi tribal women of West Pakistan, seclusion from nonrelated men is emphasized more than veiling for these women work harder than the men, carrying water, collecting firewood, grinding, spinning, making rugs, herding sheep, or helping in the fields during the harvest. In Pathan settled areas, women form only a small part of the agricultural labor force, with the exception of Mardan and Hazara districts, where the greater number of men in military service or other employment makes participation by women in agricultural work more common. Women of the poorer classes of Sind are also constrained to do menial work but whenever possible do so in the family compound.

Sexual modesty is very strongly implanted in both women and men. Religious injunction forbids complete disrobing before others, so that bathing and dressing are done in such a manner as to avoid being seen naked. Modesty in clothing requires of Moslem women that they cover the entire body to the ankle, wrist, and chin, and wear a head covering in public if they are unveiled. Children of upper- and middle-class urban families may wear Western-style children's clothing, but girls at puberty without exception assume the traditional *shalwar-qamiz* (trousers and blouse) or *sari* of adult women.

Attitudes of prudery surrounding sexual matters on the part of women result in the situation that many girls enter married life in ignorance. Nursing may be prolonged under the belief that it prevents conception, but since a woman's status as a wife and family member depends upon procreation, she is more concerned in the early years of marriage with producing children than in controlling pregnancy. Many of the women who visit the tombs of the saints are praying for the gift of children, especially sons.

There is evidence that women in the towns and villages of the Punjab are weary of constant pregnancies and seek information about birth control after they have borne three or four children. In other parts of the country there was, until recently, little interest or awareness on the part of the men or women that family planning was possible. Men seemed rather opposed to it, stating that it is against human nature or the will of God and that large families are insurance in times of need. However, beginning in 1959 the government itself began to open family planning centers. The fact that the returns of the census of 1961 indicated a much higher annual rate of population increase than had been anticipated spurred the government to expand its birth control program and by the end of 1961 some 800 family planning centers were in operation.

Marriage is viewed by Islam as the only legitimate outlet for sexual need and the injunction against any sex relations outside marriage appears to be observed to a greater degree in Pakistan than in many other societies. Premarital and extramarital sex relations of women are regarded with utmost severity, and proof of nonvirginity in a bride is grounds for divorce. In the tribal agencies of the North-West Frontier, strict application of the code of honor (*Pushtunwali*) requires the killing of an unchaste daughter and her seducer; and a man eloping with a married woman must pay her bride price to her husband or face blood revenge. Elsewhere in Pakistan the sexual code is not so drastic, but unmarried daughters are carefully protected after puberty and family members keep watch over young men to prevent them from going astray.

Exceptions to regulated sex relations through marriage are the elopements occurring from time to time (generally involving married women), the prostitutes who flourish in sections of the cities and towns, and the homosexuality popularly practiced in some parts of the country. In the Pushtu-speaking areas of West Pakistan, the unavailability and deprecation of women have encouraged the alternative practice in which the love objects are young boys and homosexual love is part of popular folklore. Homosexual practices occur in other areas of Pakistan but generally face greater social and family opposition.

Transvestites, known as *hijiras*, are organized into a caste which derives its income from institutionalized beggary, entertainment,

131

and homosexual relationships with those outside the group. By their renunciation of the male role and adoption of female clothing, the hijiras are popularly believed to change their temperamental nature as well, making it impossible for them to follow professions other than beggary. The boys who reject the male role usually abandon the family of birth and attach themselves to the household of an older hijira in order to learn the practices of their new trade.

Marriage and Divorce

Marriages in Pakistan are ordinarily arranged by the heads of the young people's families, the negotiations being conducted initially through intermediaries. It is the obligation of a father to arrange a marriage for his daughter at the customary age and in most areas he also arranges his son's marriage. The relatively few cases in which both marriage partners make the choice themselves usually occur in connection with a second marriage. The information, though inadequate, on the age of marriage indicates that girls are generally married somewhat later in West Pakistan than in East Pakistan. In East Pakistan and the Pathan areas particularly, the groom may often be ten or more years older than the bride because the required expenditure may make his family wait until it has the money in hand. According to the amendments made in 1961 to the Child Marriage Restraint Act 1929, the bride must be sixteen and the groom eighteen years old.

In theory, a Moslem girl may be married to any Moslem man and a Moslem man may marry any Moslem, Christian, or Hindu woman. In practice, custom and the Islamic injunction to "marry with one's own kind" generally operate to limit selection to a relatively small number of possible spouses. The preferred marriage "with one's own kind" is that with a near cousin in the lineage group, although there is not as much emphasis placed on marriage to the father's brother's daughter in Pakistan as in some other Moslem countries. Punjabi villagers generally observe exogamy rules which exclude the immediate lineage so that daughters marry into a family of another village. In such cases, however, there are also rules of endogamy by which she is married within her caste or subcaste or into certain specific groups slightly higher than her own.

In general, a man may marry beneath him but a woman must not be married to a man of lower traditional social status or the family loses prestige in the community. Individual exceptions, such as the marriage of a promising young civil servant of low birth to an upper-class woman, do take place but are rare. It is more common for such intermarriage to occur when the lower-class group as a whole has gradually improved its economic and educational position. Thus, in East Pakistan during the last few decades the new middle class has frequently married its sons as well as its daughters to members of the traditional aristocracy.

Islamic marriage is a civil contract rather than a religious sacrament. Both parties have the right to stipulate the terms, and the contract, currently called *nikah nama*, is not legally valid unless it includes provision of a dowry (*haq mehr*) by the groom or his family. In parts of East Pakistan it is common to demand full payment (*mu'ajjal*) of the haq mehr at marriage but ordinarily only a token payment is made then, the bulk becoming payable in the event of divorce. There are a number of ceremonies at different stages of the arrangements, which may extend over a period of several months; they vary in number and kind from one class or region to another. The essential wedding rite, at which a local imam, a *qazi*, or a licensed *nikah* registrar officiates, is the one at which the bride and groom, or their representatives, sign the *nikah nama*.

The financial features of the marriage contract may be very complicated. The customary regulations for such things as the amount of the dowry or bride-price, the proportion paid in cash or kind to the bride's family, the giving of ornaments for the bride's trousseau or settling of other property on her by the groom's family and her own family, and the provision of hospitality by each family all vary widely between the different regions and social groups. The groom's family bears the bulk of the cost under the contract, but custom may also require heavy expenditure on festivities, jewelry, and clothing by the bride's family. The marriage of daughters is the occasion for validating family status, a fact which the older female relatives of the bride do not allow her father to forget. This requires that she be married at the proper age (it reflects badly on her if her marriage is delayed for some years), that her mate be well chosen, and that the maximum haq mehr be secured, which entails an extravagance in display which may involve indebtedness or the sale of family assets.

Marriage is the most important ceremony in a woman's life. It is at this time that she anticipates the gifts of jewelry, clothing, and other perquisites which will establish her in her adult life. Under

133

Islamic law she retains separate legal entity which entitles her to hold and dispose of property, while the nikah nama may or may not state that the husband has delegated the power of divorce to his wife. Owing to her usual ignorance or diffidence, however, she very rarely avails herself of any of these prerogatives.

It is through marriage that a woman acquires social status, her position being determined primarily by that of her husband, but since Pakistanis do not have surnames, she does not adopt her husband's name. She continues to be known by her given name, with the appellation "Begum" appended to indicate feminine identity. In recent years, following the trend toward Western usage of surnames, women of social standing or pretensions thereto have employed the name of the husband and inserted "Begum" before his name as an equivalent to "Mrs." Thus, the wives of all senior government officials and married women in elite and professional groups are now addressed as "Begum."

The subjects of permissible ages for marriage, of polygamy, and of divorce have been given interpretations differing from traditional practices in the Muslim Family Laws Ordinance 1961. Islam permits a man to have as many as four wives at a time provided that he can support them all and treat them equally. In some parts of Pakistan wealthy landlords prove their status by having plural wives, but the great majority of men cannot afford the luxury. Among the educated middle class, the taking of additional wives is no longer in vogue, but some Westernized men, including high government officials, have contracted a second, or "love marriage," several years after the first marriage arranged by their parents. However, according to the Muslim Family Laws Ordinance 1961, "no man, during the subsistence of an existing marriage, shall, except with the previous permission in writing of the [local] Arbitration Council, contract another marriage. . . ."

A woman, of course, may have only one husband at a time, but since marriage is not an inviolable sacrament, she is legally free to marry again after a divorce or the decease of her husband. In practice a divorced woman finds it difficult to remarry (except in rural Bengal, where it is not uncommon for girls to be divorced and remarried while still in their teens) because of the feeling against divorce. There is no such feeling against the remarriage of a widow. The customs affecting her future status vary according to her age, whether or not she has any children, and the conventions of different Moslem groups. Depending on the circumstances, she may return to her paternal home or go to live with her brother's family, but ordinarily she remains in her husband's household, especially if she has children. A young widow is often married to the younger brother or other kinsman of the deceased, the arrangements being made by the head of her late husband's family.

Under Islamic law, divorce proceedings may be initiated by either the husband or the wife, but the rules applying to each are quite different. A wife may divorce her husband only upon the decision of a shari'a judge unless special provisions are made in the marriage contract. She must surrender all or part of the haq mehr in consideration thereof. Such divorces are very rare.

A man traditionally divorced his wife at will by pronouncing the formula *talaq*, or "I divorce thee," on three occasions in the presence of two witnesses. According to the Muslim Family Laws Ordinance 1961, he must give notice of a talaq in writing both to the Arbitration Council and to the wife. The Arbitration Council then attempts a reconciliation, and if this is successful a remarriage takes place. Should the wife be pregnant, talaq does not become effective for ninety days or until the pregnancy ends—whichever comes later. Marriage may also be dissolved by mutual agreement or by the wife, if the nikah nama includes this privilege. The divorced wife is entitled to the return of her dower and normally goes back to her paternal home. All children of divorced parents legally belong to the father and the mother must give them up, usually at the age of seven if they are boys and fourteen if they are girls. The father must support them while they are in her custody.

Divorce appears to be less frequent among the upper than the lower classes and more common in East than in West Pakistan. Since no records were kept prior to 1961 of the divorces pronounced by men, the actual overall rate is not known. It is believed to be relatively low, at least in comparison with other Islamic countries. According to the Prophet, "divorce is the most detestable of all permitted things" and in Pakistan this view has been reinforced by the legacy of Hindu attitudes against divorce and by traditional social usage. As a result, the stigma attached to divorce is more pronounced than in some other Moslem lands, especially among the higher classes. The divorce of a woman of good family is considered an insult to the family as well as to the woman, and in some Pathan areas a man who divorces his wife without a very good reason can expect to face blood revenge from her male kin. Among most Moslem groups there are customary rules and condi-

135

tions in the marriage contract which make it difficult, in practice, for a man to divorce his wife at will. The large proportion of the haq mehr which usually becomes payable in the event of divorce amounts, in effect, to a fine which most men cannot afford to pay.

As a result of these practical difficulties and social attitudes, it is much more common for a man who takes a second wife to remain married to the first one than it is for him to divorce her. The upper-class Westernized man who has taken a second wife in a "love marriage" maintains the wives in separate households. Although the feelings and prestige of the first wife are inevitably injured, it is often argued that this arrangement is kinder to her than inflicting the greater humiliation of divorce.

Changes in Family Relationships

The changes affecting the traditional Moslem family have been roughly of two sorts: those pertaining to family law and those caused by educational and economic factors. The government of Pakistan has preserved the British-derived system of law and has continued the gradual substitution of law for the customary usage of particular groups. This, combined with the increased Islamic consciousness accompanying the creation of Pakistan, has led to a wider application of shari'a law. In 1948, for example, Moslem personal law replaced customary law in West Punjab and restored to women the right to inherit property and to widows the right of a life estate rather than maintenance only. Finally, the Muslim Family Laws Ordinance 1961 enhanced women's rights through a more liberal interpretation of Qur'anic injunctions.

The most significant changes in the contemporary Moslem family have come from the introduction of Western commercial, judicial, and political institutions and an educational system designed to supply personnel for those institutions. The most dramatic change has been the emergence of a middle class of new orientation; changes within the family have been most pronounced in this group. To a lesser extent, change has occurred in families of the lower-middle class and, to a still lesser extent, among the landless laborers, especially those taking industrial jobs.

The economic base of the new middle class is not on the land but in commerce, administration, and the professions. Since Islam does not hold rigidly to concepts of traditional caste status and endogamy, families which advanced economically by the education of their members and their employment in the new technology had the possibility of significant improvement in their social position. The recent history of East Pakistan indicates that this economic advancement has often paved the way to marriage into the upper classes.

The education of its individual members has brought new relationships within the middle-class family itself. The extended family has given way very widely to the nuclear family (a man and wife and their children) because of the mobility required of persons filling professional or administrative jobs. Secondly, the economic independence of the adult son has diminished the authoritarian control of the father, which ordinarily lasted until the latter's death. Finally, there has been a marked change in attitudes toward the role of women.

The influence of Western education, together with the fact that the married couple forms its own household without constant deference to elder coresident kin, has made the husband-wife relationship more of a partnership instead of the traditional Islamic subordination of women and their confinement to home activities only. The new complexities of urban life have led to an increasing demand by educated men for an educated wife who can preside over a household alone, supervise the children's health and education by Western concepts, interest herself in social and political activities, and be more of a real companion to her husband.

Evidence of the change of attitude in the middle class is found in the boom in women's education and the emergence of a number of middle-class women from purdah to activity in social welfare work, political life, and organizations like the All-Pakistan Women's Association. While women from elite families are more visible on the national scene, the changes are more far-reaching in the middle class. Men of the intelligentsia, the professions, and the administrative services—significantly, those most affected by Western ideas—have been the active supporters of the revolution of women's position in society.

The urban lower-middle class families have been attempting to raise their social status in two ways, the one modern, the other traditional, and the two are evidently not regarded as incongruous. Considerable pressure is put on family members to acquire education and academic degrees in order to secure the white-collar jobs which advance the family in prestige. At the same time, the family observes the traditional way of achieving prestige by having its women adopt purdah. In West Pakistan, for example, certain village-level workers whose families had not observed purdah adopted purdah upon completion of training in a government Village-AID institute, since this education obviously raised them socially above the ordinary villagers.

Among the laborers, especially those in industry, family patterns have changed to the extent that urban residence and household expenses are differentiated from those of the village home. Traditionally, city work was regarded as temporary; the worker sent most of his earnings home and returned to the village for the marriage arranged by his parents. If his wife and children remain in the village home with the extended family, as is usual in East Pakistan, the worker may be dislocated and emotionally isolated, but traditional family relationships are unchanged. The man remits money for their maintenance and visits the home whenever possible, especially for harvesting and local festivals. When his wife and children join him in the city and they set up a household separate from the extended family, the alteration in relationships is more significant. The landless laborers who continue in agricultural work exhibit a similar tendency toward nuclear families, but their patterns of family life do not seem to be subject to as much change as those of the workers who move to the city.

The Family in Non-Moslem Communities

As with the Moslem majority, the Hindu, Buddhist, and Christian minorities are governed by customary law or government coded law, as seems appropriate to the case. In matters of personal law, the constitutional provision for legislation in conformity with Islam applies only to Moslems. For non-Moslems the courts of Pakistan apply separate systems of family law to each community—either the religious law of the community as a whole or the customary usage of particular groups within it, as the case may be. In this manner, the individual is reminded that his status is governed by his membership in a religious community as well as his citizenship in the nation, and the state gives precedence to family institutions as a basis of social order.

There is no single traditional Hindu family system, except in the sense of a traditional Hindu ideal. Hinduism as a religious system and a social order encompasses extraordinary diversity, much of which is correlated with caste. Nowhere is the range of variation between castes greater than in matters pertaining to the family. The caste is the group within which people marry, and each caste has its own rules for the selection of marriage partners, its marriage ceremonies, and customs or laws of authority, succession, and inheritance. Most castes have their own peculiarities of home ritual, diet, and religious observance, and their own institutions for deciding family disputes. Some of the caste variations are differences in detail only; others are quite pronounced. While some practices are given a neutral value socially, others are ranked, with the "higher" practices being those which are believed to correspond to the ideal traditional pattern. Speaking very broadly, it is the intermediate and upper castes which aspire to or practice the customs most closely approximating the traditional ideal, and the family patterns of the low castes may be altogether different.

With regard to family structure, the traditional ideal is the joint family, in which all members contribute their earnings and labor and are given maintenance according to need. The Hindu joint family functions as a single economic unit in handling funds and consumption, and its major point of difference with the Moslem extended family is that it remains undivided at the death of the father. His authority passes to his eldest son, who manages family affairs in consultation with other senior members, and inheritance is a corporate rather than an individual matter. Presumably the joint family could grow over the generations to a size of several dozen people before its cumbersomeness or a family dispute led to partition of assets and living areas. In practice, partition occurs much more frequently, and the actual composition of the family is similar to that of the Moslem extended family. As with the Moslems, the various units might continue to inhabit the same compound and share the use of some buildings or equipment, but each would have its own hearth, plots of land, and funds.

In the large intermediate Hindu ranks, it is common for married sons to live in a single household unit while the father is still living, but it appears to be much less common for them to do so after the father's death. Continuation of the joint family as a corporate unit for two or three generations seems to be more possible among the higher classes which have ample landed property. Yet these are the classes which have been subject to the same factors affecting the Moslem middle class, with the result that the influence of Western education and the mobility required of persons filling white-collar jobs have led to the creation of nuclear rather than

139

joint families. A trend toward nuclear families also appears among the low-caste families, who own no land.

The men are monogamous, although plural wives do not appear to be forbidden by the sources of Hindu law. In these sources, woman is glorified, even worshiped, in her role as mother but is granted almost no rights; her legal position, as an entity distinct from her husband, is greatly inferior to that of her Moslem counterpart under Islamic law. This does not seem to have given her a lower position within the family itself, however, and she moves much more freely in society at large than does her Moslem sister. The relations between the various Hindu family members are rather similar to those within the Moslem extended family, except that there is, perhaps, less likelihood of friction between brothers, the area of behavior permitted women is less restricted, and the roles of the two sexes are less sharply separated. It is considered a higher practice to have women work within the family compound rather than the fields, but there is no traditional emphasis on full seclusion of women and no observance of purdah. Women will do manual labor in the fields if they have to, and most of the women laborers on the plantations and tea estates are Hindus, largely from the Scheduled Castes.

Marriage practices vary widely from caste to caste. Some castes, for example, require that a person avoid marrying someone from a family with which his family has been intermarrying for several generations back; others regularly take their brides only from certain families and give daughters to certain others; other castes have customs of marriage to first cousins on one side of the family or the other. Past customs of marrying daughters well before the age of puberty appear to have diminished over the years. In urban areas, families who delay the marriage of daughters in order to complete their education are no longer subject to as much censure as they received two or three generations ago.

Like Moslem marriages, Hindu marriages are arranged by the parents and involve the giving of dowries and other financial transactions which vary with the different castes. The bulk of the expenditure for the Hindu marriage, however, is borne by the father of the bride. The bride's family generally assumes most of the cost of the several wedding festivities, provides most of her dowry or trousseau, and, among the middle and upper classes, her father often must make a payment in hard cash to the groom's family. This financial burden is one of the most common causes of indebtedness and has come in for increasing criticism in the press.

The Hindu marriage is an inviolable religious sacrament rather than a civil contract. Not only is divorce forbidden according to the traditional ideal, but a widow may not remarry. While the practice of suttee (immolation of a widow on her husband's funeral pyre) is now extinct, a widow may be poorly treated, especially if she is young and childless. Among the lower castes, divorce of some sort appears to be recognized and the custom of marrying a young widow to her husband's younger brother is not uncommon. Both are considered "low" practices, however, and, in the past at least, the upper castes and those aspiring to higher status would not allow them. Among the upper castes, the ban on the remarriage of young widows has weakened considerably under the influence of the Hindu reform movements, but the feelings against divorce continue to be very strong at the present time and divorce is quite rare.

There is no "typical Buddhist family." Buddhism, superimposed on animism, is the prevailing religion among the dozen or more tribes of the Chittagong Hill Tracts and family practices vary with the different clans and tribes. The clans may be either endogamous or exogamous; the former generally have incest taboos forbidding marriage between persons who have a common ancestor within three generations. Usually family organization is patrilineal and patrilocal but in some areas a daughter as well as a son may inherit tribal leadership. Boys commonly attend temple schools, girls do not. Women do not live in seclusion but are generally occupied with activities around the household. Marriage is a simple matter marked by the exchange of gifts. Joking relationships exist between a man and his wife's younger sister and between a woman and her husband's younger brother, both being considered potential marriage partners in the event of the death of a spouse.

The Christian family, adhering faithfully to the standards of behavior introduced by the Europeans who brought about their conversion, are monogamous and have rules of marriage and divorce governed by British law and the beliefs of their particular sects. The women have a position comparable to that of Western women insofar as personal freedom and inheritance are concerned. Upper-class Christians, descended from Eurasians or high-caste Hindus, have identified themselves more closely with Western family patterns than any other group in Pakistan, and their women are the only women of Pakistan who wear Western dress. At present there

141

is less emphasis placed on copying the British mode of living and a tendency toward assimilation as Pakistanis. Many of the lower-class Christians converted from the Scheduled Castes continue in their traditional occupation, and there is little information on the extent to which their family practices have been altered by virtue of their conversion.

Village Society in East Pakistan

In the political unit of East Pakistan a typical village society is formed of a number of extended families of greater and lesser land-holdings, whose livelihood is based on a rice economy. It is organized on the basis of structural relationships between caste groups. Those families who claim descent from the original feudal chief of the village, whether or not they now own land, are the highest social class. Generally the village is controlled by the oldest and wealthiest heads of households, who constitute an oligarchy which makes decisions on matters affecting the village. Depending on circumstances, such a group may work cooperatively or split into factions competing for prestige. All disputes are heard before this village leadership before resort is made to the courts, but the wealthy and powerful are apt to ignore adverse village recommendations, feeling that they can gain more by court action.

Ranged under the ruling oligarchy are the representatives of a priestly or learned class. The two groups cooperate to maintain the Islamic observances by the village and have a relatively close social relationship with a tradition of intermarriage. Peasant propri-etors, agricultural sharecroppers, landless laborers, and *ghulams* (former slaves) complete the general Moslem village picture. These may intermarry, except for the descendants of slaves (slavery was abolished in 1860), who marry with others of like class in other villages. The ghulams maintain a servant relationship to the first class of feudal landlords and perform many services at the dicta-tion of the latter. Those from the Chittagong Hill tribes who have been converted to Islam form their own ethnic community and seldom intermarry with other Moslems. Typically, there are occupa-tional Hindu and Moslem castes which represent the bottom range of society: weavers, net makers, potters, laundrymen, and sweepers.

The most recent social changes in rural East Pakistan are related to the advent of industrialization. Although industrialization has had little effect upon the nature of the workers' families, it has had considerable impact on the social structure. Most drastically affected were those whose land was pre-empted for factories, for they were not always fortunate enough or wise enough to buy land of equivalent value and thus retain their position in society. Land-owning agriculturalists are more highly regarded than urban industrial workers and have more freedom in their daily tasks. But the marginally employed agricultural workers and landless laborers found that factory work released them from dependence upon the wealthy landlords, and with the loss of economic control over the village the landlords lost a measure of their political and social control as well.

Commitment to urban employment inevitably draws the worker into urban patterns of action since he does not have the time to function both as industrial worker and as agriculturalist. Members of the Ashraf who have become clerks and factory workers in the cities, however, assume their old privileged position on their return to the village. This assumption of innate superiority is no longer accepted by the younger generation, which is increasingly aware of the relative unimportance of these families' power outside the village. The result of this changed attitude is a weakening of the traditional divisions of society and patterns of respect in such villages.

Some villages are located near the industrial centers and their residents include factory employees who commute to work. The status of these workers is undefined and nonfunctional at the village level and apparently the presence of a number of them is disruptive. Thus, even if the family system remains intact upon the advent of industrialization, the village social organization is changed and the feeling of unity is broken.

The influence of modern life on village economy is evident in the new systems of transportation and the availability of outside goods purchasable for cash. The development of markets and bazaar areas in larger villages has brought a new social class into being: the merchants and moneylenders. These have achieved far greater wealth and influence than they would have been able to attain in the past.

Urban Society in East Pakistan

The ties between industrial workers and the extended family remain strong, with the result that most of the urban population in East Pakistan consists of adult male workers who have not accepted the city as a permanent place of residence. As a group, however, they are a permanent part of urban life even though the individual membership is constantly changing. There is reason to believe that over a generation, more of these workers will bring their families to town and in time become part of a permanent urban labor force. The presence of such a working population makes a living possible for shopkeepers and traders, who minister to their wants and who comprise what might be called the lower-middle class, regardless of their caste affiliation. Above these would be ranged clerical workers and the educated but low-paid white-collar workers who seem to be indispensable for every government and commercial operation. Next come members of the professional middle class: lawyers, teachers, journalists, physicians, and managers of firms or higher level administrative officers. But by far the greatest economic power is held by the capitalists—the heads of large industrial establishments and the bankers.

Urban Society in West Pakistan

In the cities in West Pakistan are sophisticated, traveled, and cosmopolitan families. There are conservative, orthodox families who fulfill every command of Muhammad and faithfully adhere to the traditions of the Hadith; side by side with them are army officers whose speech, deportment, and personal ethics are modeled on the British military tradition. There is a sizable urban population with traditions of urban life which is increasing in numbers and influence.

More than any other locality, Lahore, in which are located the University of Punjab and numerous schools and colleges, is the nurturing place of the writers, intellectuals, and Western-oriented elite of West Pakistan, who are attempting a synthesis of an illustrious Moslem heritage with the new conditions of a modern state. There is continuous and often passionate discussion of politics, Islam, Westernization, and the good life among the educated and articulate elite. The use of English as the medium of instruction at the university level, and its prestige as evidence of familiarity with Western education, make it current among this educated group. To the university-educated, the reading of the English-language press is an expression of cosmopolitanism. Conversation is greatly valued as an activity, more than sports, although this class is loyal to its cricket matches, one of the most successful British imports.

144

Among educated women, the preferred professions have been medicine and teaching. In both cases the women work with members of their own sex. Women are now also entering other professions, such as social work, journalism, and government services, but their numbers are few.

Distinct from the educated middle class, yet sharing some of their activities, are the elite. These are the families whose hereditary landholdings and social position place them on the highest social level. A number of them participate in the national life through political activity, and some are patrons of religious and charitable institutions. Widely traveled, they are able to make use of Western concepts and technology as it suits their purposes. The women of this class are educated and have provided leadership in efforts toward securing women's emancipation in political and social action. It is unlikely, however, that dynamic leadership will come from a class which has so much invested in maintaining the favorable status quo.

Another and growing section of the urban population consists of the families engaged in banking and commercial establishments. These establishments include factories, shops, and the offices of numerous middlemen in the marketing of products, both local and imported. Many consumer goods must be imported from abroad, and their availability depends on a system of government allocations, which leaves business people in a state of insecurity.

The shopkeepers and business people form an identifiable class of the population although they are composed of a number of groups. The lower-middle class group is usually meticulous in observing the rituals of Islam, such as prayers, fasting during Ramazan, reading the Qur'an in Arabic, almsgiving, and maintaining their women in purdah. They live in crowded houses of the old sections of the cities, and the men work in the varied occupations which a town or city offers. To some extent, there are *mohallas*, or alleys, which specialize in particular businesses, and those of the same occupation live and work in the area. Thus, there are mohallas where the shoemakers, the goldsmiths, and rope and furniture makers predominate; others where wheat, salt, or sugar is sold. Strict separation by occupation is not possible because of the disruption at partition and the presence of incoming refugees. A characteristic of Punjabi towns is that approximately half of the population were refugees from India. Most continue to follow the occupation of their caste and family, but economic necessity has pressed some into other occupations. The caste most reduced by economic upheavel is that of handweavers, who have left the occupation by the thousands and taken on industrial or unskilled labor jobs.

In many urban centers of West Pakistan, the urban working class, or proletariat, is denied the recognition it needs to function more efficiently. The indifference shown in the matter of working conditions for employees reflects the traditional disregard for those engaged in menial tasks, and the general underemployment of the surrounding area makes it difficult for employees to secure improvement in their position. Industrial development is hampered by the cultural bias in favor of white-collar jobs. There is a dearth of foremen and supervisors with some education and skill, because men with such qualifications prefer to take a clerk's job which, in spite of lower pay, gives greater prestige to the individual and to his family.

Prostitutes occupy a unique position in the society as they live outside the accepted code of behavior. Besides those who purvey only sexual satisfaction, there is a group of entertainers in song and dance who maintain establishments which are frequented by well-to-do men in search of relaxation and pleasure. Girls of a hereditary caste of prostitutes are trained in the fine arts, and their brothers provide the musical accompaniment for their dancing and manage their financial matters. In the classical tradition of the Moghul courts when the *ahl-i-murad*, the entertainer class of dancing girls, singers, and musicians, formed a part of the upper class, these girls sing and dance before a party of patrons of prestige and wealth. Although the numbers of these entertainers are few, their significance in urban social life can be deduced from their frequent appearance in the plots of Pakistani cinema and their popularity for a social evening with the men. These women provide a sharp contrast to the passivity and compliance of "good" women and reap benefit from the difference.

As a whole the urban population increases because of the educational system; few who have had a college education in the town are willing to return to village life. College-educated men will take almost any clerical job in the city in preference to returning to the home village or rural area. This preference leads to wider separation between urban and rural populations and constitutes a divisive force in the whole society.

146

Village Society in West Pakistan

The village society of the Punjab is illustrative of the traditional social structure of the rural areas of West Pakistan. Although caste occupations are more specialized and caste customs more rigid than in Sind or the North-West Frontier, the general relationships and attitudes are comparable. It should be noted, however, that while the traditional Punjabi villages have been the subject of intensive sociological research, no comparable studies have been made since the influx of millions of refugees in 1947. As a result, there is no way of assessing the nature and extent of the impact of the refugees on rural society.

In the settled areas of the Punjab, as in other parts of West Pakistan, landowners may have holdings which include a number of villages and surrounding land. If the landlord maintains a residence in the vicinity, he is considered the most powerful and respected person. These men, if not college-trained, are now sending their sons to higher educational institutions in Pakistan or abroad to prepare them for responsible posts in government, the army, or the professions. The men wear Western-style clothing, own or drive automobiles, and often have another residence in Lahore or Karachi. Some of them are sending their daughters to the cities to be educated, but the women usually maintain purdah at their rural home, where seclusion is part of their status position. The landlords from this group run for office as representatives in the assembly. It seems apparent, however, that they have certain class interests to protect which may not be those of the electorate.

In the village, the population is divided into three groups: landowners, the *zamindars*, tenant farmers, and village craftsmen (*kammis*). The wealthiest landowners have the most prestige, and one of them is usually the *choudhry*, or chief of the village. Where there are several families of comparable holdings and social standing, there is often rivalry between them, which contributes much to the presence of factionalism in a village. Not infrequently, this rivalry is so intense that the situation resembles a feud, each side going about prepared for assault and even carrying arms for "defense."

The choudhry, also transliterated as *chaudari*, is expected to validate his position through hospitality and by his strength, which is expressed in the number of male relatives and friends who support him, or through his official connections. The center of the

147

village is the community guest house, the *dara*, or the home of the choudhry, where visitors stay, traveling holy men are entertained, and the village council meets. The family of the choudhry share in his obligations, for the people come to him or to his wife to ask for help in time of trouble, to borrow grain, money, or sugar, or to ask advice. The wife or eldest woman of the household, the *choudhrani*, handles the contributions of produce and money made to the family and is responsible for sending food to households at weddings, deaths, or in case of need.

Each farming family has contract relations, called *seyp*, with the craftsmen for certain goods and services. These services are usually paid in grain at the time of harvest. Village craftsmen in most Punjabi villages include potters, carpenters, barbers, cobblers, tailors, bakers, washermen, blacksmiths, and sweepers. The men of these contract families are the only outside men permitted to enter the houses of the village families. Craftsmen also exchange services with one another.

There is a system of ranking among the craftsmen on the basis of occupation. The barber is the confidant and messenger of the village, usually the go-between for marriages, and the cook for marriage festivities. The sweeper is universally considered of the lowest rank because of his defiling work. In social relationships, such as sitting together, smoking a common pipe, praying together, and receiving food from one another, caste status is not stringently limiting, except for the sweeper. People who consider themselves superior may exact certain respect; thus, craftsmen use deferential forms of address to the landowner and do not sit while a landowner is standing, or sit at the same level.

In these occupational castes, the wives of the craftsmen play the supporting role in the activity of the husband as they have been trained to do from childhood. Thus, the potter's wife prepares the clay and helps fire and paint the pots, while the wife of a *musalli*, or unskilled laborer, makes dung cakes, sweeps the home, and helps her husband in the fields.

The big festivities of village life, other than an occasional fair, are the weddings. A daughter's marriage is celebrated by feasting in the family and with the bridegroom's party. Much is spent on the girl's dowry and ornaments, and gifts are also given to all the craftsmen who have contracts with the family. This display is essential for achieving prestige and status on the part of the bride's family.

Validation of status, by keeping the respect of one's fellows, by greater power and wealth, or by generous distribution of hospitality, is one of the major values of village life. This is phrased differently according to the position of the individual and his family, but avenues are open to all through fulfillment of religious and personal obligations to family and to kin, as well as through the most lavish display of hospitality possible to landowners.

One change in rural social structure—and economic life—since the formation of Pakistan has been the disappearance of the Hindu moneylender. This has been a loss in some respects, such as in times of food scarcity, but the absence of ready money has prevented the villagers from incurring the heavy indebtedness which a big show at the marriage festivities would entail.

Cooperative societies have been operating in the Punjab for many years under the British and now under the Pakistan government. Despite the official encouragement, they have not flourished, although ideally they could provide the credit which farmers frequently need. Too often the landowners have borrowed on credit recklessly, thus endangering the soundness of the cooperative; or the officials of the cooperative have lent more to relatives than to nonrelatives; or other difficulties arise in the context of Pakistan's system of social obligations which do not obtain in other societies where cooperatives have been successful.

Some village dwellers have been forced by hard times to emigrate to the cities for employment, where they take up tonga driving or other unskilled work. Ordinarily, a villager returns home only to visit or to contract marriage. He usually leaves his wife and children with his family in the village when going to the city.

Tribal Society in West Pakistan: The Pathans

Tribal society among the Pathans is based on the principle of unilinear descent through males from a legendary ancestor who lived long ago in Afghanistan. In theory, all Pathans are kin to one another through this common ancestor. Although many Pathans are settled residents of the Peshawar valley they share in the social customs and heritage of the tribal group, with some modifications due to contact with administered settlements. For the individual, the significant social divisions are the tribe, the lineage, and the extended family.

149

The *qaum,* or tribe, is the largest social unit. A tribe may be distinguished by its dress, dialect, and manners and occupies a particular territory. The Pathans, also called Pakhtuns and Pushtuns, observe a tribal code called Pakhtunwali. Other than individual observance, the mechanism by which customary law is enforced is the *jirgeh,* or council, which may include all the adult males of the tribe or only a few of the elders. It is also the means of communication from government to tribesmen and can act as a judicial body. Decisions of the jirgeh are enforced by public opinion. Those who defy decisions of the jirgeh might have their house and property destroyed.

The extended lineage, *khel,* consists of all persons descended from a common ancestor more recent than the legendary tribal ancestor. These lineages may separate into smaller lineages. The latter, which are closely related, often are given to dissension and blood feuds. Marriage to close cousins is preferred among Pathans, keeping ties within a group which exists in amity at the time.

The extended family, *khandan,* consists of closely related males, their wives, unmarried sisters, and children. These live together, sometimes in a fortified residence, so long as compatibility permits. Deference of the sons to the father, of younger brothers to elder, and the separation of women's quarters from those of the men, where outside men are entertained, are observed. Polygamy is common among wealthy Pathans and produces tension within the household through the rivalry of the sons of different mothers. Disagreements over inheritance may lead to antagonism between male members of the family or lead to separation of the unit into different and often feuding family groups.

Some families have been able to secure more land than their neighboring kin, and the highest social status is given to those with the largest landholdings who thus have wealth and power. The wealthiest men have retainers and servants who help to enforce their position and who owe allegiance only to their masters. The poorer Pathans who have a reputation for integrity and courage are sought by these wealthy men as retainers and are treated in a confidential capacity as members of the household. Dependents who are non-Pathan in descent, the *ghulams* or *hamsaya,* are used as menials or craftsmen in wealthy households and their well-being depends on the good will of the master.

Among Pathans, landownership descends through males, daughters being unable to inherit as long as there are sons. The head of a lineage, the *malik,* is the most powerful and wealthy man of his lineage and has the highest social status.

The division of labor in the society leaves to men the tasks and activities outside the home. Women remain in the family quarters and are expected to go outside only to get water or gather fuel or fodder. Among families of wealth, female servants of poorer families are brought in to do the menial tasks or those which take a woman outside. This leaves the women at leisure within the compound walls, and their seclusion is a mark of the prestige of the family within the tribal area.

Pathan men prove their status by the code of hospitality, which is extended to other men of kindred lineages or to visitors. Every family maintains separate men's quarters, the *hujra,* where guests are entertained and where the men of the family spend their free time. Special prestige accrues from lavish entertainment of men of equal or higher social position, but generosity in food and drink, lodging, or protection is extended to retainers, messengers, and persons of lower social status as a matter of family pride. The hujra, although designed as a community center for the men and their guests, has been altered to serve prestige rivalry because of the competitive nature of Pathan life. The Pathan code of honor demands that retaliation, *badal,* should be exacted whenever injury has been done to the prestige of the family. This touchiness, combined with ready accessibility to guns, has been the cause of many deaths in the Pathan tribal areas, for to overlook any slight, intentional or inadvertent, violates the honor of a Pathan.

For settled Pathans, tribal membership does not retain any functional significance. Very frequently the competitive structuring of relationships makes harmonious cooperation rather difficult. Factionalism of unusually strong persuasion divides villages into wards which are often estranged from one another. Pathan landowners assume a social class superior to that of tenants of other ethnic origins, and as tenants are not owners of their homes the relationship is not permanent between any set of tenants and landowners. Only those retainers who become personal servants and sleep in the landlord's house have a close relationship which crosses class lines. The Pathan landowner prefers not to marry into the landless families. The emphasis placed on landownership and the problems of inheritance and control of family property promote increasing factionalism within the village. The Pathan family lineages may be hostile or indifferent to one another, even where marriage ties

151

exist between them. The result of this factionalism is that in times of crisis villages do not cooperate to resolve their problems but turn as tenants or as landowners to the paternalistic government to seek help. Pathan-settled village society lacks the community council, the jirgeh, which can resolve disputes and make decisions, and lacks as well a powerful representative of centralized government authority. The existing political representatives, the *lambardar* and the *chowkidar,* act to collect taxes or to report statistics respectively but have neither power nor prestige. A governing council to act for the whole village is lacking. The contacts with intermediate agents of government, who can be manipulated through bribery, reinforce the patterns of mistrust with which the Pathan views the outside government.

CHAPTER *8*

Traditional Patterns of Living

THEOLOGICAL BELIEFS, FAMILY LOYALTY AND HONOR, and concepts of status and rank constitute the primary determinants in the daily life of the Moslem community in Pakistan and, though varying according to provincial origin, class status, and degree of personal commitment to the ritual system of Islam, are expressed through generally accepted symbols. One of the central values of Islam is the equality of all men before Allah and, concomitantly, the brotherhood of all Moslems. This religious concept, reinforced by community-wide observance of the commemorative feasts and by the common discipline of Islamic prayers, fasts, and pilgrimages, continually operates against the group exclusiveness and hierarchy of Hindu society, from which the bulk of Pakistan's Moslems were long ago converted. The Moslem castes, unlike their Hindu counterparts, take meals together, engage in other forms of ordinary social intercourse quite freely, and have less objection to intercaste marriages. Yet hereditary rank and class differences do exist and are expressed by clothing and appurtenances, deportment, speech, and respect relationships.

The strong and continuing family, a major value of Pakistani life, has several important Islamic aspects. Thus modesty is enjoined as an Islamic value; the chastity of women is secured by an elaborate code of behavior and avoidance of exposure through the institution of purdah; and marriages are arranged by the families rather than the two individuals concerned. The individual is inculcated with attitudes of loyalty and obligation to his family and kinship group. The child is trained to give respect and implicit obedience to his father and other elders; and the authoritarian control of the head of the family is tempered by religious injunctions urging generosity, justice, and charity toward dependents.

153

The intensity of the allegiance given to the family, the lineage, and the ethnic group is achieved at the expense of society in general, for pride in one's own group is often phrased in terms detrimental to all the "others," whose weakness and peculiarities serve as contrast to the right behavior and action of one's own kind. These attitudes and views, which make the advancement of one's group the major loyalty in the life of the individual, lead logically to the favoritism, nepotism, and corruption that plague the administrative services of the government. The hiatus between loyalty to the kin group and loyalty to the nation or government has proved to be the source of considerable difficulty in the building of modern Pakistan, as in a number of other nations.

In the daily life of a Moslem the conscious orientation toward the supernatural, or Allah, is continually expressed in the conventions of ordinary speech, general behavior patterns, and attitudes toward natural events. There is one and only one Allah; He is all-powerful, all-knowing, just, and merciful. The success or failure of any undertaking, great or small, the bounty or destruction of nature, and the attainment of human salvation are all partially subject to human choice but ultimately dependent upon the unknowable will of Allah. The individual is free to choose whether or not to follow the path of righteousness. The Moslem, the true believer, is by definition one who submits with complete trust to Allah, lives in a prayerful relationship, and follows the commandments revealed in the Word of Allah, the Qur'an. Attainment of salvation is by Divine Grace alone, but man may make himself worthy of it; in order to do so, he needs Allah's guidance.

For the orthodox Moslem, this guidance is embodied in the Qur'an and Hadith, which set forth not only the ideals of human conduct but definite rules which enjoin certain actions and forbid others. The uneducated majority of Pakistani Moslems, while observing this formal creed, also seek additional guidance, emotional satisfaction, and even intercession with Allah—a notion unacceptable to orthodox leaders—from holy men (*pirs*) and through prayers offered at the tombs of pirs of the past.

There is a common belief that every human has a certain livelihood, *rizk*, which has been apportioned by Allah, and that it is the responsibility of the individual to seek and fulfill that livelihood. If after effort has been made the portion is small, this destiny, or *kismet*, is accepted as gracefully as possible. In such an environment as East Pakistan, where nature can be cruelly destructive through famine or flood, this acceptance can become a passive resignation so deeply ingrained as to mitigate against introduction of new ideas. In the more prosperous villages of the Punjab in West Pakistan, there is more leeway for the individual to maneuver and improve his lot. But, in the end, it is Allah rather than man who decides the destiny of the individual human being.

Social Behavior

The distinctions in social behavior between men and women are greatly emphasized in Pakistan, as in all Moslem countries. Men should be protectors, decision makers, and fighters; women should be dependent, cherishing, and nonaggressive; and it is thought to be reprehensible for members of one sex to act in the very different manner prescribed for the opposite sex.

The nature of man is accepted as strongly physical in its needs and striving; celibacy is not equated with piety as in many religions, although it is required by some of the Sufi religious brotherhoods. Sex is considered a primary function of the human being and marriage is essential for every Moslem man or woman. Procreation of children for continuation of the male family line is a major responsibility of marriage for both men and women, and failure to fill this responsibility is the source of reproach and estrangement in the family.

Woman's primary role is, of course, as a mother; her acceptance as a full member of her husband's family and her status within the family is determined largely by the bearing of children, especially sons. All activities or pleasures thought to be inimical to her biological role are censured by society. A great deal of emphasis and attention is devoted to the chastity and fidelity of women of the family in order to insure acceptable maternity and pure lineage. The value placed on chastity of women, coupled with the concept of prestige which seclusion of women gives to the whole family, provides a strong motive force for the retention of purdah in the lives of middle-class Moslems of Pakistan.

Closely connected with the values of purdah and feminine modesty is the emphasis placed by most Moslem families, particularly the Pathans, on the privacy of the home. In the villages and urban middle-class quarters, the home, especially the women's quarters, *zenana*, is a private cosmos, where duty and affection combine to provide a place of comfort and refuge for the men.

Normally, the zenana is closed to outside males, with the exception of those menials who have contractual relationships to the family. In this private world, the women may dress informally in attractive clothing and jewelry, their children play by their side, meals are prepared and eaten, and family gossip is exchanged. The men who come and go in the outside world find the attention of sisters, mother, wife, and daughters flattering and the separateness of the zenana gives it a special charm, where harmony prevails. Boldness in women is considered a great fault and it is the woman who is blamed as the temptress if informal contacts lead to sexual intimacy. Having been brought up to desire privacy and seclusion for themselves and to regard contact with nonrelated males as dangerous and un-Islamic, some Pakistan women have found it psychologically unendurable to leave purdah and enter a mixed society, even in instances where a husband's career would benefit thereby and he has encouraged her to do so.

The social bonds between men are based on behavior patterns of respect and deference. Those persons of greater age and higher social class are tendered expressions of respect from their juniors and inferiors. The hierarchical arrangement of society gives most individuals a status at the same time superior to some and inferior to others, with a range of duties appropriate to that status. Women of the higher economic and social class relegate cooking and household tasks to servants; household servants leave certain work to the village menials; the menials and craftsmen will undertake only the tasks that accord with their caste position.

In the past the owners of land held the greatest political and social power, the biggest landowners being the most powerful. Today it is still true that those who own land have greater prestige than those who merely work it as tenants. Possession of land remains a value to which most Pakistanis are committed, even if they absent themselves as individuals for employment in the cities or in government service. A person who makes his fortune in trade often attempts to consolidate his higher status by purchase of land.

The symbols of prestige for high social status are various forms of address, clothing and appurtenances, and observance of purdah. Members of the upper class are expected to validate their positions by a retinue of servants and generous hospitality. Not to do so brings censure for being niggardly rather than praise for being thrifty and prudent. Other persons in authority, such as the village headman, tribal chief, or landlord, are expected to prove their status by hospitality, even at great expense. To give to another confers power upon the giver and certain obligations of fealty upon the recipient. In a number of village and tribal communities, the strong man is the one who can win armed support or election votes by dispensing hospitality. The costs of hospitality can be recovered in various ways when political power is achieved. In part because of the code of hospitality, Moslem urban dwellers look upon the Hindu merchants' behavior as miserly in contrast to the typical Moslem's gracious generosity, appreciation of good food and a pleasant home, and willingness to spend money for personal pleasures and for the general welfare. If a Moslem bias exists, it is toward extravagance and display rather than parsimony. Individuals cite the Qur'anic proscription of usury to give a religious sanction to the code of hospitality.

The tendency toward extravagance grows out of the importance attached to proving one's position and to the popular view that a brave and decorative appearance must be maintained regardless of economies made elsewhere. Throughout the country, the furnishing of the living area contrasts with rudimentary kitchen and toilet facilities, for the public area is that which is displayed to guests, who are expected to overlook the other areas. Construction of fine and impressive public buildings may take precedence over modest housing or welfare projects, as in the almost fabulous plans for the construction of Islamabad.

Interpersonal relationships are made more agreeable by expressions of deference, and replies to questions are intended to please rather than to present objective conditions. True friends, who are of equal status, will speak frankly to each other, but otherwise a person asked for his opinion on a particular matter will say only what he believes his questioner would like to hear. A superior may often make sharp or sarcastic comments on the behavior of an inferior, but it is very difficult for one of inferior status to suggest to a superior that the latter has made an error of judgment or "taken a wrong road." This inability to criticize one's superior develops in a heavily authoritarian society where questioning the father's or teacher's judgment is not permissible behavior. Another result of the authoritarian environment is that persons who are not in a position of authority often feel little or no sense of responsibility. If responsibility is thrust upon them suddenly (as, for example, at the sudden death of a father) they may be wholly unable, or even unwilling, to assume it.

Man's Relation to Nature

The villager, above all others, has learned to live with nature and to accept it as the determining basis of life. The planting and tilling of crops occur in accordance with the season of the year and the guidance of the native calendar, as do the local festivals. The agriculturist works very hard to accomplish what he believes is necessary, yet accepts that the final disposal of his effort lies with Allah. He learns to accept the vagaries of weather and monsoon, destruction of crops and land by floods, even the total destruction of crops and conditions of famine as matters beyond his control and therefore fated to happen. Good health and longevity are valued the more because they are the exceptions rather than the rule. The sense of fatalism serves to make life bearable under conditions which appear to the agriculturist to be unalterable. It is not surprising that the initial effort of the Village-AID program was to challenge this sense of the inevitable. The attitudes which protected the stability of village life over generations have created a deterrent to progress in a democratically organized society. The extent to which innovations in practice bring material reward may be the criterion used to determine whether new relationships to nature can emerge.

Emotional Expression

Moslem Pakistanis cherish certain esthetic experiences and activities which induce pleasurable and righteous sentiments and reinforce their feeling of status. Observance of daily prayers or fasting contributes to subjective feelings of correct behavior and of religious duties fulfilled which are highly valued. Not infrequently, religious punctiliousness is combined with equally well-developed sensuality and arrogance. The giving of alms and the bestowing of hospitality produce both social and spiritual satisfaction in the giver.

To read, or better yet to hear, poetry of elevating ideas and balanced rhythm produces a beatific effect on the listeners. The *mushaira,* an event where poets declaim their own poetry, evokes cries of approval from listeners comparable to the enthusiasm shown at a championship tennis match in the West. The devotees of the mushaira are primarily of the educated class which is knowledge-able in the Persian and Urdu literary tradition. In the regional languages poetry and ballads, less formally expressed, are popular forms of self-expression which serve to dramatize the pride felt in the indigenous cultural heritage.

Although Islam does not sanction music as an approved art form, there are many Pakistanis who value music as another way of achieving esthetic experience. The folk songs of Pakistan are committed to memory and transmitted orally as part of the popular culture. Very many of them are on themes of love and romance. Although social values place great emphasis on the seclusion of women and the control of sexual selection by family-arranged marriage, the love marriage—in which the girl has at least been viewed by the man—is an aspiration of many young men. In educated middle-class circles, the romance of a non-purdah-observing girl and a man of a conservative family has often culminated in marriage; but the young wife sometimes found that her acceptance into the family was contingent upon her entering purdah.

Sexuality is more easily obtained than romance, in or out of marriage. For the orthodox, it is found with the marriage partner or partners; for the less circumspect, there are the clandestine affairs whose dangers enhance their attractiveness, the prostitutes, or the alternative of homosexual relationships.

The Historical Self-Image

Another source of esthetic pleasure to Pakistanis is the recital of the catalogue of achievements of the famous Moghul rulers of India—their attributes, conquests, architectural monuments, and constructive acts on the Indian scene. The newcomer to the Indian subcontinent might think that only the noble architectural ruins survive of that golden age, but this would be to dismiss a mystique of considerable psychological importance.

Moslem college students in Pakistan discuss the relative merits of Jahangir, Akbar, and Aurangzeb as rulers of the great empire and express admiration for these or others according to their own subjective inclination. Some prefer the rigid puritan austerity of Aurangzeb; others extol the wise catholicity of Akbar or praise the love of beauty and fidelity which was memorialized by Shah Jahan in the Taj Mahal. To the educated Pakistani, the Moghul rule stands as a bright light which illuminates all of Moslem history and represents the Indian apogee of Islamic magnificence, piety, and power with which they like to identify themselves emotionally.

Newspapers and periodicals can be counted upon to provide

articles devoted to the poets, historians, arts, and architecture of the Moghul period. The merits of the royal rulers in religious leadership or administration are discussed as seriously as questions of land reform or the foreign export market, and are probably received with more enthusiasm by a reading public which would rather think of the ideal persons of the past than consider the problems of their present political life. Yet even in the golden age, as the writers state, there were jealous and cruel rivalries in the struggle for supreme royal power. The tolerant and eclectic Akbar evokes less enthusiasm from Pakistanis than the martial, orthodox, and formally pious Aurangzeb, who killed his brothers to reach the throne. The hero, then, can combine unscrupulous maneuvering for power with formal orthodoxy and retain admiration as a good Moslem.

Discipline and Self-Control

Obedience and respect expressed by physical and verbal deference are exacted of individuals toward elders and people of superior social position. An individual, having deferred to those above him, will demand respect and service from his social inferiors. Ideally, he should exhibit justice and self-control toward inferiors, as the Qur'an enjoins considerate treatment of women and dependents upon all believers. In East Pakistan villages, for example, outward expression of hostility is strongly disapproved. Yet it can happen that suppression of resentment toward parental authority or outside control breaks out in physical aggression toward inferiors or outsiders. Male children frequently have temper tantrums directed toward the mother or servants; women express their anger by rough handling of children; teachers show hostility by cruel punishment of their students; and grown men by brutal beating of children or servants for presumed insubordination.

Aggression which the individual dare not direct toward the source of frustration appears to be displayed toward those who can be punished, including the self. Suicide of this type is not uncommon among women. The mourning and self-flagellation of Shi'as during the first ten days of Muharram has a strong element of masochism, for the cutting and tearing of the flesh is cruel treatment of the body, especially when continued to the point of exhaustion as sometimes is the case.

Self-Esteem

The emphasis on appearances is an important part of the esteem system. The individual is conditioned from childhood to look for approval from constituted authority and to live up to the social code for his role and class rather than to fulfill internal, personal standards of perfection. There is no premium on excellence of performance, of a job done for its own sake, and compromises are made in matters of personal cleanliness, order, and the finishing of products. What one is bears more relationship to self-esteem than what one does. An individual promotes his self-esteem both by fulfilling the standards of his particular lineage, ethnic, or provincial group and by emphasizing the superiority of that group over others.

For the Punjabi, the essence of life is maintenance of 'ezzat—honor or prestige—by validation of status. This can be achieved, by menials as well as landowners, through honest work, fulfilling obligations of kinship, and proper upbringing of children. Dispensation of hospitality at auspicious times, such as the wedding of a daughter, increases the sense of esteem. The landowner who uses his wealth and influence generously to help others under his protection, especially if he is the village chief, has gained much 'ezzat. Those who have fulfilled religious duties, earned an honest living, and have been characterized by upright dealings are called neyk, good, and receive particular honor.

For the Bengali, living in amity with family and neighbors is the most desired aspect of life. Membership in a social unit and correct interpersonal relations are stressed so as to promote harmony in life. The individual is important only as a member of a family, caste, or village community, and antisocial or disruptive behavior is most condemned. Life offers consolation through poetry, song, and the spiritual quest but is essentially social in its nature.

For the Pathan and other tribal groups of West Pakistan, support of the code of honor is the essence of self-esteem. This support involves the obligations of hospitality, defense of family name, asylum and safe conduct to guests in the tribal territory, and the duty of revenge in the blood feud. Life is viewed as a competitive game in which status is increased or lost by use of hospitality and by manipulation of land resources or armed might. When the act of another is construed as a personal affront, aggression is the immediate response.

For Pakistanis in general, concepts of self-esteem are threatened when the individual is faced with any unfamiliar or unexpected situation in which he may be likely to fail. Typically, the individual seeks a solution from an authority or from a superior rather than attempting to find one himself. When unexpected circumstances arise, the traditional techniques and responses no longer operate, and the individual becomes disturbed. Anxiety is sometimes met by pretending indifference—making jokes about oneself to forestall others—and at other times by avoidance of the novel and trying situation.

Time and Leisure

Attitudes toward time are characterized by considerable leniency in comparison with Western standards. The pace of living is much less hurried and apparently there is always time for brief conversation or the exchange of greetings. In the home, preparation of meals takes considerable time, but appears unhurried. It requires hours and patience to wash rice, prepare chappatties, cut up vegetables and spices, and cook the food. Western visitors note with surprise that preparations for a meal are begun after the guest arrives, rather than having food ready to serve immediately. At dinner parties, the talking comes first, the eating afterward. This custom has the virtue of allowing the guest leeway in time of arrival. There are two occasions in the Punjab and in Pakistan generally when punctuality is required: the first is the arrival of the bridegroom's party at the home of the bride; the second is attendance upon a bereaved family on the day of a death.

Although attitudes toward time are relaxed and clocks are not generally used, people recognize the time of day quite accurately according to the positions of the sun and the stars. The fixed times of prayer for an observing Moslem—five specified times during the day —demand knowledge of the time of day in order to make proper performance. When it is considered important in ritual performance, time can be observed strictly, but time scheduling is far from being practiced in most of daily life.

The year is organized on a calendrical system or, more accurately, on several calendrical systems. In rural areas the local calendar is used for the seasonal round of planting without reference to national calendars. Officially, Pakistan observes the twelve-month calendar introduced by the British. Moslem religious holidays are based on a lunar calendar and occur at different times each year. Both

Christian and Moslem dates are given on the mastheads of newspapers and magazines published in the country. Courts, schools, and other governmental agencies observe the Western calendar, and in continuance of British custom government offices and law courts observe Sunday as a holiday. Government offices close on Friday afternoons as well as on Sundays. Business firms generally adopt Sunday as a day of rest, but in the bazaars Sunday is a workday and shops are closed during the Friday noon congregational prayers.

In addition to the great festivals of Islam, a number of local celebrations, or *melas*, are held during the year, especially in the spring. These melas, ostensibly given in honor of the death anniversary of a local pir, are the occasion for secular enjoyment as well. Traveling exhibits, troupes of musicians, dancers, and assorted entertainers arrive at the site of the shrine for a few days or a week. The local villagers flock to the shrine to see the sights and hear the sounds—sounds which in recent years have been augmented by public amplifiers—and to spend a bit of money. These melas are especially popular in West Pakistan and the more revered the holy man, the larger the mela and the attending crowds. Secular holidays, proclaimed by the government, are of more importance to the urban population who can witness the pomp and circumstance of military parades than they are to villagers.

The favorite leisure-time activity for adults of all classes is conversation. Groups of men gather at the teahouses in towns, in the guest house of the village chief in rural areas, or in the men's *hujra* (community house) of the tribal area to smoke and exchange views. Women receive female callers in their own quarters or pay visits to women in other households. The educated class form loose friendship groups, which customarily meet at the teashop or restaurant after the day's work. These associations provide a rallying point and escape from the demands which family and work place upon them. The closest bond is between those who have been schoolfellows together on a basis of equality, and there is a warmer tie than usually exists between brothers. These groups are all-male, of course, but smaller groups might be mixed when they are held in the home and the persons are related to one another or stand on the basis of long friendship between the families.

Young men enjoy hunting as a sport, and in those areas which have game this is a common entertainment. Birds are the usual game since rabbits and boar are proscribed foods and other large

163

game is scarce. Horseback riding is liked because of its utility in getting around the countryside and the correlation of riding with a manly and martial tradition. There have been excellent horsemen coming from the Punjab especially, and at fairs and exhibitions sports such as polo and tent-pegging draw huge crowds. Wrestling and quail fighting have their groups of enthusiasts, quail fighting being very common. In the Punjab *kabaddi,* a form of wrestling and physical strength testing, is engaged in by competing teams of young men from neighboring towns or villages. Children have no organized games. Small children are free to play in the courtyards or streets, but by the age of seven or eight boys help their fathers and girls assist with younger siblings or help in cooking and household tasks.

In general, agriculturists are too occupied to seek further physical exercise, and the urban young men, with some exceptions, lack facilities and the motivation for group sports. In college, there have been excellent sportsmen in cricket, field hockey, squash, and tennis, in the British tradition, and considerable public attention and national pride are involved in the international contests. As in India, field hockey is a man's game, and in international matches the superb Pakistani and Indian teams know no rivals except each other. The organized recreation program of the Boy Scouts, Girl Guides, and the schools is available to only a small educated elite group. The goal of the service units for the men in military training is physical fitness, gained by marching or riding, but this experience is not extended into civilian life.

The movies are a favorite diversion of the urban residents and movie houses are numerous. The educated class attends the imported foreign films, but for the non-English-speaking majority, there are a number of Pakistani-produced films or Indian imports in Hindi which provide familiar themes.

Residential Patterns

The census of Pakistan of 1961 lists 86.9 per cent of the population as rural. This rural majority resides primarily in village communities, since the single dwelling apart on the land has never been traditional on the Indian subcontinent for reasons of security and social cooperation. A village has from several hundred to three or four thousand people, but the average is probably four to five hundred people. There are many types of villages, whose composition

164

depends on the geographical area, on whether it is a landowner village or one of independent holdings, and on the productivity of the area.

In the settled areas of West Pakistan, most structures are made of mud or sun-dried brick with a plastered mud finish, although wealthy families may have homes of kiln-dried brick. Typically, each house in the village adjoins the next one, often with a common wall, and there is a courtyard before every house where the women perform their daily tasks. Animals belonging to the family, such as cows and buffalo, are brought into one section of the courtyard every night. Several trees may provide shade but there is usually no other vegetation in the compound. A mud wall surrounds each courtyard to give privacy to the home and protect its occupants from the gaze of passersby. The streets or alleys of such villages are bordered by high walls on both sides. There are general social boundaries within the village, landowners being in a different quarter from the village menials or the landless laborers. As the alleys are unpaved and there are open drains, passage along the streets becomes difficult during the rainy season.

Moslem villages usually have a mosque, if the village can support it, which is a simple brick structure with a courtyard in front where community prayers can be said. The center of community life is the guesthouse of the village headman or the guesthouse of the local landowner, where the men gather to exchange news and visitors are entertained. The fields worked by the villagers, consisting of many small and irregular plots of land, surround the village. These are marked off from one another by ridges and water channels and are traversed by footpaths and dirt roads which lead to main roads. The fields of each village adjoin fields of neighboring villages of comparable type. In the Himalayan foothills of West Pakistan hamlets tend to be smaller with houses ranged along the water course, and terraced agriculture is usual.

In East Pakistan, the typical Bengali village consists of houses of bamboo matting and mud with thatch or corrugated iron roofs. These villages are located along water systems and rivers in order to use this network of communication. Earth from the digging of water storage tanks has been used to raise the level of the houses above the annual flood waters. Here too each rural household has a courtyard where the women can do their chores in privacy.

Towns, distinguished as urban areas with five thousand or more residents, furnish goods and services not ordinarily available in villages, such as factory-milled rice or wheat and the imported wares of the shops. The town may also be the administrative center of an area, with local courts, police station, and government offices to which the villagers must repair on occasion. There are likely to be more multistoried houses of brick than in the villages and no courtyards in the more congested areas.

The cities of Pakistan often have considerable historic continuity. Hyderabad, Lahore, Multan, and Peshawar in West Pakistan, and Dacca in East Pakistan, have been important centers of administration and trade for hundreds of years. These cities possess mosques and forts of great historical interest which are still standing. The old urban areas of these cities were constructed on adjoining land, but many of the buildings have been replaced over the years. Typically, these older sections consist of several-storied brick houses built to use the land fully and crowded along winding alleys and streets.

During the British administration, new areas were constructed near the urban centers to provide for the military and administrative personnel and their dependents. Complete military cantonments with barracks and living quarters were constructed adjoining the old cities of Lahore, Rawalpindi, Peshawar, Nowshera, Mardan, and Quetta. In addition, courts, legislative buildings, and new residential sections with paved streets were erected at provincial capitals during the British period. Although designed primarily for Europeans, wealthy families with Western orientation were attracted to these more spacious and modern living areas, and with the departure of the British an increasing number of well-to-do Pakistanis moved from ancestral homes in the rural area or the old city to these modern cantonments. In Karachi, with its new administrative and commercial importance, hundreds of housing units of modern style have been built since it became the national capital. In this instance, the original city is not ancient nor does it contrast so sharply with the newer areas. Refugee camps still exist on the fringes of Karachi and in some other areas of Pakistan.

In the cities there is a great range in the quality and type of structure. The poorer refugees construct a shelter out of any scraps of wood, pieces of gunny sack, cardboard, straw, or sticks that can be found. These are supplemented by mud and stones. The resulting huts have roofs of straw—occasionally corrugated iron—and are frequently located in areas subject to flooding.

The prosperous, on the other hand, may live in elaborate brick or concrete structures that would be impressive in any country. Modern plumbing, electrical fixtures, garages, servants quarters, paved driveways, and elaborate gardens characterize these houses and the entire property, referred to as a compound, is surrounded by a wall approximately six feet high with an iron gate at the entrance. Houses of this type, usually called bungalows regardless of their size, are owned by the more successful businessmen, land-owners, and high-ranking government officials and many are rented by foreigners.

Except for the refugees, whose ties with the ancestral village have been broken, most urban residents maintain contact with their family in the village. From the village they secure some of their food supply, such as wheat flour or rice, and marriages are often arranged through the resident village family. City-dwelling members of a family are obligated to entertain relatives who come to the town or city for visits or to seek employment.

Many of the urban workers are men who have come to town or city because of economic pressure on land in the family holdings and unemployment in the countryside. Leaving a wife in the village, they take whatever employment can be found. These workers, especially in the factories of East Pakistan, do not lose their orientation toward the land, and the low prevailing wages and difficult living conditions do not predispose them to accept urban life permanently. They continue to return to the village to participate in the harvesting or in local festivities and marriages, and save in anticipation of purchasing land on which to settle.

Some urban dwellers belong to the urban tradition, in that the family has sold or lost its village lands, and commercial or professional employment has become the mainstay of family income. The educated young men from this background, intellectuals whose experience with rural life has been minimal, find no attraction in living in the villages, and prefer any employment in the city to what they regard as exile. There is a danger that these men, who occupy some of the top administrative posts in the government and are the writers and journalists who speak for the literate minority, may become estranged from the culture of the majority, those who live in village communities at such a different level and with such different traditions from the Western-educated elite. This cleavage between educated minority and land-based majority is not unique to Pakistan but is characteristic of several nations of Asia and the Middle East.

Clothing Customs

During most of the year very little clothing is required in Pakistan. Even in the winter months the temperatures are mild in East Pakistan and along the coast in West Pakistan. In the northern part of West Pakistan, however, temperatures just above freezing are common in December and January, and at the higher elevations the temperatures drop much lower. Cotton cloth is used everywhere though woolen coats and blankets are not uncommon in the colder areas.

In West Pakistan the men ordinarily wear the loose, pajama-type cotton trousers known as the *shalwar*, which is usually white or grey, very full at the top, gathered at the waist by a drawstring, and tapered at the ankles. Worn over it is the *kurta*, a white or grey cotton shirt somewhat longer than its Western counterpart. Generally made with buttons on a band that extends only part way down the front to a pleat, this shirt must be pulled over the head and is not tucked in at the waist. A vest or sleeveless sweater is occasionally worn in cold weather, frequently with the addition of a wool suit coat or jacket, which is shorter in length than the kurta. For more formal occasions, and among well-to-do Moslems generally, a long coat known as a *sherwani* is popular. It buttons at the neck and reaches down to the knees. Black is the usual color for a sherwani, but grey and white are also worn. With the sherwani, tighter trousers are worn, but these are still gathered slightly at the waist and tapered to the ankle and therefore also give a wrinkled effect.

In East Pakistan the Moslem men generally wear a *lungi*, a length of colored or patterned cloth which is wrapped tightly around the waist, extends to the ankles, and resembles a skirt. The Hindu male may wear a *dhuti*, like the lungi a long piece of cotton cloth, usually white, which is wound around the waist and passed between the legs from back to front and tucked in at the waist. A white tunic-like shirt without a collar is frequently worn.

Although turbans are occasionally worn by tribal and other rural leaders and by many Punjabis from hotel servants to members of the president's mounted bodyguard, the almost universal head-dress of West Pakistan is the Jinnah cap, named after Pakistan's leader. In shape the Jinnah cap resembles the overseas cap of the American soldier, but it is much more substantial and made from sheepskin or lambskin dressed as fur or, more elegantly, of the most expensive karakul. In the extreme northern mountainous regions of West Pakistan the Gilgit cap is the prevalent headgear. Made of thick, woven woolen cloth and in its unrolled form often several feet long, the Gilgit cap is rolled in much the same manner as a stocking cap. In West Pakistan a bareheaded man is a rarity.

Most of the population, both male and female, goes barefoot but those who can afford to do so wear sandals or shoes. Some type of footwear is worn by most adults in urban areas. Perhaps the most popular, at least in the northern sections and mountain areas of West Pakistan, is the *chapli,* a very practical type of sandal in which two strips of leather cross over the toes and buckle behind the heel. Often these have very heavy, substantial soles. There is a variation of this style of shoe which the women wear. Fancy slippers with long pointed toes, heavily embroidered or gilded, are often seen on both men and women and are sold in large numbers to tourists.

The most conspicuous woman's garment in West Pakistan is the tent-like *borqa',* usually made of white cotton, which is worn over the other garments and completely conceals the wearer's body. A square of loose netting in front of the eyes permits some vision. Borqa's are worn by those Moslem women who observe purdah or who, in deference to conservative custom, prefer to remain inconspicuous in public places. Many of the upper-class women wear a two-piece borqa' of thin silk or crepe, usually black but occasionally navy blue, dark red, or tan. This type of borqa' consists of a long, sleeveless tunic, with a separate headpiece which has a veil that drops over the face. Some of the more educated women, especially those in the urban areas who are teachers or social workers, or whose husbands are businessmen or government officials, no longer wear the borqa'. At the other end of the social scale, the borqa' is not worn by the peasant women in rural areas who work in the fields or by the women coolies or sweepers.

There are three types of dress commonly worn by Pakistani women. The most popular, and perhaps the most practical, is the *shalwar-qamiz,* which was originally a Punjabi dress. It consists of the shalwar trousers, which are exactly the same as those worn by the men; the qamiz, which is a fitted garment reaching below the knees with long sleeves; and a *dupatta,* or large scarf. The dupatta, made of very light material, is about two and a half yards long and is thrown over the shoulders and sometimes used to cover the head. Depending on the material, the shalwar-qamiz can be

169

worn for any occasion from sports or gymnastics to a formal dinner or wedding. Simple cotton versions are used as the uniform of the Women's National Guard, the Women's Naval Reserve, and the Girl Guides as well as Pakistani nurses and airline hostesses. The daytime qamiz of most women is made of a bright print cotton or silk with contrasting solid color or white shalwar. For evening and formal wear, it will be made of fine silk, usually red, white, or pastel colors, and elaborately embroidered in silver or gold thread and decorated with sequins.

As in India, the *sari* is a popular woman's garment in East Pakistan and in West Pakistan among the women who migrated from areas of India other than the Punjab. The sari consists of a piece of cloth usually about five or six yards long and forty-four inches wide which is draped around the waist, pleated, tucked into a tight petticoat band, and brought up across the front and over the shoulder. It is worn with a short blouse called a *choli*. A day-time sari may be made of inexpensive cotton in white or bright colors with a woven border of contrasting hue, but the more prosperous women may wear silk saris delicately embroidered with wide bands of gold or silver thread in intricate designs to give a shimmering effect. Here again, the ornamentation and materials used depend on the financial resources of the wearer as well as the occasion.

The third type of dress is the *gharara*. It consists of a very full, divided skirt which reaches below the ankles. It is worn with a short qamiz and a dupatta gracefully draped. The gharara is especially worn for formal functions.

The variations in costume among the peasant women throughout Pakistan are too numerous to mention in detail. The Sindhi dress, outstanding in color and design, consists of three pieces—a backless choli, a long full skirt, and a dupatta—all made of coarse cotton in brilliant colors such as red, yellow, and green in distinctive native prints. On festive occasions, the Sindhi woman will wear over her shalwar a long loose kurta or shirt elaborately embroidered with bright colored thread and little mirrors. In the northwest tribal areas, the Afridi woman's costume shows a marked Central Asian influence. She will wear a shalwar with a skirt on top, and over all a kurta with a high neck and long, full, loose sleeves. The bodice of the kurta may be ornamented with embroidery and silver buttons for festive occasions or be plain black. She wears a small pillbox-type hat with a veil hanging from it down the back and sides. The Bengali village woman of East Pakistan wears a sari of cheap mill cloth or khadi and a short choli. Except among the Eurasian community, women, even in the cities, rarely wear Western clothes, and Western headgear is almost never seen.

Jewelry plays a very important role in the Pakistani woman's costume. Especially among nomadic tribes and in poor villages, women in shabby dress will be seen wearing heavy silver jewelry, handmade by village craftsmen, that was given to them at the time of their marriage. Very wide silver armbands or heavy silver anklets are frequently worn by peasant women in villages. In the moderate income brackets, the jewelry may be made of solid gold and ornamented with precious stones.

Pakistani women usually wear their long hair drawn back smoothly in a flat bun and decorated with silver hairpins or flowers. Western make-up has yet to be entirely adopted by even the most modern Pakistani women and the popularity of many indigenous cosmetics that have been used for centuries continues unabated. For example, *kohl* is used as eye make-up—even on small babies— and the palms of the hands and the soles of the feet are sometimes stained with henna dye on festive occasions.

The Concept of Pakistan

There is little if any national consciousness among the rural population of Pakistan, a result primarily of the traditional social emphasis on family and tribal obligations at the expense of those of the general community. Local affairs understandably play a predominant role in the lives of people who have never been more than ten miles from their native village. The most likely source of change in this situation is the tremendous influx of refugees, particularly into West Pakistan, which has created a new element in the community—people whose interests are of necessity tied to the success of the state and who can no longer return to their villages.

Aside from the refugee element, urban and rural populations have only a superficial divergence of interests despite occasional incidents of hostility. An exception would be the real differences of attitude and interests between the great majority of the population who are villagers or lower-class urban dwellers and the small group who now hold economic and political power. To bridge this gap and build a foundation for true nationhood poses a real challenge to the country's present leadership.

CHAPTER 9

Education

As in many other countries of Asia, formal education in Pakistan is underdeveloped and inadequate to the needs of the new nation. Although learning is highly valued and scholars are regarded with esteem by other members of the society, educational facilities are limited and the standards generally low. Private support is given to some schools and colleges but the bulk of the financial burden falls on the provincial governments, whose budgets are already strained, with the result that allocations for education have been quite limited. The total public expenditure on education in 1960-61, by both the central and the provincial governments, amounted to only about $13.5 million—a situation made somewhat more encouraging, however, by the steady rise in the percentage of provincial budgets going to education.

There is general recognition of the importance of education for economic development and an increasing awareness of the need for a well-trained corps of personnel to meet the vastly enlarged obligations of Pakistan as an independent nation. Ambitious plans have been drafted for increasing the country's educational resources. In 1959 a Commission on National Education submitted a series of recommendations that were adopted by the government. While the universities are to be developed into more effective teaching and research centers, the new educational program stresses the development of personal character and leadership, the concept of national service, and recognition of the value and dignity of manual labor.

The government meanwhile faces the fact that the majority of the people of Pakistan are illiterate. Using as criterion the ability to read with understanding a short statement on everyday life in any language, the 1961 census listed as literate 28 per cent of the males, 9.3 per cent of the females, and only 19.2 per cent of the total population over five years of age. A conditional literacy was attributed to some 5.6 million people who can read the Arabic script of the Qur'an for devotional purposes without actual comprehension of the words. In the 1961 census the schedule included space for data on nine languages, as well as for additional ones, as follows:

	Bengali	*Punjabi*	*Pushtu*	*Sindhi*	*Urdu*	*Baluchi*	*Brahui*	*Arabic*	*English*				
Mother tongue	1	2	3	4	5	6	7	8	9	10	11	12	13
Other languages	1	2	3	4	5	6	7	8	9	10	11	12	13
Write and read	1	2	3	4	5	6	7	8	9	10	11	12	13
Read only	1	2	3	4	5	6	7	8	9	10	11	12	13

However, in the census bulletins issued or in preparation, no summary of linguistic statistics has been included. Apparently only the very detailed district census reports, which are planned for each of the sixty-eight administrative districts, will include material on languages.

According to the 1951 census, with literacy defined as the ability to read and write, 5,948,000 people had fluency in Bengali, 2,360,000 in Urdu, and 1,953,000 in English. Since then the national languages, Bengali and Urdu, have been given increasing emphasis in teaching. Bengali is now compulsory in East Pakistan; Urdu is compulsory after Class VI in West Pakistan except in the Sind. However, English remains a major language of administration, of the law courts, and of the National Assembly, as well as the primary language of all college-level teaching. Current recommendations are to continue English as a compulsory language in all schools in Classes VI through XII.

The central and provincial governments have both declared themselves in favor of universal compulsory education and some progress in this direction has been made (see Table 4). Thus the total number of primary schools increased from 38,122 in 1948-49 to 44,200 in 1959-60. In the same period enrollment increased from 3,057,000 to 4,706,000, so that by 1959-60 about one-third of all children between the ages of six and eleven were in school and it is probable that the length of time that the students remain in school has also increased somewhat. On the other hand, there is still considerable waste of resources by students who attend school intermittently over several years and never manage to attain higher levels.

A major bottleneck in the development of education has been the limited supply of trained teachers but this situation may be changing. Although the number of primary teacher training institutions declined from 125 to 75, chiefly as a result of consolidation, the enrollment increased from 6,145 to 7,140, and the total number of primary school teachers from 92,053 to 123,310. The number of institutions training secondary school teachers jumped from 11 to 23, with an increase in enrollment from 785 to 1,841 and in the total number of secondary teachers from 46,229 to 52,294.

History of the Educational System

The earliest system of education known to have existed on the Indian subcontinent was the Brahmanical. At first, learning was imparted only to Brahmans or priests, but sometime before 500 B.C. members of the Kshatriya (warrior) and Vaishya (merchant) and agriculturalist castes were also permitted to receive instruction in preparation for their respective vocations. Three types of institutions gradually emerged: the *parishads* (assemblies of the elders, almost exclusively Brahmans); the *tols* (Brahman schools for Sanskrit learning, training centers for the priesthood); and the *pathshalas* (primary schools open to all Caste Hindus).

These primary schools gave instruction in reading, writing, and arithmetic and were open to all except the untouchables and the aboriginal inhabitants of the country. The primary schools existed in all the large villages and usually consisted of twelve to twenty pupils with a teacher, assembled under a tree or in a temple, shed, or other building set apart for the purpose. The teacher was regarded as a public official who was primarily the village priest and then the teacher. He was maintained by the community through provision of rent-free lands or a share in the village harvest.

With the advent of Buddhism, the position of the Brahman priest-teacher was greatly shaken. The Buddhists did not recognize a separate priestly caste nor did they base their teachings on the Vedas. The goal of Buddhist education was primarily a preparation for the life of meditation as a monk. The Buddhist schools were open to all, including the untouchables, and were usually located in monasteries. Youths who intended to pursue the monastic life remained in these schools from the age of six to twenty. Those who were destined for a lay life left at the age of twelve.

The Moslems, who invaded India in successive waves from the beginning of the tenth century to the establishment of the Moghul empire in the sixteenth, brought with them their own educational system. Schools were generally attached to mosques, and the Qur'an together with the heritage of Arabic and Persian literature formed the basis of the curriculum. Although government patronage was extended only to the Moslem schools, Hindus and Buddhists were permitted to continue their traditional forms of education. Sometimes instruction for Moslem children was simply given in the mosque, with the *imam*, or individual in charge of the mosque, serving as teacher. This education usually imparted little more than the rudimentary 3 Rs and sufficient Arabic to read the Qur'an. The school attached to the mosques was known as the *maktab* (plural, *makatib*). The *madrasas*, or higher schools, were usually independent institutions in which the various branches of Islamic learning and literature—both Arabic and Persian—were intensively studied.

Still a third system of education was private tutoring in the home, customarily resorted to among the wealthy and the only way in which women could be educated.

With the decline of the Moghul empire in the eighteenth century the schools lost a good measure of their economic support, and to this loss was coupled the general instability introduced by the advent of the British. As the fortunes of the Moslems declined so did the standards prevailing in the makatib and madrasas. While the Hindus were quick to avail themselves of the new educational opportunities introduced by the British, it was not until the second half of the nineteenth century that the Moslems, under the leadership of Sir Sayyid Ahmad Khan and Abdul Latif, began to make serious efforts to do so. Sir Sayyid Ahmad Khan, convinced that Western science and the principles of Islam were not antagonistic but could be integrated in a new Islamic humanism, urged Moslems to emerge from their intellectual isolation and partake of the new knowledge. In 1875 he founded the Mohammedan Anglo-Oriental College at Aligarh, an institution that soon became the intellectual center of a renascent Moslem culture and political consciousness.

175

In recognition of its growing stature and scope the college in 1920 was renamed Aligarh Moslem University.

The introduction by the British of a Western educational structure took place in stages beginning with primary schools and followed by secondary schools, colleges, and universities. Both the vernaculars and English were used in the primary schools, with emphasis usually on English, but from the secondary school level up instruction was almost wholly in English. The system of primary schools gradually spread and in 1930 those in Bengal were released from the provincial government and placed under the administration of district school boards. This decentralization of administration and the resultant haphazard financing led to uneven development of facilities. In addition, the desire for universal compulsory education spurred a too rapid expansion and the influx into the school system of many untrained teachers.

World War II had an adverse effect on the educational system in that it induced many teachers to leave their posts for more lucrative employment elsewhere. At the same time, the general rise in the cost of living reduced the income of the schoolteacher to below subsistence level, and most teachers found themselves forced to devote much of their time to other means of livelihood. As a consequence, teaching posts in the primary schools now hold much less attraction for qualified persons.

The Educational System

According to the system now in force, most children start their education at the age of six years, although there are a few institutions in the country which accommodate pre-elementary or kindergarten students (see the chart, Organization of Elementary, Secondary, and Higher Education). The elementary or primary schooling usually covers Classes I to V, or from ages six to ten years. It is followed by middle schools (equivalent of the junior high school) using either vernacular or Anglo-vernacular, which normally cover Classes VI to VIII or ages eleven to thirteen years, but in some cases may start a year earlier. Next come the secondary or high schools, covering Classes IX to XI, or ages fourteen to sixteen years. The middle schools are gradually being absorbed by the secondary schools. At the successful completion of this level of education, the student is known as a Matriculate, the lowest qualification generally demanded for clerical employment. Those

ORGANIZATION OF ELEMENTARY, SECONDARY,[a] AND HIGHER EDUCATION IN PAKISTAN

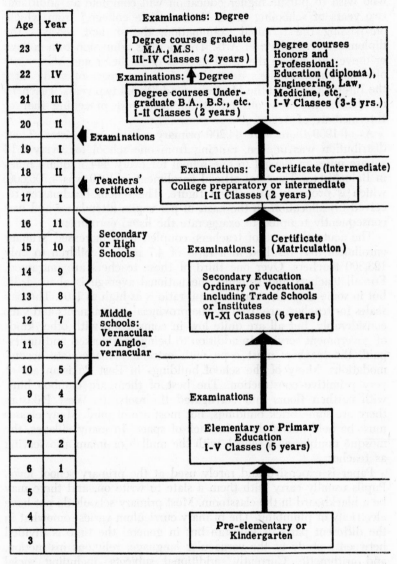

(a) The pattern of secondary education and the significance of terminology vary from province to province.

From Abul H. K. Sassani, *Education in Pakistan.*

who wish to pursue higher education will complete an additional two years of schooling in an "intermediate college," from which, on passing the terminal examination, the student receives the diploma, Intermediate of Arts. This permits admission to a college or university, where the usual degrees of Bachelor and Master are offered. The Bachelor's degree requires two years of study after the Intermediate and the Master's an additional two years. Teacher's certificates are now offered at the level just preceding that of Intermediate of Arts.

As of 1959 there were 44,200 primary schools in Pakistan. Their distribution was uneven, ranging from one school for every 3.14 square miles in Bengal to one school for every 444.5 square miles in Baluchistan. The total official enrollment in 1959 was 4,706,000, which is probably an inflated figure. The school headmaster received his allocation on the basis of per capita attendance and was consequently tempted to exaggerate the listed enrollment.

The acute shortage of teachers, coupled with increased primary enrollment, has resulted in a ratio of 4.7 million children to only 123,300 teachers. Over one third of these teachers are untrained. For all teachers and students the national average is about 1:38, but in some areas the teacher-pupil ratio is as high as 1:64. The pay scales for teachers are fixed by the provincial governments and vary considerably, but all are quite low in comparison with other kinds of government service. In addition to being overworked and underpaid, the teachers must cope with extremely inadequate accommodations. Many of the school buildings in East Pakistan are of very primitive construction. The best of them are bamboo huts, with earthen floors and corrugated tin roofs. In West Pakistan there are some brick buildings, but most are of mud. Many classes must be held out of doors for lack of space. In many villages, the mosque doubles as a school, with the mullah or imam also serving as teacher.

Paper is expensive and rarely used at the primary school level. Pupils usually carry with them a slate to write on, and there may be a blackboard in the classroom. Most primary schools do not have electricity or plumbing. The primary curriculum varies somewhat in the different parts of Pakistan but in general the time is divided between a study of the vernacular language, religious instruction, and arithmetic. Currently, additional subjects, including social studies, physical training, music, arts and crafts, and hygiene, have been introduced.

178

Secondary education generally extends from Class VI to Class XI, but this is not uniform throughout the country. Over half of the secondary teachers are trained. In general the middle schools may be divided into two main categories: Anglo-vernacular and vernacular. The aim of the Anglo-vernacular schools is to prepare students for college or university training, while the vernacular schools are very largely considered terminal. In the vernacular school the medium of instruction is almost invariably the local mother tongue, whereas English is a compulsory subject in the Anglo-vernacular school. Differences between these two types of schools seem to be slowly disappearing.

Though the course of study of the lower middle school is very much the same as that of the vernacular elementary school, there are variations in the curriculums of both the upper middle school and high school throughout the country. Some of the middle schools are self-terminating, others prepare pupils for high school. Required subjects generally include Urdu, mathematics, general science, history, geography, religious education (for Moslems), and language—vernacular or foreign. Advanced Urdu is offered for those whose medium of instruction is Urdu, and elementary Urdu for those whose medium of instruction is either English, Sindhi, Punjabi, or Bengali.

Until recently the secondary schools were under the control of both the government and the universities and seem to have suffered from the dual administration. Generally, the secondary schools were inspected both by the provincial departments of education and the universities; conflicting authorities created a good deal of friction and misunderstanding. At present, each provincial department of education prepares a list of the so-called accredited secondary schools, and the universities add these to their list of affiliated schools.

Unlike primary education, secondary education is financed chiefly by private societies, by local bodies such as municipalities, and by religious organizations. As a result, schools have arisen only in localities where private enterprise and benevolence are active factors. High schools are not well distributed geographically, and the rural areas have been largely neglected. Partly the same factors account for the small number of girls' schools. In addition, the orthodox Moslem prejudice against women's education is particularly strong in rural areas. Even in the cities, women's education remains restricted, though it has made considerable advances in the

179

past decade. Custom demands rigidly segregated conditions for boys' and girls' schools, and coeducation is usually found only at the university level.

Technical and vocational education has been relatively neglected in Pakistan (see Table 5), although there are plans for extensive developments in this field. The first technical high school was established at Karachi in 1951 and there are polytechnic institutes at Karachi and at Dacca. There are in addition perhaps two hundred or more nonstandardized trade, technical, and vocational schools.

Primary teachers are trained in normal schools maintained by the department of education in each province. Students are admitted after either the eighth or tenth grade, the former taking a two-year course and the latter only a one-year course. Those who pass the examination are then given a Junior Vernacular Certificate. In 1959 there were 75 normal schools with an estimated 7,410 students.

Teachers for the middle schools are trained in separate schools or in departments attached either to normal schools or to teachers' training degree colleges. The certificate granted at the end of a one-year course is known either as Senior Vernacular, Junior Anglo-Vernacular, or Certificated Teacher, varying in the different parts of Pakistan. Except for the Certificated Teacher course, which is given in the colleges and open only to those who have passed the intermediate examination, candidates are required to have passed the matriculation examination held at the end of the tenth grade. About a thousand teachers are trained annually in these courses.

High school teachers are trained in teachers' training colleges, of which there were 23 in 1959, and in education departments at the universities of Peshawar and Sind. Candidates who already hold a Bachelor's degree in arts or science are admitted to the course, which lasts one year, and upon successful completion are awarded the Bachelor of Teaching degree. About five hundred students receive this degree each year.

In 1959 the 209 nonprofessional colleges included both degree colleges, some of which offered graduate work at the Master's level, and intermediate colleges, equivalent to the American senior high school. The degree colleges also offered courses at the intermediate level. The combined enrollment for all colleges in 1959-60 was 116,442. Two-thirds of these colleges were privately maintained and had varying standards. An indication of the relative follow-through in the educational system is reflected in the fact that the total college enrollment equaled about 10 per cent of the high school enrollment and only 2.5 per cent of the primary school enrollment. The colleges do not hold their own examinations, nor do they grant their own degrees. These functions are performed by the universities to which the colleges are affiliated. The universities were originally formed on the model of the University of London, a nonresidential examining institution to which were affiliated various colleges with English as the medium of instruction. Even after the University of London was changed into a teaching institution, the principal function of such a university was to prepare syllabuses and conduct examinations for its member colleges. In the past few decades, however, these affiliating universities have also assumed teaching functions.

The University of the Punjab at Lahore, founded in 1882, has 33 affiliated colleges, and 47 colleges are affiliated with the University of Dacca, founded in 1921. The universities of Karachi, of Peshawar, of the Sind, and of Rajshahi in East Pakistan were established after independence. The universities, as set up by the British, were autonomous bodies even though they received their financial support from the government. All the universities have been affected by the political turmoil since independence, with the result that political authorities have been able to exert an increasingly large influence in university affairs. University officials have shown relatively little inclination to defend their autonomy, although the degree to which the government has been able to dominate has varied from university to university.

The publicly maintained colleges are financed and managed by the provincial governments through their departments of education, except for the engineering, agricultural, and medical colleges, which are usually financed and managed through the ministries of public works, agriculture, and health. The exception is the University of Karachi, which obtains all its funds from the central government. The private colleges are aided by government grants. Additional revenues are received from tuition fees and examination fees. Tuition fees are retained by the college or university where the student registers, but the examination fees are paid by the colleges to the university to which they are affiliated. These fees, in turn, are paid to the individual university examiners on a piece-work basis over and above their regular salaries.

The chancellor is the titular head of the university and, following British practice, is customarily a highly placed dignitary. The most frequent choice is the provincial governor. The actual administration is handled by the vice chancellor, who corresponds in responsibilities and functions to the American university president. Overall control of the university is vested in the court, or senate, which includes both university and nonuniversity personnel. As the senate meets only occasionally, sometimes only once a year, the more immediate working body is the executive council or the syndicate, which consists of senior university staff members, representatives of the affiliated colleges, and representatives of the government. It is the executive council that most nearly resembles the board of trustees in the American system.

Religious education is given emphasis in the makatib and, at a higher level, the madrasas and the Dar ul-Ulum. Most of these institutions are in East Pakistan. Their primary purpose is the teaching of Islam, including the Qur'an, the Hadith, religious law, and related subjects. Students sit for examinations conducted by the Madrasa Education Board. Madrasas are maintained by both public and private funds. In East Pakistan they fall into two categories: the Old Scheme madrasas and the Reformed Scheme madrasas. The graduates usually become teachers or assume the post of imam at a mosque. Often they do both, since many of the primary schools are located in the village mosques. The Dar ul-Ulum offer private Moslem training at a higher level, and more advanced education in Islamic studies is available at the universities, which have special departments for this purpose. Criticism has been leveled at the Old Scheme madrasas, which devote 75 per cent of the curriculum to the teaching of Islam and related subjects.

While there are separate schools maintained privately by the Hindus for the teaching of Sanskrit, there are no institutions of higher learning devoted to it. The University of Dacca, however, maintains a combined department of Bengali and Sanskrit, where higher degrees are offered for studies in either language. Schools for the study of Pali are maintained by the Buddhists in East Pakistan, but there are no institutions of higher learning devoted to Buddhist studies, and Pali is not currently offered in the universities. A number of schools and colleges are maintained by Christian mission organizations. These institutions have a high percentage of foreign staff members and their standards are high. Usually the majority of the students are Moslems. The government has welcomed these institutions with the understanding that Christian religious education will not be offered non-Christians.

Current Educational Problems

Education and scholarship are firmly entrenched values in Pakistani society. There have always been in the Moslem societies of South Asia those groups of learned men known as the ulama whose lives are dedicated to the study of the classical literary tradition of Islam. High honor for these men, often with direct support by the rulers of the land, is a centuries-old tradition. Their potential contribution to a smooth transition to the study of modern European culture, or to a synthesis of Islamic and Christian philosophy, was initially thwarted by political factors. British power was imposed on the subcontinent largely at the expense of the Moslem ruling class. Moslems chose to express their hostility toward the British by withdrawing from contact with the conquerors and in particular by not assimilating the new culture introduced by them. As a result, while Hindus flocked to the new schools set up by the British, Moslem youth continued to attend the deteriorating madrasas. As the political, economic, and social fortunes of the Moslems declined, so did the number of Moslem schools and students.

By the end of the nineteenth century, however, Moslems had started to enter into the educational system established by the British, and some had reached high levels of scholastic attainment. A sharp distinction arose between the education of the traditional scholars in the madrasas, where Urdu, Arabic, and Persian were the vehicles of a traditional body of knowledge, and the modern scholars in the colleges and universities, where English provided the key to new subjects and new ideas. Since modern education, under British rule, opened the way for economic and social advancement, it came to be highly valued. The traditionally educated ulama steadily lost prestige and influence as the modernists rose to positions of power and wealth.

Attempts were made to rectify the situation by modernizing the curricula of the madrasas on the one hand and by adding departments devoted to Islamic studies to the various universities on the other. Separate institutes also have been set up to pursue Islamic studies. None of these steps have as yet proved successful in bringing traditionalist and modern elements toward fusion, yet the need for doing so is widely recognized. Traditional education contained many anachronisms and did not serve to adjust the individual to a rapidly changing world. In seeking some type of accommodation, it was recommended that there should be an Islamic bias to education on all levels and that the universities, institutes, or departments of Islamic studies "should visualize themselves as centres from which light should radiate so that our sense of purpose and direction should remain firm and clear."

The traditionalist scholar is still a respected member of society and, in parts of West Pakistan, has demonstrated strong political influence. The modern scholar, largely because the nature of his studies tends to alienate him from the traditional culture of the masses, has not been able to attain a comparable status. For one thing, modern scholars do not command the same degree of respect and support of government officials and men of wealth as traditionalist scholars. While there is still a considerable reservoir of respect for any form of educational attainment, the modernist tends to be regarded more for his technical accomplishments than for authentic scholarship. A strong factor in distinguishing between the traditionalist and the modernist is language. The modern scholar must have a good technical command of English, which is spoken by a very small though influential segment of all Pakistanis; the traditionalist uses Arabic, Persian, and Urdu, which are spoken by a larger percentage of all Pakistanis and with which the indigenous culture has much greater affinities.

The seriousness of the handicap resulting from the use of English as the medium of modern higher education should not be underestimated in its effect on standards or as a factor in attitudes toward modern education. Experience indicates that to cover the same ground and a similar course of study, a student of average ability would take a much longer time to read books in the English language than a student of similar intellectual capacity who received his education in his mother tongue. Thus a frequent result is a high proportion of failures in examinations and a generally low standard of performance. The obstacle presented by pursuing studies in a foreign language, coupled with the many economic and social difficulties to be found in Pakistan, has partially resulted in inferior education and a progressive decline in standards since the withdrawal of the British. In 1950, the Pakistan Public Service Commission sought to test the equivalence of standards by sending the best results of their examination to be re-examined by the examiners of the Civil Service Commission of the United Kingdom. The general conclusion was that even the best products of the Pakistani educational system merited third-class marks by British standards.

Prior to independence, most of the students who pursued higher education were children of government officials or of families with considerable wealth. In almost all cases, the family had already had strong contacts with British culture, and in many instances English was spoken in the home. A significant change has taken place in the complexion of the student body since independence. For one thing, far more Moslems are pursuing higher education than previously. Many of the present students come from middle-class families, which have enjoyed rapid upward mobility since independence—some through unexpected opportunities in government service and others through equally new opportunities in commerce and industry. Most of the elder members of such families have little or no knowledge of English with the result that for a large number of students the language is even more purely academic than it was for their predecessors.

The examination system, particularly on the university level, has done much to inhibit the creative functions of education. The uniform final examinations, administered by an outside agency (the university) were the decisive factor in the student's academic—and frequently personal—life. Failure meant bleak prospects for his future. At best, he could hope for only a mediocre, low-salaried job and little bargaining power in the arrangement of his marriage.

The whole course work is tailored to fit the examinations. The syllabus is fixed and the function of the teacher is to impart to the student the precise knowledge required for passing the examinations. This allows little room for improvisation or experimentation. As there are no internal tests, relatively little studying is done during the year and there is a period of intense cramming during the few weeks before the final examinations. Guides to successful studying and "short-cuts" to memorization of material are heavily relied on, and preparing them often provides an extra source of income to underpaid teachers. The net result of all this is that the student faces his examination under conditions of severe physical fatigue and nervous tension that greatly reduce his efficiency. His preparation has given him neither the time nor the incentive for digestion and assimilation of knowledge. He can only hope to disgorge as many facts as possible from the crammed storehouse of his memory.

Reliance on memorization is found at all levels of the educational system. Once the prescribed method of learning traditional religious texts, memorization has been carried over to modern

Western-type education and encouraged by the examination system. Other factors favorable to the reliance on memory are the lack of textbooks, particularly on the primary level, and the use of a foreign language—English—as the medium of education.

The examination system has dictated the form of instruction as well as the content. Classes are almost exclusively in the form of lectures, and there is little contact between teacher and student. Foreign observers and Pakistanis who have studied abroad have frequently remarked on the difficulty of conducting seminars and encouraging student participation as a result of this system.

Studies have recognized the examination system as "the major institutional barrier to higher learning" and suggested a number of remedial measures, including a closer collaboration between the college principals and teaching staff and the examining bodies; a periodic revision of syllabuses, with a shift in emphasis from memorization to understanding; a more careful selection of students for colleges and universities; and, finally, a reconsideration of the relation between higher education and employment, i.e. the orientation of the whole educational system toward the requirements for government service. Such changes, if effected, should "provide a much improved environment for the student to develop qualities of industry, intellectual curiosity, and moral strength."

The number of girls attending schools and colleges has increased rapidly in the past decade. For example, in 1961-62 at the University of Peshawar, 74 of 430 candidates for the Master's degree were women, and the colleges affiliated with the university enrolled 3,296 boys and 719 girls. The major obstacles to the education of women continue to be poverty and social prejudice expressed in the institution of purdah. Even in a liberal family, consideration of a girl's education will be secondary to that of her brothers, whose earning capacities will depend on the amount or quality of their education. Of the families in a financial position to educate their daughters, the majority are still sufficiently influenced by tradition to demand separate facilities for girls. As these are frequently not available, many prefer to keep the girls at home.

The education of girls in middle-class families had been given a fillip by the increasing demand of educated men for wives with whom they can share their intellectual and cultural interests. This is particularly true for those who have been educated abroad. On the other hand, in orthodox circles there are still doubts about the value of having an educated wife, who might prove too difficult to "control"—and perhaps even be a competitive threat. Moreover, because of the social requirement of universal marriage for women and the restrictions of purdah, there is a great problem of wastage connected with the education of women. There have been few jobs they could take without incurring social censure. However, this situation is rapidly changing as talented, attractive girls appear in shops, in offices, and on the planes of the country's airline.

Pakistan's First and Second Five Year Plans have taken cognizance of all the major problems in education. Recommendations for the establishment of technical schools; government aid to private educational bodies; promotion of teacher training; a reorganization of school administration, with a scholastic rather than the present managerial bias in the directorates of education; a revision of curriculums with a view to giving greater emphasis to science and technical subjects; an increase in the quantity and quality of teachers at all levels of the educational system through training, better salaries, and educational research; a more even geographical distribution of schools; and an overall consolidation and expansion of the educational system, including an intensified program of adult education, were financed by these plans. The First Five Year Plan spent 400 million rupees on the improvement of the educational system, and the Second Five Year Plan envisages expenditures of 890 million rupees toward the implementation of the recommendations of the Commission on National Education. Support also comes from institutions and organizations abroad. For example, the Ford Foundation has contributed $1,081,000 for educational projects. With concerted effort significant changes may result in the Pakistan educational system in the near future.

CHAPTER *10*

Art and Literature

THE RICH CULTURAL HERITAGE of Pakistan covers a period of more than five thousand years and archaeological evidence of the earliest known civilization in the subcontinent has been found in West Pakistan. Pakistanis are fond of pointing out that Sind, Sindhi, Hind, Hindu, Ind, Indus, and India are all related words originally applied by early invaders to the area that is now West Pakistan. During this long history the main sources of Pakistan's artistic and intellectual expression have been the Indic civilization of the northern plains, Islamic civilization, and, for relatively shorter periods, the cultures of Iran, Greece, Rome, and Western Europe. The Islamic tradition has, of course, been the most important, and it permeates the art and thought of Pakistan today.

In both wings of Pakistan virtually all forms of artistic and intellectual expression have been primarily religious in character. This has been true throughout history, whether the artists and thinkers were Moslem, Hindu, or Buddhist. The content of their work was primarily spiritual and in most cases the manner, purpose, and act of expression were essentially religious.

In terms of the broad sweep of cultural history, West Pakistan has been characterized by the importance of influences coming from outside and East Pakistan by its isolation and the predominance of its own local genius. West Pakistan has been the scene of the influx of numerous peoples and cultures, for all the overland invaders of the subcontinent entered through this province. When it was not independent, it was as often annexed to lands in western Asia as it was to empires centered in northern India. Iran often exerted a strong influence, especially during the period of Moslem rule. To the present day, West Pakistanis feel themselves closely identified with the western Islamic world. East Pakistanis, by comparison, are much less likely to identify themselves with peoples and events outside Bengal. East Pakistan has been much more isolated than West Pakistan, and every movement of cultures into it has been molded into a distinctively Bengali form.

Indus Valley Civilization

Archaeological excavations made in the Indus valley during the 1920s resulted in the discovery of remains of a great civilization which flourished during the fourth and third millenniums B.C. The two major cities excavated are Harappa in the Punjab and Mohenjodero (almost four hundred miles away) on the Indus river in Sind. The antecedents of this culture are unknown, but the artifacts reveal many elements similar to those of Mesopotamian civilization. The pictographic script used on the seals has not been deciphered but the people are believed to have been Dravidians. Although the Dravidian peoples now live only in southern India, there is one Dravidian language still spoken near Mohenjodero, the tongue of the Brahui tribes of Baluchistan.

The Indus valley people reached a stage of development in architecture and town planning far in advance of anything which was to appear on the subcontinent for many centuries. Two- and three-story houses were built of burnt brick; public baths and elaborate drainage systems were constructed; and towns as a whole were remarkably well laid out. The absence of any adornment on the buildings is conspicuous, but their interiors have yielded terra cotta and bronze figurines, seals, and other art objects which display an extraordinary degree of artistic sophistication, technical mastery, and variety of style. The antecedents of later artistic styles have been detected in Indus valley art, and so have many symbols and motifs echoed in later Indic civilization.

These evidences of the continuity of civilization in the subcontinent are more important to modern Indians than to Pakistanis. Pakistan does not consider its culture to be descended in any way from that of the Indus valley but is, rather, quite conscious and proud of the fact that within its borders are the remains of an advanced society contemporary with the traditionally recognized "centers of civilization" such as Egypt, Sumer, Iran, and China. Available evidence indicates that the Indus valley civilization came to an end around 1500 B.C. It is not known whether this culture had already decayed or whether it was destroyed violently, but it appears to have fallen before the seminomadic Aryan tribes who entered from the northwest at about that time.

Indic Civilization

The pastoral Aryan tribes who entered the subcontinent from the northwest gradually and relentlessly spread eastward across the Punjab and along the Gangetic plain, conquering or peacefully absorbing the indigenous peoples or pushing them farther south and east. Although the characteristic Indic civilization of the sub-continent is now believed to be a blend of Aryan and non-Aryan elements, it was the Aryans who came to dominate the society and its culture. The artistic and intellectual expression of northern India is primarily that of the Aryans, however much it may have imbibed from Dravidian and other pre-Aryan sources.

In regard to material culture, the period from the fourth century B.C. to the Aryan invasion (*ca.* 1500 B.C.) presents a great gap in knowledge, for the buildings and artifacts of this millennium were evidently made of perishable materials. In regard to religious, philosophical, scientific, and poetic literature, however, this was the formative period of indigenous Indic civilization. A large body of this literature has survived, much of it with remarkably few corruptions despite its oral transmission. It is the fountainhead of later Indian religious and intellectual expression.

The classical period of Indic civilization may be dated roughly from 500 B.C. to 700 A.D. During this period Hinduism developed its characteristic forms; Buddhism and Jainism rose, flourished, and declined; and there was an immensely rich and varied development of philosophy, literature, and the arts. The areas which later became Pakistan were, of course, a part of this culture, but its geographical center was the middle Gangetic plain, known as Aryavarta (land of the Aryans), which now belongs to the Union of India.

Culturally speaking, the ancient province of Gandhara was the most important region in Pakistan before the coming of the Moslems. Gandhara was centered on the great corridor reaching from Rawalpindi across Peshawar to Kabul and nearby areas. Its early capital was Taxila, an educational, commercial, and administrative center of antiquity, the ruins of which lie about twenty miles northwest of Rawalpindi. The stage for the rise of Gandharan culture was set by the spread of Hellenism from the west under Alexander the Great, the spread of Buddhism from the southeast during the third century B.C., and the subsequent invasions by several Central Asian peoples. The height of Buddhist art and learning in Gandhara was reached in the first few centuries A.D. under the patronage of the Kushans, who ruled a huge empire from their capital at the site of modern Peshawar.

The sculptures and monuments of this period exhibit styles and motifs from various Indian schools as well as influences from Greece, Rome, Iran, and western China. This is partly because Gandhara was a major center of trade and partly because the Kushans patronized a number of artistic traditions. The single art style which was most prominent under the Kushans and which is today identified with the name of Gandhara is an eclectic "Greco-Buddhist" style. The content is Indian Buddhist but the form and execution are distinctly Hellenic or Roman. The rise of Gandharan art coincided with the beginning of the representation of the Buddha in human form and the growing prominence of Mahayana and other Buddhist schools in which worship centered around the Buddha image. In Gandhara these Buddhas have all the traditional signs and poses of Buddhahood but their features and dress are more Greek than Indian. Of all the pre-Moslem cultures, Pakistanis are proudest of Gandhara.

During the Gupta period (320–490 and 606–647 A.D.) Indic civilization flourished in every field of artistic and intellectual expression and classical Indian art and literature reached their highest levels. The areas that are now the two wings of modern Pakistan were at times under the suzerainty of the Gupta monarchs but only at the periphery of the Gupta culture. Buddhism appears to have died out of West Pakistan during this period but survived in East Pakistan until the Moslem conquest in 1200 A.D.

The cultural history of Bengal during the formative and classical ages of Indic civilization is largely unknown. Intersected by numerous rivers and covered with dense forests, East Bengal appears to have been rather sparsely populated. In large areas stone is not available for building and, even where it has been used, many monuments have succumbed to the ravages of the climate, floods, and fast-growing vegetation. Much of what is assumed to have been created in early Bengal has perished; the ancient sites which have survived have not been as fully excavated and studied as those of the Indus valley and Gandharan civilizations.

The golden age of Buddhism in Bengal occurred during the

Pala dynasty (*ca.* 800–1100 A.D.) which ruled both Bengal and Bihar. The Bengali tradition of philosophy and art which flourished under the Palas is sometimes called Tantric Buddhism. On a popular level it was a complex, non-Aryan, polytheistic mystery cult interspersed with many animist elements and associated with the worship of village fertility goddesses.

On the philosophical level, Tantric Buddhism combined the world-denying disciplines of mysticism and an emphasis on the duality of the universe. The dual principles, which came to be defined as consciousness and activity (or energy), were identified with the male and female principles respectively. The devotee, by submitting himself to the particular discipline of his guru, or spiritual preceptor, would seek to cut off the thirty-two nerve channels to the brain and attain supreme bliss through participation in the divine intercourse of the male and female principles. Salvation could be attained not only through asceticism but through a perfect realization of love and its sensual enjoyment. On their lowest levels Tantric rites sometimes gave rise to the mystery cults and debased sexual practices by which Tantrism is known in the West.

The emphasis on mysticism, love, and a close relationship with nature probably antedates Buddhism and has remained characteristic of Bengal to the present day. These themes are prominent, in various forms, in the great Hindu and Islamic traditions which succeeded Buddhism and are expressed in countless Bengali poems, ballads, dances, dramas, and songs.

The sculpture of the Palas, a late development of the Gupta style, is represented in numerous smooth black slate images of high technical accomplishment. These elegant images suggest metalwork in their clear-cut outlines and lack the sense of a dynamic surge of the life-force from within which is so important in most Indian art.

The architecture of the Buddhist rulers of Bengal was on an immense scale. The three main archaeological sites so far discovered are Paharpur, Pattikera, and Mahasthan. At Paharpur, in Rajshahi district near the western border of East Pakistan, are the remains of the largest Buddhist monastery south of the Himalayas. It was first built around 800 A.D. and underwent extensive rebuilding about two centuries later. The nearly three thousand sculptured panels on the walls date from the original construction of the building and were reset later without consideration of subject order. The lower series, of stone, is devoted primarily to Hindu divinities, with emphasis on the Krishna legends. The jumble of

192

terra cotta panels in the upper levels portrays all manner of Buddhist and Hindu divinities, humans, animals, and symbols. Many of the stone sculptures are done in the elegant court style; others, together with all of the terra cottas, are done in a vigorous, crude, folk style which appears to be characteristic of Bengal.

Pattikera, which may have been a medieval provincial capital, is located in the Maynamati-Lalmai ridge near Comilla in Tippera district. The site was accidentally discovered during trench-digging operations in World War II and only four of its eighteen mounds have been excavated. They reveal extensive monasteries and palaces decorated with numerous terra cotta panels in the vivid folk style. The buildings appear to be roughly contemporary with those of Paharpur. The Pakistan government is continuing the excavations at the present time, and it is expected that when they are finished much more will be known about early Bengal. Mahasthan, the ancient Pundranagar, is in Bogra district. It was a Gupta city, capital of the Pala kingdom, and became an important place of Moslem pilgrimage to the tomb of a warrior saint. Below the tomb and mosque is a Hindu temple of Siva and below that a Buddhist building.

No Buddhist literature has survived in Bengal, but Hindu Sanskrit literature flourished under the Brahman Senas, who replaced the Palas around 1100 A.D. The most outstanding court poet was Jayadeva, author of the *Gita Govinda,* perhaps the most famous love poem of India. It is not known to what extent Jayadeva was influenced by Tantrism. Bengali Hinduism itself, however, shows definite Tantric influence.

Culture under Moslem Rule

The Arabs brought Islam to Sind before the Pala dynasty was established in East Pakistan, but the cultural effects of this first Islamic penetration were slight. A Moslem empire was established throughout the northern plains in about 1200 and, although the greatest buildings of the next three centuries were in India, important literary developments occurred during this period in Pakistan. The greatest age of the Moslems on the subcontinent came during the Moghul empire of the sixteenth and seventeenth centuries. The height of Moslem cultural achievement was reached during the reigns of Akbar (1556–1605), Jahangir (1605–1627), and Shah Jahan (1628–1658). Although the Moghul capitals and most important monuments, with the exception of Lahore, were in what is now India, the Moslems of Pakistan look upon their period as their golden age.

Some of the greatest achievements of the period of Moslem rule were in architecture. Moslem architecture introduced and featured the elements of the dome, the minaret, and the pointed arch.

In general, Islamic architecture on the Indian subcontinent, as elsewhere, was an adaptation to the requirements of the Moslem religion of elements taken over from the peoples the Moslems conquered. Some of these adaptations and structural solutions had already been worked out when Islam came to India. In buildings of brick and tile the Moslems borrowed heavily from Iran; early buildings in stone were greatly influenced by the Seljuk architecture of Asia Minor; other adaptations were distinctively Indo-Islamic. In the erection of Islamic mosques and tombs, the Moslems called upon Indian workmen whose working experience in stone rested on centuries of tradition. Both in carved or inlaid stone decoration and later in form, the hand of the Indian craftsman is evident in the Moslem buildings.

Initially the architectural traditions represented by the Moslems and the Hindu workmen were complete opposites: the Islamic mosque is a simple group of cubes with clear, rigid outlines interrupted only by dome or minaret and with light, open courts. The Hindu temple has a profusion of sculpture, a dark and mysterious interior, broken outlines, and a piling up of diverse forms. Gradually, however, these traditions were reconciled in a multitude of ways. In the Moghul tombs and other buildings the dome no longer rises in isolation over a single chamber but is the culmination of a complex, carefully coordinated design of gates, gardens, and pavilions. The so-called "Hindu pavilion," a circular cupola in various sizes, was widely used for this purpose. Prominent examples of a synthesis, in which the basic plan is Islamic but the details are Hindu, are found in some of Jahangir's buildings in the Lahore fort described below.

The two wings of Pakistan represent provincial schools in this development, with architectural styles varying from time to time according to individual tastes and the relative strengths of the indigenous regional tradition, influences from other countries, and contact with the imperial court at Delhi or Agra.

In West Pakistan, especially in Sind, the Iranian tradition was ascendant. Apart from the dominant dome and the use of arcades,

194

a conspicuous feature of Iranian architecture is the way in which brilliantly colored tiles are used to give surface variety to an otherwise simple, geometric structure. This Iranian style, with little modification, is evident in the lovely tiled mosques of Tatta in Sind. Sind is, in fact, famous for its tilework, and the craft is still followed, though somewhat precariously, in the vicinity of Hyderabad. The designs on the Sindhi tilework consist primarily in varieties of the ancient arabesque, a complex abstract design of linear and floral patterns.

In Bengal, as in Sind, stone for building is scarce, but here the regional tradition alternated in influence not with a foreign tradition but with the style of the imperial court, depending on how much contact that court had with its Bengal viceroys. Prior to the Moghul conquest of Bengal in 1575, Islamic building there was derived from the early architecture of Delhi. The native genius of the Bengali craftsman for terra cotta carving is seen in the luxuriant surface decoration of the buildings. The most important pre-Moghul buildings, which are partly in ruins, are massive structures mostly of brick, with some features reflecting the forms derived from bamboo construction. A case in point is the use of a convex roof with projecting eaves, which resembles that of the Bengali hut.

In the latter part of the century the Moghuls built a number of mosques in the vicinity of Dacca, their capital, and some Bengali traits were adopted in the west. An exquisite example of the convex "Bengal roof" is found on the white marble Naulakha pavilion built by Shah Jahan at the fort in Lahore. The finest examples of Moslem architecture in what is now Pakistan are the Moghul buildings in Lahore, which cover the whole range of the metropolitan Moghul style. Lahore is the only city in Pakistan which was a front-rank center of administration, trade, art, and learning under the Moghuls and it retains its pre-eminent position as the cultural center of West Pakistan today.

The most important secular buildings are those of the palace-fortress just inside the old city of Lahore. Most of the fort was built by Jahangir, and the Akbar-Jahangir phase of Moghul architecture is reflected in the use of Hindu pavilions, rich red Mathura sandstone varied with patterns inset in black and white marble, and the brackets of the columns which, in the Hindu style, include carvings of animal figures, contrary to the injunctions of Islam. The buildings added by Shah Jahan are of gleaming white marble rather than sandstone, and their style and decoration show a strong

195

Persian influence. The decoration characteristic of Shah Jahan consisted of inlays of semiprecious stones in floral patterns or mosaic tilework. On the outside wall of the fort is a remarkable series of mosaic tile panels done by a master Iranian craftsman which (contrary to Moslem convention) depicts human and animal forms in a lively, entertaining fashion.

The Moghuls' love of beauty is proverbial. Of the many formal gardens they built for the enjoyment of the court, one of the most famous is Shalimar (a Sanskrit word meaning "garden of bliss"). Just outside Lahore, it presents today only a vestige of its former beauty but is still the treasured resort of many thousands, particularly on holidays.

The religious buildings—tombs and mosques—exhibit the same variety of styles and the same combination of grandeur and grace. The most famous is the Badshahi mosque, adjacent to the Lahore fort, which has the largest open court of any mosque in the world. The Badshahi mosque, erected by Aurangzeb, lacks the eager invention of Akbar's period or the studied elegance of Shah Jahan but is still a monument of great dignity.

There are a few examples of mural painting on the interiors of some of the Moghul tombs, but the great bulk of the famous Moghul painting is in miniature. The delicate ornamental conventions of Moghul painting are of Persian derivation. As far as India was concerned, this introduction of Persian miniature art meant a fundamental change in subject matter and function as well as size. Because Islam forbids the depiction of humans and animals in religious art, the new painting was entirely secular; the figures were courtiers rather than gods. The scenes were those of aristocratic life: royal hunting parties, idyllic love scenes, episodes at court, harem festivities, and portraits of princes and nobles. In addition, skills in the decorative use of calligraphy and abstract and floral patterns were highly developed in the surface decoration of the buildings and in painting, furnishings, textiles, jewelry, and other handicrafts.

The artists and artisans were clustered in the urban administrative centers, for their art, which existed primarily for the adornment and enjoyment of the courtiers, was dependent on court patronage. The nobility were often connoisseurs of art and many were painters and poets in their own right. Similar to Versailles in many respects, court life was far removed from that of the ordinary folk. The courts had their full complement of painters, craftsmen, poets, philosophers, and—since the Moghuls were not averse to the pleasures of wine, women, and song—musicians, dancing girls, bards, and entertainers.

The reign of Aurangzeb (1658–1707) meant a severe setback for the court arts, for he reimposed the Islamic injunctions against music, art, wine, and extravagance in secular as well as religious life. Initially the artists and musicians simply went to other courts, but after the establishment of British rule their production declined with the decline in the ability of the aristocracy to patronize it and was further hurt, eventually, by competition with Western goods. A number of these crafts are still pursued, of course, often with workmanship of a high caliber. But artistic creativity in this field today is but a shadow of what it was under the Moghuls.

The Literary Heritage

The official and literary language of most of the Moslem rulers of India was Persian and in both style and content the rich literature which flourished in Moslem India was heavily indebted to Persia. Of the early Indo-Persians at Delhi, Amir Khusru (1253–1325) was unquestionably the greatest. A renowned poet, mystic, and historical scholar, he also evolved new dances and melodies, reputedly invented the popular musical instrument, the sitar, and composed song forms for the expression of mystical sentiments and classical Indian themes which are now part of the repertoire of Indian classical music.

Amir Khusru is also credited with being the first man to use Urdu as a literary language. Urdu gradually developed a rich literary tradition which was quite different in form and content from the devotional and aesthetic Hindu poetry flourishing during the period. One verse form still very popular is the *ghazal,* a series of lyrical couplets usually about love.

The Moslem rulers introduced the writing of history in India. Before the Moslems there was no religious interest in historical scholarship, and historical accounts of the Buddhist and Hindu kingdoms came from Greek and Chinese travelers. The bulk of the Moslem histories are court chronicles which are characterized by the religious bias and fulsome flattery of their authors, but in Abu'l Fazl, the Moghuls produced a historian of note. His vast

197

Akbar Nama, describing the reign of Akbar and of his predecessors, has been called the most important historical work which India has produced.

Nonhistorical literature was greatly influenced, both in content and in language, by the religious movements of the period. The twelfth through the sixteenth centuries were characterized by the prevalence of notable saints who carried messages attempting to transcend the parochial limits of religion, caste, and sect and emphasizing direct devotion to Allah. In Hinduism there arose many saints who taught in the vernacular rather than the classical Sanskrit language, preaching a message to all castes of bhakti, or faith in a personal deity, rather than dependence upon the complicated Sanskrit rituals of the Brahmans. A somewhat similar mystic devotional tradition was flourishing in Islam. In addition, individuals arose who attempted to combine the two religious traditions and spread an eclectic Hindu-Moslem faith.

A prominent example of the eclectic leaders was a Moslem weaver named Kabir (1440–1518), who was initially a disciple of the famous Hindu saint, Ramananda. To Kabir, all institutional religions were a sham; the barber, washerwoman, and carpenter were nearer to God than the priest "who leaves Brahma to worship a stone" or the ascetic "with his great beard and matted locks, looking like a goat." "God is One," he sang, "whether we worship Him as Allah or as Rama. . . . There is One Father of Hindu and Mussalman, One God in all matter." Today Kabir's followers, the Kabirpanthis, number millions (largely among lower Hindu castes) and his songs of religious ecstasy and the oneness of mankind are sung all over northern India. One of Kabir's followers was Nanak (1469–1538), the founder of Sikhism. In view of the intense hostility between Sikhs and Moslems during the last century it is interesting to note that Sikhism was originally a reforming sect which included many Islamic elements in its teachings.

Another such attempt was Akbar's *Din-i-Ilahi* ("divine faith"). Akbar was distinguished politically by his efforts to build a united realm and he included several non-Moslems in his government. In religion he was generally tolerant and, although he never learned to read, took part eagerly in the religious discussions of the Moslem, Hindu, Parsi, Jain, and Jesuit theologians and saints who gathered at his court. Owing partly to his own experiences and partly to his desire to unite all of his subjects, he tried to found a new eclectic religion and issued in 1579 an Infallibility Decree by which he made himself the sole arbiter of religious disputes. But the Din-i-Ilahi perished at Akbar's death. Modern Moslems have often pointed to Akbar's failure as proof of the strength of Islam in resisting Hindu absorption and of the impossibility of a reconciliation between the Hindu and Moslem ways of life. In general, the reconcilers have done less to bring the two faiths together than to add new sects to the variety of religions of the subcontinent.

More important to Moslem literature and philosophy than these eclectic movements was the profound influence of Sufism. This tradition, which emphasizes individual devotion to Allah, love, and mystic disciplines, grew up outside the subcontinent. The missionaries who brought Islam to the Indian masses were primarily Sufis—particularly those who went to Bengal, where the Sufis were extremely successful. Of the two sides of Islam, the legalistic and the mystical, the former has produced notable scholars, historians, and jurists, while the latter has been more conducive to art and creative thought. It was generally the men inspired by Sufism who were the most outstanding poets. During the twelfth to sixteenth centuries Sufi Islam was brilliantly expounded by such Persians as Sa'di, Jalal ud-Din Rumi, Hafiz, and Amir Khusru, who lived at the Moghul courts.

Cultural influence did not spread entirely from West to East under the Moslems. During the later centuries, when it appeared that Islam was being corrupted by non-Islamic cults that had entered under the aegis of Sufism, a group of remarkable scholars, partly inspired by higher Sufi ideas, strove to restate orthodox theology with emphasis on the psychological and ethical side of religion and thus break away from the formalism of the theologians on the one hand and the excesses of the popular cults on the other. Two of the most outstanding were Indians: Ahmad Sarhindi (1563–1624) and Shah Vali Allah of Delhi (1702–1762), whose followers are active today.

In the Vaishnava tradition of Hinduism the Supreme Deity, Vishnu, is worshipped in his major incarnations, Rama and Krishna. The devotional Bhakta cults are usually associated with Vaishnavism and especially with worship of Krishna. The Bhakta movement had an important effect on literature, for its emphasis on the spiritual unity of man (which challenged the exclusiveness of caste and the supremacy of the Brahmans), its mass appeal, and the tendency of its saints to teach in the vernacular resulted in the beginning of vernacular literatures in most of the regions of the subcontinent. In this respect it resembles the Protestant Reformation of Europe.

The Krishna cult spreading throughout northern India was carried by Chaitanya (1486–1533) to Bengal, where it had a close "affinity to the dreamy and emotional Bengali character" and met with a ready response. Vaishnavism already existed in Bengal— Jayadeva's *Gita Govinda* is considered an early Vaishnava poem— but under the influence of Chaitanya, who brought it to the lower classes, it became a popular movement and Bengal underwent a religious revival. The growing Vaishnava movement was greatly influenced by Sufism in Bengal. In fact, the two traditions, with some differences but many similarities, have throughout the religious and literary movements of Bengal interacted with each other. In their literature both use the imagery of ordinary life and human love to express man's relationship with the divine; in both the influence of mysticism has made the poets devotional and their poetry lyrical.

Before the coming of the Moslems, the literary language of Bengal was Sanskrit. During the first century of Moslem rule there was no literary production to speak of, but during the fourteenth and fifteenth centuries the Moslem courts became centers of literary activity, primarily in Persian. Moslem rulers patronized not only the Persians who migrated to Bengal but the native Hindu poets. There was considerable translation of Sanskrit religious works into Persian, and Moslem poets wrote on Hindu as well as Moslem religious themes. Under Chaitanya's influence, Vaishnava poets translated the Sanskrit epics into Bengali. The Moslem kings also encouraged the development of Bengali as a literary language. Gradually a large number of Persian and Arabic words became a part of Bengali, and these centuries were marked by the growth of an extensive Bengali literature of anonymous folk ballads known as *puthhis*. Many hundreds still exist, as embellished by successive generations, and their recitation is a popular feature of village entertainment.

The Moslem poets who flourished from the fifteenth to the seventeenth century brought about a major change in the subject matter of poetry. Formerly the poems had dealt with religious themes, gods, and spirits; now the Moslem poets, drawing partly on puthhi legends, added themes of ordinary humans and daily life. This secularization of literature is considered a major contribution of the Moslem writers.

200

The literature of West Pakistan, in closer touch with the court of Delhi and developments in Iran, has a less regional flavor than that of East Pakistan. While there is much oral literature in the Punjabi tongue, written Punjabi literature appears to be largely that of the Sikhs and is written in the Sikh Gurumukhi script. In Punjab and the rest of West Pakistan the literary languages of the Moslems were Persian and Urdu. Urdu literature generally remained Persian in tone, but along with Persian and Arab themes and images the poets used local subjects, metaphors, and similes.

Like the puthhis of Bengal, the works of a more regional character deal with the hopes, joys, and sorrows of the people and most of the narratives are about popular figures of legend and history. The favorite stories of West Punjab and Sind are tragic love stories analogous to Romeo and Juliet. The Laila-Majnoon, Hir-Ranjha, Sassi-Punhun, and Sohni-Mahival stories have undying appeal and exist in many versions. The great poet of Sind was Shah Abdul Latif (1689–1752). His thought and poetry are woven into the ordinary Sindhi's life today. His *Risalo* is the only classic of imaginative literature produced in the Sindhi language. Shah Abdul Latif was a Sufi and his poetry, often sung, expresses the love and longing of a mystic for reunion with his Maker. He had a genius for using well-known folk tales as allegories to express religious truths. His versions of Sassi-Punhun and Sohni-Mahival are especially popular.

The national poet of the Pathans, or Pushtuns, is Khushhal Khan Khattak (1613–1687), a warrior-poet who rebelled vigorously against Moghul rule. His songs of love, mysticism, war, and adventure, composed in Pushtu, remain immensely popular among the Pathans of the North-West Frontier today.

Moslem Literature under British Rule

Clive's victory at Plassey occurred in 1757 and thereafter the administrative and cultural center of Bengal was Calcutta, the capital of British India until 1911. Bengal was the first province to feel the full impact of British rule and the first to develop a Westernized intellectual class. It was also the province in which the Moslems suffered the greatest economic, political, and cultural decline. Some of the emerging Hindu leaders were themselves Persian scholars, but the major characteristic of nineteenth-century Bengal was the interaction of Indian culture with that of the West.

The leaders of the great nineteenth-century Bengal Renaissance were Hindus, and the Moslems, who initially held aloof from Western education, did not produce comparable figures until the twentieth century.

The Moslems did respond to the Bengal Renaissance, and Moslem Bengali literature reflects the influence of the Hindu writers. The most important of these was Rabindranath Tagore (1861–1942), the prolific poet, dramatist, and educator, who won the Nobel Prize in 1913 for his humanistic lyric poetry and is still the most popular literary figure among Moslems as well as Hindus in Bengal.

Second only to Tagore in the esteem of the Bengali Moslems is Nazrul Islam (1899), who flourished between the two world wars and is no longer writing. His work reflects his belief that Bengali literature is the joint creation of Hindus and Moslems and that neither should hesitate to use the legends and myths of the other. Yet, although not consciously antithetical to the Tagoric tradition, his pride in his Moslem heritage, his frequent use of Arabic and Persian words and images, and his passionate call for a Moslem awakening gave rise to a new Moslem literary cult. A rebel and romantic, Nazrul Islam traveled from village to village singing songs of revolt against British rule, and most of his published words were proscribed by the British government.

Elsewhere in the subcontinent a less severe malaise set in among the Moslems during the nineteenth century. Their cultural decay was halted largely through the efforts of Sir Sayyid Ahmad Khan (1817–1898), who did for the Moslems what had been done for the Hindus a generation or two earlier. A great admirer of the British, Sayyid Ahmad Khan urged his fellow Moslems to take to Western education. In 1875 he founded what became Aligarh University and the reform movement he led is known as the Aligarh movement. He applied reasoned historical criticism to Islamic theology, exalting the Qur'an and attempting to modernize the existing code along Western lines.

Another reaction to Western penetration moved in the opposite direction. Various fundamentalist reform movements arose which attempted to purify Islam from Western and Hindu "corruptions" and re-establish the orthodox code. The fundamentalists were active among the masses but few intellectuals were influenced by them.

The two outstanding literary figures of the late nineteenth century were Altaf Husayn Hali (d. 1914), biographer, critic, and poet; and Muhammad Shibli Nu'mani (1857–1914), poet, historian, biographer, and founder of modern literary criticism in the vernacular. Both were more or less associated with the Aligarh movement and worked with Sayyid Ahmad Khan to establish Urdu as a language for the dissemination of new ideas. Neither man, however, went as far as Sir Sayyid in adopting Western standards. While Sayyid Ahmad Khan approached Islam from the values of the modern West, they tended to approach Western values and contemporary Moslem society from the viewpoint of early Islam. Hali's major epic poem, *Musaddas* (1886), written at the urging of Sayyid Ahmad Khan, was a moving lament of vanished Islamic glory in which Hali urged Moslems to emulate their past greatness. Shibli worked out a program of liberal reform from within, proving through careful historical research that the early theologians had approved of rational philosophy and engaged in it brilliantly.

Another Moslem leader, Sayyid Amir 'Ali (1849–1928), was also active in the Aligarh movement but partly diverged from it to become a romantic and apologist. His major work, *The Spirit of Islam* (1891), glorifies early Islam and the life of the Prophet but emphasizes the rational content of Islam to show its compatibility with Western ideas. While others argued that Islam did not oppose progress, Amir 'Ali held that the spirit of Islam is progress. He presented an Islam that was already so admirable that it made few demands for reform on its adherents. His followers carried this further and maintained that the best in Western culture itself actually had an Islamic source, the Arab civilization of the Abbassides.

The giant among the Moslem poets and thinkers of the twentieth century was Muhammad Iqbal (1876–1938), who overshadows his predecessors in current esteem. A highly gifted poet writing in Persian and Urdu, he said with eloquence and passion what his fellows were beginning to feel but could not formulate and had a very great influence on Moslem thought. His main contribution was a spirit of dynamic activity. He called not for a revival of the past or an accommodation to the present but for the creation of a new society. For Iqbal the universe was process; life was movement; history was unfinished evolution; action was a virtue in itself. "An infidel before his idol with a wakeful heart," he wrote, "is better than the religious man asleep in the mosque." He rejected various forms of dualist thinking, making Allah immanent rather than transcendent. His work reflects his study of the Persian

Sufi poets, but he rejected the side of Sufism which emphasizes asceticism and contemplation. The ideal, he said, was not self-negation but self-affirmation, not withdrawal from the world but restless, passionate involvement in it and conquest of it. Man was not to submit to Allah's will in the usual Moslem sense but to absorb Allah's will into his own and be the copartner on earth.

Iqbal was greatly influenced by Nietzsche and Bergson and by his studies in England and Germany in 1905-08. His society of the future, however, would not be a copy of the West. From the West he wanted Moslems to adopt scientific learning and the spirit of restless initiative, but all else should be shunned. He was against capitalism because he saw it associated with individual frustration and intense competition between men and nations. He was a vigorous opponent of imperialism, aggressive war, and all forms of exploitation. Because he saw some sham in the democratic institutions of his day he condemned democracy as a system and favored a dictator-savior for society. He called for a union of Western intellect and Eastern love, a society of brotherhood, social service, spiritual warmth, and especially a union of strong personalities. He called for the rise of supermen capable of selflessly guiding the community but had no solution for conflicts between them—the problem of one man's development at another's expense.

Iqbal created an enthusiasm for dynamic righteousness among the Moslems but did not say what right was. He gave a poetic vision of the ideal Moslem society but was vague or contradictory when dealing with the political and economic means of achieving it. His dynamism, furthermore, is evident more in his ideas than in his practice. Although he argued vigorously for the principle of Ijtihad ("individual reinterpretation"), when it came to specific issues he argued for conservatism and was reluctant to innovate. His views were not consistent, but Moslems of many kinds find inspiration in his writings.

Today he is revered as the national poet of Pakistan. In 1930 he gave a speech as president of the Moslem League in which he advocated a Moslem India, with the Punjab, North-West Frontier, Sind, and Baluchistan amalgamated into a single state. Pakistanis now credit him with having been the first prominent Moslem to call for a separate Moslem nation. His calls for a Moslem state, a Moslem revival, and a new kind of society tended to coalesce in the minds of his followers, with Pakistan as the homeland of the new society. His sayings on the importance of the community and his reluctance to advocate controversial reforms within that community encouraged people to compose their differences and concentrate on the winning of Pakistan. His stress on the importance of the leader tended to enhance the position of Jinnah and to encourage unquestioning submission to Jinnah's leadership.

Iqbal is still widely read in West Pakistan, and an Iqbal Academy has been set up for the study of his works. One has the impression that today Iqbal the thinker is much less influential than Iqbal the symbol of Pakistan.

Contemporary Intellectual Movements

Intellectual expression in Pakistan has been concerned primarily with the religious issues surrounding the establishment of an Islamic state. The three groups most active in this respect are: the ulama, who tend to identify the Islamic state with official recognition of their own traditional authority; the liberals and politicians, who identify it with parliamentary democracy through their own interpretation of the doctrine of consensus (*ijma*); and an organization called the Jama'at-i-Islami, which identifies it with a kind of orthodox caliphate.

It has already been noted that the most prominent thinkers of the past century were generally those of a liberal, modernist view. Their main center, Aligarh, is now in India and so are some of their most learned representatives, but many leaders of the Pakistan movement also held modernist views in regard to constitutional matters. However, the adoption of the constitution of 1956 and then the constitution of 1962 did not resolve all the religious controversies. In Pakistan today, the liberals are strong but liberalism is weak and has little mass support. The civil servants and the younger generation of a progressive bent are tending more and more to express their modernist views in secular terms, rather than attempting to evolve a distinctive Islamic liberalism.

Perhaps the most significant orthodox Moslem movement is represented by the Jama'at-i-Islami founded in 1941. Its actual membership of 1,000 men is an elite corps of initiates somewhat analogous to the Jesuits. It has a large body of supporters with ample funds, is well organized, and engages in propaganda and social service, especially among the urban refugees.

The leader of the Jama'at, and virtually its sole spokesman, is Maulana Abul 'Ala Maudoodi (1903), a former journalist who is a skillful and effective writer in Urdu. Maudoodi is largely self-taught, but he is a very learned man. His thought is logical rather than apologetic or romantic; his program is one of fundamentalist reform. Unlike most of the ulama he does not accept the whole corpus of Moslem law with all the adjustments and compromises that have been made over the years but goes directly to the Qur'an, the Sunna, the conventions established under the first four caliphs, and the rulings of the great jurists of early Islam. Prior to partition he opposed the creation of Pakistan, since he rejects the concepts of a geographical or national basis for a Moslem state. He holds that in Islam all rights of legislation and all power to give commands rest not in humans, individually or collectively, but in Allah alone. Society is to be regulated and the government administered by the Qur'an and Sunna with only devout Moslems in the administrative posts of the state. The head of state would be an *amir* ("leader") who would be Allah's vice-regent on earth, as the first four caliphs were in early Islam. In administering the Qur'an and Sunna, questions of interpretation would be settled by the consensus of the amir and a council of learned men. These views have been called fascistic, but Maudoodi would grant certain limited powers to a democratically elected assembly. He lays great stress on the piety and integrity of the amir, who would be a sort of philosopher-king.

Maudoodi was jailed from 1948 until 1950 and then again in connection with the Punjab Disturbances of 1953. After his release his influence increased for a time—especially among the middle-class urban discontents, refugees, and idealistic but frustrated students—but declined sharply following the imposition of martial law in October 1958.

Educated Pakistanis appear to care a good deal about their literature, past and present, and increasing attention is given to developing literature in the regional languages. The government has recently begun subsidizing institutions developing and publishing works in Sindhi, Pushtu, and Bengali. As these efforts are in the early stages, the bulk of the literary production continues to be in the two national languages, Urdu and Bengali. A conspicuous feature of Urdu and Bengali literature, in turn, is the virtual replacement of the prepartition generation of writers by younger men of a different bent. Contemporary Urdu writers in Pakistan tend to specialize in humor or in social messages (the more radical

Urdu writers generally stayed on the Indian side of the border). Humorous essays and short stories are the most popular literary forms, with the best-known humorists being A. S. Bokhari and Shaukat Thanvi.

The novel was almost completely absent as a form of Urdu literature prior to partition. A pioneer effort was made in those years by Faiyaz 'Ali, but it is only in recent years that Urdu novels of significance have emerged, some of the leading novelists in Pakistan at present being women. Among those Urdu writers of the prepartition period who still have influence is the novelist Aziz Ahmad. Hasan Askari has concentrated upon critical essays. Ghulam Abbas, although his output is now small, shows a continued capacity for social satire. Perhaps the most prolific writer is Saadat Hasan Manto, who has concentrated on the theme of the communal riots in a wide variety of stories. Two of the younger writers, A. Hamid and Ashfaque Ahmad, have already attracted attention. The former has a rare gift for lighthearted satire woven into intriguing plots; the latter tends toward romance as found in the everyday life of the peasants.

The most significant development in poetry has been the successful adaptation of the Persian ghazal so that the Urdu poet can use it without discomfort. English as well as Persian poets have great influence and a number of Urdu poets have forsaken the ghazal form in order to experiment with the modern techniques of Western literature.

While Urdu literature suffers from its small audience and publishing difficulties, Bengali literature was adversely affected at partition by the political controversy over the state language issue. Writers who tended to use pure Bengali were accused of being pro-Hindu, and those who tried to use an Urduized Bengali had little success with their readers. This setback has been largely overcome and some of the most interesting literary developments are occurring in Bengal.

The outstanding contemporary Bengali writer and musician is undoubtedly Jasimuddin, who was already famous before partition. He has retained close touch with the village life of East Pakistan and his poems, almost always about the life of the rural people, are usually written in a peasant idiom. For many years now he has been engaged in collecting and recording the traditional ballads of the countryside, many of which have provided inspiration for his own work. His songs are particularly noted for their dramatic quality and their poignant portrayal of the deep loves and sorrows of the villagers.

The leading woman poet of Bengal is Begum Sufia Kamal, whose general theme is love and separation; the leading male poet is probably Farrukh Ahmad, a romantic who strives to awaken a sense of revival among Moslems.

There is a strong tradition among Bengali prose writers to address themselves to social problems, most frequently with a Marxist bias. Moslem writers in East Pakistan since partition, however, have not distinguished themselves as social critics, probably due to known government antipathy under Moslem League rule. Most of the contemporary stories are woven around the theme of love.

A widely popular form of entertainment in Bengal is the *jatra,* or dramatic performance, based on traditional myths and legends. Jatras may be given by amateur groups within a village for some special occasion or by traveling troupes, the performance usually starting in the evening and frequently continuing for eight hours or more. These dramas are characterized by the colorful costumes and backdrops, which are used whenever available. As the audience knows the story by heart, the actors must be careful to represent the heroes properly and references to local events are sometimes woven into the plot.

Dancing is not generally favored among Moslems and in many parts of West Pakistan is not tolerated at all, with possible exceptions made for children. Professional dancers are usually assumed to be associated with prostitution. West Pakistan has a number of folk dances, however, which are performed by men and women separately (mixed dancing is considered immoral), the most famous being the vigorous formal Khattak dance of the North-West Frontier tribesmen. Upper-class girls and women in purdah often entertain themselves with dance dramas and songs, especially in connection with weddings. Dances, largely based on folk styles, are also widely employed in the films.

Films have been very popular in the urban centers of the sub-continent for a number of years. Movie production became an important industry in the early 1930s and by 1946 the annual production of about three hundred films made India the third most important film-producing country in the world. The bulk of the pictures were made in cities now in India; at partition, Pakistan inherited only four studios, all in Lahore, which were manned primarily by non-Moslems. With the departure of the staffs and removal or destruction of much of their equipment, the studios produced no films for more than a year. The government banned the import of Indian films and, as a result, many cinemas also had to close.

By 1949, many Moslem producers, directors, artists, and technicians had moved from Indian film centers to begin building up a Pakistani industry. Their output from 1949 to 1952 was less than a dozen pictures per year. During this period the government rescinded its ban on Indian imports and the lack of Pakistani expansion was largely due to competition from Indian films. The government then reimposed the embargo, with the result that a large number of films were produced in 1954. In 1956 the government approved an agreement made earlier by Indian and Pakistan producers which provides for an annual exchange of up to thirty-four movies between the two countries. The star system, which obliges producers to collect a cast of big names, prevails in Pakistan. As the country has only about two dozen name artists, a top artist may make several pictures simultaneously with the result that production costs soar and quality suffers.

Pakistani films cannot be considered either an "artistic" or an "intellectual" form of expression, but they are an extremely popular form of public entertainment in the urban areas. By Western standards, they are characterized by melodrama, repetition, and excessive length. The subject matter is usually a romantic fable of medieval heroes or the doings of the pseudo-Westernized "fast set" in imitation of Hollywood. The films have been roundly criticized in the press for their lack of any reflection of genuine Pakistani life or culture, but apparently the unreal world depicted by them is what the ordinary moviegoer wants to see. He also expects, and receives, music and dancing in every film. Whatever the story happens to be about, a locally produced movie must be a musical or it will not sell. The films have developed a hybrid, undemanding musical style of their own which is easily recognized. The songs are quite singable and very popular.

Music is widely enjoyed in Pakistan although among some sections of the population it has the same moral stigma as dancing. But, from Amir Khusru on, Moslems have made great contributions to the classical music of the northern plains, though the leading Moslem exponents of this art remained in India at partition. What classical music there is in Pakistan is supported largely by Radio

Pakistan. Film music, a mixture of folk and Western popular styles, is considerably more widespread. Each linguistic region of Pakistan has its own distinctive folk song literature. The variety ranges from the pipe and drum accompaniment of the Khattak dances to the broad, sweeping melodic line and rhythmic subtlety of the Bhatiali boatmen's songs of East Pakistan. The Bengali songs are most appealing to a Western ear. The instruments used in Pakistani music are usually strings, plucked rather than bowed, and percussion, especially the *tabla* or drums, but solo singing remains the most common form of musical expression. While American music stresses harmony and new tunes, Pakistani music is characterized by melodies based on fixed patterns. The scale patterns allow for considerable improvisation and it often happens that performers will compete with one another in a manner reminiscent of an American jazz session.

There are two groups of painters in Pakistan: those basing their work on the Persian and Moghul tradition and those painting in new forms. Among the latter, abstraction, stemming not from the ancient Arabesque but from Western painting, is increasing in popularity, the work characterized more by experimentation than by definite schools or personal styles. Abdur Rahman Chughta, born in 1897, is the leader of the traditionalists and has a distinctive style. His people are those of a romantic past, with large bodies, small heads, and broad areas of drapery; his interest is subjective content and overall, two-dimensional design rather than objective reality. What is a pleasing combination of large luminous color areas of shaded washes, delicate and elegant flowing line, and a mysterious romantic quality in Chughta's work often becomes unrelieved sentimentality in the hands of lesser artists. Of the other traditionalists, Fyzee Rahamin is also worthy of note for his portraits and elaborate murals. Recently he has begun experimenting with modern idioms. Zainul Abedin of East Pakistan is unquestionably the leading experimentalist. He has confined himself almost exclusively to drawings, etchings, and watercolors, but with extraordinary effect. Some of his best work depicts the tragic famine scenes of 1943 in his most characteristic style, a combination of brief heavy lines and effective use of unpainted space. From his university post in Dacca, and as president of the Dacca Art Group, he has done much to encourage young Bengali painters. K. M. Sultan is the leading landscape artist, and the leading woman painter is Zubeida Agha, an abstractionist.

Both contemporary painting and the surviving traditional handicrafts suffer from the lack of patronage in Pakistan. Generally, wealthy Pakistanis still prefer cheap sentimental versions of Eastern art or shoddy imitations of Western products. Apart from a few individuals like Zainul Abedin, interest in encouraging contemporary artists through exhibits and employment comes largely from members of foreign missions resident in Pakistan. Some of the leading Moslem painters remained in India at partition and have received financial encouragement from the Indian government. Until recently the Pakistan government did little to support its contemporary artists, partly because it lacked the resources and partly because of the religious feelings against representational art. However, it has established two funds, one for the award of prizes for individual achievement in the arts and sciences, and the other for grants to bereaved families of artists, journalists, and men of letters. It is also considering the award of annual prizes to the best films in order to stimulate production of better quality pictures.

The government has made efforts since 1947 to publicize the quality and variety of the existing arts, especially through the *Pakistan Quarterly,* which publishes numbers of excellent, well-illustrated articles. It maintains and publicizes the collections in its museums of antiquities, particularly the fine Gandharan sculptures in the Peshawar Museum and the rich collections in the Taxila Museum. Another field for which government grants are given is archaeology, which gets by far the largest amount of money. Aid is given to the Archaeology Department for such undertakings as the preservation of the Moghul buildings in Lahore, work on the Buddhist sites at Maynamati, and to conduct excavations at Kot Diji, a pre-Harappan site in Sind.

Modern architecture displays almost no influence from the great monuments of the Moghul empire, with the exception of the mausoleum of Mahomed 'Ali Jinnah at Karachi which reflects the traditional feature of a square structure crowned by a lofty dome. Contemporary buildings are illustrated in a periodical, *Engineering Forum,* published at Karachi. The bulk of new construction has been at Karachi and includes office buildings, government structures, school and university buildings, hotels, industrial complexes, refugee colonies, and private residences. Most of this work is of reinforced concrete in the so-called "international style." Foreign architects of international renown have been engaged by the government to design the overall plan and some of the major structures

211

for the vast new capital at Islamabad, as well as to design the national assembly complex at Dacca.

Recently the government has increased its efforts to expand markets for the many handicrafts through greater publicity and economic missions. Still in their early stages, these efforts have not got to the point of finding new expression for the traditional crafts to meet the tastes of foreign consumers. In addition to its grants for developing vernacular literature, encouraging artistic production, archaeology, and expanding handicraft markets, the government has subsidized institutes for Islamic research and culture in Karachi, Lahore, and Dacca.

CHAPTER 11

Political Dynamics

A SUCCESSFUL POLITICS OF PROTEST and a familiarity with the administrative and judicial institutions of the British colonial government in India were the chief heritage of the new Pakistan government. The legislative function, by contrast, was only very poorly understood beyond the essentially advisory role the British had permitted to native legislative bodies. The subcontinent had offered few opportunities for experience in the intricacies of government. Nor had there been much leeway for political activity of any other kind.

It was perhaps predictable that the early years of Pakistan would be characterized by the rule of one party—the Moslem League responsible for the creation of the country—and the rise and decline of this party under its founder, Mahomed 'Ali Jinnah, lies at the core of political dynamics in Pakistan. A number of other political parties did arise and their proliferation attested to a political awakening. But their inherent weakness stemmed from the absence of a broad popular base. The politically competent few wielded influence through landownership or official position or administrative ability; the population at large remained overwhelmingly illiterate and uninformed, content with the fact of independence. This situation gave the illusion of a political vacuum and seemed to encourage the adventurous.

By 1957 the new political ferment had reached crisis proportions. In West Pakistan, parties and politicians were attacking each other with increasing violence, to the accompaniment of demonstrations, strikes, and clashes with the police. A similar trend in East Pakistan culminated in a disorder on the floor of the provincial assembly in September 1958 during which the deputy speaker was killed. A month later General Ayub Khan took over as chief martial administrator and promptly banned all political party activity. The next year, as president, Ayub Khan promulgated the Basic Democracies Order, a blueprint for the creation of basic democratic institutions throughout the country, and somewhat later initiated a program of land redistribution in West Pakistan to help the peasants but also to reduce the power of the large landowners. Political parties returned to the scene only in July 1962 following passage of a special bill by the National Assembly.

This was the larger pattern of political activity in the first decade of Pakistan's existence. As we shall now see, the political tension of this period was sustained by a diverse array of personalities and parties all forcefully pursuing their own objectives.

The Moslem League

Moslems first began taking a serious interest in politics during the early years of the twentieth century and in 1906, led by the late Agha Khan, successfully campaigned for the right to elect their own representatives and to have separate electorates for this purpose. That same year the All-India Moslem League was founded in Dacca to promote the interests of the Moslem community though for the next thirty years or more the League, overshadowed by the much more powerful Indian National Congress, was to have relatively little influence.

The Moslem League's rise to power started when Mahomed 'Ali Jinnah resumed the presidency at the League's Bombay session in 1936. Jinnah was then sixty years old and a highly successful lawyer. Born in Karachi of a merchant family, the young Jinnah received his higher education in England, won immediate prominence on his return to Bombay to practice law, and was soon a wealthy man in his own right. His first venture into politics came as a member of the Congress party, followed in 1913 by membership in the Moslem League as well. Three years later Jinnah was elected president of the League for the first time and proved to be an able speaker and parliamentarian. Jinnah combined active participation in innumerable conferences emphasizing Moslem interests with an ardent nationalism and advocacy of Hindu-Moslem cooperation, though in his opinion Gandhi's tactics were irresponsible and divisive. But by 1932 he was practicing law in England, having become disgusted with the "spineless" Moslems and the "shortsighted" Hindus. His return to Bombay four years later came in response to the persistent urging of a group of his colleagues to accept a position of leadership in Moslem politics.

The Moslem League in 1936 was little more than a pressure group acting in the interests of the more prosperous Moslems. It was hardly active in the elections at all—especially in the Moslem-majority provinces where it was content to leave such matters to individual Moslem politicians and their provincial organizations. In 1936, however, Jinnah persuaded the League to participate actively in the 1937 provincial elections, which had been scheduled in accordance with the Government of India Act of 1935. The campaign for election forced middle- and upper-class Moslems to appeal to the millions of less fortunate Moslems, many of whom had turned to the Indian National Congress because of its more effective political activity. The Moslem League succeeded in winning most of the seats which it contested in the 1937 elections, but on an overall basis its showing was not impressive. The Congress formed ministries in seven of the nine provinces—including the overwhelmingly Moslem North-West Frontier province.

The Moslems became united to a considerable extent because of the mistakes made by Congress once in power. The Congress ministries soon demonstrated their insensitivity to Moslem feelings and in many cases a Moslem Leaguer found his position in a Congress cabinet dependent on an agreement to accept the discipline of the Indian National Congress, which was controlled by a relatively small group of Caste Hindus. This the Moslems were naturally reluctant to do. Spurred by the obvious need for greater political leverage, Jinnah conducted an active and successful recruiting campaign to enlarge the membership of the League. Then at a mass meeting in Lahore in 1940 the All-India Moslem League, led by Jinnah, adopted the now-famous Pakistan Resolution advocating a separate homeland for the Moslems of India in the Moslem-majority areas of the subcontinent.

The overwhelming success of the Moslem League dates largely from the adoption of this resolution. Stressing "faith, unity, and discipline" Jinnah devoted himself to attaining the goal of an independent Pakistan. In the 1946 elections the Moslem League made Pakistan an election issue and won all of the 30 Moslem seats in the central legislative assembly of India and 427 out of the 507 Moslem seats in the provincial assemblies. The will of a majority of Moslems had been clearly demonstrated: by 1947 Pakistan was a reality. As the organization that had succeeded in bringing Pakistan into existence against overwhelming odds, the Moslem League enjoyed tremendous prestige. There was, during the first years of Pakistan, no effective opposition. Jinnah served in triple capacity as governor general of the new nation, president of the constituent assembly, and president of the Moslem League. Yet many diverse interests had worked together within the frame work of the Moslem League to attain Pakistan and to ensure its survival during the early period of confusion and emergency. This emergency psychology could not be long maintained.

Jinnah's death in 1948 marked the end of the coalition and the beginning of factionalism. The most influential person in Pakistan in the next few years was Prime Minister Liaquat 'Ali Khan, who had been Jinnah's principal lieutenant. His background followed the familiar pattern: son of an aristocratic Moslem landowning family, Liaquat 'Ali Khan had been educated at the Moslem university at Aligarh, then Oxford, obtaining his law degree in England. His interest in politics grew from his more than twenty years of experience as a provincial and central legislator before partition. Although unable to stem the increasing factionalism within the Moslem League, he was a competent and respected prime minister and after Jinnah's death made that office the dominant one. His assassination in 1951 left no nationally recognized leader to succeed him as the country's political chief. The internal differences within the Moslem League led to defections, struggles for power, and new political parties. This political instability tended to shift the balance of power back to the governor general.

In 1951 most of Pakistan's problems were still unsolved: no constitution had been adopted; the Kashmir, canal waters, and refugee and evacuee property problems continued to contribute to a tense situation between India and Pakistan; and the country's economy still had no sense of direction. Under these circumstances the politicians picked Ghulam Muhammad, a senior civil servant and economist, for the role of prime minister as a replacement for Khwaja Nazimuddin, the devoutly religious Moslem Leaguer and veteran Bengali politician who had succeeded Jinnah as governor general and then followed Liaquat 'Ali Khan as prime minister. Food and economic crises and his failure to deal decisively with the Punjab riots finally resulted in Nazimuddin's dismissal by the governor general in April 1953. He was replaced by another Moslem Leaguer who had been active in Bengal politics prior to partition: Muhammad 'Ali Bogra. The new prime minister—who at the time of his appointment was the ambassador to the United States—was fifteen years younger, more sophisticated, more energetic, and more Westernized than his predecessor.

At the time of Nazimuddin's dismissal as prime minister, there was no indication that he did not have the support of the legislature. The dismissal occurred because the governor general had concluded that his cabinet was "entirely inadequate to grapple with the difficulties facing the country." The new prime minister does not appear to have been a party choice, because he had not been active in internal politics for several years. This in itself was an indication of the decline in power and lack of leadership of the Moslem League. From this period the governor general and later the president emerged as the country's most powerful officers.

Muhammad 'Ali Bogra worked energetically to improve relations with India and inside Pakistan tried to secure the compromises that might facilitate the adoption of the constitution. Nevertheless East Bengal repudiated the leadership of the Moslem League in the March 1954 elections and the following September the constituent assembly adopted legislation intended to ensure that the governor general would act in political matters only with the approval of the cabinet, specifying further that cabinet members, in accordance with the usual practice in parliamentary governments, had to be selected from the membership of the national legislature. The governor general responded by dissolving both the constituent assembly and the incumbent cabinet a month later.

For more than eight months (October 1954–July 1955) the country was governed under emergency clauses by the governor general without benefit of a central legislature. Muhammad 'Ali Bogra headed a cabinet which included Dr. Khan Sahib, a popular former Congress leader in the North-West Frontier province; H. S. Suhrawardy, leader of the Awami League; two former provincial governors; General Ayub Khan, commander-in-chief of the army, as minister of defense; Iskandar Mirza as minister of interior; and a number of Moslem League stalwarts. During this period a vigorous and ultimately successful effort was begun to get the individual units of western Pakistan to join together into "one unit," i.e. the single province of West Pakistan.

In August 1955 Governor General Ghulam Muhammad, seriously ill, was replaced in office by Major General Iskandar Mirza, a retired army officer and experienced administrator. Meanwhile, the Moslem League transferred its support from Muhammad 'Ali

Bogra to Chaudhri Muhammad 'Ali, the able finance minister and former civil servant, who formed a coalition government with the assistance of the United Front (see below). Under this administration the second constituent assembly finally adopted a constitution and Iskandar Mirza became the first president of Pakistan in March 1956.

As indicated in Table 6, the two years following adoption of the constitution were marked by political instability in the central government, with a succession of four prime ministers and as many different coalition cabinets. The Moslem League, which had lost control in East Pakistan in 1954, became a minority party in West Pakistan following the defection of a large number of its members to the new Republican party in 1956. By September of that year the Moslem League found itself excluded from both the central cabinet and the two provincial cabinets—replaced by the Republican party, which for several years maintained control of the West Pakistan government and was a major participant in the central cabinet. For more than a year the Republican party shared power with East Pakistan's Awami League, supporting H. S. Suhrawardy, the Awami League leader, as prime minister. But a resurgence of the "one unit" controversy caused a split between the Awami League and the Republican party and resulted in a new short-lived coalition cabinet headed by the Moslem League. This cabinet fell when the Republican party refused to support the Moslem League's stand in favor of separate electorates.

On December 17, 1957 Pakistan's seventh government in ten years took office, with Republican leader Malik Firuz Khan Noon as prime minister. The sixty-four-year-old Punjabi landlord and politician was supported by a coalition which included—in addition to the Republicans—the National Awami party, the Krishak Sramik party, and the Awami League. Both the National Awami party and the Awami League, however, refused to participate in the cabinet. Although the coalition was supported by at least fifty members of the Assembly's total membership of eighty, the situation so deteriorated that parliamentary government seemed on the verge of collapse. President Iskandar Mirza declared martial law, naming General Muhammad Ayub Khan chief martial law administrator on October 7, 1958, and, on October 24, prime minister. Three days later Ayub secured Mirza's resignation and assumed sole control of the state. On February 14, 1960, he was elected president.

Politics in East Pakistan

The Indian province of Bengal, out of which East Pakistan was carved, was in many ways the most important province of India. It was the first to come under British control in the last half of the eighteenth century and until 1911, Calcutta, the provincial capital, was also the national capital. One of the first modern universities in India was established there in 1857. With more than sixty million persons in 1941, Bengal was the most populated province on the subcontinent and a major commercial and industrial center.

In many districts of Bengal the Moslems constituted a majority of the population and as early as 1937 a Moslem ministry took office. The commerce of the province, however, was clearly dominated by the Hindus: at the time of partition only 358 out of 2,237 large landholders in Bengal were Moslem; the Hindus controlled the large and profitable jute business; the professions and moneylending were mostly Hindu occupations; and Hindus held most of the higher civil service posts. Although some of the Moslem political leaders in Bengal were enthusiastic about the idea of Pakistan, all were extremely reluctant to see the province partitioned. Yet to most Moslems an Islamic state seemed to be the only answer to the long-resented domination by the Hindus, even at the price of the partition of the province. The appeal of Pakistan was for Bengal's Moslems both religious and economic.

At partition Bengal was divided and the Moslem-majority areas became East Bengal, a province of the new state of Pakistan. Large numbers of Hindu business and professional men emigrated from the province as Sir Frederick Bourne, who had been governor of the Central Provinces in undivided India, became the new governor of East Bengal and Khwaja Nazimuddin, Cambridge-educated Moslem League leader and former minister in the Bengal government, head of a Moslem League cabinet. Khwaja Nazimuddin, named governor general of Pakistan in September 1948, was replaced by Nurul Amin, a member of the East Bengal cabinet.

The most important action taken by the Moslem League government in East Pakistan was the adoption of the land reform bill called the East Bengal Estate Acquisition and Tenancy Act of 1950, passage of which was facilitated by the fact that most of those who would lose land through nationalization were Hindus. The act eliminated large numbers of rent receivers and limited the amount of land held by one family to a little more than thirty acres.

219

For six years following the creation of East Pakistan, the same legislative assembly continued in session, with the central government reluctant to schedule new elections. As it became increasingly evident that the creation of Pakistan was in itself no panacea, the province became more and more critical of the central government. The deliberations of the constituent assembly constantly added new sources of irritation; there was an effort to make Urdu—a language few Bengalis know—the national language; almost all of the officers that occupied the higher civil service posts came from outside Bengal; and, on a very practical level, most of the government's development expenditures were going to West Pakistan. With growing conviction the politically sensitive Bengalis argued that the province was not getting a fair deal from the center and should be given broad powers to handle its own problems.

Concerned by the situation H. S. Suhrawardy, who had operated so effectively as a lawyer and politician in undivided Bengal, decided to promote a new party in opposition to the Moslem League. In 1950 about 1,500 delegates met in Lahore to set up the All-Pakistan Awami Muslim League with Suhrawardy as president. By 1953 Suhrawardy's party was actively campaigning throughout the country against high taxes, landlordism, and corruption and in favor of democracy. The attempt to be all things to all people inevitably had repercussions. In West Pakistan the word "Muslim" had been included in the name of the party; in East Pakistan, eager to gain the support of the substantial non-Moslem minority, the party council changed the name to the simpler Awami League. It also advocated joint electorates, which were popular in the eastern province but less so in the west. Generally speaking, the Awami League had little success in West Pakistan and subsequently devoted its major energies to the eastern province.

In 1953 a second party came into existence in East Pakistan in opposition to the Moslem League. This party was built around one strong and well-known personality, Fazlul Huq, who had devoted most of his eighty years to Bengal politics and had been, at various times, president of the All-India Moslem League (1916-21), mayor of Calcutta (1935), chief minister of Bengal (1937-43), lawyer, and editor. As a member of the Bengal cabinet he had been instrumental in the passage of legislation favorable to the tenant farmers. In 1941, while chief minister of East Bengal, he incurred Jinnah's wrath by flouting the rigid party discipline which the national Moslem League leader was determined to impose on the provincial leaders of the party. As a result, he was expelled from the League and in 1943 ceased to be chief minister of Bengal through loss of Moslem League support. By 1946 tempers had cooled and he was readmitted into the Moslem League. Noted for his hospitality and generosity, and for his remarkable capacity to communicate with the peasantry, he was undoubtedly the best known and most popular figure in East Bengal politics.

Although he spent most of his political career as a member of the Moslem League, Fazlul Huq at one time had formed and led the Krishak Praja movement, which later became a party to promote the interests of the Bengali cultivator. More radical than the Moslem League, it had by its success effectively forced the latter to take a stronger stand in matters of land reform. In 1953, he resigned from the Moslem League and reassembled his old political associates to form the Krishak Sramik (Peasants' and Workers') party. The new party advocated provincial autonomy and announced that it would cooperate with other minority parties—the most important being the Nizam-i-Islam, representing the ultrareligious Moslems.

Before the 1954 elections an agreement was reached with the Awami League to join forces in opposing the Moslem League. The resulting coalition of parties, campaigning as the United Front, had a platform calling for the election of a new constituent assembly; recognition of Bengali as an official language on a par with Urdu; autonomy for East Bengal except in matters of defense, currency, and foreign policy; noninterference from the central government in matters related to the export of jute; devaluation of the rupee; and the abolition of certain restrictions on travel between East Pakistan and India. In addition, the Moslem League was criticized for its laggard implementation of the 1950 land reform legislation. Incumbent Prime Minister Muhammad 'Ali Bogra, himself a Bengali, made a speaking tour of East Pakistan, and the Moslem League appeared to be confident of victory despite evidence of a vigorous and effective campaign by many students in behalf of the United Front. Sixteen parties were participating in the election, with 1,285 candidates running for 309 seats. The election drew about 65 per cent of the 19,677,013 electors (both men and women) and turned into a complete rout of the Moslem League. The chief minister of the Moslem League cabinet, Nurul Amin, was defeated by an eighteen-year-old student. Of the 237 Moslem seats, the United Front won 223 and the Moslem League 10.

At the request of Governor Khaliquzzaman, Fazlul Huq formed

a coalition cabinet consisting of seven members of the Krishak Sramik party, five members of the Awami League, and two members of the Nizam-i-Islam. The following two months brought three labor riots in the province involving the jute and paper mills and a match factory, with a total death toll of more than six hundred. The central government later alleged that the riots were inspired by Communists. There had been increasing reports that the Communists, who had won only four seats in the 309-man provincial legislature, had increased their propaganda efforts substantially since the elections and that Hindu members of the Communist party from Calcutta had been providing leadership to the striking workers.

The cabinet might have survived this crisis except that, during the same confusing weeks, Fazlul Huq made a widely publicized statement that he was in favor of making East Bengal an independent state. This was too much for the central government. Fazlul Huq was charged with "treasonable activities" and his entire cabinet dismissed on May 30, 1954 by Governor General Ghulam Muhammad under his emergency powers. A new provincial governor, Major General Iskandar Mirza, was directed to administer the province by "governor's rule" under which the legislature and cabinet ceased functioning, and only the courts continued to operate. Army contingents in East Pakistan were reinforced. Coincidentally, the monsoon floods were unusually severe and, as epidemic conditions threatened, hundreds of American military personnel were flown in to assist with this aspect of the emergency. The new governor, an experienced administrator, acted with dispatch. The authority of the higher civil servants was reaffirmed and they were prodded into making decisions with a minimum of red tape. More than a thousand persons were arrested, though most were released shortly afterward.

The United Front had thus been successful in the elections only to be thwarted by the intervention of the Moslem League-dominated central government. United Front spokesmen constantly reminded the national government leadership that the elections had clearly shown that the constituent assembly—at least as far as East Pakistan was concerned—was no longer representative and should be dissolved. Shortly thereafter, for a variety of reasons, the governor general complied with their request. The central cabinet was revised at the expense of the Moslem League. Suhrawardy became minister of law, Abu Husayn Sarkar joined the cabinet as a representative of the Fazlul Huq group, and Major General Mirza relinquished the governorship of East Pakistan to become the central minister of the interior. Governor's rule was terminated in East Pakistan on June 5, 1955 and parliamentary government restored. There had been considerable speculation as to whether the Awami League or the Krishak Sramik party would emerge as the dominant group within the United Front as the voting had indicated that the two parties were of almost equal strength, but the Krishak Sramik party turned out to be the more successful in getting the support of the Hindu and other minority groups.

Abu Husayn Sarkar left the central ministry to become chief minister of the province. His new cabinet excluded the Awami League, which thereupon announced that it was no longer a part of the United Front. The East Pakistan legislature elected sixteen members of the United Front, twelve members of the Awami League, and a smaller number of Moslem League and independent candidates to the new constituent assembly. Shortly afterward, the Moslem League and the United Front formed a central coalition cabinet with Chaudhri Muhammad 'Ali as prime minister.

On March 5, 1956 Fazlul Huq, who had been labeled a traitor in 1954 for advocating an independent East Pakistan and later made central minister of the interior, was appointed governor of the province. In September the provincial assembly again was permitted to meet, and the Awami League set up a cabinet headed by Ataur Rahman Khan. When Fazlul Huq arbitrarily dismissed Ataur Rahman Khan in 1958, President Mirza countered by reinstating the chief minister and removing Fazlul Huq from the governorship of East Pakistan for unconstitutional action. Interparty friction continued to build until, in September, the Awami League succeeded in having the speaker of the provincial assembly declared insane. The tragic climax came in a resultant outbreak of physical violence on the floor of the assembly during which the deputy speaker was so severely beaten that he died a few days later.

Politics in West Pakistan

Any explanation of politics in West Pakistan must begin well before 1955—the year the several provinces and states in western Pakistan were integrated into "one unit"—for the former Sind, Punjab, and North-West Frontier had never had much in common in political matters and still approach politics in their own characteristic ways.

The North-West Frontier province had a reputation for doing the unexpected. A number of its spokesmen were independent tribal leaders prior to becoming landlords and 60 per cent of the cultivators in the province owned their own land, albeit the average holding was too small to support the cultivator and his family. Until aroused by Jinnah the overwhelmingly Moslem North-West Frontier province had not taken very seriously the threat of Hindu domination in a united and independent India, being much more attracted to the anti-British and social reform slogans of the Indian National Congress. Their principal prepartition leader, Abdul Ghaffar Khan, was an admirer and friend of Gandhi, even to winning the friendly epithet "Frontier Gandhi." Consequently the Red Shirts, as Ghaffar Khan's followers were called, were the last to break with the Congress party despite their dedication as devout Moslems to the goal of a purely Islamic egalitarian society in the Frontier province. Once introduced into the province, however, the concept of an Islamic state had immediate appeal and in July 1947 the province voted to join Pakistan. The Pathans have been more aroused over the Kashmir question than any other group in Pakistan even though Ghaffar Khan had opposed their participation in the fighting in Kashmir.

After partition the central government viewed the independent activities of Ghaffar Khan's Red Shirts with increasing disapproval —largely because the group tacitly endorsed the creation of an independent state, to be known as Pushtunistan, consisting of the Pathan areas on each side of the Afghan-Pakistan border. The pro-Congress cabinet of Dr. Khan Sahib (a brother of Ghaffar Khan) was dismissed shortly after partition and a new one formed by the Moslem Leaguer, Khan Abdul Qayyam, who proved to be an energetic and forceful administrator. In June 1948 Abdul Ghaffar Khan was arrested for inciting against the government and imprisoned for six years. By 1956 he was again active in politics as one of the founders of the National party, which joined forces with a group of dissident Awami Leaguers in East Pakistan to form the National Awami Party. His rearrest followed.

Under pressure from the central government, Sardar Abdur Rashid, the premier and a former police official, agreed in behalf of the North-West Frontier to endorse the integrated province of West Pakistan with the condition that, until 1965, not more than 40 per cent of the members of the new provincial legislature could come from the Punjab. Rashid was later dismissed from his post when he reportedly developed misgivings about the execution of the "one unit" plan, which of course had in 1955 ended the separate existence of the North-West Frontier province.

The province of Sind, which had been carved out of the province of Bombay in 1936, brought to the new province of West Pakistan a reputation for unsavory politics. There were 7,000 landlords in Sind who owned more than 5,000 acres each—a few far more—and 72 per cent of the agricultural laborers were tenant farmers. The leading political figure of Sind for many years was M. A. Kuhro, one of the large landowners. At the age of twenty-three a member of the Bombay Legislative Council, Kuhro worked constantly for a separate province of Sind and was elected to the first legislature of Sind in 1937, joining the Moslem League two years later. After partition he was either a member of the provincial government or a leading member of the opposition.

His career in the first years of independence was marked by repeated charges of venality. When Jinnah ordered his dismissal as premier of Sind in 1948, the charge sheet contained sixty-two specific allegations of maladministration, misconduct, and corruption. Kuhro was sentenced to two years' imprisonment, only to be acquitted on appeal to the chief court of the province. Premier again by early 1951 Kuhro was forced to resign later the same year in the face of further allegations of corruption and maladministration. In 1953 on the recommendation of a special tribunal the governor general disqualified Kuhro from holding any public or representative office for six years, but the act under which his disqualification had been ordered was repealed the next year and Kuhro resumed his post, having meanwhile gained the endorsement of the central authorities by espousing a single province of West Pakistan. In passing, we might note the docile nature of the Sind legislature as illustrated by its voting record on this issue: under Pirzada Abdus Sattar's premiership, 74 members supported his opposition to the plan; under Kuhro the members quickly reversed themselves and endorsed the "one unit" resolution by 100 to 4. In October 1958 Kuhro was again arrested on charges of corruption and again disqualified from holding public office.

In the undivided Punjab province of prepartition India, the Moslems constituted a majority of the population but, lacking unity, were only slightly more powerful politically than the Hindus. The balance of power fell to the Sikhs, a very cohesive group on occasion. Nearly four million of India's six million Sikhs lived in the Punjab and controlled some of the best land in the province.

In 1923 the conservative Moslem landowners joined the landed Hindus in founding the Punjab National Unionist party, which held sway over Punjab politics up to 1942 with the Moslem League, the Congress party, and the militant Sikh wing known as the Akalis reduced virtually to satellites. The sudden death of the highly respected Unionist premier and Moslem League restiveness threatened the delicate balance among the communal groups in the Unionist party and with the elections in the Punjab in 1946 (about 15 per cent of the population was eligible to vote) the Moslem League replaced the Unionist party as the strongest political group in the province. The Moslem League won 75 seats; Congress elected 51 members; and the Sikhs and Unionist party elected 22 and 20 legislators respectively. But neither the Congress party nor the Sikhs would agree to join a cabinet containing members of the Moslem League. When the Unionist party leader, Sir Malek Khizar Hyat Khan Tiwana, formed a government excluding the Moslem League, the League turned to communal agitation in an effort to unseat the premier. The Unionist government, sensing possible violence, jailed some of the Moslem League leaders, including Malik Firuz Khan Noon and Mian Iftikharuddin, but could not halt a widespread civil disobedience campaign, which finally brought the premier's resignation in March 1947. The governor then asked the Moslem League to form a government. The Sikhs, alarmed at the prospect of partition, prepared to resort to civil war. A leader of the Sikh Akalis announced: "The time has come when the sword alone shall rule." Instead, governor's rule was imposed and remained in effect until August 15, 1947.

With partition, a Moslem League government was established in which the landlords played the major role. The Khan of Mamdot, a landlord, became the first chief minister and a retired British officer of the Indian civil service, Sir Francis Mudie, governor. An inexperienced ministry was faced with problems of unprecedented difficulty. For a time over 50,000 refugees were entering Lahore, the provincial capital, every day. Under Mudie's guidance rapid progress was made in resettling these refugees. His zeal also extended to a strict watch over the allocation of land and property, which predictably made enemies of those politicians and civil servants caught profiteering. At the same time Mamdot's political authority was being undermined by Mian Mumtaz M. Daultana, who had been elected president of the Punjab Moslem League by a 198-176 vote after openly opposing Mamdot. The tense situation provoked a strongly worded statement by the governor general who "viewed with growing concern the state of public administration in West Punjab." Observing that the discipline of the services had been "destroyed" and public life "demoralized by corruption," the governor general castigated those who would conduct the administration for the benefit of a few and cited the behavior of the elected representatives as a principal factor in the breakdown of public morality. In January 1949, acting on instructions from the governor general, Mudie dissolved the provincial legislature and established governor's rule—which was to continue until the provincial elections in March 1951. Meanwhile, a judicial inquiry into charges of misconduct partly exonerated Mamdot, but Mudie, who had incurred the hostility of the provincial Moslem League, was subjected to a critical press campaign and resigned soon afterward. His successor as governor of West Punjab was Sardar Abdur Rab Nishtar, a Pathan from the Frontier area and one of the most experienced and popular of the Moslem League politicians.

The 1951 elections to the Punjab legislative assembly were the first direct universal adult suffrage elections ever held in Pakistan. A total of 8,847,911 persons were eligible to vote, including 3,593,339 women and a substantial proportion of refugees and landless peasants. Out of the 197 seats to be filled, some were designated for special groups, e.g. 44 seats for refugees from India and 5 seats exclusively for women. Four parties contesting Moslem League supremacy entered the elections, the most important being the Jinnah Awami Moslem League. This party was an amalgamation of two groups, one led by the previous Moslem League chief minister (the Khan of Mamdot) and the other by Suhrawardy, both of which had broken away from the Moslem League on the grounds that it was no longer following Jinnah's program. A second party, under the leadership of Maulana Abul 'Ala Maudoodi, was a conservative religious organization known as the Jama'at-i-Islami. A third group, the Azad Pakistan party of Mian Iftikharuddin, advocated Pakistan's withdrawal from the British Commonwealth, radical agrarian reforms, and the nationalization of industry. The fourth, the Communist party, also campaigned but did not succeed in electing any candidates.

It was a Moslem League victory. Although League candidates received only about half of the votes cast—with a low 30 per cent

227

of the electorate voting—the Moslem League ended up winning 143 seats to the Jinnah Awami Moslem League's 31 (the Khan of Mamdot and five of the Lahore representatives were reelected) and one each for the other two parties. Of sixteen persons elected as independents, half went over to the Moslem League following the election, as did two of the Jinnah Awami Moslem League's winners. But in a report issued several years after the event the Electoral Reforms Commission referred to this (along with other 1951 provincial elections) as an "absolutely unsatisfactory" election that had "totally failed to achieve a true representation of the people."

Named as the new chief minister, Mian Mumtaz M. Daultana formed the first cabinet since the governor's suspension of parliamentary government two years before. An intelligent, personally ambitious young landlord, Daultana won wide popularity among the refugees for his espousal of moderate land reform legislation. However, there were more urgent matters—increasing anxiety and unrest over Kashmir, religious extremism, food shortages—and his disinclination to make politically unpopular decisions proved to be his undoing. Daultana was finally dismissed by the governor after failing to take necessary preventive measures at the time of the Punjab riots in 1953 despite strong recommendations from his police and civil officers. His successor was Malik Firuz Khan Noon.

Factionalism within the provincial Moslem League—fomented in large part by Daultana—soon threatened Noon's ministry, but the Khan of Mamdot chose this time to bring his fourteen followers in the provincial assembly back into the Moslem League in support of the chief minister. Noon's ministry nevertheless came to an end in 1955 with his dismissal by Governor Gurmani. The new chief minister, Abdul Hamid Khan Dasti, had been a minister in each of the three preceding provincial cabinets. Dasti's premiership lasted only a few short months—until the formation later that same year of the "one unit" of West Pakistan.

The first governor of the new province was M. A. Gurmani, an experienced politician and administrator first elected to public office in 1926 at the age of twenty-one and four years later a member of the Punjab legislative council, who after many years of participation in Punjab politics became the chief minister of Bahawalpur State in 1945. With approximately another five years as a minister in the Pakistan national cabinet, Gurmani was chosen in November 1954 to be governor of the Punjab and by the following April had already been designated as the future governor of

West Pakistan—a post retained until his replacement in 1957 by Akhtar Husayn, a senior civil servant.

Dr. Khan Sahib was selected as the new chief minister of integrated West Pakistan. Born in the North-West Frontier province in 1882, he received his medical training in London, on his return entered the Indian Medical Service, but resigned in 1921 to engage in private practice. His quiet entry into politics in 1930 was followed by ministerial posts in the North-West Frontier in 1937 and again in 1945, but for a time after partition he was out of favor with Pakistan's political leaders because of his long association with the Indian National Congress. Back as a member of the national cabinet in 1954, not affiliated with any particular party at the time, a proved administrator, a popular figure among the Pathans of the Frontier—Khan Sahib had suddenly loomed as the best possible compromise candidate for chief minister.

The problem of representation in the assembly of the new province was settled by having the former provincial legislators each select members of the new assembly from his own district. These indirect elections took place in January 1956 and, not surprisingly, a majority of the "new" members were—whatever their factional allegiance—Moslem Leaguers.

A move to unseat Khan Sahib came in April 1956 from Sardar Bahadur Khan, brother of General Muhammad Ayub Khan, Moslem Leaguer, and last chief minister of the Frontier province, who had maneuvered a party resolution calling for the chief minister's resignation. Khan Sahib calmly dropped his challenger from the cabinet along with two other Moslem Leaguers, Daultana and Kuhro, also noted for their political conniving. Replacing these three were Mamdot, Kazi Fazullah, and Abdur Rashid, former chief ministers of the Punjab, Sind, and the Frontier province respectively. Before the slow-settling political dust had cleared, Khan Sahib had created a new Republican party and won a test of strength by one vote. The provincial Moslem League lost a substantial portion of its membership to the new party and never recovered its previous position; the Republican party retained control of the provincial government and, by 1958, headed the national government as well.

There was one early threat to Republican control of the provincial government when on March 21, 1957 some members publicly joined the opposition. Khan Sahib asked the governor to dissolve the legislature and hold a direct general election. In an advisory opinion the Supreme Court concluded that the governor did not have the power to dissolve the provincial assembly, which had been given a special role by the constitution and could not be terminated without a regular general election. Sardar Abdur Rashid, a member of the Republican party, succeeded Khan Sahib later in 1957 and was, in turn, replaced by another Republican, M. A. Qizilbash, in March 1958. In May 1958 Dr. Khan Sahib was stabbed to death by an assassin.

Other Political Forces

In the first decade of Pakistan's existence politics and political parties were the reflection of personalities—of the leaders in the fight for independence. These individuals followed their own convictions and their own ambitions, sometimes cooperating with, sometimes opposing the government, forming new political parties and alliances as their interest dictated, and, in general, exhibiting less devotion to working for a united nation than to enhancing personal power.

The Communist party of Pakistan, a relatively feeble offshoot of the powerful Communist party of India, made little headway in this period. Four Communists were elected to the provincial assembly of East Pakistan in 1954. The government stated that Calcutta was the base from which propaganda and Communist agents invaded East Pakistan. In the autumn of 1954 a decree was issued banning the Communist party in Pakistan.

The Communist line was reflected by the Azad Pakistan party, founded in West Pakistan in 1950 by Mian Iftikharuddin. In 1954 about half the members of the council of the party resigned, stating that it was controlled by the Communists. However, Iftikharuddin continued to propagate the Communist line and to publicize Communist-front groups in the *Pakistan Times* and *Imroze*. In East Pakistan the Communist line was supported by the Ganatantri Dal (Democratic party), founded in 1953 and moderately active into 1956.

Some of the most important religious figures of Pakistan engaged in political activity designed to impose conservative religious views on the country. In 1952 fourteen religious parties and societies came together to establish the short-lived Majlis-i-Amal, or Council of Action, whose purpose was to brand the Ahmadiyas as heretics and have them declared a non-Moslem community.

Prominent in this council were the Majlis-i-Ahrar-i-Islam, the Jama'at-i-Islami, the Jami'at ul-Ulama-i-Pakistan, the Jami'at ul-Ulama-i-Islam, and the Jami'at-i-Ahl-i-Hadith. Most of them took part in the anti-Ahmadiya riots at Lahore and other towns in March 1953. The court of inquiry established to determine the causes for the disturbances took a long, hard look at the beliefs and motives of these groups and their leaders and commented wryly that "provided you can persuade the masses to believe that something they are asked to do is religiously right or enjoined by religion, you can set them to any course of action regardless of all considerations of discipline, loyalty, decency, morality or civil sense." The report also stressed the great divergencies of views among the religious leaders and encouraged the government to proceed with necessary programs in the certainty that the religious groups lacked the cohesion and ability to arouse effective opposition. Although carefully preserving a conciliatory attitude toward these leaders, particularly with reference to the concept of the Islamic state, the government did take a firmer position in dealing with potential agitation against public order by some of these leaders.

Dynamics of the Peaceful Revolution

General Muhammad Ayub Khan's assumption of control under martial law in October 1958 was termed a peaceful revolution. His first action was to ban the activity of political parties and in successive statements General Ayub made clear his belief that the activities of politicians had brought the nation to the verge of disintegration. A June 1960 speech offered this succinct analysis: "These people had made politics a profession and democracy a toy to fondle with. Their only business was to misguide the people by making fiery speeches and raining empty slogans from time to time and acquire personal power and benefits under cover of patriotism. . . . Their only wish is that the same outmoded system should again return to the country wherein disruption, misguidedness, and selfishness should have their play, enabling them once again to stage the drama of personal aggrandizement at the nation's cost." In September 1961 he remarked: "Politics in our part of the world is still regarded as a means of livelihood, not as an honourable profession, nor service in the cause of the masses. It is still regarded as a means of getting to a position of vantage from where you can exploit the rights of others."

231

General Ayub set as his goal a fundamental change in the bases of political power and in the political dynamics of Pakistan. The Public Offices (Disqualification) Order 1959 and the Elective Bodies (Disqualification) Order 1959 were designed to bar public officeholders and politicians convicted of corrupt practices from standing for election for a period of seven years. Special tribunals heard charges against those accused under the orders: some agreed voluntarily to retire from public life, many others were convicted. In addition, under the second of these orders politicians and others who had been arrested under security regulations were automatically disqualified from elective posts. In January 1959 the government adopted a program of land reform for West Pakistan. As this program was put into effect the long-established system of land tenure was radically changed. Without examining the details of the program at this point, it may be said that one of its chief effects was to strip the large landowners of their power to influence and instruct the peasant farmers at the time of elections.

Ayub himself characterized his purpose shortly after taking control: "Our ultimate aim is to restore democracy, but of a type that people can understand and work." The Basic Democracies Order was promulgated on October 27, 1959 "to provide for the constitution of basic democratic institutions throughout Pakistan." Ayub explained that the numerous reforms instituted by his government had been "designed to prepare the base on which an upward pyramid of a sound political system can be developed."

A new National Assembly was elected on May 28, 1962 by the Basic Democrats and its convocation marked the end of martial law, though President Ayub's continuing concern for political stability was evident in his remarks to the opening session on June 8: "We cannot take one step forward if governments come and go with dishonest alliances and postelection expansions or contractions of political parties to exploit particular occasions. For these reasons, I am personally opposed to the idea of political parties of this nature and a parliamentary executive." Nevertheless in July 1962 the National Assembly passed a Political Parties Bill, which permitted the revival and formation of parties while introducing two significant new safeguards. The formation of parties prejudicial to Islamic ideology or to the stability and integrity of Pakistan was prohibited—clearly ruling out any activity by the Communist party of Pakistan—and individuals disqualified from public office were forbidden to join political associations.

232

Although Ayub did not actively oppose passage of the bill, he may have believed it could lead to a return of political strife. Indeed, its passage was followed by the appearance of active political opposition within the National Assembly and the resurgence of several allegedly discredited old-guard politicians who began addressing public gatherings. The late H. S. Suhrawardy, for example, who had been barred from political office in 1960 and detained for "treasonable activities" from January until August of 1962, was active through most of 1963 advocating the formation of a National Democratic Front, a coalition of opposition elements. One of his major goals, shared by other opponents of the regime, was to force a revision of the constitution that would subordinate the powers of the president to those of the elected bodies of the country.

Political party activity soon assumed forms unwelcome to the government and in May 1963 six opposition leaders, members of the Moslem League, the Awami League, and the Jama'at-i-Islami were arrested. In the same month the government moved to participate in a reorganized Moslem League (Conventionist), with President Ayub Khan first a member and later president of this body, while opposition elements called their offshoot the Moslem League (Councilors). Early in 1964 Maulana Maudoodi and sixteen other members of the executive committee of the Jama'at-i-Islami were arrested and the organization was declared to be illegal. While the future of political parties in Pakistan remained uncertain, it was apparent that groups and individuals, some favoring an Islamic state and some opposed to the presidential system of government, intended to remain hostile to the regime.

CHAPTER 12

Theory and Structure of Government

IN MARCH 1956 Pakistan welcomed the completion of a constitution that had been in the making for more than eight years and, with its adoption, ceased to be a Dominion and became an "Islamic Republic" within the British Commonwealth of Nations. The constitution of 1956 provided for a federal government of the parliamentary type with a single national assembly, in which the two provinces of Pakistan were equally represented, and two provincial assemblies. The president of Pakistan, to be elected by a majority of the votes of the legislators in the combined provincial and national assemblies, was in turn to appoint a prime minister and cabinet "likely to command the confidence of the majority of the members of the National Assembly." This constitution divided the functions of government between the national and provincial governments, but the balance of power rested clearly with the central government.

In October 1958 the constitution of 1956 was abrogated and not until February 1960 was a constitution commission appointed to draft a new document. Its report, submitted in March 1961, was reviewed and discussed, and on March 1, 1962 President Ayub Khan enacted the Constitution of the Republic of Pakistan. Its description of the federal government parallels that of the constitution of 1956 and, as between the national and provincial governments, the balance of power remains with the central government. The powers assigned to the president are much broader and stronger than those allocated in the first constitution. For example, there is no prime minister, and the president presides over a council of ministers which he himself names.

Both these documents incorporated many ideas and institutions first introduced into India by the British, although the second constitution owes more to the example of the American presidential system of government. The administrative and judicial structure through which the British ruled in the nineteenth century was adopted with very little change. The civil service system, for example, was taken over virtually intact after being given constitutional status as the All-Pakistan Service. Representative government, on the other hand, was a comparatively recent development. During the latter part of the last century, the British permitted Indian representation on various councils, but these councils were either purely advisory or else dominated by a government-appointed majority. In 1919 a step forward was taken when the provinces were authorized to set up governments with elected legislatures and ministers responsible to the legislature. The franchise was based on a property qualification which restricted the electorate to less than 3 per cent of the population. The jurisdiction of these representative governments was limited to such departments as education, agriculture, and health. The British administrators carefully retained full control over the instruments of power—including the police, justice, finance, and the armed forces. Even in their limited area of jurisdiction, the representative governments could be overruled by the British-appointed governors if the dictates of imperial administration appeared to require it.

The Government of India Act of 1935 was adopted by the British Parliament after nearly eight years of study, investigation, and debate. It was one of a series of constitutional reforms designed to give Indians a greater part in the government of their country and experience in parliamentary government with a view to India's eventually becoming a self-governing nation. As enacted, the Government of India Act envisioned a Federation of India comprising the provinces of British India and such princely states as might accede—each of the provinces of British India, previously only administrative subdivisions of India, to be given a separate constitutional personality with definite rights, powers, and obligations.

The federal government for which the 1935 act provided was never brought into existence during British rule, but the provisions for it became the basis for the Federal Government of Pakistan. Although the provinces elected their legislatures and were responsible for such functions as health, education, agriculture, police, land revenue, and local government, the 1935 act gave a variety of controls over the provinces to the federal government, and similar controls—particularly emergency controls—appear to have become an established feature of Pakistan's constitutional system.

Apart from its federal feature, and those features designed to preserve the substance of British control over India, the constitutional system envisioned by the 1935 act was similar to that of Great Britain. In the provinces the system of government was of the responsible parliamentary type, in which a representative of the Crown was the constitutional chief executive and a cabinet drawn from, and responsible to, a directly elected legislature was the effective executor and the initiator of legislation. Almost 15 per cent of the population were eligible to vote in the provincial elections.

A feature of the 1935 act which deserves mention is the system of election it provided. The system of separate, or communal, electorates had been a characteristic of British India's constitutional law since the Morley-Minto reforms of 1909 and was maintained and elaborated in the 1935 act. Under this system representatives of a minority community (such as the Moslems) were elected by constituencies composed exclusively of members of the community to be represented. The last elections to the provincial assemblies prior to the granting of independence took place in 1945-46.

In July 1947 the British Parliament enacted the Indian Independence Act, which terminated the control of the British Parliament over Indian affairs, gave statutory recognition to the constituent assemblies of the two dominions, and empowered the governors general to adapt or eliminate those provisions of the Government of India Act of 1935 that were inconsistent with independence. Accordingly, the Pakistan Provisional Constitution Order was promulgated in August 1947, thus providing a legal base for the functioning of the government until Pakistan could adopt its own constitution.

First Constituent Assembly

A constituent assembly for undivided India had been formed in 1946, its members elected by communal groups in the provincial assemblies on the basis of one representative for every one million members of that community in the province. When a separate constituent assembly for Pakistan was created, the members from those provinces that lay entirely within the borders of Pakistan automatically became members of the Pakistan constituent assembly, but in the Punjab and Bengal provinces new elections were held. Legislators representing districts falling within the jurisdiction of Pakistan constituted an electoral college for purposes of selecting the members of the Pakistan constituent assembly from these two partitioned provinces. The initial membership reflected the system of voting by religious communities (see Table 7); the Sikh members never participated and the later influx of Moslem refugees from India resulted in adding ten more Moslem seats in 1950.

Under the terms of the Independence Act of 1947 and the Government of India Act of 1935, the new constituent assembly was empowered to act as the national legislative assembly and, when functioning in this capacity, was to be bound by the 1935 act. The 1947 act also conferred constitution-making powers on the constituent assembly, including the authority to amend the 1935 act, though no provision specifically required the assembly to submit a constitution to the country for ratification.

The constituent assembly first met August 10, 1947 and on the following day unanimously elected the governor general, Mahomed 'Ali Jinnah, its president. Several months later Jinnah observed that the framing of a constitution was a "stupendous task" that might take eighteen months or two years, probably basing this estimate on the fact that no other country had ever taken longer than two years. But this first constituent assembly still had not adopted a constitution after more than seven years of deliberation.

Many factors contributed to this failure. Jinnah, although an able and respected leader, was a sick man overburdened with executive duties, whose death in September 1948 came just over a year after the assembly was convened. Without his unifying influence, internal dissension increased and the power of the Moslem League declined steadily. Although many Moslems agreed that Pakistan should be an Islamic state, there was endless discussion and no agreement as to just what an Islamic state was and what constitutional provisions were required to make it Islamic. Spokesmen for the western portion of Pakistan, which contains more than five times the area of East Pakistan, demanded the right to elect a majority of the representatives to any national legislative body that might be set up; East Pakistan's advocates insisted with equal fervor that the greater population of the east should give it the right to a preponderant voice in national affairs. The proposition that minority religious groups vote as a separate electorate for a specific number of reserved legislative seats proved to be highly controversial. An attempt by the representatives of western Pakistan to have Urdu adopted as the national language aroused the Bengali-speaking population of eastern Pakistan to riots and widespread protests. Moreover, the assembly members were anything but diligent. In their constitution-making role they met, on an average, less than ten days per year during the assembly's first six years of existence. Even at these meetings attendance was poor. Twenty members (out of sixty-nine) also held office in either the central or provincial governments. Some were perhaps reluctant to terminate such an influential and profitable assignment.

In March 1954 elections to the provincial assembly were held in Pakistan's eastern province and almost all of the members affiliated with the Moslem League were defeated. Since most of the members of the constituent assembly were members of the League, this defeat in a province that contained a majority of Pakistan's population opened the constituent assembly to the charge that it was no longer representative. On October 24, 1954 Governor General Ghulam Muhammad declared a state of emergency throughout Pakistan and dissolved the constituent assembly. The constitutional machinery, he announced, had broken down and the constituent assembly had lost the confidence of the people.

But although the first assembly had failed to adopt a constitution, its work contributed greatly to the success of the second assembly. Its Objectives Resolution—with slight alterations—became the preamble to the constitution of 1956. The principle of equal representation or parity between the two wings of Pakistan ultimately found its way into the final document. Likewise its language formula, which recognized Urdu and Bengali as equal state languages and provided that English would continue to be used for official purposes for twenty years, was finally adopted.

Second Constituent Assembly

The dissolution of the first constituent assembly by the governor general touched off a chain reaction of judicial activity which, but for the good judgment of the Federal Court and the patience of the governor general, might have resulted in complete legal chaos in Pakistan.

The president of the first constituent assembly challenged the power of the governor general to dissolve the assembly and requested the provincial court to issue writs of mandamus and quo warranto which, if granted, would have enabled the assembly to reconvene without interference. The court upheld the president of the assembly, but since an important question of law was involved it authorized an immediate appeal to the Federal Court. The latter declared that the provincial court had no authority to issue such writs because the 1954 amendment to the Government of India Act, which ostensibly granted such authority, had never received the assent of the governor general.

Since the assembly for seven years had assumed that the assent of the governor general to "constitutional" legislation was not required, the Federal Court's decision created general consternation. Altogether, forty-four acts of far-reaching legal consequences suddenly were found to be invalid. The implications were staggering. The provincial legislatures had been elected under voided procedures. The governors of three provinces, under emergency conditions, had issued 143 acts, all of which were invalid. The State Bank of Pakistan had been regulating the currency and exercising exchange controls under invalidated legislation. The administration of Karachi had been illegal since 1948. Many persons had been imprisoned, including some convicted of conspiracy, under invalidated laws. It was even discovered that one of the federal judges in the case had been appointed under one of the invalidated acts. (He was promptly reappointed under a different law.)

The governor general reacted by declaring another emergency and, with authority from the Government of India Act of 1935 to assume legislative powers under such conditions, promulgated an ordinance retroactively validating thirty-five of the forty-four invalidated laws and, at the same time, amended certain provisions of the existing Constitution Order to preclude suits against the government in respect of any acts arising out of the emergency proclamation. The Federal Court within a few weeks declared that the governor general had gone beyond his legislative powers and threw out the emergency ordinance.

The governor general's next step, on April 15, 1955, was to summon a new constituent assembly for a meeting in May. He also issued a proclamation assuming to himself, until other provision could be made by the constituent assembly, such powers as were necessary to validate and enforce laws designed to avoid a breakdown in the constitutional and administrative machinery of the country. He then again validated retroactively most of the laws in question. This time, however, he also submitted several questions to the Federal Court and requested advisory opinions. Was the first constituent assembly rightly dissolved? Would the second constituent assembly have the same powers as the first? Under what authority could the laws be validated pending action by the new assembly?

The Federal Court, ruling for the first time on this particular point, upheld the governor general's right to dissolve the first constituent assembly. It inferred that there was a clear assumption in the 1947 act that the assembly would frame a constitution and then dissolve itself; since it had not done so in more than seven years and had assumed the form of a legislature for an indefinite period, the governor general had the right—as the Crown's representative —to dissolve it. An irremovable legislature, said the court, is the very antithesis of democracy. The court also upheld under the common law of necessity the temporary validation of the laws and gave its support to the new constituent assembly, but added that the governor general could only specify the electorate—not nominate individuals.

In the more than six months that passed between the dissolution of the first assembly and the convening of the second the nation had no legislature and all legislative power remained in the hands of the governor general. While the Federal Court was deliberating, politics was in ferment and administrative changes of great importance were being planned. The most radical of these changes pertained to the integration of the many provinces and other units of western Pakistan into the single province of West Pakistan—the so-called "one unit" scheme, which had first been announced to the public by Prime Minister Muhammed 'Ali Bogra on November 22, 1954. Shortly afterward the governor general had set up a council composed of governors, ministers, and high-ranking civil servants to work out the administrative problems involved in the integration. By the following April the governor general was ready to abolish the old units and, since there was still no assembly, sought to bring the "one unit" into being by edict. But, as described above, the Federal Court declared that the governor general had no power to ordain such "constitutional legislation," and the plan to create a province of West Pakistan had to await the creation of a second constituent assembly.

The events which took place between October 1954 and May 1955 clearly established the Federal Court (referred to as the Supreme Court after the adoption of the 1956 constitution) as a major factor in the government of Pakistan. The prestige of representative legislative bodies had declined as it became evident that even after seven years the politicians could not agree on a constitution. At one time or another during this period governor's rule prevailed in three of the four provinces. Ministries were dismissed and their powers assumed by the various governors who administered the provinces as agents of the governor general at the center. Under this arrangement the civil courts continued to function, serving as a check on the administrators. Considering the legal complications and frustrations to which the overburdened administrators were subjected, martial law might have been declared and the civil courts and civil law replaced by courts martial and martial law. Instead, the rulings of the Federal Court were respected and constitutional government prevailed. The decisions of the highest court reflected a high degree of judicial ability and a clear appreciation of the complicated constitutional questions involved.

In the summer of 1955, complying with an order from the governor general, the provincial legislatures elected a new constituent assembly consisting of eighty members evenly divided between the two wings of Pakistan, with eleven seats reserved for non-Moslems (see Table 8). About thirty of the eighty members were lawyers, all but a few having had considerable political experience. Perhaps twenty members could be described as career politicians who typically got their start in local politics. At least eight were influential landlords, mostly from West Pakistan. There were also several former civil servants, businessmen, tribal leaders, journalists, educators, and Moslem religious leaders.

The new assembly met for the first time on July 8, 1955. It subsequently validated most of the legislation about which there had been so much controversy and on September 30 passed the "one unit" bill establishing the province of West Pakistan. Then in quick succession a new constitution was presented to the assembly (January 9, 1956), adopted (February 29), and put into effect (March 23).

The Constitution of 1956

Pakistan's 1956 constitution was a rather lengthy and detailed document of some one hundred pages which in most of its details bore a strong resemblance to the Government of India Act of 1935 and the Indian constitution. The essence of the 1956 constitution was the provision for a federal republic of the parliamentary type with a strong central government and two provincial governments. Following an impressive preamble came thirteen parts entitled: I. The Republic and Its Territories; II. Fundamental Rights; III. Directive Principles of State Policy; IV. The Federation; V. The Provinces; VI. Relations between the Federation and the Provinces; VII. Property, Contracts and Suits; VIII. Elections; IX. The Judiciary; X. The Services of Pakistan; XI. Emergency Provisions; XII. General Provisions; and XIII. Temporary and Transitional Provisions.

Since this constitution was in force for only nineteen months, there is no value in reciting its details. However, it must be pointed out that its adoption failed to resolve a number of issues which were to generate much political heat during the months which followed, namely, the "one unit" controversy, the language issue, implications of an "Islamic state," the electorate question, and provincial autonomy.

As described above, one of the first constitutional questions taken up by the second constituent assembly related to the integration of West Pakistan into a single unit. During the period between the two constituent assemblies, every prominent political figure of the western portion of Pakistan seemed to be endorsing the abolition of the various separate legislatures and administrative organizations in the several provinces and states. By December 14, 1954 the merger had been approved in principle by the legislators or rulers of all the units concerned. But this apparent unanimity had been achieved and maintained under great pressure from the central government. All three provincial chief ministers were at one time or another dismissed by the governor general either for failing to endorse the scheme or for withdrawing endorsements once given. The central government prevailed and the second constituent assembly, as we know, passed the West Pakistan Act of 1955. As adopted, the constitution referred to two provinces: East Pakistan and West Pakistan.

Many individuals had lost position or prestige by the integration of West Pakistan and continued to agitate against it; the advantages claimed for the integration did not materialize as quickly as some had expected; and there was considerable administrative confusion in connection with the change-over. It soon became popular for politicians to vie with one another in denouncing the scheme. In 1957 the West Pakistan assembly voted 170 to 4 (with 121 abstentions) in favor of a resolution recommending that West Pakistan be reconstituted as a subfederation with four or more fully autonomous provinces. At the same time, the major political party of West Pakistan forced the resignation of the prime minister, ostensibly because of his opposition to any change in the provincial arrangements.

The central government tried to stay out of the controversy—partly to avoid involvement in the closely related and explosive issues of parity of representation between East and West Pakistan and the choice of a national language. If West Pakistan were to revert into several provinces, each unit would probably demand that its particular language be officially recognized by the national government, thus further confusing an already complicated problem. Before his death in 1948, Mahomed 'Ali Jinnah had openly favored the adoption of Urdu as the national language of Pakistan but this idea later became anathema to the Bengali-speaking citizens of East Pakistan. The constitution effected a compromise by declaring both Urdu and Bengali to be state languages with the status of English, which meanwhile would continue to be the language of higher education and commonly of administration and legislation, to be determined later.

Another source of controversy was the concept of an "Islamic state." The 1956 constitution labeled Pakistan an "Islamic Republic" and provided that the president must be a Moslem. It prohibited any law "repugnant to the Injunctions of Islam as laid down in the Holy Qur'an and Sunna" and stipulated that the president appoint a commission to report within five years on how best to give legislative effect to the injunctions of Islam. The difficulty of the task will be immediately apparent. To begin with, the verses of the Qur'an, like those of the Bible, can be used to support almost any point of view. Nor is the Sunna by any means a precise body of doctrine; "the Sunna" can mean simply the traditions of the Prophet or these together with the additional traditions of one or more Moslem sects. Ancient injunctions require extensive interpretation before they can be applied to modern conditions. What group or organization should have the authority to make these interpretations? Islam has many sects, none willing to let any other interpret the Qur'an and Sunna for all Moslems.

The question of electorates was closely related to the religious question. Should religious minority groups have their own reserved seats in the legislature or should all citizens constitute a common electorate, without regard to religion? The 1956 constitution left this question to be settled later after consultation with the provincial assemblies. Early in 1957 the National Assembly decided on a common voters' list for all citizens, but the issue would not die. The movement to reconsider the decision for joint electorates was the principal source of political unrest in the latter months of 1957. Generally speaking, East Pakistan favored the joint electorate system and West Pakistan favored separate electorates. The minority religious problem is more critical in East Pakistan, where there are a considerable number of Hindus, and evidently the politicians attached importance to the Hindu vote. Certainly a united East Pakistan would be in a stronger position vis-à-vis West Pakistan than an East Pakistan divided along communal lines. Communal friction tended to increase under the system of separate electorates, in which the minority group was set off as a special community. However, separate electorates could be defended in West Pakistan on the ground that the minorities were so small that they would never be able to elect any candidate under the joint electorate system.

An undercurrent in all these political controversies was the lingering question of provincial autonomy. The 1954 elections in East Pakistan demonstrated a remarkable shift in political opinion. The defeat of the Moslem League, which had previously been the ruling party, was complete. Clearly, the victorious United Front had correctly gauged public opinion with the plank in its political platform advocating complete autonomy for East Pakistan except in matters pertaining to defense, foreign policy, and currency. A related plank emphasized provincial freedom to export jute without interference by the central government. The spokesmen for East Pakistan continually expressed the opinion that both the central and provincial governments had been dominated by West Pakistan and that progress in the East was held back by excessive interference from Karachi.

244

The Constitution of 1962

In March 1956 the second constituent assembly had elected Major General Iskandar Mirza, then governor general, as president of Pakistan. For reasons noted elsewhere, on October 7, 1958 President Mirza declared martial law in an order which also abrogated the constitution, dissolved the central and provincial assemblies, dismissed the central and provincial cabinets, and outlawed political parties. General Muhammad Ayub Khan was appointed Chief Martial Law Administrator and on October 24 Mirza named him prime minister. Three days later General Ayub forced Mirza's resignation and, assuming the office of president, announced that his ultimate aim was to restore democracy in Pakistan.

The first step was taken on October 27, 1959 when President Ayub promulgated the Basic Democracies Order designed "to provide for the constitution of basic democratic institutions throughout Pakistan, and to consolidate and amend certain laws relating to local government." In December 1959 some 80,000 so-called Basic Democrats were chosen in a nationwide election; in February 1960 the Basic Democrats elected Ayub as president for a term of five years.

Immediately thereafter the president appointed a constitution commission which was to submit proposals for establishing a democracy based upon Islamic principles of justice, equality, and tolerance—a democracy that by providing a firm and stable system of government would also strengthen national unity. The constitution commission study, submitted in March 1961, was considered by several committees and reviewed in detail by Ayub Khan, who made very clear his preference for the presidential form of government as operated in the United States over the British parliamentary system. Finally, after lengthy deliberation, a new document was drafted and on March 1, 1962 Ayub Khan enacted the Constitution of the Republic of Pakistan. The major divisions were as follows:

Part I. The Republic of Pakistan

Part II. Principles of Law-Making and of Policy

The Principles of Law-Making

1. Islam [No law should be repugnant to Islam.]
2. Equality of Citizens

3. Freedom of Expression
4. Freedom of Association
5. Freedom of Movement and Right to Acquire Property
6. Freedom to Follow Vocation
7. Freedom of Religion
8. Safeguards in Relation to Arrest and Detention
9. Protection against Retrospective Punishment
10. Regulation of Compulsory Acquisition of Property
11. Protection against Forced Labour
12. Public Educational Institutions
13. Access to Public Places
14. Protection of Languages, Scripts and Cultures
15. Protection against Slavery
16. Practice of Untouchability Forbidden

The Principles of Policy

1. Islamic Way of Life
2. National Solidarity
3. Fair Treatment to Minorities
4. Promotion of Interests of Backward Peoples
5. Advancement of Under-privileged Castes
6. Opportunities to Participate in National Life
7. Education
8. Humane Conditions of Work
9. Well-being of the People
10. Opportunity to Gain Adequate Livelihood
11. Social Security
12. Provision of Basic Necessities
13. Administrative Offices to be Provided for Public Convenience
14. Entry into Service of Pakistan Not to be Denied on Grounds of Race, etc.
15. Reduction in Disparity of Remuneration for Public Services
16. Parity between the Provinces in the Central Government
17. Service in the Defence Services
18. Elimination of Riba [Usury]
19. Prostitution, Gambling and Drug-taking to be Discouraged
20. Consumption of Alcohol to be Discouraged
21. Strengthening Bonds with the Muslim World, and Promoting International Peace

Part III. The Centre

Part IV. The Provinces

Part V. Provisions Applicable Generally to the Centre and the Provinces

Part VI. Relations between the Centre and the Provinces

Part VII. Elections

Part VIII. The Services of Pakistan

Part IX. The Comptroller and the Auditor-General

Part X. Islamic Institutions

Part XI. Amendment of the Constitution

Part XII. Miscellaneous

The Schedules

First Schedule: Oaths of Office

Second Schedule: Remuneration and Terms and Conditions of Judges

Third Schedule: Matters with Respect to Which the Central Legislature Has Exclusive Powers to Make Laws

Unlike the first constitution, the 1962 constitution does not define the state as an "Islamic republic," but the preamble and the section (Articles 1 through 8) dealing with the principles of law-making and policy—including the statement that no law may be repugnant to Islam—closely echo the corresponding parts of the earlier version. The balance of the document (Articles 9 through 250) is quite different, particularly in regard to the theoretical structure of the new government.

The 1962 constitution states that Pakistan has two capitals: Islamabad, seat of the central government, and Dacca, principal seat of the National Assembly. While construction continues at the site of the new city of Islamabad—at an estimated cost of 900 million rupees—the central government is officially located at Rawalpindi, just to the south. In practice, the offices of the ministries and other organs of the central government are still at Karachi, the former federal capital, as are the embassies of the foreign nations.

According to the constitution, the executive authority of the republic is invested in the president, who may exercise this authority either directly or through subordinate officers. As the Central Legislature consists of the National Assembly and the president, a close link between the legislative and executive branches of the government is assured. The relation of the executive to the judiciary has been established by empowering the president to name the judges of the Supreme Court, and the president's position vis-à-vis the provinces through his power to name, give direction to, and dismiss the provincial governors. A relationship between the executive and the duty of the state to promote Islamic principles appears in the right of the president to name the members of the Advisory Council on Islamic Ideology.

The president of Pakistan must be a Moslem, must have attained the age of thirty-five, and must be qualified to be elected a member of the National Assembly. He is elected by the votes of the members of the Electoral College of Pakistan, with this body currently consisting of the Basic Democrats. His term of office is five years. The president is the supreme commander of the defense forces, with full authority to grant commissions and to name service commanders. He has the power to grant pardons and reprieves and to remit or suspend any sentence passed by any court. The votes of at least three-quarters of the total number of the members of the National Assembly are required for impeachment of a president, and a similar vote is required for his removal from office on the grounds of physical or mental incapacity. If the office of president is vacant or if for any reason he is unable to discharge the duties of his office the speaker of the National Assembly shall act as president. The president determines the number of divisions of the central government, appoints the members of the president's council of ministers from among individuals who are not members of the National Assembly, and may name parliamentary secretaries to the divisions, i.e. ministries, of the central government from among the members of the National Assembly.

The president calls the National Assembly into session and may send messages to it or appear before it in person. He submits the annual budget statement to the National Assembly, and no bill may be introduced in the National Assembly which would involve expenditure of central government funds except on his recommendation. The president may also dissolve the National Assembly, but following such action a national election must be held to elect a president and a new National Assembly. When the National Assembly is not in session or stands dissolved, the president may promulgate ordinances which have the same force as bills passed by the National Assembly. At a later date such ordinances must be laid before a session of the National Assembly. If the president is satisfied that a grave emergency exists—if, for example, Pakistan is threatened by war or external aggression or if the security or economic life of the country is threatened by internal disturbances beyond the power of a provincial government to control—he may issue a proclamation of emergency and under such a proclamation promulgate ordinances necessary to meet the emergency, regardless of whether or not the National Assembly is in session.

Clearly, the president of Pakistan has very broad and extensive powers. Many were included in the 1956 constitution; others reflect the personal convictions and desires of Ayub Khan. In an official publication entitled *The Constitution: A Study,* the point is made that if the president is to function effectively as the chief administrator of the nation he must have the authority to determine the main lines of administrative policy, to coordinate the activities for which he is responsible, to appoint and remove the personnel of the administrative agencies, to control finances and lay down financial policy, and to give the lead in matters of legislation. These requirements have all been met in the 1962 constitution.

The National Assembly comprises 156 members, half from East Pakistan and half from West Pakistan, elected by the Basic Democrats. Three seats in each province are reserved for women, who are also eligible for election to any other of the seats. Unless dissolved sooner, a National Assembly continues for a term of five years. The Central Legislature, composed of the National Assembly and the president, has exclusive powers to make laws required by the national interests of Pakistan in respect to the security of the country, including its economic and financial stability, and to enact bills relating to planning and coordination and to the achievement of uniformity in respect of any matter in different parts of the country. More specifically, the Third Schedule of the constitution details many matters with respect to which the Central Legislature has exclusive powers to make laws. Bills passed by the National Assembly are presented to the president for his assent. If he withholds assent to a bill, and the bill is again passed by the votes of two-thirds of the body, it is returned to the president. If he refuses assent to a bill presented a second time, the conflict must be referred to a referendum by the members of the Electoral College.

249

East Pakistan and West Pakistan have provincial legislatures, each consisting of the governor of the province and a provincial assembly of 155 members, with three seats reserved exclusively for women. As in the National Assembly, members are elected by the Basic Democrats. Unless it is dissolved sooner, a provincial assembly continues for a term of five years. The relationship of the governor to the provincial assembly and his powers in this respect parallels that of the president to the National Assembly. In a similar manner, the governor names his council of ministers and the parliamentary secretaries.

The judicial branch of the government is headed by the Supreme Court made up of judges, appointed by the president, who serve until they reach the retirement age of sixty-five. This court has exclusive original jurisdiction in any dispute between the central government and a provincial government and between the provincial governments; it has appellate jurisdiction to hear appeals from the judgments of a High Court; and it has advisory jurisdiction with regard to questions of law which are referred to it by the president. Each province has its own High Court, composed of judges who are appointed by the president and who serve until they attain the retirement age of sixty years. The jurisdiction of these High Courts is that conferred by the constitution and may be extended by law: it includes initial jurisdiction.

In addition to the Supreme Court and the High Courts, there are such other courts as were previously established by law: they are not described in the constitution. Pakistan inherited from British India a strong tradition of the independence of the judiciary, and this tradition has been recognized and reaffirmed by the constitution. For example, a judge of any court cannot be removed from office except through a special process in which his conduct on the bench is examined by a Supreme Judicial Council comprising the judges of the Supreme Court and the chief justice of each High Court.

According to the constitution the Advisory Council on Islamic Ideology consists of between five and twelve members appointed by the president with the purpose of making recommendations as to means of encouraging the Moslems of Pakistan to order their lives in all respects in accordance with the principles and concepts of Islam, and of advising the central legislature and the provincial legislatures in cases where proposed laws may not be in accordance with the basic principles of lawmaking.

According to the constitution, elections are supervised by election commissions, headed by a chief election commissioner appointed by the president. An election commission is brought into being for the purposes of each election of a president, each general election for members of the National Assembly, and each referendum. The electoral rolls may include any citizen who is not less than twenty-one years of age and who is a resident of the electoral unit wherein his or her name is enrolled. (Thus, there is a joint electorate for the entire country.)

The electors for all electoral units in both provinces (not less than 40,000 units in each province) together constitute the Electoral College. This college is defined as consisting of the Basic Democrats and such other persons as are chosen in such a manner as the chief election commissioner may direct. The Electoral College elects the president by the votes of its 80,000 or more members.

The chief election commissioner arranges the 40,000 or so members of the Electoral College of each province into 155 groups in such a way that each group contains the constituents for one seat in the provincial assembly. In similar fashion the members are arranged into seventy-five groups for each province, each of these groups made up of the constituents for one of the 150 seats in the National Assembly. In both cases the constituents elect from among themselves the persons who are to fill seats in the National Assembly and in the provincial assemblies.

The constitution sets forth the terms and conditions of employment of persons in the service of Pakistan who are members of the All-Pakistan Service, of any of the defense services, and of the civil services of the central and provincial governments. Appointments to these posts are made by the president or his representatives, except that the governors name members for provincial civil posts. Examinations for and supervision of service personnel is conducted by a central public service commission and provincial public service commissions. Certain safeguards are provided against arbitrary dismissal and other actions unfavorable to the interests of the personnel.

The constitution provides for its amendment. A bill to amend the constitution must be passed by at least two-thirds of the members of the National Assembly prior to its presentation to the president for his assent. Should he withhold assent and should the bill be again passed by not less than three-quarters of the members of the National Assembly, it is again presented to the president. The

251

president may then assent or he may choose to refer the conflict to a referendum of the votes of the members of the Electoral College. Approval of the bill by a majority of the Electoral College is to be regarded as carrying the president's assent, and the bill becomes an amendment to the constitution.

Earlier in this chapter it was pointed out that certain issues remained unsolved or unsettled after the adoption of the 1956 constitution. These included the "one unit" controversy, the language issue, the implications of an Islamic state, the question of joint versus separate electorates, and the issue of provincial autonomy. Only that concerning the electorate was resolved in the 1962 constitution, but there has been comparatively little debate or discussion of them in the National Assembly or the provincial legislatures. With reference to the "one unit" controversy, the constitution states that a bill to amend the constitution that would have the effect of altering the limits of a province shall not be passed by the National Assembly unless it has been approved by the votes of not less than two-thirds of the members of the assembly of the province. As concerns the language issue, the constitution states that the national languages of Pakistan are Bengali and Urdu. As noted earlier, the constitution provides for an Advisory Council on Islamic Ideology, but the functions of this body are not such as to permit it to define the features of an Islamic state. With regard to earlier demands for provincial autonomy, the 1962 constitution yields no more ground to these demands than did the 1956 constitution.

Reforms of Ayub Khan

After Ayub Khan assumed the office of president in October 1958, he set to work to establish the reasons for the failure of parliamentary democracy in Pakistan and to determine a new course for the country's development. On the one hand, he was concerned with making reforms and fostering innovations that would overcome existing obstacles to orderly development. On the other hand, he sought a way to institute a workable type of democracy.

With reference to the first of these major objectives, Ayub Khan took advantage of the powers he possessed as chief martial law administrator to overhaul and reorient the political, social, and economic institutions of Pakistan. A series of martial law regulations covered subjects such as black market operations, smuggling, tax collection, and tax arrears. In addition, a series of ordinances dealing with public and private corruption, dishonesty, and activities against the interests of the state were promulgated. The Public Conduct (Scrutiny) Ordinance and Rules empowered special committees to screen the records of all civil servants in a search for evidence of corruption and incompetence. As a result, nearly three thousand individuals were either dismissed from service, retired, or reduced in rank. The Public Offices Disqualification Order and the Elective Bodies (Disqualification) Order were used to disqualify political leaders and politicians from standing for elective offices for a period of seven years if clear evidence of corruption had been presented against them or if they had been arrested under existing security laws. Other ordinances were directed against the activity of Communists and Communist fronts and enabled the government to acquire the press assets of these groups and to eliminate such individuals from public life. The imposition of these ordinances served the dual purpose of removing from the political arena both subversive and reactionary elements and of enabling Ayub Khan to proceed with his plans free from hostile criticism.

Ayub Khan appointed a number of commissions staffed by specialists to examine basic problems of the country. Separate commissions investigated such subjects as land reforms, law reforms, press reforms, education, food and agriculture, medical reforms, and social evils eradication. The lengthy reports of these commissions were promptly published and then considered by the president and his council of ministers. In nearly every case the reports were approved by the president and their recommendations drafted as orders and ordinances, which were then promulgated under martial law authority. As Ayub Khan pointed out, through the use of this method it was possible to implement fundamental and necessary reforms without encountering the opposition and delays incidental to the presentation of reform bills to the central and provincial assemblies. Also, he indicated his belief that no successor regime would be able to turn the clock back by nullifying these reforms.

Basic Democracies

In an article for *Foreign Affairs* in July 1960, Ayub Khan had announced that his ultimate aim was to restore democracy of a type that people can understand and make work. Before long he came to the conclusion that there were four prerequisites of a successful democratic system in a country like Pakistan: it should be simple to understand, easy to work, and cheap to sustain; it should put to the voter only such questions as he can answer in the light of his own personal knowledge and understand without external prompting; it should ensure the effective participation of all citizens in the affairs of the country up to the level of their mental horizon and intellectual caliber; and it should be able to produce reasonably strong and stable government.

President Ayub Khan drew up his version of such a democratic system and presented it to experienced legal associates for drafting in a definitive form. On October 27, 1959 he promulgated the Basic Democracies Order, which was "to provide for the constitution of basic democratic institutions throughout Pakistan, and to consolidate and amend certain laws relating to local government." In pertinent statements he indicated that all the changes and reforms that had been introduced or contemplated in the agrarian, educational, local, and economic spheres were designed to prepare the base on which an upward pyramid of a sound political system could be developed. He pointed out that this type of democracy would go up from below, not be imposed upon the people from above, and that the people would choose from among their own neighbors the persons they wanted to elect.

The structure of the Basic Democracies (see the plate, A Structural Chart of Basic Democracies) has four tiers: (1) union councils in rural areas and town committees or union committees in urban areas; (2) *thana* councils in East Pakistan and *tehsil* councils in West Pakistan; (3) district councils; and (4) division councils. At the lower tier there are about 8,000 union councils, town committees, and union committees. Each represents a population area averaging ten thousand people, who elect some ten members of the body—one for each constituency in the area. In addition to the elected members there are appointed members. The typical council or committee has two-thirds elected to one-third appointed members. The 80,000 or so members of the bodies of this tier constitute the Electoral College of Pakistan. Forming the basis of the second tier are the chairmen of all the union councils, town committees, and union committees, who automatically become members of the thana councils or the tehsil councils and who comprise 50 per cent of the total membership; the balance of these councils is made up of 25 per cent appointed members and 25 per cent local government officials. On the third tier the chairmen of

A STRUCTURAL CHART OF BASIC DEMOCRACIES

DIVISIONAL COUNCILS (15)

CHAIRMAN: COMMISSIONER (EX OFFICIO)

This council consists of chairmen of all district councils in the division and representatives of nation-building departments together with an equal number of nonofficial members. Of the latter, at least one-half are appointed from among chairmen of union councils and union/town committees.

DISTRICT COUNCILS (76)

CHAIRMAN: COLLECTOR (EX OFFICIO)

This council is composed of chairmen of all tehsil/thana councils in the district and representatives of nation-building departments. In addition, there is an equal number of nonofficial members, of whom at least one-half are drawn from among chairmen of union councils and union/town committees.

TEHSIL/THANA COUNCILS (599)

CHAIRMAN: TEHSIL/SUBDIVISIONAL OFFICER (EX OFFICIO)

This council includes chairmen of all union councils and town committees in the tehsil/thana plus an equal number of representatives of nation-building departments and appointed nonofficial members.

UNION COUNCILS AND UNION/TOWN COMMITTEES (8,216)

CHAIRMAN: ELECTED BY THE COUNCIL/COMMITTEE FROM AMONG ITS MEMBERS

This body consists of representatives of the people elected on the basis of adult franchise and nonofficial appointed members, numbering not more than one-half of the elected members, each of whom represents between 800 and 1,000 persons.

the thana councils and the tehsil councils become members (25 per cent) of the district councils, an additional 25 per cent are appointed members, and 50 per cent are government officials active at the district level. On the fourth tier—the divisional councils—the relative percentage of chairmen of councils, appointed members, and official members corresponds to that of the district councils. As originally promulgated, the apex of the structure of the Basic Democracies was to consist of provincial development councils, with a membership similar in general composition to that of the district and divisional councils. However, the functions of these councils were later transferred to the provincial assemblies.

The structure of the Basic Democracies is intended to display an integrated concept of relationships: direct, personal contact between tiers; appointed members who can lend their special experience to the less experienced; government officials in a position to respond to reasonable suggestions and proposals; and the encouragement of initiative at the lower levels, along with reviews and controls emanating from the upper tiers.

The functions of the bodies comprising the various tiers are clearly defined in the lengthy Basic Democracies Order. The union councils, for example, are to carry out agricultural, industrial, and community development projects; to establish cooperative societies; to plan and construct community projects such as roads, wells, irrigation facilities, schools, and clinics; and to enact local regulations relating to public health, sanitation, building construction, and the conduct of businesses and occupations. Funds are derived from taxes, rates, tolls, and fees imposed by the union councils as well as from grants made by the provincial and central governments.

President Ayub Khan, in a typical speech on the virtues and objectives of the Basic Democracies, explained:

> The most important aspect . . . is that for the first time an attempt has been made to build up a structurally sound political system to connect villages with the capital of the province. . . . The new system also opens up new channels of communication between the governors and the governed and introduces an element of stability in the government, which had so far suffered from the weaknesses of the monolithic type of government.

On another occasion he remarked:

> All nation building departments of the government, such as agriculture, health, cooperatives, animal husbandry, etc., with whom our

people have to come in daily contact have been represented on the upper-tier councils. This close association of the people with their government will result in a twofold benefit. On the one hand, it will make available in local communities the technical and managerial skills of government and other public agencies for the more skillful management of their affairs, while, on the other, the work of the administrator will be subjected to public scrutiny and discussion leading to greater responsiveness of the departmental activity to the real needs and wishes of the local people.

The Basic Democracies came into operation early in 1959 and for the first two years the central and provincial governments provided all the funds required for supervisory staff, training seminars, and development projects, but thereafter the councils began to employ their taxing authority to make their own substantial contributions to the program. In another aspect of the developing program, teams of sociologists visited many areas to study the impact of the scheme and its program and to query people as to their understanding of the purpose and values of the councils as well as their attitude toward actual programs. One objective was to ascertain whether the people considered local officials more responsive to local needs. These studies continue and may in time lead to certain changes in the functioning of the structure. The first tentative conclusion seems to be that the masses still lack understanding of the concept but that the elected members of the union councils are concerned with their responsibilities and include many natural leaders.

In another chapter mention is made of the role of the Basic Democracies in the fields of agriculture, community development, and social welfare. Here interest is in the Basic Democracies as a political institution—as a part of the structure of government—beyond its function as the Electoral College. Some foreign observers have expressed doubt that the concept and structure of the Basic Democracies was, in fact, the personal creation of President Ayub Khan, and have looked elsewhere for possible sources of inspiration. In Pakistan they are informed that the tiered structure of the Basic Democracies resembles one existing in Bengal prior to partition, and the point is made that the Basic Democracies Order repealed fifteen acts concerned with local self-government, village councils, and local tax rates, some of which dated back to 1856. Near the end of the nineteenth century the British administration of Bengal enacted legislation providing for the grouping of a number of villages into a "union," with each group supervised by a five-member union committee, which was empowered to hire police and pay them from locally assessed taxes. Later the union committees were renamed "union boards" and a second tier (local boards) and a third tier (district boards) were established. Two-thirds of the members of these boards were elected and one-third appointed by officials of the government. The peak of this activity came in the 1930s when the district boards gave active financial support to the union boards, but in the years of agitation for a Moslem state these boards almost ceased to function.

Looking outside of Pakistan, observers have remarked upon the general similarity of the structure to that of democratic centralism as practiced in the so-called "people's democracies." Comparisons have also been made with the structure of the National Union, brought into being in Egypt by President Nasser some years earlier. The National Union displayed the same pyramidal structure, the same division into tiers, and the similar aim of drawing the mass of people into cooperation for their mutual interests. However, the National Union served additional purposes: its tightly-knit structure served as a channel for conveying the socialistic ideology of the regime and was intended to be the supreme political corps of the regime, more powerful than the administrative structure of the regime. The Basic Democracies are not intended to convey a unified ideology, nor are its members conceived as members of a political party. It is probable that President Ayub Khan believed that the method of elections would work to eliminate the discredited politicians from office and militate against the re-establishment of the political parties they had headed. However, in the summer of 1962 the National Assembly passed a bill providing for the formation of political parties and a number of these politicians resumed their activity.

The Structure of the Central Government

The administrative structure of the central government consists of the president's secretariat, which comprises the council of ministers and five divisions. The council of ministers—each of whom may hold several portfolios—directs the following ministries:

Commerce	Fuel, Power, and Natural Resources
Communications	Health
Defence	Home and Kashmir Affairs
Education and Information	Industries
External Affairs	Labour and Social Welfare
Finance	Law and Parliamentary Affairs
Food and Agriculture	Rehabilitation and Works

In addition, the president may name ministers of state to assigned tasks, a distinction here being that ministers of state do not have the right of appearing before the National Assembly to explain the policies and actions of the government as do the holders of regular portfolios. Ministers may be selected for their regional influence or personal popularity and are not always specialists in their assigned fields. Further, they may not remain very long in the same post. Ministers are primarily concerned with political and major policy decisions.

To assist them in formulating specific programs, and in coordinating, controlling, and implementing these programs, there is a nonpolitical civil servant who, in most ministries, has the title "secretary to government." He is assisted, in turn, by a hierarchy of joint secretaries (in the larger ministries), deputy secretaries, and under or assistant secretaries. These officers supervise a considerable number of office personnel—called superintendents, assistants, upper division clerks, and lower division clerks—whose time is spent mostly on the "files." They start files, make notes and drafts, trace and summarize precedents and previous references, locate the pertinent statutes, and recommend the action to be taken. If his superiors are preoccupied with other matters, the casual note of an ill-informed clerk may determine an important case, but more commonly the clerk's notes are reviewed and initialed by one echelon after another until, months later, action is forthcoming. The files accumulate in deep piles on countless desks, where they may remain for long periods gathering dust, disturbed occasionally by some clerk in search of a special case in which a superior officer has shown an unexpected interest.

The five "divisions" of the president's secretariat are named Cabinet, Establishment, Planning, Economic Affairs, and States and Frontier Regions. Most influential is the Cabinet Division (or Secretariat) which keeps the cabinet's minutes and records, provides staff for ministers, acts as a communication and coordination agency between the cabinet and the ministries, and is the president's personal department. Second most important is the Establishment Division, which is responsible, in association with the Central Public Service Commission, for all matters concerning the higher civil service and includes the Organization and Methods Unit, which studies and attempts to improve the structure and procedures of government. The Planning Division is in close touch with the National Economic Council, a body whose duties are specified in the constitution, and with the Planning Commission, a government organization which drafts and supervises the execution of the five-year plans. The States and Frontier Regions Division is concerned with those areas of both provinces which have not as yet been fully integrated into the systems of provincial government.

The National Assembly meets alternately at Rawalpindi and Dacca. Its legislative procedure is patterned after that of the British House of Commons. The National Assembly elects its own speaker and deputy speaker and frames its own rules of procedure. Committees are used to expedite the work of the Assembly and to study and present reports on particular bills. Most bills originate in the cabinet. The majority of the speeches are made in English, but Urdu and Bengali are also spoken. The meetings have a tendency to become disorderly, and at such times the rulings of the speaker are challenged continually. There is a question hour in the Assembly during which members may ask oral and written questions of the ministers—much like the British practice.

The Structure of the Provincial Governments

The structure of each of the provincial governments is similar to the central government: a governor, council of ministers, unicameral assembly, secretariat, various departments, and a public service commission. The governor's powers and duties with regard to the provincial assembly are almost identical to those for the president and National Assembly. Similarly, the size and procedures of the provincial assembly are virtually the same as those of its counterpart at the central level. The activities of the two levels of government are, of course, quite different. The provincial governments have jurisdiction over such essentially internal matters as the maintenance of public order, agriculture and land revenue, local government, education, water resources, public health, roads and railways, welfare, and the generation of power.

The governor is appointed and may be dismissed by the president. As the executive authority of the province, administrative action is taken and government orders are issued in his name. Like the president's, his term of office is five years and he cannot serve as a member of either the national or provincial assemblies. The governor, at his discretion, appoints his council of ministers. In general, the number and names of the ministries are similar to those of the central government.

The permanent head of the administration in both provinces is the "chief secretary," who is responsible for general administration and the proper functioning of the secretariat and who also handles many civil service matters, keeps cabinet minutes, and issues orders in behalf of the cabinet. Much of his authority is derived from his responsibility for exercising administrative supervision over the division commissioners and district officers in the province. The chief secretary is usually head of the Home Department, which is responsible for law and order.

Each province is subdivided, for administrative purposes, into divisions which are, in turn, made up of districts. A typical district would contain about 4,000 square miles and a population of one to two million persons. Districts in East Pakistan have a bigger population, and one of them—Mymensingh—has more than six million inhabitants. In West Pakistan there are 51 districts (including political agencies) grouped into 12 divisions. In East Pakistan there are 17 districts and 4 divisions (see the plates, Territorial Administrative Structure of Pakistan and Pakistan Administrative Divisions and Districts).

The division, headed by a commissioner, is an administrative echelon which has increased in importance since West Pakistan has been made a single province. Provincial departments maintain regional offices at division headquarters which are coordinated by the commissioner. The latter also supervises and hears appeals from the deputy commissioners.

Several of the departments of the provincial government have their representatives at district headquarters. Normally these include a superintendent of police, a district inspector of schools, a district health officer, an officer of the agricultural department, and others—all appointed by, and under the administrative control of, the respective departments of the provincial government. At the same time such officers are under the general supervision of the deputy commissioner in charge of the district, who has special powers with regard to the police.

The deputy commissioner, whose role has not changed substantially since the British regime and who is by all odds the most important official in the district, has two primary functions: the collection of the land revenue and the maintenance of law and order. Under his magisterial powers he can impose a sentence of up to two years in criminal cases; he is required to tour his district periodically and is the principal channel of communication between the district and higher levels of government; increasingly he assists in the developmental activities of the Basic Democracies.

The assessment and collection of land revenue is one of the major functions of the provincial governments and in West Pakistan has become a highly organized and meticulous affair. Each district is administered according to the tehsils, which are headed by a *tehsildar* and *naib* (deputy) *tehsildars*. The naib tehsildars are in turn assisted by *qanungas*, who supervise ten to fifteen *patwaris*, the ones directly involved with the people. The patwari maintains a complete record of the landholdings in his area and the amount of revenue due from each farmer. The actual collection of the revenues is the responsibility of one or more headmen in the village, each of whom receives a commission as compensation. Although his office is usually hereditary, the headman can be removed by the deputy commissioner.

The patwari, as the lowest ranking literate person in the government hierarchy, is a person of considerable importance and influence. Recruited by the revenue officer assisting the deputy commissioner, after an interview and a written test, the patwari is given three months of training in a special school and then appointed to a specific location by the district administration. His critical importance can be deduced from the fact that in any dispute over land ownership his land and crop records may be the deciding factor.

In East Pakistan, by contrast, the system of land revenue collection is in a state of transition. Until 1956 most of the land was held by large landowners known as *zamindars*, whom the government held responsible for the payment of a land tax. But the amount of this tax had been fixed in perpetuity by the "Permanent Settlement of 1793" and the zamindar customarily collected a considerably greater amount as rent from his several hundred tenants—a situation partly responsible for the poor financial resources of the provincial

TERRITORIAL ADMINISTRATIVE STRUCTURE OF PAKISTAN

FEDERAL GOVERNMENT

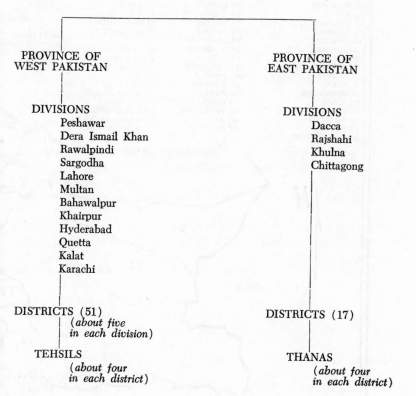

PROVINCE OF
WEST PAKISTAN

PROVINCE OF
EAST PAKISTAN

DIVISIONS
Peshawar
Dera Ismail Khan
Rawalpindi
Sargodha
Lahore
Multan
Bahawalpur
Khairpur
Hyderabad
Quetta
Kalat
Karachi

DIVISIONS
Dacca
Rajshahi
Khulna
Chittagong

DISTRICTS (51)
*(about five
in each division)*

DISTRICTS (17)

TEHSILS
*(about four
in each district)*

THANAS
*(about four
in each district)*

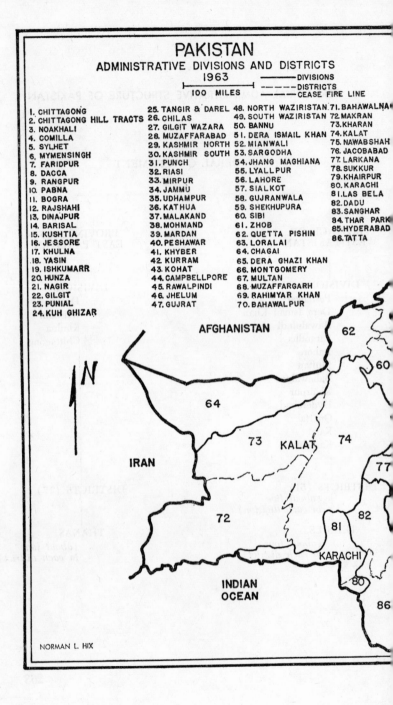

PAKISTAN
ADMINISTRATIVE DIVISIONS AND DISTRICTS
1963

——— DIVISIONS
– – – DISTRICTS
—·—·— CEASE FIRE LINE

100 MILES

1. CHITTAGONG
2. CHITTAGONG HILL TRACTS
3. NOAKHALI
4. COMILLA
5. SYLHET
6. MYMENSINGH
7. FARIDPUR
8. DACCA
9. RANGPUR
10. PABNA
11. BOGRA
12. RAJSHAHI
13. DINAJPUR
14. BARISAL
15. KUSHTIA
16. JESSORE
17. KHULNA
18. YASIN
19. ISHKUMARR
20. HUNZA
21. NAGIR
22. GILGIT
23. PUNIAL
24. KUH GHIZAR

25. TANGIR & DAREL
26. CHILAS
27. GILGIT WAZARA
28. MUZAFFARABAD
29. KASHMIR NORTH
30. KASHMIR SOUTH
31. PUNCH
32. RIASI
33. MIRPUR
34. JAMMU
35. UDHAMPUR
36. KATHUA
37. MALAKAND
38. MOHMAND
39. MARDAN
40. PESHAWAR
41. KHYBER
42. KURRAM
43. KOHAT
44. CAMPBELLPORE
45. RAWALPINDI
46. JHELUM
47. GUJRAT

48. NORTH WAZIRISTAN
49. SOUTH WAZIRISTAN
50. BANNU
51. DERA ISMAIL KHAN
52. MIANWALI
53. SARGODHA
54. JHANG MAGHIANA
55. LYALLPUR
56. LAHORE
57. SIALKOT
58. GUJRANWALA
59. SHEKHUPURA
60. SIBI
61. ZHOB
62. QUETTA PISHIN
63. LORALAI
64. CHAGAI
65. DERA GHAZI KHAN
66. MONTGOMERY
67. MULTAN
68. MUZAFFARGARH
69. RAHIMYAR KHAN
70. BAHAWALPUR

71. BAHAWALNA
72. MAKRAN
73. KHARAN
74. KALAT
75. NAWABSHAH
76. JACOBABAD
77. LARKANA
78. SUKKUR
79. KHAIRPUR
80. KARACHI
81. LAS BELA
82. DADU
83. SANGHAR
84. THAR PARK
85. HYDERABAD
86. TATTA

AFGHANISTAN

IRAN

INDIAN OCEAN

KALAT

KARACHI

NORMAN L. HIX

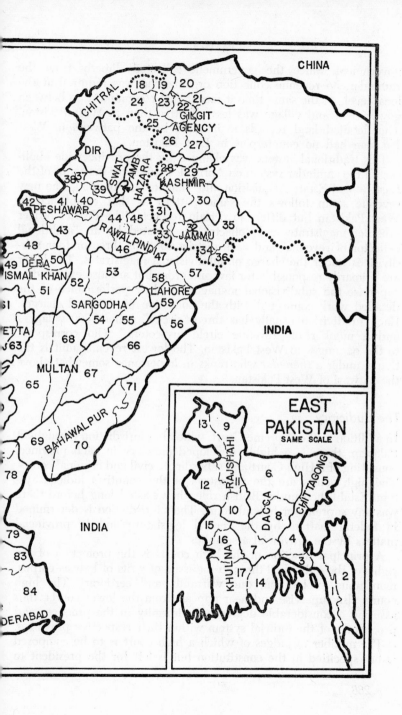

government. Since the government collected directly from the zamindar, no revenue collection organization was required at the local level. At the same time it meant that communication between government and village was less effective than in West Pakistan. The detailed land records maintained by the patwaris in West Pakistan had no counterpart in East Pakistan.

This traditional system was changed by the provincewide abolition of the zamindar system on April 14, 1956 under the terms of the East Bengal Estate Acquisition and Tenancy Act of 1950. The new revenue setup follows the same pattern as that established in West Pakistan but differs in certain respects. The district officer (district magistrate and collector) is assisted by an "additional collector of revenue" and each district contains three or four subdivisions under the charge of subdivisional magistrates. The latter are primarily responsible for law and order but are also expected to supervise the subdivisional managers in their performance of the detailed work connected with the collection of the land charges. Each subdivision usually has three "circles" (about 300 villages) and a number of "revenue circle inspectors," who correspond to the qanungas in West Pakistan. The lowest revenue unit is the thana, under a *thanadar* who ranks in importance somewhat above the patwari of West Pakistan.

The Judiciary

In addition to the Supreme Court, which has jurisdiction throughout Pakistan, there is a highly developed judiciary in each province, consisting of a High Court and subordinate civil and criminal courts. The high courts are the mainstays of the country's judicial system. Established under British rule, they existed long before there was any supreme or federal court. Their jurisdiction is determined in federal matters by the central legislature and in provincial matters by the provincial assemblies.

A principal function of the high courts is the protection of the rights of the individual through the issue of writs of habeas corpus, mandamus, prohibition, quo warranto, and certiorari. The high courts also supervise and hear appeals from the lower courts, thus assuring a considerable degree of uniformity in the practices and procedures of the judicial system within their respective provinces.

The number of judges of which a high court is to be composed is not specified in the constitution but is left for the president to determine. Judges are appointed by the president after consultation with the chief justice of Pakistan, the governor of the province to which the appointment relates, and the chief justice of the high court of that province. Qualifications are similar to, but less strict than, those for supreme court judges. Roughly, the requirement is ten years of legal experience, although members of the civil service of Pakistan of ten years' standing with three years' experience as a district judge are also eligible.

The district judge is the principal judicial authority in his district in civil cases and supervises the subordinate judges and *munsif* courts. Subordinate judges are promoted from the rank of munsif by the high court; the munsifs are appointed to the judicial branch of the provincial civil service by the provincial government and are then assigned by the high court. The munsif's jurisdiction does not extend to suits exceeding 2,000 rupees ($400).

The sessions judge is the ranking judicial authority in criminal matters in the district. Sessions courts may inflict any punishment authorized by law, but a death sentence must be confirmed by higher authority. Most of the sessions judge's time is spent hearing appeals from magistrates. The deputy commissioner of the district is also "district magistrate" and has a limited power to hear appeals from second- and third-class magistrates.

Special Areas

There are certain parts of Pakistan—the so-called "tribal areas"—to which the authority of the provincial assembly and provincial courts does not automatically extend and which are administered under the executive authority of the president. The constitution provides that no central law shall apply to a "tribal area" unless the president so directs and no provincial law unless the governor, with the approval of the president, so directs. Unlike most other parts of the country, the tribal areas have no system by which the provincial government levies land revenue.

These areas include some of the wildest and most scenic as well as strategically most important parts of West Pakistan. They contain over five hundred miles of the Pakistan-Afghanistan border and mountain ranges over 20,000 feet high. Specifically, these areas are: the states of Amb, Chitral, Dir, and Swat; the political agencies of Khyber, Kurram, Malakand, Mohmand, North and South Waziristan; and the tribal areas attached to the districts of Bannu, Dera

Ismail Khan, Hazara, Kohat, Mardan, and Peshawar. Each political agency is headed by a "political agent" who is usually a member of the civil service of Pakistan. The attached tribal areas are administered by the deputy commissioners of their districts.

The four states each have rulers who formally acceded to Pakistan in 1947. Of the four, Swat is the most populated (552,000), accessible, and developed, and its ruler, the Wali, has worked closely with the Pakistan government. The Mehtar of Chitral, largest of the states, died in an airplane accident in 1954 and a political agent appointed by the central government is acting as regent for the Mehtar's infant son. The ruler of Dir has remained relatively isolated and uncooperative, obviously reluctant to modify his absolute powers. Amb is a tiny state which is under the political jurisdiction of the deputy commissioner of Hazara district.

The political agencies and tribal areas include belligerent tribes that the government premits a large degree of autonomy, ordinary means of administration having proven impractical. Some tribesmen attempt to cultivate the rocky soil; others have become tradesmen, mechanics, or small-arms manufacturers. During 1954 a Tribal Advisory Council was formed which later elected tribal representatives to the 1955 constituent assembly. The Division of States and Frontier Regions of the central government maintains contact with these areas.

In addition to the above, there is Azad (free) Kashmir, which has relations with the central government's Ministry of Home and Kashmir Affairs even though it is not constitutionally a part of Pakistan.

Local Self-Government

The description of local self-government which follows reflects the situation prior to the promulgation of the Basic Democracies Order, since it is impossible at this time to determine what changes have been made at this level.

In general, the machinery of local self-government is not well regarded. Promising young administrators generally show no enthusiasm when careers in local government are discussed, pointing to the extremely low salaries and lack of security. There is a hint that local governments are corrupt and at the mercy of district officers and politicians. Just as the central government has been reluctant to grant broad power to the provincial governments, so have the latter kept the control over local government in their own hands. The local authorities have practically no powers which cannot be immediately withdrawn by the district officer or the provincial government. Elected local boards can be, and have been, abolished at slight provocation. Provincial authorities can remove local staff, grant exemptions from local taxes, charge any expenditure to local funds, and suspend any local regulation. Officials of the provincial and central governments say that authority cannot be delegated to local bodies lest it be abused. Such an attitude of mistrust is hardly conducive to efficiency and initiative at the local level, and yet the central government's development programs call for just such initiative and administrative capacity.

Many groups in Pakistan pay lip service to the cause of local government but few actually work to extend its authority. For more than a century the district officer has had great power within his area and is understandably reluctant to promote any reduction in that power; the large landowners apparently feel that strong local government might detract from their own positions of power and influence; local residents fear that more local functions may bring higher taxes; the provincial civil services sense that the development of services at the local level may somehow diminish their own importance; and even the local government's own employees, who plead for more local independence, want to be considered as members of the provincial civil service because their security, retirement, and other benefits would be enhanced thereby.

The principal organ of local self-government in the rural areas of West Pakistan is the district board, which may have as many as one hundred members, all directly elected by adult franchise. Its most important functions are the construction and maintenance of public roads and ferries, the administration of the primary schools, and the supervision of public health. Its principal source of income is the local rate, which is levied on all landowners, collected by the revenue administration of the provincial government, and handed over to the district board periodically. In 1956 in certain areas the levy was 6 annas per rupee of land revenue paid by the owner. Provincial grants in aid are an additional source of revenue.

District board administration is complicated by the fact that several of its department heads, being also employees of the provincial government, operate in a dual capacity. The following officials, however, are strictly employees of the board and report directly to its chairman: the secretary, the taxation officer, the district engineer, and the head supervisor of arboriculture. The deputy commissioner has wide powers to veto actions of the district board. The provincial government can supersede a district board and has frequently done so in recent years. When this occurs the deputy commissioner becomes responsible for the board's functions. Some deputy commissioners consider the district board superfluous. The public does not appear to have much respect for it as a representative body—perhaps because new elections have not been held in some cases for many years.

At the village level, there is very little self-government. At one time, the *panchayat* (a five-man council of elders) discussed controversial village matters until unanimity of opinion was reached. Under British rule the government-appointed headman became the most influential person in the village, and the prestige of the panchayat declined. Today, in spite of the sporadic attempts by the government during the last fifty years to reverse the trend, only about a fifth of the villages in the Punjab area have active panchayats. In the frontier areas of West Pakistan, the tribe rather than the panchayat is the local unit.

Existing laws governing panchayats provide for a three- to seven-man council. Members are elected by adult suffrage on the basis of ward representation in villages of more than 3,000 population. The panchayat's functions include maintenance of the water supply, poor and sick relief, the development of agriculture and industry, and judicial decisions in minor civil cases. The deputy commissioner and district board exercise general supervision over these activities.

In East Pakistan the district boards are smaller in size and have fewer functions than those in West Pakistan. Its members are elected by members of the union boards described below. A special school board in each district administers primary education, and the field of public health is gradually being taken over by the provincial government.

The smallest units of local government in East Pakistan are the union boards, which superseded the panchayats in 1919. A union board, which usually consists of between eight and ten members, has jurisdiction over approximately twenty villages containing a total of about 8,000 persons. In 1954 there were 3,621 such boards. They are responsible for village police, roads, bridges and ferries, sanitation, water supply, and primary schools and exercise some minor judicial functions. Most of the members are elected by secret ballot in what is usually a lively contest. The members, in turn, elect a president from among themselves. The circle officer (a provincial employee) works closely with the union boards.

Sometime after the population of a village reaches 5,000 and before it passes 30,000 it officially becomes a municipality and, as such, may elect its own municipal committee, set up its own administration, and perform for itself those functions which the district board and—in East Pakistan—the union board have previously performed for it: road building and maintenance, public health and sanitation, water supply, fire fighting and prevention, and education and libraries. Three out of four of Pakistan's more than two hundred municipal committees are in West Pakistan.

The provincial governments have passed elaborate legislation describing in detail their relationship to these municipal committees. In essence, this legislation reserves to officers of the provincial government the right to make all important decisions. For example, the budget of the municipal committee must be approved by the division commissioner acting as the representative of the provincial government; the provincial government, on the other hand, can charge an expenditure to local funds whether the municipal committee approves it or not. The demarcation of wards, preparation of electoral rolls, and conduct of elections are performed by provincial officials. The elected candidates cannot assume office until the election results are published by the provincial government in its official gazette. In spite of these provisions, considerable bogus voting has taken place. Decisions on municipal affairs are made in the form of committee resolutions which are subsequently forwarded through the deputy commissioner to the division commissioner. They become effective only after the approval by the latter. Decisions are carried out by the president, who is elected by the committee from its own membership, and the executive officer. There are various other officials: a secretary, municipal engineer, waterworks superintendent, and health officer.

The principal sources of revenue are the property tax, taxes on utilities, and grants from the provincial government. In West Pakistan a major source of income is the octroi—a tax on goods transported into the municipality. Two cities in Pakistan—Lahore and Karachi—are classified as municipal corporations. In contrast to the administrative procedure in other municipalities, the 70 or 100 members respectively of these municipal corporations elect their mayors and theoretically wield legislative control within their own cities. But in practice both corporations have on occasion been superseded and placed under an administrator appointed by a higher level of government.

Municipal administration in Pakistan generally is then handicapped by inadequate powers, outdated laws and procedures, civic apathy, the absence of local police and local courts with summary powers to enforce local laws, and inadequate authority. Nevertheless, there are many competent employees at the local level. Proposals made at their occasional conferences evidence considerable discernment in the administration of local affairs.

The Civil Services

Pakistan inherited one of the most remarkable civil service systems in the world. Installed in India by the British during the nineteenth century, and for many years open at the higher' ranks only to the British, the civil service had as its function control of the entire subcontinent and its members constituted an administrative elite.

After World War I an increasing number of Indians entered the higher services—most Hindu, but a small number Moslem. At the time of partition it was this group which managed to set up a central government for Pakistan and many still occupy key administrative jobs. At one time or another even the positions of prime minister, president, and governor have been occupied by former civil servants.

The better paying administrative jobs today are filled by persons who have entered the Superior Civil Services through competitive examination. A number of these services are primarily financial and their members hold responsible positions involving accounting and the collection of federal taxes; the most coveted are the Civil Service of Pakistan, the Pakistan Foreign Service, and the Police Service of Pakistan.

Some of the higher posts and most of the junior posts in the provinces are filled by officers of the provincial civil services. Almost all of the provincial administrative posts below the district level are normally filled by officers recruited by the respective provincial Public Service Commission.

For the administration of the domestic affairs of Pakistan, the Civil Service of Pakistan is by far the most important of the services in that it supplies officers to both the central and provincial governments—an important characteristic which distinguishes it (together with the Police Service) from the other services. Thus most of the key administrative and police positions of the provincial governments are held by officials who have been recruited and selected by the president, acting on the advice of the federal Public Service Commission. Only the president has the authority to discharge or reduce the rank of a member of these services, and the constitution specifies that the central legislature shall have the exclusive power to make laws with respect to them. The Establishment Division of the President's secretariat has the responsibility for training officials and maintaining the personnel records with respect to these services. While an officer is assigned to a province, the governor is responsible for his promotion and transfer and for any disciplinary action against him. Thus the province has only a limited control over many of its key personnel.

Persons desiring to enter the Superior Civil Services must take the competitive examination before reaching the age of twenty-four, although some extensions are allowed for persons from backward and isolated areas. In the written examination the candidate selects from an approved list the three or four academic subjects in which he chooses to be tested. Additional questions are given to examine the "general knowledge" and writing ability of the candidate. If he passes this written examination he is given psychological tests and finally is subjected to an oral interview by a board of experts. About sixty applicants per year are successful in entering the Superior Services, of which approximately a third enter the Civil Service of Pakistan. The latter are sent to the Civil Service Academy in Lahore for nine months to receive instruction in law, horseback riding, the Bengali or Urdu language, government procedures, surveying, accounting, typing, and administration. They then proceed to East Pakistan, where they receive their first experience—under supervision—in trying criminal cases. Next comes a trip abroad, usually to England, for several months of further training. Upon returning to Pakistan they are each assigned to a district where as assistant commissioners they deal with the simpler revenue cases and exercise magisterial powers. After a few years, perhaps with an intervening period as under-secretaries in the provincial secretariat, they become deputy commissioners. As such, they are the principal link between the government and approximately one million people and exercise great power and responsibility. From time to time they may be assigned to the central secretariat for a tour of duty or they may be promoted to division commissioner. A Civil Service officer is assured of increasing responsibility, great prestige, good pay, free medical treatment for himself and his family, a high degree of job security, and retirement with a pension at fifty-five years of age. On January 1, 1957 there were 287 officers in this service.

Despite many accomplishments the Civil Service of Pakistan has been subject to criticism. There are those who feel, for example, that an examination at twenty-three cannot measure the extent to which a man will apply himself to the job in his thirties or forties. Others object that the system, designed primarily to maintain order and collect land revenue during the British rule, does not meet the developmental requirements of Pakistan today. Yet the consensus among informed observers seems to be that the so-called "steel frame" must continue, that the maintenance of order remains one of the country's vital problems, and that the district officer needs great powers in order to eliminate excessive red tape. Perhaps an expanded training program, with increased emphasis on training in developmental programs and administration, and increased opportunities for promotion from the other services are required.

Certainly the present system effectively reduces—at least within the Civil Service—the ever-present tendencies toward nepotism and corruption. The former is largely eliminated by means of the competitive examinations, and the latter is minimized because an officer would hesitate to risk his present advantageous position by engaging in questionable activities.

Clerical personnel are also recruited by competitive examinations; most of the better clerical jobs require a Bachelor's degree. Theoretically a member of a clerical service may be promoted to one of the positions customarily held by a member of the Civil Service, but in practice this rarely occurs and then only when the employee is approaching retirement. The difference in the status, prestige, and pay of the two services is very great and the personal relationships reflect this, considerable deference being shown to a member of the Civil Service. Still lower in the scale there is a small army of chaprassis who carry messages and files and serve tea.

With the exception of the Central Engineering Service, which is selected by competitive examination, most of the technical positions are filled on an ad hoc basis on the advice of the Public Service Commission. The positions are advertised, the applications are reviewed, and frequently interview boards are constituted. There is

274

a shortage in Pakistan of almost all types of technical personnel, including those with training in administration. The Planning Commission described these shortages as the most serious impediment to the fulfillment of the five-year plans—more serious than the shortage of natural and financial resources. At the same time there exists the anomaly that qualified persons cannot readily find suitable employment, especially in the government, because the need for such technicians has not been recognized by formally establishing suitable positions in the organization.

Public Order and Safety

The maintenance of public order and safety has long been recognized on the Indian subcontinent as the primary function of government. Since the British constituted a foreign minority of less than 300,000 persons amidst a population of 300 million, public order was essential to their very survival. Any doubt there may have been on this score was eliminated during the so-called Mutiny of 1857. The British installed an elaborate system of police administration and this system was retained by the Pakistan authorities after partition. To operate this system, Pakistan could call on a substantial number of experienced police officers inherited from prepartition India, where nearly half of the police force had been Moslem. The police today are a professionally trained group, with the higher officers selected on the basis of a competitive examination conducted in English. The assistance of a well-trained army is available in the event of widespread disorder.

In spite of several conspicuous instances of public disorder, the normal situation in Pakistan today is one of tranquillity. Mass demonstrations in the major cities in protest of some government action or international incident continue, but violence rarely results. There is usually adequate warning of impending trouble and one can easily avoid the areas in which disorder is likely to flare. Foreigners who take normal precautions are seldom involved in the disturbances and travel freely and without untoward incident throughout most of Pakistan.

The rule of law is well recognized and the customary legal remedies are available throughout most of Pakistan. The lower courts are slow and their dockets are overcrowded with minor legal matters, but the higher courts are staffed by a trained and professional judiciary. Theft is widespread in the urban areas, where masses of refugees live under extremely crowded and unsatisfactory conditions, but for the most part it is petty in nature.

Because the police were for many years associated with the harsher aspects of alien rule, there is general fear and distrust of the police among the public, particularly persons of low income and status, and many crimes, in the villages especially, undoubtedly go unreported for this reason. Fearing reprisals, people frequently fail to report instances of police corruption, which—particularly in the lower ranks—continues to be a major problem. This failure to gain the confidence of the great mass of the population is perhaps the most serious shortcoming of the police system in Pakistan.

Under the constitution, the responsibility for maintaining internal peace and tranquillity rests with each provincial government, whose principal instrument for this purpose is the police force. Should the police force become inadequate to a situation the provincial government can request the central government for the assistance of the army. The home minister in the provincial cabinet has the political responsibility for public order, but in practice this portfolio is frequently retained by the chief minister. The chief secretary and the home secretary are the civil servants who exercise general administrative supervision over the police function.

The inspector general of police, whose office is in the Home Department, is head of the police force in the province. He is assisted by deputy inspectors general, one of whom is in charge of intelligence and criminal investigation for the province; others are given responsibility for the larger territorial divisions, or "ranges," which are usually identical to the commissioners' divisions.

At the district level, the district officer in his capacity as magistrate has general control and direction of the police force and also heads the criminal administration of the district. Responsible for the maintenance of law and order, he is the one who must decide if a proposed public meeting should be banned in the interests of public tranquillity or give the order to fire on a threatening mob. It is this combination of executive and judicial powers which—though in operation throughout most of the Indian subcontinent—has evoked considerable criticism from observers of Pakistan's judicial and legal system. The district magistrate's role has been described as that of policeman, prosecutor, and judge. The constitution of 1962 directed that judicial and executive functions be separated—an indication that the district magistrate may lose the power to hear cases and retain only his responsibility for the maintenance of the peace. The relationship between the district magistrate and his superintendent of police has not always been harmonious.

The senior officer in the police force at the district level is the district superintendent of police. Other police officers have charge of district subdivisions, which are further divided into circles and thanas. Each thana has a police station manned by an inspector or subinspector and a number of constables. At the village level are *chowkidars* (watchmen), maintained by the Union Councils. The size of a thana varies considerably but in East Pakistan averages about 134 square miles with perhaps 150 villages. An important function of the thanadar, who is in charge of the thana police station, is the investigation of criminal and other cases reported to him. His staff may consist of twenty men, mostly constables. A considerable amount of time must be devoted to keeping track of recent refugees from India and investigating the antecedents of newly appointed government employees. Official reports have attributed the low efficiency of the thana police to overwork and inadequate supervision by the circle inspectors, the latter often described as inexperienced officials with a tendency to peruse and initial the case histories from the vantage point of an armchair.

The chowkidar is an old village institution. Formerly, he was appointed, paid, and dismissed by the village community and acted as its agent. In recent times the chowkidar has been appointed—in East Pakistan—by the district magistrate on the recommendation of the president of the union board. Now he is appointed by the Union Council. The chowkidar is paid the equivalent of a few dollars per month.

Police functions of an intelligence nature—i.e. criminal investigation, internal security, and anticorruption activities—have been given considerable emphasis in Pakistan. The provincial government in East Pakistan alone has an anticorruption staff of about three hundred persons headed by a deputy inspector general. At the federal level there is a Central Intelligence Bureau in the Home Ministry which is in communication with the provincial governments and also conducts its own investigations. At the provincial level there is a Criminal Investigation Department in the Home Ministry which performs a similar function. A technical branch of this department controls the police wireless system, which connects all districts, and the police transport facilities. Habitual

277

offenders or "bad characters" are kept under surveillance and their movements reported in detail. Each district headquarters has an attached central investigating agency which maintains criminal records and issues (in West Pakistan) a weekly gazette to all thana officers to keep them posted on the latest developments.

The higher police positions throughout Pakistan are held by members of a national career service originally selected by a competitive examination conducted by the federal Public Service Commission. Even though the constitution lists the police function as a provincial responsibility, the Police Service of Pakistan, like the Civil Service of Pakistan, is controlled as to appointment, conditions of service, and removal by the central government. The details of recruitment and selection are substantially the same for both services. Usually the candidates with higher scores request and obtain assignment to the Civil Service and those with somewhat lower standing become police officers. The competition is such, however, that only those who are well above average scholastically would normally qualify for police appointments.

About fifteen are taken into the Police Service each year. Following appointment, the first year of their two-year probationary period is spent at the Police Training College at Sardah, East Pakistan, where the officers are given instruction in criminal law, medical jurisprudence, languages, and other subjects. During the second year their time is divided between a military unit and a district headquarters. On completing probation, an officer is given the rank of assistant superintendent of police and placed in charge of a subdivision or a set of police stations from which he is expected to control the entire police force in an area of about a thousand square miles. Normally an officer will become a superintendent of police in charge of the police force of a district after about seven years. This promotion is made on the basis of seniority and most of his career is spent at this post. Intermediate positions in the police force (subdivision officers and inspectors) are held by officers of the provincial police services; constables are recruited on a semimilitary basis at the district level. All members of the police force receive at least six months of training.

The jurisdiction over criminal law and procedure in Pakistan belongs concurrently to the national government and the provincial governments. Each is empowered by the constitution to define crimes and penalties relating to those matters in which it has legislative jurisdiction. Pakistan incorporated into its own legal system the Penal Code of 1860 and the Criminal Procedure Code, both with amendments, which the British provided as the basic criminal law for British India.

The Penal Code was originally drafted by Lord Macaulay, the eminent English jurist and essayist, in 1837. The provisions, drafted with great skill, were patterned after the prevailing British law and the concepts embodied therein are very familiar to any Western jurist. As might be expected, considering the problems faced by the British colonial administration, the penalties are somewhat more harsh and rigid than is customary in the West, and more attention is given to the problem of preventing incipient crime by restricting the movements of those whose actions promote criminal activity. Thus, a police officer can ban a meeting if he believes it is likely to endanger public peace, or he may make an arrest without a warrant to prevent the commission of a serious crime.

Since partition, legislation in Pakistan has made some additions to the criminal law, notably in the Pakistan Criminal Law Amendment Act of 1948, designed to tighten the law against corruption and malpractices in government. But the fundamentals of the criminal law remain the same.

A serious criminal case normally goes first to a magistrate who, after a prima facie case has been established, refers it to a court of sessions. If the offense carries a penalty of not more than two years imprisonment or a fine of not more than 1,000 rupees it can be tried by a magistrate. The provincial government appoints public prosecutors from among the members of the bar in the district to be served. These prosecutors conduct the cases before the sessions courts. In the case of the magistrates' courts, however, the prosecution is conducted by subordinate police officers who have received some practical training under the public prosecutors.

Pakistan's penal system is organized on a provincial basis. Prison administration, like the police force, comes under the home department of the province. There is a separate inspector general in charge of prisons. Inspectors general of police may also be prison inspectors for the central jails, as the district magistrates are for the district jails. The system has undergone little change in Pakistan since the period of British rule. Its purpose is to confine prisoners effectively and cheaply, and in this it is reasonably successful. Generally speaking, the public appears to consider this to be the proper function of a penal system, for little is heard in Pakistan in the way of agitation for prison reform.

279

Pakistan has borrowed the concept of preventive detention from British Indian law, in spite of the distaste with which that concept was regarded during British rule by many of those who are now governing Pakistan. Faced with some of the same problems that confronted the British, the leadership in Pakistan has retained some of the British methods for solving those problems. Preventive detention—that is, imprisonment in order to prevent violation of the law—has proved a convenient method by which the government in Pakistan may meet certain problems of public order and safety.

At the same time, however, preventive detention has by its very nature presented temptations to governments to abuse this power for reasons of political gain. One of the complaints against government most frequently heard both in the central and provincial legislatures has been the abuse in application of preventive detention laws. Every province has had its public safety act, under which preventive arrest has been easy; and the jails of the provinces have seldom been without their quota of political *détenus*. East Pakistan and the former North-West Frontier province have been notorious for their use of preventive detention against opposition political parties. In East Pakistan, in fact, even members of the constituent assembly have been arrested and detained under the public safety act.

Some effort has been made in the constitution to limit the possibilities of abuse of preventive detention laws. A clause under Fundamental Rights states that no preventive detention law shall authorize the detention of a person for more than three months unless the appropriate advisory board reports that there is sufficient cause for further detention. The advisory boards are appointed in the provinces by the governors and chief justices of the high courts and at the center by the president and the chief justice of Pakistan. This would appear to put a limit of three months on any possibility of abuse of preventive detention. In the past, however, when time limits have been set, the practice of immediate rearrest after release has sometimes been used.

The Foreign Service

The president and the various prime ministers of Pakistan have played a very active role in promoting and implementing the country's foreign policy. Most of the diplomatic activity, however, is carried on through Pakistan's ministry of external affairs and by the various missions of Pakistan established throughout the world. Except for a few appointments at the ambassadorial level, these activities are conducted by the officers of the Pakistan Foreign Service.

These officers are recruited through an annual competitive examination, with about six being appointed each year. Candidates may be sent abroad to study international law, diplomatic history, and foreign languages for about eighteen months. Upon their return to Pakistan they are trained in government procedure and sent on a study tour to that province of Pakistan with which they are least familiar. The Foreign Service is very popular in Pakistan and the foreign posts are made particularly attractive by the provision of substantial living allowances while abroad.

CHAPTER 13

Mass Media

SEVERAL FACTORS have militated against a more rapid development of the information and entertainment media in Pakistan since partition: the particularly low level of education among Moslems in prepartition India and continued widespread illiteracy in the new Pakistan; the economic dislocations of partition which, at least initially, severely limited the country's ability to fill the equipment and material needs of the emergent publishing, broadcasting, and film industries; and the special geographic and linguistic problems presented by a predominantly rural and ethnically diverse population.

Least affected by such factors has been the press—the oldest and best developed of the mass media in Pakistan and, partly because of the premium attached to literacy and the printed word, the most influential. Though the ratio of newspapers to inhabitants is one of the lowest in the world, even lower than in many other countries in Asia, the number of readers for each copy is high and the role of newspapers in the people's lives has a long tradition.

The Moslem Press in India and Pakistan

Much of the character of the Pakistan press today can be traced to the partisan press that developed in British India in the period immediately preceding independence. The first Indian-owned and Indian-language papers on the subcontinent had appeared early in the nineteenth century but, for historical and educational reasons, tended to be Hindu rather than Moslem enterprises. Of the few Urdu newspapers founded as early as the 1820s, none was particularly identified with territory now in Pakistan or with the espousal of Moslem causes.

As the freedom movement gained strength toward the close of the last century, providing the first real challenge to the Indian press, Moslem-oriented papers made a tentative appearance and from about 1910 on became more common. But only after Mahomed 'Ali Jinnah launched the struggle for a separate Pakistan did a militant Moslem press develop. By the early 1940s Moslem politicians had become aware of the need for a strong press to advocate their point of view. The result was the emergence of a primarily partisan Moslem press, which the Hindus promptly labeled the "League press."

Its birth coincided with one of the most difficult periods in the recent history of the subcontinent. It had to labor under the double disadvantage of competing with the press of the much more powerful All-India freedom movement—bitterly opposed to the formation of a separate Moslem state—as well as of fighting for freedom from foreign domination. Furthermore, the Moslem community was generally less wealthy even in proportion to its numbers than its Hindu counterpart and was, therefore, not in a position to proffer the financial support that would have established a really powerful Moslem press. Its circulation was rather meager. Notwithstanding these limitations, it did succeed in consolidating much of Moslem public opinion in favor of Pakistan and was an effective medium for convincing others of the feasibility of partition.

The material situation of the Moslem press was not improved by the two-way migration which accompanied partition. Although West Pakistan inherited Lahore, one of India's leading publishing centers, the majority of those engaged in journalism, publishing, and printing had been Hindus or Sikhs who migrated to India. In addition, most of the major printing establishments were within the territory of the new India. As the areas now constituting Pakistan were among the least industrialized in prepartition India, the manufacture of spare parts also became a serious problem. However, between 1947 and 1950 the material situation of the Pakistan press improved to such an extent that enough presses were imported to permit the leading newspapers to be printed separately.

Without a paper industry at the time of partition, much less a newsprint factory, Pakistan had to make its way in the newsprint market at the time of an already existing worldwide shortage. For some years newsprint had to be rationed and allotted by a central agency, thus limiting the size and scope of the papers. However, the Khulna newsprint mill now turns out over 25,000 tons of news-print annually, a figure far above domestic requirements.

Published information on the Pakistan press is rather scanty. In 1952 Pakistan was reported to have 76 daily newspapers. By 1958 the figure stood at 103 (see Table 9) but by 1960 had dropped to 95 papers. Reliable circulation figures are not available. By 1960 a total of 1,374 separate publications were appearing in Pakistan. Some 901 were in Urdu, 226 in English, 155 in Bengali, and far smaller numbers in Sindhi, Gujarati, Pushtu, Persian, Punjabi, and Arabic.

Among the newspapers only some of the Urdu, English, and Bengali papers can claim circulation figures of more than a few thousand. Newspapers and periodicals published in Urdu are re-ported to have a combined total circulation of over 300,000. Next in importance are the English-language papers with a combined circulation of between 125,000 and 160,000. Readers of the English-language papers are by far the most influential persons in the coun-try. Potential readers of this press are university graduates, civil servants, politicians, and professional people. Since the constitution states that English may be used for official purposes until at least 1972, the English-language press has a sound basis for pre-serving and even for expanding its influence. On the whole, the press is dominated by political and international news, followed by news on sports and business affairs.

A striking feature of the press in Pakistan is the proliferation of publications in West Pakistan by comparison with the dearth of publications in East Pakistan. The reasons for this disparate dis-tribution are without doubt largely economic: low industrialization and urbanization coupled with the general poverty of the peasant in East Pakistan militate against the expansion of the newspaper industry. By and large, newspaper publication is concentrated in the big cities. The capital and largest city in West Pakistan, Karachi, has twenty-eight daily papers; Lahore, the second largest, has twenty-two. Similarly, in East Pakistan almost five-sixths of all the dailies and one-half of all other publications are published in Dacca, the second capital.

Many of the outstanding daily newspapers are organs of political parties or leaders and may be more readily compared to the French press than to newspapers in the United States. Owners and editors are known to represent the interests of certain political groups, and readers know the political overtones they may expect to find in a certain newspaper.

The more detailed examination of the press begins with the English-language papers. *Dawn,* once the official newspaper of the Moslem League in Delhi, was founded in 1942 by Mahomed 'Ali Jinnah to propagandize the idea of Pakistan, and after partition moved to Karachi. Edited by Altaf Husayn, it has a circulation of 38,000 copies and is widely read among government officials and civil servants as well as by business people in Karachi. The paper tends to support the policies of the government in office. *Dawn* has correspondents in the major cities of the country and in England and the United States. Its owners, Pakistan Herald Publications, Ltd., also publish the *Evening Star* at Karachi, the *Illustrated Weekly,* a Gujarati edition of *Dawn,* and *Vatan,* also in Gujarati.

The *Pakistan Times,* founded in 1947 in Lahore by Progressive Newspapers, Ltd., was for some years the country's leading opposition daily. Together with its sister publications, the Urdu daily *Imroze* (published simultaneously in Lahore and Multan) and the magazine *Lail-o-Nahar,* the *Pakistan Times* was controlled by the late Mian Iftikharuddin, long a controversial political figure because of his leftwing and pro-Soviet leanings. Coming from a family of wealthy landowners, Iftikharuddin was able to invest considerable funds in his newspaper ventures.

Perhaps as a result of its dynamic and enterprising owner, who quickly managed to purchase modern printing presses from abroad, the paper became the best-produced in the country from the professional point of view and could claim a circulation of 34,000 copies. Politically the paper was on the extreme left wing and usually followed the Communist line, as did its European correspondent, and cartoons reprinted from the London *Daily Worker* were a regular feature. Its line was deplored by successive governments until, following establishment of martial law in October 1958, the government forced Iftikharuddin to sell his newspapers to new owners more acceptable to the new regime. Currently it is published simultaneously in Lahore and Rawalpindi and has correspondents in England and the Middle East.

The *Morning News* was published in Calcutta prior to partition. The first editor was Abdur Rahman Siddiqui, one of the elder politicians associated with the Moslem League. Now published in Karachi and Dacca, the paper is controlled by Khwaja Nooruddin, managing editor, and the industrialist Adamjee under the ownership of National News Publications, Ltd.

The *Pakistan Observer*, published in Dacca, was started in 1949 by Hamidul Huq Chowdry. Consistently advocating the cause of provincial autonomy, it has a circulation of about 10,000 copies.

Two other English-language dailies deserve mention for their special roles prior to the independence of Pakistan. The *Civil and Military Gazette* of Lahore was the oldest paper in what is now Pakistan and was at one time prominently associated with Rudyard Kipling. From British control it went into Hindu hands just before partition, and was widely read by civil servants in the Lahore area. After partition it steadily declined until it acquired new type faces and a more aggressive management. Printing 13,000 copies, it appeared to be in a healthy condition until it suddenly ceased publication in 1963.

The *Khyber Mail*, published in Peshawar, was originally a weekly that was popular among the British in the North-West Frontier province. At present it is a daily, and the only English-language paper of the area.

Among the papers published in Bengali, *Azad* is undoubtedly the most spectacular, if only by virtue of its circulation, which is about 20,000 copies. Its owner and editor, Maulana Muhammad Akram Khan, is himself a very colorful figure whose career proceeded from newsboy to newspaper owner. The *Azad* was originally published in Calcutta, where it was a very prosperous paper, its owner being then president of the provincial Moslem League. At partition he left Calcutta, abandoning his printing plant, and started anew at Dacca. Moslem League interests became subordinate to commercial interests. It has both London and Karachi correspondents and carries provincial and national news. Over the years *Azad* has been an important medium for Bengali literature.

Sangbad was founded in Dacca in 1950 as the official Moslem League paper in Bengali, but later its tone turned against the League and still later it moved more sharply to the left. *Ittifaq*, also published in Dacca, is edited by Tufazzal Husayn and has been sympathetic to the Awami League.

Among the several score of Urdu newspapers only a few are worthy of mention. In any discussion of the Urdu press it is useful to keep in mind the special difficulties which are encountered in the printing of publications in Urdu. Urdu readers have a strong prejudice against linotyped script, and the publishers of Urdu papers are forced to use lithography, a process by which hand-written text is transferred to printing plates. Not only is the process time-consuming, but the quality of the end product often compares unfavorably with typescript. Apart from this, most Urdu news has to be translated from the English texts supplied by the news agencies. As a result, even the best Urdu papers come out later than their English-language counterparts.

The daily *Jang,* published in Karachi and Rawalpindi, is controlled and edited by Mir Khalil-ur-Rahman. It claims a daily circulation of 60,000 and a Sunday circulation of 100,000 copies. *Imroze,* published in Lahore and Multan by Progressive Newspapers, Ltd., has a circulation of about 35,000.

The *Zamindar,* established in 1910 in Lahore, owed its popularity to its founder, the late Maulana Zafar 'Ali, a well-known poet, writer, and politician. It is now published by his grandson, Mansur 'Ali Khan. *Nawa-i-Waqt* was established in Lahore by the late Hamid Nizami, secretary of the old Punjab Moslem Student's Federation, and Shaikh Hamid Mahmud to propagate the teachings of Muhammad Iqbal, and was a staunch supporter of the concept of Pakistan. At present it is published simultaneously in Lahore, Lyallpur, and Rawalpindi. An independent, nationalist publication, it has a circulation of about 19,000 copies. *Anjam,* formerly of Delhi, is now published in Karachi and Peshawar. *Kohistan,* printed in Lahore, Rawalpindi, and Lyallpur is run by Nasir Hejari, a prolific writer of Islamic historical novels.

The Pakistan army publishes the Urdu daily *Hilal* in Rawalpindi. A sober and well-edited paper, it is influential because it reaches military personnel from small villages who would not normally come in contact with a daily newspaper and who, when on leave, spread information to their even more isolated village relatives and friends.

Periodicals

Among the periodicals of a general information type, the monthly English-language *Pakistan Review,* edited by S. D. Zafar and published by the firm of Ferozsons, may be termed the best effort in this field. It aims at providing general cultural, educational, and political information. Apart from articles and editorials, it contains photographs and drawings as well as film and book reviews. *Contemporary Arts,* a quarterly, and *Scintilla,* a quarterly sponsored by the University Women's Art Group, feature excellent articles on literature and the arts, well illustrated in black and white and color. Other popular magazines include *Vision Monthly, Illustrated Weekly,* and *Women's World.* The monthly *Mirror,* owned and edited by Begum Zebun-Nisa Hamidulla, reports society events and appeals mainly to the begums of the country.

News Services

Pakistan has had its own national news services since 1948. The Associated Press of Pakistan (APP) was created by Malik Tajuddin, its managing director, and is owned by the nonprofit Eastern News Trust. Its activities are supervised by an eight-member board, seven of whom are elected by the subscribing newspapers, the eighth being nominated by the government in its capacity as a subscriber to the APP news service. The government pays the subscription fees of APP to Reuters and the Associated Press of America and also pays for news supplied to ministries of the government and to Radio Pakistan. Financial matters are controlled by a finance committee which has a government official as its adviser. Although the APP is nominally an independent business enterprise, the government in its role as an important subscriber and as the source of loans and subsidies wields considerable influence over the policies of the news agency. More specifically, in 1961 the government, concerned with evidence of mismanagement in the form of large debts to foreign news services and to the posts and telegraph services of Pakistan, appointed an administrator to supervise all its operations.

The head office of the APP is in Karachi and there are branch offices in Lahore, Peshawar, Rawalpindi, Lyallpur, Hyderabad, Multan, Bahawalpur, Dacca, and Chittagong as well as a correspondent at New Delhi. Foreign news as obtained from Reuters and the Associated Press is distributed within the country solely by the APP. Serving about fifty newspapers, it operates an internal teleprinter service connecting its offices with each other and with subscribers and a radio teleprinter circuit between Karachi and Dacca. Stringer correspondents away from branch office towns communicate with zonal offices by telegram or telephone, but this coverage of home news has not been too satisfactory. The agency finds it difficult to maintain other than part-time stringers in the small towns and rural areas; most correspondents either have other jobs or are forced to work for several publications.

Second oldest is the United Press of Pakistan, Ltd. (UPP), a private company founded at the end of 1949 to take over coverage of Pakistan from the United Press of India. The UPP has offices at Karachi, Dacca, and Lahore but depends on press telegrams for news from other towns in East and West Pakistan. Some seventeen papers use its service. It has news exchange agreements with the United Press of India and the Pan-Asian Newspaper Alliance of Tokyo. Recently it has started to distribute the reports of the Star News Agency, a subsidiary of Near and Far East News, Ltd., of London.

The Pakistan Press Association (PPA) is a private company established in 1956 with a head office in Karachi and branch offices at Lahore, Hyderabad, Rawalpindi, Peshawar, and Dacca. In addition to local correspondents, it has one foreign correspondent— in Istanbul. Foreign news is obtained from the Agence France Presse, the Deutsche Presse Agentur (West Germany), the Agenzia Giornalistica Italia (Rome), and the Middle East News Agency (Cairo). Thirty newspapers subscribe to its services.

The APP, the UPP, and the PPA use English as the only medium of news transmission. Up to now no news agency has transmitted news in any of the vernacular languages.

The Press and the Government

Part II, Article 3 of Pakistan's constitution states that "no law shall impose any restriction on the freedom of a citizen to express his thoughts," except that this principle may be departed from in the interests of the security of Pakistan, friendly relations with foreign states, public order and decency or morality, or for the purpose of ensuring the proper administration of justice, and for the purpose of preventing the commission of offenses. A series of laws and ordinances, of which eleven had already been enacted under British rule, enabled the government of Pakistan to curb the freedom of the press. These included the Pakistan Public Safety Act and the West Punjab Safety Act.

Some of the laws enacted by the British in the last century and incorporated into Pakistan's present Penal Code merely dealt with routine matters, such as the registration of printing presses and newspapers, the preservation of copies of publications of all types, defamation, criminal intimidation, and imports of publications. Others, like the Press (Emergency Powers) Act of 1931, the Pakistan Public Safety Act of 1949, the Security of Pakistan Act of 1952, and the Official Services Secrets Act of 1923 (as amended in 1955), provided constant reminders to publishers and editors to exercise restraint and caution.

The Press (Emergency Powers) Act of 1931 (as modified up to January 10, 1954) empowered the government to ask newspaper publishers and keepers of printing presses to furnish security deposits, which were liable to forfeiture without a judicial trial. Encouraging or inciting any person to interfere with the administration of the law or with the maintenance of law and order, as well as the selling, distributing, or publishing of unauthorized newspapers, were offenses under the Public Safety Act of 1949.

Under the Security of Pakistan Act of 1952, the government could ban a paper for a considerable period of time or institute precensorship if a paper published "any news, report or information likely to endanger the defense or external affairs or security of Pakistan or any part thereof or maintenance of supplies and services essential to the community, or the maintenance of public order." The act also provided for the maximum penalty of three years' imprisonment for breaches of this statute. However, in 1957 the supreme court ruled that sections of the act which conflicted with constitutional guarantees of freedom of speech were invalid.

After 1949 a number of newspapers were banned for various periods and their owners and employees jailed, warned for the publication of objectionable material, or required to deposit security. The papers also suffered the withdrawal of government advertising and other forms of patronage. Successive governments attempted to coerce, persuade, and win the support of various papers through placing advertisements, buying copies on a regular basis, and even—in the provinces—making direct payments.

President Ayub Khan took a fresh approach to the question when he appointed a Press Commission. Its report, published in 1959, recommended the repeal of sections of existing laws and ordinances and the consolidation of some of their provisions. As a result, the Press and Publications Ordinance 1960 did consolidate numerous provisions relating to the press and repealed two of the laws enacted in British India.

On September 2, 1963 the government promulgated the Press and Publications (Amendment) Ordinance 1963, which included four major amendments to the 1960 ordinance. One prohibited publication of any except authorized, certified accounts of proceedings in the National Assembly, the provincial legislatures, and the courts and required that newspapers publish government press releases without cutting or editing. Another provided for the appointment of commissions for inquiring into the affairs of any printing press or newspaper and empowered the government to take punitive action should such reports be unfavorable. The other amendments concerned penalties to persons and companies contravening the terms of the ordinance.

In response to protests from owners and editors of papers, these amendments were suspended pending discussions with officials of the government. On October 9, 1963 the government issued the Press and Publications (Second Amendment) Ordinance 1963, which eased the restrictions on the reporting of legislative and court proceedings and the handling of government press releases and which eliminated the arbitrary powers of the commissions of enquiry.

Influence of the Press

In actual fact the influence of the press in Pakistan—as in other economically underdeveloped countries—is much greater than either the volume of the papers or their circulation figures would indicate. If one newspaper is purchased per family it may be read by as many as three or four adults, even in the cities; in the rural areas the family readership might be even greater; in small towns and rural centers newspapers are found in municipal reading rooms and have a large volume of readership. It may be estimated that the readership is anywhere from three to four times as high as the actual circulation figures of the newspapers.

Foreign Media in Pakistan

Reuters, the Associated Press of America, the Agence France Presse, the Star News Agency, and the United Press International of America maintain offices in Pakistan. The last three have distributed news directly to local subscribing newspapers, but a government decree of October 1963 requires that all foreign news services must distribute their material through a national news agency.

The circulation of foreign newspapers on a relatively large scale takes place only in East Pakistan. Some of the interests of the Bengalis remain oriented toward the great commercial city of Calcutta and it is not surprising that the Calcutta English-language daily, the *Statesman*, commands a respectable circulation in Pakistan. Owing to regular air service between Calcutta and Dacca, the *Statesman* is actually in a position to compete with the *Morning News* and the *Pakistan Observer* on the Dacca newspaper market. Another Calcutta daily, the Bengali-language *Loka-Sevak*, commands a circulation of several thousand copies in Pakistan. In West Pakistan the Bombay edition of the *Times of India* is popular among the numerous businessmen who migrated from Bombay to Karachi.

Among foreign periodicals, the *Illustrated Weekly* of India with its well-presented feature articles is a serious competitor for Pakistan's *Illustrated Weekly*. Of all the overseas foreign publications, the *Reader's Digest* is undoubtedly the most widely read and displayed. Especially popular among the younger generation of the English-reading public, it is sold not only in the bookstores but even by hawkers at provincial railway stations throughout the country. *Time, Newsweek, Life,* and the *Saturday Evening Post* can be seen displayed in bookstores and stalls and are available in library reading rooms. British publications have been familiar to readers of English for years and enjoy considerable popularity. These publications include the *Economist*, the *New Statesman, Illustrated, Argosy, Daily Mirror* (weekly edition), *Women's Own*, and the *Lady*.

A number of foreign countries—and the United Nations—maintain press attachés or information services in Pakistan. These organizations produce and distribute a variety of information materials, written and spoken as well as visual. Their activities are largely confined to the important cities and towns and to the mass media of information. The Chinese Information Service (Communist China), for example, has distributed a great deal of material about Chinese Moslems, most of it in Urdu. This also applies to the publications of the Egyptian, Tunisian, and Russian information services. Paperback works by Chinese and Russian authors are sold at low prices in many bookstores, especially in East Pakistan. Among the services provided by Western countries, the British Council, the British Information Service, and the United States Information Service have libraries at Karachi, Lahore, and Dacca. The largest proportion of visitors are students and their main interests appear to be centered on technical subjects. Art classes and public lectures arranged by these organizations are also well attended. The United States Information Service, moreover, has at its disposal a number of mobile vans to carry documentary films into the rural areas. Mobile exhibits produced by some of the foreign services are in great demand by schools, universities, and cultural organizations throughout the country. According to the experience of the United Nations Information Center at Karachi, the effectiveness of press releases and abstract information is limited by comparison with that of visual media (films, film-strips, and exhibits).

The Cinema

Films have provided a highly popular form of entertainment in the urban centers of the subcontinent for a number of years. With the gradual growth of the motion-picture industry in Pakistan, it became increasingly apparent that, to enable local films to compete with Indian productions, it was imperative that their quality be improved. At the same time there was increasing official awareness of the potentiality of the cinema as a powerful medium for mass communication. The government-sponsored National Film Conference of 1956, therefore, recommended establishment of a corporation which would extend technical and financial assistance to existing studios, of a Motion Picture Academy, and of two new pilot studios. It was decided to organize an annual film festival and to arrange for presentation of presidential awards to the best motion pictures of the year.

The resulting increase in domestic film production and the lifting of a protective ban against the import of Indian films had a favorable effect on viewing facilities. In 1948 Pakistan had 280 cinemas, in 1956 there were 320, and the number has continued to increase.

Film censorship was one of the many legacies of British rule in India and the government of Pakistan has experimented with approaches to the subject. For some years the provincial governments operated separate censorship boards; then an ordinance of 1961 allocated this task to the central government; finally, with the promulgation of the 1962 constitution responsibility was returned to the provinces. But legislation enacted in 1963 brought the matter once again into the hands of the central government, which is currently empowered to appoint regional censorship boards. Censorship standards relating to moral codes do not seem to be applied as strictly to films with a foreign setting as to films with a Pakistan background.

Other Media

One striking aspect of life on the Indo-Pakistan subcontinent is the rapidity with which large crowds will gather at the slightest provocation. Meetings of all kinds are a welcome interruption of the drab existence led by the majority of the people and are usually well attended. It is therefore not surprising that all types of organizations, whether religious or political, have recognized meetings as an important channel of communication with the illiterate masses. Whether they are religious or political in character, public meetings will generally start with a recitation from the Qur'an. If it is a political meeting the organizers may end it by taking their followers, accompanied by a loudspeaker-van blaring slogans, in procession through the town or village. For the purpose of political information on the village level and at fair times, the usefulness of meetings cannot be denied, as they frequently provide one of the villager's rare contacts with personalities outside his immediate world. It is to be noted that President Ayub Khan follows a consistent program of addressing mass meetings throughout Pakistan.

Pamphlets are a very widely used medium of information in Pakistan, an important reason being the absence of any censorship over pamphlets. An inquiry into the Punjab Disturbances of 1953 revealed that pamphlets played an extremely important role in inciting the public to acts of violence. Equally important, however, is the fact that pamphlets normally carry no date and, unlike newspapers, are apt to be preserved by the recipient, particularly if they contain some form of religious material.

Billboards are used for advertising purposes in the large towns and along main highways. Frequently Urdu slogans for better health and education can be seen stenciled on house walls in West Pakistan. Both billboards and posters are usually covered with a fair amount of text and, more often than not, are not conceived visually enough to appeal to a largely illiterate public. An interesting use of billboards is made by the motion-picture industry. To promote a new film a man carrying a poster advertising the film wanders through a town followed by a small band of musicians playing tunes from the picture.

Loudspeakers are widely used for political as well as advertising purposes. Frequently they are mounted on cars or mobile vans which can be seen covering the countryside—to the extent that it is accessible by road—as well as the towns. Loudspeakers are especially noticeable in market towns and at fairs. Apart from the fact that they are not dependent on literacy, loudspeakers are a sufficiently informal medium to permit the use of local languages and dialects, which greatly enhances their effectiveness.

The people in the villages rarely benefit directly from the dissemination of information through the mass media, such as the press, radio, or films, although each union council is alleged to be provided with a radio set. In the villages the age-old familiar methods of face-to-face communication continue to prevail. Market towns and villages are among the most important places for the dissemination of news. Here people exchange information about the events affecting their lives while congregating to buy or sell things. These visits are usually confined to the male head of the family but, on his return, he will pass on what he has learned to his customers, relatives, or friends.

Village fairs and *urs* also constitute important centers for the diffusion of news. While a market town or village fair may cater to the needs of thirty to a hundred villages, a country fair, depending on its reputation, may be attended by people from a hundred to a thousand. Not all the people in a village get a chance to visit the fairs regularly but many attend them at least a few times in the course of their lives. The performances they attend or some new agricultural equipment they see may leave an indelible impression on their minds, profoundly affecting their attitudes toward certain problems.

Itinerant bards and storytellers are also important carriers of information. Their repertory may range from mythological stories to information about locally important families.

Inside the villages the *hookah* group meetings constitute the most important opportunities for interaction between people. A hookah group is a sort of informal village club: the men will gather, perhaps at the house of one of the wealthier members, to discuss affairs of interest to the community. This is the place where news from the outside is discussed or where important strangers may visit and speak. In some of the bigger villages the hookah groups are gradually being abandoned for the informal gatherings at the tea stall or coffeehouses, some of which have radios.

Friday or holiday services at the local mosque are also important occasions for imparting information or propaganda. Mullahs frequently refer to public affairs and politics in their sermons and in the course of special addresses which often precede the Friday prayer services.

Women have their own channels of communication. Elderly women may be important bearers of news in the course of their roving or friendly visiting. Midwives who are on constant rounds relay information acquired in the course of their work. The village well or canal is an important place for gossiping and passing on information. School children learn about the affairs of other families in the play hour at school and may pass on to their parents knowledge and information imbibed from their teachers. In the normal course of events news is propagated on a sex basis in villages, men communicating mostly with men, women with other women.

Few newspapers reach the villages. They are received by members of the educated elite—someone who has lived in the town for a while or a schoolteacher. In a village with a postoffice the postmaster may receive a copy or open some other person's paper to read the latest news and pass it on; many people make a point of visiting the postoffice at least once a day for "news." Villages which do not have a postoffice are occasionally—and some of them regularly—visited by the *dakia*, the postman, who is always assured of a good reception. While some villagers actually come for mail, others gather just to hear the news.

It goes without saying that in a country characterized by a dearth of organized media of communication, rumor provides an important source of correct, but more frequently of misleading, information. Servants, for example, eagerly exchange during their daily shopping rounds at the bazaar bits of conversation picked up at their masters' homes. So-called *bazaar gup*, or gossip, has been the source of some of the wildest rumors circulated among the population in times of war and political stress.

Official Information Media

In the light of the factors of relative political instability and the geographical, social, and political cleavage between East and West, no government of Pakistan has been successful in evolving a propaganda focus commensurate with the need to rally the nation for internal development. The Islamic concept was sufficiently powerful to win mass support for establishing the nation, but not for inculcating in the people a sense of purpose and direction for the future. In foreign affairs, on the other hand, constant fear of India has provided a rallying point enabling the various governments to evolve a consistent, though ambivalent, line of internal and external propaganda. Limited emphasis is placed on external propaganda, as is demonstrated by the relatively small sums allotted to information services abroad.

Official information programs of the central government are the responsibility of the Division of Information and Broadcasting of the Ministry of Education and Information (see the chart, Organizational Structure of the Ministry of Education and Information). The central ministry also maintains regional information offices in each province, but for certain types of information activities the provinces have their own organizations.

In each province a Directorate of Public Relations, under the Information Office, handles all types of government propaganda and publishes a weekly magazine. Special importance is attached to internal and external public relations activities in regard to Kashmir. The Ministry of Home and Kashmir Affairs includes a Chief Advisor to the Azad Government of the State of Jammu and Kashmir. The Director of Information of the Azad Government publishes, at Rawalpindi, a biweekly *Azad Kashmir News,* and the Department of Films and Publications of Pakistan proper puts out a great deal of material on Kashmir.

For propaganda connected with foreign affairs the Ministry of Education and Information maintains liaison with the Ministry of Foreign Affairs. A deputy secretary of the Ministry of Foreign Affairs is usually attached to the Ministry of Education and Information to guide and supervise foreign publicity. At a lower echelon, foreign publicity is carried out by press attachés in important capitals of the world. For example, the Embassy of Pakistan in Washington publishes a biweekly, *Pakistan Affairs.*

Direct and indirect relations between the government and the press are maintained by the Press Information Department of the Division of Information and Broadcasting. Apart from arranging press conferences for prominent government officials, this department distributes photographs and press releases concerning activities of the government. Most of this material is released in English

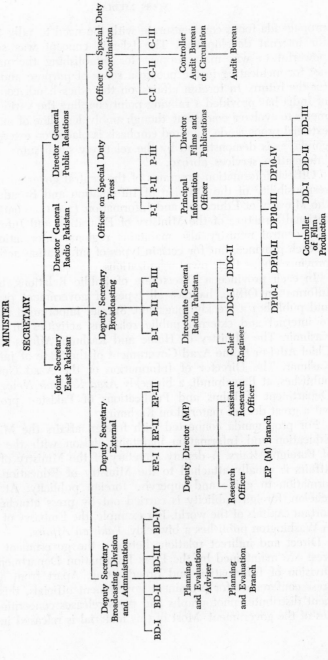

MINISTRY OF EDUCATION AND INFORMATION

Information and Broadcasting Division

MINISTER

SECRETARY

Joint Secretary East Pakistan

Deputy Secretary Broadcasting Division and Administration
- BD-I
- BD-II
- BD-III
- BD-IV

Planning and Evaluation Adviser

Planning and Evaluation Branch

Deputy Director (MP)

Research Officer

Assistant Research Officer

EP (M) Branch

Deputy Secretary External
- EP-I
- EP-II
- EP-III

Deputy Secretary Broadcasting

Directorate General Radio Pakistan

Chief Engineer

DDG-I

DDG-II

- B-I
- B-II
- B-III

Director General Radio Pakistan

Officer on Special Duty Press

Principal Information Officer
- P-I
- P-II
- P-III

Director Films and Publications
- DP10-I
- DP10-II
- DP10-III
- DP10-IV

Controller of Film Production
- DD-I
- DD-II
- DD-III

Director General Public Relations

Officer on Special Duty Coordination

Controller Audit Bureau of Circulation

Audit Bureau
- C-I
- C-II
- C-III

—Urdu and Bengali being used only where the original text was in these languages. Speeches by ministers or other important officials are frequently released in the vernacular languages and in pamphlet form. The smaller vernacular publications tend to be more dependent on official press releases as sources of stories than the large metropolitan papers with their access to news agency stories.

The Press Information Department also issues the semimonthly *Pakistan News Digest* designed for citizens of the country living abroad. It is an eight-page tabloid, well illustrated and printed on airmail paper. It contains speeches by important officials, economic and political news items, and a digest of domestic and foreign newspaper editorials. Heavy emphasis is placed on Pakistan's foreign relations, with special reference to Kashmir.

Publications of a general informational and tourist variety generally carry the imprint of the Department of Films and Publications or of the Department of Tourism. Publications directly concerned with government activities, such as reports of the ministries, the annual budget, and statistical and census reports are published by the Manager of Publications, Karachi.

By far the most widely distributed publicity periodicals and publications are, however, issued by Pakistan Publications, a Karachi publishing firm which is controlled by the central government. The presentation and make-up of these publications are of high quality, though this does not always apply to the contents. The many books and magazines which this firm has to its credit include the *Pakistan Quarterly,* a high-class cultural periodical, several books of the literature and arts of Pakistan, and such handbooks as *Ten Years of Pakistan, Pakistan: Basic Facts, Pakistan Miscellany,* and an annual, *Pakistan.*

The Bureau of National Reconstruction publicizes the Basic Democracies through a variety of publications, including the weekly, *Pak Jamhuriat: The People's Paper,* which appears in English, Urdu, and Bengali editions.

Broadcasting

Radio broadcasting is a government monopoly. It traces its history to the development of broadcasting in India where it had begun as a private enterprise in 1926. Financial difficulties had induced the British government of India to assume direct control and at partition Pakistan assumed the monopoly for its areas.

Radio Pakistan came on the air for the first time at midnight on August 14, 1947 over three low-powered medium-wave stations at Lahore, Peshawar, and Dacca with a total output of 20 kilowatts. By 1960 the government had at its disposal a total of 204 kilowatts for the operation of 19 transmitters and was able to broadcast 143 daily program hours in 17 different languages. Today Radio Pakistan is an organic system with medium-wave transmitters at Karachi, Lahore, Peshawar, Rawalpindi, Quetta, Hyderabad, Dacca, Rajshahi, Sylhet, and Chittagong, and short-wave transmitters at Karachi, Lahore, Dacca, Peshawar, and Rawalpindi. The first effective east-west link between the two wings was provided by the installation of a 100 kilowatt short-wave transmitter at Dacca. Stations within West Pakistan are linked by teleprinter service, as are Karachi, Dacca, and Rawalpindi. Broadcasting House, headquarters of Radio Pakistan, is located in Karachi and its fourteen air-conditioned studios and eight booths are equipped with the latest sound apparatus and the most modern studio devices.

In 1959 the listening audience of the country was estimated at 1.5 million people. The number of licensed sets in 1959 was 227,000 but it is certain that the number of sets in operation far exceeded those for which licenses had been obtained. At present three foreign companies operate receiver assembly plants in Pakistan and meet the current demand without additional imports. Future development under the Second Five Year Plan aims at serving the entire population through medium-wave transmitters, as well as stressing the domestic manufacture of inexpensive listening sets and batteries. It is important to note that only battery-powered radios can be used in the vast unelectrified rural areas.

The programs of Radio Pakistan are produced by two parallel services, one for home listeners and the other directed at listeners abroad. Broadcasts in the External Service are prepared in English, Arabic, Urdu, Persian, Afghan-Persian, Pushtu, Gujarati, and Burmese; they are beamed to the United Kingdom, the Middle East, South Asia, Southeast Asia, East Africa, and Southeast Africa. News and music are the mainstay of these broadcasts.

Programs in the Home Service are made up of about 30 to 35 per cent spoken material and the balance music. Only about 10 per cent of the musical programs offer indigenous classical music, the remainder being devoted to film or folk music.

Spoken programs of national interest originate in Karachi and are relayed by regional stations. This applies, for instance, to broadcasts by leading public figures and to radio plays, which Karachi broadcasts about once or twice a week. It applies above all to news broadcasts which are all prepared in Karachi. Local news is broadcast in English, Urdu, Bengali, Pushtu, Baluchi, and Kashmiri. News in Sindhi, Punjabi, and Pushtu is broadcast from the regional stations at Karachi, Lahore, and Peshawar respectively.

Apart from subscribing to the national and foreign news agencies operating in Pakistan, Radio Pakistan has its own Central News Organization, which maintains correspondents in important centers and dispatches others, whenever possible, to cover important national as well as international events. News broadcasts, however, reflect the official point of view and may perhaps be termed the purest form of government propaganda.

Rural broadcasts are an integral and most important part of regional programs and are alleged to be very popular. The rural programs broadcast from Lahore have the reputation of attracting listeners on the Indian side of the border, while the folk music programs from Dacca have a considerable audience in West Bengal. For the purpose of popularization, news broadcasts are dramatized by having the announcer enact a village character who tells a story.

Regional stations also broadcast religious, women's, children's, school, and armed forces programs and include market bulletins, weather forecasts, and special programs for tribal areas.

At present commercial advertising over Radio Pakistan is limited to a total of one hour a day, with the messages grouped in units rather than coming at frequent intervals throughout the day. Six journals, one each in English, Urdu, Bengali, Arabic, Persian, and Burmese, publish the programs of Radio Pakistan.

Documentary Films

Few documentary films were made during the first years of Pakistan's existence. Initially, in the absence of a documentary film laboratory, the few films produced on behalf of the government had to be farmed out entirely to foreign companies or at least had to be processed abroad. However, following the installation of a film processing laboratory in Karachi the Department of Films and Publications has been very active in this field. The 1962 edition of its *Film Catalogue* lists 70 documentary films and 35 documentary-cum-newsreels. In addition, this department issues a weekly newsreel as well as a variety of newsreels on special events

and subjects. Many of the documentary films are produced in both
35 mm. and 16 mm., and in both black and white and color. All
carry English-language sound tracks and are also available in local
languages. These films include travelogues, studies of agricultural
and economic development, cultural subjects, and didactic films.
Many are available on loan from the offices of the press attachés
abroad.

CHAPTER 14

Foreign Relations

IN THE FIELD OF FOREIGN RELATIONS the new state of Pakistan faced the problem of creating an attractive image of the power and prestige of the country—a task all the more difficult because the world tended to identify the new India and its well-known leaders with the entire subcontinent. Pakistan had to start from a handicapped position in publicizing its position and its views in early disputes with India and, within a relatively brief period, had to make policy decisions and choices certain to affect the foreign relations of the country over a long period. While the disputes with India were a major concern because of the possibility that they could result in open warfare, there was also, from the beginning, friction with Afghanistan. With its very large Moslem population, Pakistan felt the urge to take the initiative in promoting closer ties among all the Moslem nations. It was at the same time confronted with a choice between following a neutral policy and entering into alliances with other countries. The decision to join CENTO and SEATO was of particular importance as concerned long-term relations with the United States, the Communist powers, and India.

Relations with India were fraught with danger from the moment of partition. It was perhaps inevitable that the partition of the subcontinent along religious lines in 1947 would be accompanied by dissension and bitterness—although the chaos and bloodshed that actually resulted exceeded the expectations of the most pessimistic. Boundary disputes, arguments over the disposition of property left behind by the refugees, and the division of the assets and liabilities of prepartition India between the two countries could hardly be resolved to the satisfaction of all, but it was the accompanying violence that left a bitter residue of mutual hostility.

Problems of Accession

According to the Indian Independence Act, the rulers of the 562 Indian states, populated by about 90 million people, were to choose whether to retain autonomous status or to accede to either Pakistan or India. Lord Mountbatten, then governor general, recommended to these rulers that the religious composition and wishes of the populations and the geographical locations of the states be taken into consideration. Before partition actually took place in August, most of the states had come to a decision. Bahawalpur, Khairpur, and the states of the North-West Frontier province and Baluchistan joined Pakistan. Most of the remaining states chose to become a part of India. The three states that had not acceded to either India or Pakistan by Independence Day were Junagadh, Hyderabad, and the State of Jammu and Kashmir. Two of these, Junagadh and Hyderabad, have no contiguity with Pakistan and their populations were predominantly non-Moslem, but the Moslem monarchs who ruled them did not wish to accede to India.

Junagadh was a small state on the west coast of India about 210 miles south of the nearest Pakistan territory. On September 15, 1947 its ruler signed an instrument of accession to Pakistan and a controversy followed immediately. India took the position that the question of Junagadh's accession should be settled by a plebiscite; Pakistan held that, with the ruler's signing of an instrument of accession to Pakistan, Junagadh became a part of Pakistan and that legally and constitutionally there could be no question of limiting the ruler's right to accede to Pakistan. India brought military forces to Junagadh's border; the ruler of the state fled to Pakistan; and the Dewan, or prime minister, invited the Indian forces into the state. The Dewan later stated that this invitation was in response to a threatening ultimatum from an organization known as the Provisional Government of Junagadh, which had been formed in India and was led by Samaldas Gandhi, a nephew of Mohandas K. Gandhi. The Junagadh affair came to an end when Indian troops entered Junagadh on November 9, 1947. A plebiscite held later overwhelmingly favored accession to India. In Pakistan, however, the accession to Pakistan by Junagadh's ruler is still regarded as legally valid—although the government has given less and less voice to this claim.

The Hyderabad dispute also involved a state having a predominantly Hindu population with a Moslem ruling dynasty. But the

ruler of Hyderabad, a large state in the southern part of the subcontinent surrounded by India, sought to remain independent rather
than accede to either dominion. Pakistan was thus not directly concerned in the Hyderabad affair. Yet Pakistanis took a lively interest in Hyderabad—a long-established seat of Moslem culture
and living link with Moghul times—and generally favored its independence, fearing that the Moslem elements in the state would
be quickly submerged if it were to become integrated with India.
A standstill agreement between the government of India and the
ruler of Hyderabad was signed at the end of November 1947. Although negotiations between the two governments continued actively for almost a year, no negotiated agreement for Hyderabad's
accession to India was reached. Furthermore, feelings between
India and Hyderabad were becoming embittered by growing disorder within the state as opposing Moslem and Hindu extremist
elements clashed. Along with these disturbances frequent clashes
occurred on both sides of the state's borders with India. In this
situation, and with negotiations getting nowhere, India began to
prepare for military action against Hyderabad. The ruler of Hyderabad reacted by appealing to the United Nations Security
Council, but before the appeal could be considered India sent her
troops into the state and quickly overcame the state's forces. Despite
the subsequent withdrawal of the appeal by the ruler of Hyderabad,
Pakistan proceeded to protest India's action in taking over the
state and in May 1949 brought the matter again before the Security
Council. Pakistan's position was that India's action in Hyderabad
constituted aggression against an independent state and therefore a
threat to the maintenance of peace. India claimed that Hyderabad
had not become a fully independent state after the withdrawal of
the British and that therefore Indian action in Hyderabad was solely
an internal affair. Here the matter rested.

Pakistan might perhaps have lost interest in Junagadh and
Hyderabad after these relatively far-removed Hindu-majority states
had been taken over by India had it not been for the Kashmir
dispute. Instead of a Moslem dynasty ruling Hindus, in Kashmir
a Hindu dynasty, with its seat at Srinagar, ruled a state in which
three persons out of four were Moslems; instead of being an area
far away in India, Kashmir was contiguous with Pakistan. In
short, the situation was the reverse of that in Hyderabad or
Junagadh. The name "Kashmir" is commonly, if loosely, used to
refer to the State of Jammu and Kashmir and includes far more

than the famous Vale of Kashmir, although that is the most important part. The State of Jammu and Kashmir comprises a total area of more than 84,000 square miles—an area much larger than East Pakistan and approximately the size of Minnesota—made up of several parts: Kashmir province, Jammu province, the state of Punch, the Gilgit Agency, and the regions of Baltistan and Ladakh. Those parts other than Kashmir and Jammu provinces—i.e. the so-called Frontier Districts—contain 75 per cent of the area and 7 per cent of the population and consist of vast areas of Himalayan peaks and arid valleys (see Table 10).

Maharaja Sir Hari Singh, the ruler of Kashmir, and his predominantly Hindu administration had no enthusiasm for joining either a Moslem Pakistan or an India moving in the direction of democratic socialism. Thus, in spite of pressure from Lord Mountbatten to join one of the two countries, the Maharaja procrastinated during the summer of 1947, hoping to remain independent of both. Soon after partition, Gilgit and the Skardu region of Ladakh revolted against Kashmiri rule and acceded to Pakistan. These districts were far removed from Srinagar and their overwhelmingly Moslem population was in no mood to tolerate the few non-Moslem officials stationed there. A similar attitude in Punch, a small district in the southwest, caused the Punchis to revolt following the violent suppression by Hindu authorities of their pro-Pakistan demonstrations, and much of the district came under rebel control.

By October 1947 Moslems living in the districts of Kashmir near the Pakistan border had set up an Azad (Free) Kashmir government at Muzaffarabad and organized an independent army made up of ex-servicemen from Punch and the Mirpur district of Kashmir. Many Moslem refugees from Kashmir who had fled to Pakistan also joined this army which ultimately received supplies from Pakistan. At the same time some 2,000 tribesmen from Pakistan's North-West Frontier province were preparing to enter Kashmir—evidently neither supported nor opposed by Pakistan's officials, who were in any case deeply preoccupied with the immense task of bringing order out of the chaos that followed partition. The tribesmen met with little resistance and plundered and massacred their way up the Jhelum river valley toward Srinagar, the capital of Kashmir. The Maharaja first became aware of the proximity of the tribesmen when the lights went out in the palace at Srinagar and the trouble was traced to the power plant thirty miles away which the tribesmen had captured.

The Maharaja acceded to India on October 26, 1947 stating that "the alternative is to leave my state and the people to freebooters." Lord Mountbatten accepted the next day in behalf of India, promising: "It is my Government's wish that, as soon as law and order have been restored in Kashmir and its soil cleared of the invader, the question of the State's accession should be settled by a reference to the people." Prime Minister Nehru accepted the principle of plebiscite under Lord Mountbatten's proviso. The same day Indian troops were flown into Srinagar to bring the tribesmen under control. Disorganized and preoccupied with loot, the latter were no match for a disciplined force, although they continued to be reasonably effective in guerrilla activity.

For its part, Pakistan refused to recognize the Maharaja's accession to India. As Indian troops advanced in the direction of Pakistan's borders, the Pakistan government became increasingly alarmed. At first the Pakistan army units were merely stationed in strategic locations inside Pakistan in case an Indian break-through should be attempted, but in May 1948 troops crossed into Azad Kashmir and actively participated in holding the line against the Indian army. Neither side, however, wished to engage in any major offensive effort which might extend the fighting into either Pakistan or India. Anxious to find a solution, Pakistan's Prime Minister Liaquat 'Ali Khan agreed to a plebiscite on condition that Indian troops be withdrawn, state troops immobilized, and a coalition government with representatives of the Azad Kashmir government placed in charge of the government at Srinagar. Prime Minister Nehru refused and intermittent warfare continued.

Early in 1948 India presented to the Security Council its charge that Pakistan had committed an act of aggression against it in Kashmir, recommending that the United Nations condemn Pakistan for the invasion of Kashmir and request Pakistan to withdraw its forces so that a plebiscite could be held. The United Nations was to be invited to observe and advise. Pakistan countered by challenging the Maharaja's accession to India and submitting charges of its own against India. The Security Council refused to condemn Pakistan for aggression and instead offered its good offices to aid in restoring law and order and for arranging a plebiscite in Kashmir. A United Nations Commission for India and Pakistan was duly set up on April 21, 1948 to investigate the facts and determine the conditions under which a fair plebiscite might be held. In July its members visited Kashmir and on January 1, 1949, with the assistance of the commission, a cease fire was arranged along a stabilized military front. Teams of United Nations observers remained in the area to report any violations.

The cease-fire line left India in control of the fertile Vale of Kashmir and the mountainous regions to the east and southeast, while Pakistan controlled most of the mountainous areas to the northwest and a narrow and hilly strip of western Kashmir bordering Pakistan. At the time hostilities ceased Pakistan had an estimated 81,000 soldiers on its side of the cease-fire line and India 130,000 troops on the eastern side of the line. Three-fourths of the population and most of the cultivable land of Kashmir lie on the Indian side.

The UN has tried continually, but without success, to arrange a plebiscite. Two of the resolutions adopted by the UN have been agreed upon by both countries and have formed the basis of most of the subsequent attempts to obtain a satisfactory settlement. The first of these was adopted on August 13, 1948 and provided for (1) a cease-fire order, (2) UN military observers, (3) the withdrawal of all of Pakistan's troops, citizens, and tribesmen, (4) the withdrawal of the bulk of Indian troops—leaving a number (to be agreed on by the United Nations commission) sufficient to enable India to maintain law and order and guarantee political rights, and (5) the joint determination, by the two countries and the commission, of the conditions prerequisite to an impartial plebiscite. However, India interpreted this agreement to mean that the Azad Kashmir government would surrender the areas under its control to the Kashmir government; Pakistan would not agree to this.

A second resolution, adopted on January 5, 1949 and endorsed by both India and Pakistan, reaffirmed the principle that the question of accession was to be determined by plebiscite and provided for a plebiscite administrator who, together with the commission, would act as arbitrator in the final distribution of the armed forces and other matters. Disagreements again arose over the disposition of the Azad Kashmir forces and the jurisdiction of the Azad Kashmir government. In February 1951 the Security Council resumed debate on the issue and a month later once more urged that a plebiscite be held under UN auspices. Dr. Frank D. Graham, appointed as arbitrator, went to Kashmir to arrange for its demilitarization but was unsuccessful.

Left with no alternative, the Security Council adopted in December 1952 a resolution calling on both parties to the dispute to reach an agreement on demilitarization. Pakistan and India did engage in discussions and again went on record as agreeing in principle to the holding of a plebiscite under a plebiscite administrator to be named by the UN. Concrete action was not forthcoming, however, and in January 1957 Pakistan renewed its appeal to the Security Council, stating that it had accepted all the recommendations of the UN but that India had not done so. Prime Minister Nehru defended India's position by pointing out that Pakistan's action in joining CENTO and SEATO, with the concomitant acceptance of arms from the United States, had radically altered the situation prevailing at the time the recommendations were made. The Security Council, with the USSR abstaining, thereupon adopted a resolution giving broad powers to a UN representative who was to negotiate a settlement with both parties. Early in 1958 Dr. Graham was in contact with both governments, asking them to accept a five-point proposal for these negotiations: India refused.

In April 1962 Pakistan again requested the Security Council to take up the issue and in June debate began on a resolution which once more offered the good offices of the UN in the resumption of negotiations. In this debate Krishna Menon stated that the accession of Jammu and Kashmir to India was "full, complete and final" and that any form of intervention was unwelcome to India. When the resolution came to a vote a few weeks later, it was vetoed by the USSR. At that moment the prospect of direct negotiations between Pakistan and India seemed very remote. Yet, under circumstances which are more appropriately discussed in a later paragraph, before the end of the year delegates from the two nations began such negotiations—only to break off their talks once more after several rounds of meetings during the spring of 1963.

During the more than a decade in which the Kashmir issue had been repeatedly examined and discussed by the UN, both Pakistan and India had taken steps to strengthen their control over the areas contiguous to these countries. In 1951 the son of the former Maharaja, who had replaced his deposed father as head of state, defied the Security Council and called for the election of a constituent assembly for Kashmir. All seventy-five seats were subsequently won by the National Conference party. (It appeared that no opposition party was allowed to organize an election campaign; in any case only two seats were contested.) The leader of the party was Shaikh Muhammad Abdullah—the "Lion of Kashmir"—who had been jailed in 1946 for campaigning against the Maharaja but, generally assumed to be pro-India because of his role in the Indian National Congress, had been released a year later and made prime minister of Kashmir. The newly elected constituent assembly dutifully deprived the long-absent Maharaja of his powers and confirmed his son as "head of state" but balked at ratification of a tentative agreement with India which virtually extended Indian sovereignty to Kashmir. When Shaikh Abdullah insisted that a plebiscite be held he was removed from office and imprisoned without trial in 1953. His deputy, Bakshi Ghulam Muhammad, became the new prime minister and soon afterward the agreement was ratified by the unanimous vote of all members present (six of the eleven absent members were in jail). Henceforth India claimed—much to Pakistan's irritation—that Kashmir's constituent assembly had voted for accession to India and that the integration of Kashmir with India was complete.

After four and a half years of detention, Shaikh Abdullah was released from prison early in 1958. His first act was to denounce Kashmir's constituent assembly as unrepresentative and incompetent: "The front-rank members of the body were put in prison. . . . Those who were not in prison were forced into submission by threats . . . and irresistible temptations were thrown in their way. . . . There was no contact between these members and their constituents." The ultimate decision on accession, in his opinion, could only be decided by a vote of the people under impartial international supervision. However, in some remarks he seemed to propose that a plebiscite should offer three alternatives—accession to Pakistan, accession to India, or independence for Kashmir. Several months after his release he was again placed under arrest. In 1961 he was brought to trial on charges of conspiracy to overawe by criminal force and in 1962, still on trial, was charged with having conspired to wage war. Bakshi Ghulam Muhammad was replaced as prime minister in October 1963 by Sham al-Din, and in April 1964 all charges against Shaikh Abdullah were dismissed and he was released from detention.

On its side of the cease-fire line, Pakistan lends support to the Azad government of the State of Jammu and Kashmir, currently headed by President K. H. Khurshid, who presides over a State Council.

The Problem of Water Rights

Next to the Kashmir issue the most important cause of friction between Pakistan and Inda has been control of the waters of the Indus river and its five tributaries: the Jhelum, Chenab, Ravi, Beas, and Sutlej rivers. The British in India constructed barrages and an extensive network of canals in the upper basins of these tributaries —the region of the Punjab, or "five waters." Partition conveyed most of the irrigated land of the Punjab to Pakistan, while the headwaters and some canal headworks went to India. On April 1, 1948 India shut off the supply of water to major canals leading into Pakistan, depriving the country of 1.7 million acre-feet of water. Pakistan initiated discussions, claiming that the rights of established users of the water must be recognized, and a month later India restored the supply to the canals. However, India insisted that it had exclusive rights to the Ravi, Beas, and Sutlej rivers and declined Pakistan's proposal that the matter be referred to the International Court of Justice.

A way out of the impasse came with the visit in 1951 of David E. Lilienthal, a former chairman of the Tennessee Valley Authority, who subsequently published an article suggesting that the International Bank for Reconstruction and Development be invited to intervene in the dispute and take the lead in preparing a plan for the joint development of the resources of all the rivers. Responding to Lilienthal's suggestion, Eugene Black, president of the International Bank, conferred with officials of Pakistan and India, and negotiations were opened.

These negotiations dragged on and on until on September 19, 1960, the Indus Waters Treaty was signed by the governments of India and Pakistan, by the International Bank, and by those governments—including the United States, the United Kingdom, Australia, Canada, New Zealand, and the Federal Republic of Germany—which had agreed to supply grants or loans toward the financing of the irrigation works, estimated cost $1,070,000,000. The treaty allocated the waters of the Indus, Jhelum, and Chenab to Pakistan; those of the Ravi, Beas, and Sutlej to India. It also spelled out the location of huge new storage dams and the course of major canals. Pakistan having given up rights to the three eastern rivers, India agreed to supply a larger proportion of the total cost of the integrated development.

311

The Pakhtunistan Dispute

The frontier between Pakistan and Afghanistan is over a thousand miles in length. Most of its course was demarcated in 1893 as the result of an agreement between the then amir of Afghanistan and a British mission headed by Sir Mortimer Durand—hence its name, the Durand Line. Closely related tribal peoples overlap the Durand Line: in Pakistan they are called Pathans and in Afghanistan Pakhtuns or Pushtuns. A turbulent group, long relying upon sporadic warfare to supplement their income from sparse fields and numerous flocks, they consistently resisted efforts by the British forces in India to penetrate and pacify their areas. The British established the North-West Frontier province as a major administrative unit, with the areas immediately adjacent to the Afghan frontier controlled by five Political Agencies.

Prior to partition the government of Afghanistan suggested that the Pathans be allowed to decide whether to accede to India, accede to Pakistan, or become independent. This suggestion, outlined in diplomatic notes, was later rejected on the ground that the inhabitants of the North-West Frontier province had already voted in favor of joining Pakistan. (One consequence was that in October 1947 Afghanistan cast the only vote against the admission of Pakistan to the United Nations, although it did vote in favor of admission at a later date.) The Afghan government sponsored propaganda calling for the creation of an autonomous state of Pakhtunistan, or Pushtunistan, which would include all the Pathans within Pakistan. Maps of Pakhtunistan depicted an area stretching east to the Indus river and south to the Arabian Sea and may have reflected the wish of landlocked Afghanistan to gain direct access to seaports.

As had been the case prior to partition, most of the foreign trade of Afghanistan moved through the port of Karachi and by rail to its frontier. However, as the Afghan government pressed for Pakhtunistan and allegedly inspired tribal dissension within Pakistan, the government of Pakistan retaliated by halting the movement of Afghan goods, with the first such action occurring in 1950. The USSR responded by offering Afghanistan transit rights and in 1955 moved to exploit the increasing dependence of Afghanistan upon the route through the Soviet Union by extending financial credits to Afghanistan. Also, Soviet leaders openly supported Afghanistan on the Pakhtunistan issue.

The incorporation of all the administrative units of West Pakistan into the "one unit" in 1955 was denounced by Afghanistan as a deliberate attempt to put an end to the special status of the Pathans, and the Afghan government stated that it no longer regarded the Durand Line as the boundary between Pakistan and Afghanistan. With mounting frequency there were clashes along the frontier and raids on police posts and other installations within Pakistan in the area the Afghans called "occupied Pakhtunistan." In September 1961 Pakistan asked the Afghan government to close its consulates and trade agencies in Pakistan, claiming that their personnel was directing hostile activity. Afghanistan immediately broke off diplomatic relations with Pakistan and declared that it would not move goods through Karachi until it was permitted to reopen the consulates and agencies. Concerned over the halt in the movement of supplies and equipment for American aid programs into Afghanistan and by the increasing reliance of Afghanistan on the Soviet Union as the only outlet for its trade, the United States offered its good offices as a mediator in the dispute between Pakistan and Afghanistan. Its representative met with members of both governments but no agreement was reached. In 1962 the Shah of Iran was accepted as a mediator, and in May 1963 representatives of Pakistan and Afghanistan met at Tehran and agreed to the immediate resumption of diplomatic relations. However, this agreement was concluded without reference to the still unresolved Pakhtunistan issue.

Relations with Moslem States

From the very beginning Pakistan's foreign policy has reflected a desire for close and friendly relations with other Moslem countries. This desire has found expression in several treaties of friendship and in the encouragement of various nongovernmental international Islamic organizations devoted to cultural, intellectual, or economic matters. It has supported the stand of the Arab states against Israel, encouraged independence movements in Tunisia, Algeria, Morocco, and Indonesia, and condemned "imperialism" in international disputes affecting the interests of Moslem nations.

Pakistan's consistent efforts to promote strong diplomatic and cultural ties with all Islamic countries have been hampered by the rising tide of Arab nationalism. There are more Moslems in Pakistan than in all of the Arab countries combined, but Pakistan is a newcomer to international society and few of its inhabitants can read or speak Arabic, the language of the Qur'an. Egypt has emerged as the leader of the Arab bloc and would reject any suggestion that it share the leadership of the Moslem world with Pakistan. Faced with a choice of friendship with either Pakistan or India, Egypt has indicated that it would choose the latter and has refused to support Pakistan in the Kashmir dispute. Pakistan supported Egypt vigorously during the Anglo-French invasion of the Suez in 1956, but President Nasser spurned Pakistan's offer of armed aid and even rejected the suggestion that Pakistanis participate in the United Nations force that was stationed in Egypt after the cease fire. This incident drew the following comment from a Karachi newspaper: "Nasser will never be our friend; he will never think in terms of Islam except when it suits his own interest."

Relations with the British Commonwealth

For historical reasons, Pakistan has more friendly ties with Great Britain than with any other country. In the decades preceding the final partition of the subcontinent, the British tended to side with the Moslem League in its disputes with the more anti-British Congress party. The friendship was enhanced by the cooperation of this section of India, which supplied many excellent soldiers during World War II. Most of the influential landowners of West Pakistan could trace their position of affluence to privileges granted to them by the British. Thus Pakistan began its existence with a reservoir of good will for Great Britain that was not seriously diminished by the several decisions made in 1947 by Sir Cyril Radcliffe and Lord Mountbatten that Pakistan regarded as blatantly pro-India. Most of Pakistan's resulting ill will was focused on Lord Mountbatten rather than on Great Britain.

There was little hesitation in Pakistan's decision to remain within the British Commonwealth of Nations. Most of the higher ranking civil servants in Pakistan had, at one time or another, been to England for training and Pakistan's leading lawyers, many of them active in politics, had all been educated at Cambridge or Oxford. The chief source of bitterness against the British had disappeared when independence became a reality. Many high-ranking English civil and military officers stayed on after partition to assist the new state in solving its difficult problems, although most have by now returned to Great Britain.

Pakistan had expected, however, that the Commonwealth would be of some assistance in settling disputes among its own membership. In this it was doomed to disappointment. Repeatedly at conferences of Commonwealth prime ministers Pakistan has attempted to introduce the Kashmir dispute, but it has become increasingly evident that the various dominions are reluctant to introduce dissension into Commonwealth meetings and, in any case, are not willing to go beyond the discussion state; some of Pakistan's spokesmen believed that the dispute should be judged by disinterested members of the Commonwealth and that failure to implement their recommendations should result, as a last resort, in the expulsion of the defaulting member from the Commonwealth.

Pakistan has also been disturbed by the failure of the Commonwealth to adopt an anticolonial policy or to vigorously oppose racial prejudice and segregation in South Africa. Nevertheless, it decided to remain within the Commonwealth as a republic when it adopted its first constitution.

In 1950 the Commonwealth countries were instrumental in establishing the Colombo Plan for Co-operative Economic Development in South and South East Asia. In this organization the United States and several Asian countries are associated with the members of the Commonwealth in planning and financing development projects. Pakistan has benefited from the Colombo Plan in the areas of financing and of technical assistance and training.

Relations with the United States

Although the mass of the Pakistani population is probably incapable of distinguishing one English-speaking country from another, those who speak English themselves appear well-disposed toward the United States. Many find a common bond in the fact that the United States, like Pakistan, was ruled for many years by Great Britain before achieving independence. Others get from American motion pictures a distorted impression of everyday life in the United States or, reflecting the views of a former teacher or newsstand pamphlet, envision the United States as an amalgam of Wall Street, capitalism, and racial prejudice. Most educated Pakistanis are aware that Pakistan is receiving substantial amounts of aid from the United States but have difficulty understanding why much more aid goes to India—which Pakistan sees as the country most likely to encroach upon her sovereignty.

Prior to 1950 the only Americans who knew much about Pakistan were those reporters, diplomats, and educators whose jobs

315

required such knowledge. Then Prime Minister Liaquat 'Ali Khan visited the United States and used every opportunity to acquaint Americans with the importance and viability of Pakistan. Two years later Muhammad 'Ali Bogra, as Pakistan's ambassador to the United States, proved to be an able spokesman for his country: "Do not count Pakistan as a neutral nation of Asia. Our basic sympathies are strongly with the West."

Several factors were stimulating Pakistan's attempt to win assistance from the United States at that time. It was becoming evident that substantial aid was soon to be given to India; unless Pakistan benefited similarly her relative position would be weakened. Secondly, Communist aggression in Asia, demonstrated by the Korean war and the conflict in French Indochina, had served to alarm Pakistan. In the third place, the end of the war in Korea had affected Pakistan's markets for jute and cotton adversely, and her economic difficulties were increasing.

By 1953 the United States had become anxious about its position in the strategic Middle East and, hoping to promote an interest in the common defense problems of this area, proposed the establishment along with other Western powers of a Middle East defense organization. But the Arab countries were so embittered over Western policies toward Israel that the proposal failed to gain support. At this point a unilateral military pact between Pakistan and the United States began to receive serious consideration. Pakistan's initial reluctance disappeared after the United States gave over 600,000 tons of wheat to Pakistan to alleviate a food crisis in 1953. The Mutual Defense Assistance Agreement with the United States was signed in May 1954 and Pakistan, now a participant in the Defense Support Program of the United States, had received the first shipments of military equipment by November.

Pakistan agreed that none of the aid would be used for aggressive purposes, and America in turn made it clear that Pakistan was under no obligation to provide military bases or to side with the United States in any future war. To Pakistan the pact was important as a means of increasing her military strength and thereby reducing the threat of aggression from India. To the United States, Pakistan seemed to be a "dependable bulwark against Communism" —in the words of Secretary of State Dulles—because of the "strong spiritual faith and martial spirit of the people." Vice President Richard Nixon later volunteered that the United States would "stand by" Pakistan and protect it against "forces working for its destruction."

The United States, trying to assist India and Pakistan, faced a difficult and serious dilemma. As today, both countries were in economic straits and yet both were expending far more on their armed forces than they could afford. Without economic assistance from the United States or other countries, such large military expenditures would not be feasible. Yet the growing bitterness between the two neighbors over the Kashmir question made it increasingly evident that their anxiety was occasioned primarily by a fear and distrust of each other. Thus, the more the United States aided these countries, the more they were able to increase their military budgets, and the more devastating any future conflict between them might become. On the other hand, to withdraw all support from both countries would invite economic collapse and Communist penetration. However, this estimate of the situation was to become outdated in the autumn of 1962.

Military Alliances

When the defeated Japanese forces withdrew from Southeast Asia and the South Pacific after World War II, a political vacuum was created which provided a constant temptation for the forces of insurrection, aggression, and subversion. In view of this situation, representatives of eight countries—Australia, France, New Zealand, Pakistan, the Philippines, Thailand, the United Kingdom, and the United States—met at Manila in September 1954 to consider measures designed to preserve peace in the area. The result was the South-East Asia Collective Defense Treaty Organization, known as SEATO.

The signatory nations agreed "to refrain in their international relations from the threat or use of force in any manner inconsistent with the purposes of the United Nations" and to "maintain and develop their individual and collective capacity to resist armed attack and to prevent and counter subversive activities directed from without against their territorial integrity and political stability." Each party to the treaty further agreed to take action "in accordance with its constitutional processes" to meet the common danger in any territory which the parties might designate by unanimous agreement. The "States of Cambodia and Laos and the free territory under the jurisdiction of the State of Vietnam

317

[South Vietnam]" were so designated. The council, the secretariat, and the special committees of SEATO meet at Bangkok, its permanent headquarters. Unlike CENTO, SEATO has no unified military command and its members are not obligated to come to the aid of any member which is attacked by another power.

In February 1955 Turkey and Iraq concluded a Pact of Mutual Cooperation which related to their mutual defense and security and invited other countries with interests in the region to participate in the pact. Pakistan, Iran, and the United Kingdom accepted this invitation and the new agreement became known as the Baghdad Pact. The United States has declined to become a full member, although it takes part in the meetings of the major committees of the governing council of the pact. In August 1959, following the withdrawal of Iraq, the name was changed to that of the Central Treaty Organization (CENTO). In March 1959 Pakistan, Turkey, and Iran signed Bilateral Agreements of Cooperation with the United States, thereby strengthening the military potential of CENTO and providing for American military aid in case of an attack on any CENTO member.

Pakistan's adherence to SEATO, CENTO, and the Bilateral Agreement with the United States stems from the conviction of its leaders that the future security of the country will be better served through military alliances than by a posture of neutrality and nonalignment. On several occasions President Ayub Khan has equated neutralism with opportunism, as in a July 1960 article:

> Moreover, in the context of present-day world politics Pakistan has openly and unequivocally cast its lot with the West, and unlike several countries around us, we have shut ourselves off almost completely from the possibility of any major assistance from the Communist bloc. We do not believe in hunting with the hound and running with the hare. We wish to follow, and are following, a clear and unambiguous path. . . . As a student of war and strategy, I can see quite clearly the inexorable push of the north in the direction of the warm waters of the Indian Ocean.

Or again in a speech in September 1961:

> There is a definite need for Pakistan to make friends—powerful friends—who are interested in the security of Pakistan. As far as we are concerned, we cannot match the big countries around us in military strength. We just haven't got the means. Even what

we are spending is beyond our capacity, but we have to develop a deterrent power, a deterrent military power so that if anyone commits aggression against us we are in a position to effectively reply.

Relations with Communist Powers

Relations with the Communist countries were influenced, on the one side, by the distaste of the Pakistanis for Communist ideology and by their concern over Communist expansion and, on the other side, by the hostility of the Communist bloc toward CENTO and SEATO. The USSR attacked Pakistan's presence in CENTO on the ground that it served as a cover for the establishment of American military bases directed at the Soviet Union; Pakistan denied that such bases existed or were contemplated. In 1960, after an American U-2 plane which had allegedly taken off from Peshawar was shot down over the Soviet Union, these attacks turned to threats against Pakistan. Pakistan was concerned over the mounting Soviet presence in Afghanistan, including the equipment and training of the Afghan army, and it resented the fact that the USSR had sided with Afghanistan on the Pakhtunistan issue and with India on the Kashmir issue. However, relations between the two countries remained correct, if not cordial. Trade agreements were concluded, and in 1961 an agreement which provided for the exploitation of the oil and gas reserves of Pakistan by Soviet technicians was reached.

The People's Republic of China had been recognized by Pakistan as early as 1950 and in the same year Pakistan voted in favor of admitting that country to the United Nations. Communist China attacked SEATO on the ground that its purpose was to establish new military bases in Asia but refrained from strong criticism of Pakistan's role in this organization. In 1956 Prime Minister Suhrawardy visited China and later in the same year Chou En-lai came to Pakistan. Suhrawardy had hoped to win the support of Communist China in the Kashmir dispute, but the Chinese leaders stated that their country would maintain a neutral position.

Search for an "Independent" Foreign Policy

In 1959 Pakistan began to question the soundness of its foreign policies. A reappraisal was undertaken and this reappraisal, along with a parallel search for an "independent" foreign policy, con-

319

tinues. One factor which led to the reappraisal was criticism expressed in the United States in 1958 and 1959 of what was alleged to be excessive American military aid to Pakistan; it was said that India had been forced to meet this challenge by diverting funds from economic development to strengthening its own military machine. This criticism may have had something to do with the proposal made by President Ayub Khan on November 3, 1959 that India and Pakistan join in a common defense pact "to defend respective frontiers and the frontiers of each other in the case of aggression." This proposal was rejected by Nehru.

In July 1961 President Ayub Khan visited the United States and met with President John F. Kennedy. A joint communiqué stressed the value of existing alliances and stated that Pakistan would continue to receive American military and economic aid. In a public statement President Ayub warned of the severe strain that would be placed on Pakistan-American relations should the United States extend military assistance to India. In the months that followed, Pakistani officials questioned the value of the country's military ties with the United States, insisting that the United States was far more interested in India than in its ally, Pakistan. In September 1962 President Ayub Khan was again in the United States. His stay was a brief one, and the communiqué issued after a meeting with President Kennedy was very similar to that of a year earlier.

During this period, while Pakistan was expressing increasing concern over the value of its treaty relations with the United States, it appeared to turn toward the People's Republic of China. Possibly Pakistan felt that such a move would result in a reaction on the part of the United States in the form of more favorable treatment. Possibly, too, Pakistan sensed the desirability of attempting to replace India in China's friendly affections. (Prior to the border incidents of this period Nehru had consistently praised the warm Chinese-Indian relations.) Pakistan took the initiative in proposing the demarcation of the frontier between the countries, and in 1961 the Chinese accepted this proposal. In May 1962 Pakistan and Communist China announced their decision to enter into negotiations for an agreement on "the location and alignment of the boundary between China's Sinkiang and the contiguous areas the defense of which is under the control of Pakistan and to sign on this basis an agreement of a provisional nature." It was also stated that after the settlement of the Kashmir dispute, the sovereign authorities concerned would reopen negotiations with the Chinese government to sign a formal treaty regarding the boundary of Kashmir.

So matters stood at the time of the Chinese military campaigns against Ladakh and the North-East Frontier Agency of India in October and November 1962. India's urgent, successful appeal to the United States and the United Kingdom for immediate military assistance aroused antagonism against the Western powers in Pakistan, and at the end of November the National Assembly met in emergency session to review the country's foreign policy. Speakers were unsympathetic toward India, stating that there had been no Chinese "invasion," that the bulk of India's armed forces were still stationed along the frontier with Pakistan, and that military equipment supplied to India by the Western powers might well be turned against Pakistan at a later date. During the debate the foreign minister said that Pakistan would not hesitate to withdraw from CENTO and SEATO if it should appear that membership in these pacts was no longer in the national interest.

American and British special representatives strove to find ways to allay Pakistan's feeling of betrayal and to bring the countries together. Near the end of December 1962 Nehru suggested the possibility of a confederation of India and Pakistan, but Pakistan rejected this concept. The Western representatives were successful in persuading both powers to hold bilateral discussions on the future of Kashmir. The first in a round of meetings took place near the end of 1962 and others in the opening months of 1963; they were broken off without agreement having been reached. In March 1963 Pakistan and the People's Republic of China signed an agreement covering the location of the boundary between the two countries.

Throughout 1963 Pakistan took steps designed to "normalize" its relations with Communist countries, while high officials denied that the country intended to obtain arms from those powers or to seek a military alliance with the People's Republic of China. Pakistan concluded an air agreement with Communist China which gave Pakistan International Airlines landing rights at Canton and Shanghai, while the Chinese received similar rights at Karachi, Dacca, and Lahore. Later in the year, in October, Pakistan and the USSR reached an air agreement which provided for overflights of each country to points in third countries. Specifically, the planes of the Soviet Aeroflot may land at Karachi en route to Rangoon and Jakarta and will no longer be forced to overfly China on this route.

Pakistan concluded a barter agreement to exchange jute for cement from China as an extension of the trade agreement made in January 1963. Comparable barter agreements were reached with the USSR, Hungary, Poland, and Czechoslovakia to exchange jute and chrome ore for cement and manufactured items.

Whether the agreements mentioned above are to be considered as expressions of an independent foreign policy seems open to question, since they neither enhance Pakistan's image on the international scene nor contribute materially to its economic development. To a certain degree these actions may represent a deliberate reaction to the arming of India by the United States and the United Kingdom. On the other hand, Pakistan expressed its continuing dependence on development aid from the United States and sought increased American military assistance to counterbalance the arms supplied to India. It is probable that the government of Pakistan seeks to illustrate that future decisions in the field of foreign relations will be based on enlightened self-interest, although no shift toward a policy of neutrality and nonalignment has occurred.

CHAPTER 15

Labor

THE LABOR FORCE OF PAKISTAN is overwhelmingly rural, agricultural, and ill-educated. It is also overwhelmingly male (see Table 11). The low proportion of women in the labor force is in part due to the seclusion of women enjoined by Islam. For a woman to work outside the home was long considered shameful and non-Moslems as well as Moslems would try to conceal such work, even from the census investigators. The nature of the economy and a lack of labor-saving devices also help to explain why in the past women rarely worked outside their homes and so were not counted in the labor force. However, each year more young women take up clerical work, the service trades, factory employment, and the professions.

The fact that one in every five of the urban workers reports that he is engaged in agriculture also reflects the close relation between agriculture and the towns. Even the larger cities contain dairy herds and many of the people living in towns work in the surrounding fields during the busy season. At the same time it should be pointed out that some at least of those reporting themselves as farmers are recent immigrants to the towns who prefer to call themselves farmers even though they are really dependent upon low-status urban jobs.

Until partition there was a strong tendency for the agricultural and nonagricultural workers to belong to different castes, and often to different religions. In what is now Pakistan the small shops in the villages were practically a monopoly of the Hindus or Sikhs. More often than not the village shopkeeper would be the only non-Moslem in a Moslem village. But the mass emigration of the Hindus and Sikhs from West Pakistan at partition, and the continuing emigration from East Pakistan, left a gap which could only be filled by some of the Moslem farmers becoming shopkeepers. As a result there is a growing community of interest between the producer and trader groups in the countryside.

This feeling of community has undoubtedly helped the development of Pakistan both by making the labor force psychologically better able to undertake future changes in occupations and, what is of more immediate importance, by facilitating the spread of new ideas about crops, methods, and markets from the merchants to the farmers. This is particularly true in West Pakistan, where good transport facilities enable the merchants themselves to be alive to wider market possibilities.

In the nineteenth century, when large portions of the cultivated areas of what are now East and West Pakistan were taken under cultivation by jungle clearing and irrigation respectively, the expanding populations occupied new farms which were usually as large as the peasants could comfortably handle, and relatively compact. But in many areas the present level of agricultural production was achieved fifty years ago by about three-quarters as many workers. With the increase in population has come an increasing fragmentation of the land, causing much land to be wasted in ridges between the fields, so that today a larger labor force works at least as hard, but less efficiently, on the same acreage of land. It is extremely difficult for productive industrial and commercial employment to increase fast enough to actually draw off some of the potentially surplus rural labor. A survey made in 1959 indicated that the labor force had increased to an estimated 26,900,000 as compared with the figure of 22,699,000 for 1951. Of this new total 18.1 million persons were engaged in agriculture (Table 12). Some persons could be employed in the kind of village reconstruction envisioned in the Village-AID and Basic Democracies programs, but this would also require a raising of additional funds by land taxation.

It is very difficult to estimate the money value of the incomes of the farm population since a large part of income is received and consumed in kind. Figures of farm incomes are even more unreliable than most Pakistani statistics. Even the relatively few hired laborers are paid more in kind than in cash. Estimates of the money value of annual agricultural incomes vary from about 200 rupees ($42) to 620 rupees ($130) against a per capita income for the entire population in 1960 of 247 rupees ($52). In the poorer districts of both wings, there are workers who receive nothing but their food, one suit of clothes a year at the Id festival, and a place to sleep. Incomes seem usually to be lower in East Pakistan. This is probably counterbalanced, in part at least, by the fact that the milder winters in East Pakistan mean that less food, less clothing, and less shelter are needed for survival. Comfort is not the issue at such low levels of income. The hired laborers are at the bottom of the income as well as the social scale, but the lot of the smaller sharecroppers and owner-cultivators is little better. However, incomes vary a great deal from district to district or even within a village. The poorest village is likely to have at least one family who eats well; the wealthiest districts nevertheless include an undernourished majority of the people.

While about 70 per cent of the labor force is engaged in agriculture, the balance is distributed in a great variety of occupations. More than half work on their own account in cottage industries or as small traders, craftsmen, and casual workers—skilled or unskilled. The rest are regular employees. Industrialization may have increased the proportion of those in regular employment a little, but it seems unlikely that there has been any great change.

The term "independent workers" is something of a catchall covering all individuals who do not consider themselves in regular employment. Most of the "independent workers" are either village menial servants—sweepers, barbers, washermen, domestic servants, and so on—or else workers in the cottage industries, which are suffering from the competition of the new factories.

In both the villages and towns of Pakistan many are still employed in traditional crafts. The peasants, particularly of West Pakistan, need a village carpenter and blacksmith to keep their simple tools in repair. One of the few luxuries that the better off can enjoy are the services of a barber. Carpenters, blacksmiths, and barbers were traditionally paid in kind at harvest time. Payments in kind are still sometimes made to the producers of cooking and storage pots or of handspun and handwoven cloth, to the sweepers for garbage and nightsoil collection, and even to a village bard. Increasingly, however, such services are being paid for in cash, particularly as the products of the traditional village crafts are replaced by the products of factories, both foreign and Pakistani. Some small towns have decayed because of the falling markets for their craft products, others simply because they have been bypassed by buses and lorries in favor of larger centers more favored by the road system. But the passing of small towns and village craftsmen is lamented in Hazara or Sylhet today just as it was in Maine or Vermont some fifty years ago.

In contrast to the situation in the traditional crafts there has been a very rapid growth in the labor force employed in large-scale industry. At partition the industrial labor force numbered around 100,000 and in 1959 was estimated to number about 600,000.

The proportionate rate of expansion of Pakistani industry has been very great, and Pakistanis are duly proud of the fact. They are not proud of the conditions in which many of the industrial workers live, particularly the refugees around Karachi, the main industrial center. The refugees often supplied the technical leadership required to start new factories at Karachi and elsewhere, but the great bulk of the new industrial labor force outside Karachi has been drawn from the villages of Pakistan. In a few cases these villages are located close to the factory and the worker may even still live in his village and commute to work on foot, by bicycle, or by bus. More frequently, however, he will live under appalling conditions of overcrowding in miserable tenements and seek every opportunity to return home to visit the family he left in his native village.

There has been an almost continuous shortage of skilled workers for Pakistan industry, but there has never been any difficulty in obtaining unskilled workers. While some factories in East Pakistan recruit their workers directly by the management interviewing applicants and selecting from a back file of such applicants, a more usual system is for the *sardar* (foreman) or the *mistri* (skilled workman who in a factory would be in charge of the setting and, perhaps, maintenance of a group of machines) to be the deciding factor in the employment of labor. Very often he will train some workers without pay for about two months, then allow them to do the work of absentees, and finally promote them into the ranks of the permanent labor force. In the absence of any records on such *badli-wallahs,* as these casual workers are called, the door is left wide open to the practice by the sardars and mistris of selling jobs. On the other hand it does provide the foreman with an incentive for teaching the former peasant the techniques needed for work in a factory. Similar methods were widely practiced in both India and Western countries in the earlier stages of their industrial evolution. The present industrial labor force has, therefore, a predominantly rural and agricultural background, and these factory workers seem to regard trade as preferable to either farming or industrial labor (see Table 13).

Industrial workers are usually more literate than the farming element of the population but, even so, half of those surveyed in East Pakistan were illiterate. However, as long as the industrial labor force is relatively small, the factories can skim the cream of the labor force by offering monthly wages above the prevailing average.

The biggest problem that Pakistani industry faces is the supply of craftsmen with the skills that are needed in modern factories. The craftsmen, though often very highly skilled at their traditional crafts, are largely illiterate and unable to read blueprints, which are usually in English. The problem is accentuated by the low prestige of manual labor and the unwillingness of employers to pay wages sufficiently above what they pay their clerks to make better educated youths willing to dirty their hands in working with machines. The government has opened a number of technical high schools and polytechnics to fill the gap but is reportedly finding it difficult to enroll students of a sufficiently high caliber since the potential jobs have less prestige than that of government clerk.

Perhaps paradoxically, a supply of engineers and scientists has been easier to obtain. Both parents and students are very anxious to secure one of the very limited number of places in engineering or medical colleges and despite some political favoritism these colleges recruit only from the best of the young men. The real problem is that it takes a long time to train engineers, doctors, or other scientists, and at times there may not be enough graduates in any given field. It also costs a great deal of money to give good practical training, particularly in a country where almost all the equipment has to be imported. However, foreign aid programs have been particularly valuable in supplying equipment and advice.

The biggest problem with such technicians is that they lack the kind of wide practical experience that could be expected in a Western country. In part this is inevitable when the students may never have seen even a railway train before they came to college and in part it is due to the expense and time involved in providing the buildings and equipment needed by engineering and other colleges.

It is difficult to estimate the incomes of the industrial workers. In 1955 monthly wages varied from 110 to 154 rupees in the major industrial towns. Wages and salaries are normally paid monthly, and may include a "dearness allowance" worth as much as, sometimes more than, the basic salary. Bonuses of approximately a month's salary are paid by successful businesses at the end of the busy season. Seasonal factories may pay such bonuses at the start of the next busy season, but only to those who report back for work. Such bonuses are regarded by the management as measures to ensure that trained workers do not leave when most wanted and by the workers as part of their normal pay.

Equal in importance to the industrial workers is the army of clerks in industry, trade, and, most important of all, government service. Some say that the greatest monument the British left to their rule is the *babu*, or clerk, who keeps the office registers and files. The typical babu learns by rote the actions required of him, very few ever understanding what the system is all about. As a result office procedure in Pakistan is completely archaic and amazing to anyone acquainted with developed practices.

Most of the babus trained by the British were Hindus or Sikhs, who almost all left Pakistan. After partition, although untrained Moslems had to take over the desks left by the Hindus, the machinery of government and commerce did not completely break down, thanks largely to the self-sacrificing devotion of the few remaining trained clerks, who alone had any idea of the necessary procedures. In the struggle to avoid a breakdown, however, improvement or modernization was too much to expect. Just to keep things running proved enough of a challenge.

By about 1954 the situation had improved to the point where the industrialization program could be undertaken without undue strain on the economy. But one of the weakest points in the Pakistan economy is the under-trusted, inkstained babu, sipping cups of tea amidst innumerable dirty, dusty, and incredibly untidy files and registers, obeying orders without real understanding of what they are about—the despair of all those who wish for a modernization of Pakistan, and the envy of all the peasants and laborers, whose one wish is that their sons might also one day be called Babu-Ji (Sir Clerk). The monthly wages of this class of government employee varied from 172 to 280 rupees in 1955, while clerks in commercial enterprises received from 172 to 333 rupees.

Labor and management relations have been complicated by many problems and sources of friction or misunderstanding. In the initial years of the new state most employees had no previous experience in industrial management since they came largely from the commercial and landowning class. Often foreign experts and technicians aided in the establishment of industrial enterprises, but they did not speak the languages of the factory workers and could be of little help in the establishment of modern labor relations. However, problems of communication existed at other levels.

The labor force in any one factory is very often drawn from many different language areas, or at least from areas with dialects so different that there is a serious communication problem. Great difficulties have been reported by Bengali refugees from the Calcutta area trying to make themselves understood in Chittagong, or even in Dacca-Narayanganj. A laborer from one of the Punjabi-speaking villages of Hazara finds it difficult to make himself understood in Multan, in the southern Punjab, or even in Lahore. The problem is much worse when the same factory employs Urdu-speaking refugees from India, Pathan watchmen, and perhaps some Sindhis and Baluchis, as well as Punjabis and Bengalis. The situation in some Karachi factories is not too different from the situation in many an American factory at the turn of the century with its polyglot and largely immigrant labor force; and as in America there have been some riots which were largely movements of protest against the employment of nonlocal labor. The 1954 riots in Dacca-Narayanganj were believed to have started because of bitter feelings between Bengalis and non-Bengalis: in the riots at the Chandraghona Paper Mills many Pathan *chowkidars* (factory guards) were murdered by Bengali workmen. In both cases Communist agitation has been blamed, but never proved; in both cases there was a long history of bad feeling which finally boiled over.

Labor relations are further complicated by the fact that the language of administration and the courts is English, thus giving the employers, fluent in English, an important advantage over their workers in any dispute. The workmen are forced to rely as a rule upon outsiders to present their cases to their employers. This procedure is in line with the government's encouragement of arbitration and mediation (see below).

The trade union movement in Pakistan includes some 300,000 members from the industrial labor force of the country and an unknown number among the government employees and professional workers of the country. Since registration with the government is not required, the total number of trade unions can only be estimated but is probably about 500. Dominating the trade union movement with the largest total membership are the unions representing railway workers and textile workers. Their history goes back to the period before partition when the anti-Communist Indian Federation of Labor controlled most of those areas now making up West Pakistan and the leftwing All-Indian Trade Union Congress was strong in East Bengal. The membership of both was drawn largely from the many railroad and maritime unions. At partition the leadership, preponderantly Hindu, for the most part emigrated and twenty-two unions claiming 50,000 members in West Pakistan acted to fill the vacuum by forming in 1947 the Pakistan Federation of Labor under a veteran union leader, the late M. A. Khan. In a similar move, the East Pakistan trade unions combined to form the East Pakistan Trade Union Federation under the presidency of Dr. A. M. Malik, who had been president of both the Indian Quartermasters' Union and the Indian Sailors' Union. In 1950 those bodies combined to form the All-Pakistan Confederation of Labor, with Dr. Malik as its first president.

The All-Pakistan Confederation of Labor (APCOL), an affiliate of the International Labor Organization, has retained the East and West Pakistan Federations as branches and, though originally identified with the Moslem League government, is now relatively independent of political parties. Like a number of other All-Pakistan organizations in other fields, APCOL is a very loose confederation whose fundamental purpose is to provide unified representation at the government level and at international conferences. Real executive capacity rests primarily with the almost autonomous constituent federations, e.g. APCOL does not charter, organize, or affiliate unions, leaving this to the two provincial federations. The executive power of APCOL is in the hands of an equal number of representatives from each of the constituent federations, and officers of APCOL are usually also powerful in the provincial federations and in the stronger unions. The East Pakistan Federation of Labor, like many another Bengali organization, is particularly concerned with the maintenance of provincial autonomy and has achieved equality of representation in APCOL despite a smaller number of members.

In opposition to APCOL is the Pakistan Mazdoor (Workers') Federation started in Lahore in 1947 as the Pakistan Trade Union Federation and powerful for a time among the railway workers of the Punjab and among some of the textile workers. It reached its peak of popularity in 1950, when an East Pakistan federation merged with it, but its popularity declined after most of its leaders were arrested as suspected Communists in 1950. After that date it had connections with the leftwing National Awami party.

The Pakistan Mazdoor Federation leaders formerly complained of harassment by governmental authorities. The government, on the other hand, has accused its leaders of pro-Communist and subversive activities. At present the Communist element is believed small but probably most industrial disputes are due to its activities. A change in the political climate leftward might reveal it as extremely powerful; a shift to the right might wipe it out entirely.

The authorization for the formation of trade unions is contained in the Pakistan constitution (Part II, Article 4, Freedom of Association): "No law shall impose any restriction on the freedom of citizens to assemble peacefully and without arms, or to form associations or unions." The position of the government with respect to trade unions and labor in general was defined in 1955 with the publication of a paper entitled "Labor Policy." In February 1959 it was replaced by a more detailed document called "Revised Labor Policy." This policy is defined as bringing local regulations in harmony with the conventions and regulations of the International Labor Organization. Many of the ILO regulations have been adopted and additional ones are to be implemented with the eventual aim of a complete parallelism. The document favors the growth of healthy trade unions, while stressing the need to maintain industrial peace, described as a lack of disturbances and disputes between labor and management by means of the orderly settlement of points of friction and tension. The employers must recognize the trade unions and must, within a period of five years, provide housing for at least 25 per cent of their permanent employees. In a number of industries provisions are in effect for annual leave, holidays, sick leave, and minimum wages, and the goal is to extend these benefits to all plants. Trade union officers must either work in the plants where the unions are located or be full-time trade union workers.

The history of the industrial development of Pakistan has been marked by many strikes, some accompanied by extreme violence—such as those at the jute mills in the vicinity of Dacca in 1954 in which scores of people were killed. In some cases minor irritations were the cause of industrial labor unrest, and eventually strikes. This was true of the prolonged and bitter strike at a sugar mill in

West Pakistan. The management was frankly at a loss to discover the real cause of the strike. The strikers, who had demanded similar conditions to those in a neighboring mill, were much taken aback when shown that their own pay and conditions were in fact better. The management felt, probably rightly, that they offered the best pay and working conditions in the area and, probably wrongly, that the strike was all due to Communist agitators. The prime cause was more likely the great difficulty both sides experienced in adjusting to the demands of a large industrial plant.

To resolve disputes and to avoid strikes the government employs the machinery of the Industrial Disputes Act. This act, inherited from that in force in British India, was amended in 1956 to broaden its application and to extend the definition of a "public utility" to cover not only railways, ports, communications, and power and defense industries but practically all major industries, and the government is empowered to extend the definition if "public interest so requires." Strikes in the field of public utilities are not permitted nor are irregular and illegal strikes. Disputes are referred to industrial courts and any strike or lockout during conciliation proceedings or during the period when a settlement or award is in effect is prohibited and ipso facto illegal.

CHAPTER 16

Public Health and Welfare

ALTHOUGH APPRECIABLE PROGRESS HAS BEEN MADE SINCE 1947, health standards in Pakistan remain extremely low as a result of inadequate nutrition, unsanitary conditions, and insufficient medical facilities. Health statistics are incomplete and unreliable, but life expectancy appears to be about thirty years—one of the lowest figures in the world—and estimates place the death rate at almost double and infant mortality rates at nearly five times those of developed countries or among the highest in the world. Scores of thousands are killed or incapacitated every year by malaria, tuberculosis, malnutrition, and dysentery. Water supplies are rarely potable but, even when the source is pure, the water is usually contaminated during distribution. Underground drainage for sewage is available to only about 2 per cent of the population. Between 30 and 50 per cent of the population, according to some estimates, are afflicted with bowel diseases. Even those who take the most meticulous precautions rarely escape occasional attacks of dysentery.

At partition, India fared better than Pakistan in the distribution of institutions and personnel in the public health field. Relatively few doctors were of the Moslem faith and most of the organizations engaged in health research were situated on the Indian side of the new border. There were almost no nurses. Since 1947, however, major attacks on malaria and tuberculosis have been made and new medical training schools have been established.

Diet

Sample studies indicate that the average Pakistani family spends more than half of its income on food (see Table 14). Nevertheless, the amount of food consumed is considerably below that necessary for normal health. The average daily calorie intake per person in

Pakistan has been estimated at 2,030, with West Pakistan faring somewhat better than East Pakistan. The Pakistani diet, in addition to its inadequacy from an energy standpoint, is not well balanced—particularly in East Pakistan. There is an excessive reliance on rice and wheat in the two provinces. Except on holidays and ceremonial occasions, the consumption of meat is a luxury denied most of the population. Storage, refrigeration, and canning facilities are inadequate so that the supply of fruit and vegetables is sporadic and seasonal. As a result the diet is deficient in calcium, fats, and proteins and in most of the vitamins.

The eating habits in both wings of Pakistan have certain similarities beginning with the main food item, an inexpensive cereal, which is consumed in large quantities. Such spices as curry, onions, garlic, peppers, chilies, and ginger are liberally used by all Pakistanis and hot tea diluted with boiled milk is the popular beverage. Pork in any form is completely avoided by Moslems. Hindus, on the other hand, will not eat beef and rarely any other meat but may be fond of fish. Fruit is not often available at a price the average man can afford. An almost universal practice at the end of the meal is the chewing of betel leaf (*pan*), the rolled leaf usually holding areca nut, unslaked lime, catechu, and cloves and other spices. The red juice stains the teeth after long use. Tobacco, smoked in a hookah or as a cigarette, is widely used throughout the country. The consumption of alcohol is contrary to the teachings of Islam and most alcoholic beverages are too expensive for all except the wealthy few, but in East Pakistan a local brew derived from the fermented juice of the palm tree is heavily consumed by lower-caste Hindus and by many Moslem villagers as well and beer is produced at factories in West Pakistan.

Though the two wings share a reliance on wheat or rice and a preference for spiced foods, sweet tea, and the betel leaf, important differences between the two provinces do exist. East Pakistan, for example, has access to large quantities of excellent seafood along both coasts and from the rivers. Unfortunately, rapid spoilage in the warm climate and extremely limited food storage or refrigerated transportation facilities preclude wide consumption beyond the immediate fishing areas. The drying and salting of fish for preservation, though more common in East than in West Pakistan, remains largely unexploited except among the tribes of the Chittagong Hill Tracts. Other dietary differences between the provinces tend more toward traditional habits.

The staple food in West Pakistan is wheat, which is customarily served in the form of a *chappatty*—a large, flat, unleavened loaf. In the former North-West Frontier province, *atta*, a mixture of wheat and other grains, is made into a round loaf of coarse bread referred to as *nan*. In the Punjab the peasant may start the day with chappatties and milk or tea. At noon he will usually have chappatties with *dal*, a high-protein vegetable not unlike the lentil, which is cooked in the form of a very thick soup, and a spinach of rape leaves. In the evening he will have either chappatties or rice, and just before retiring maybe a glass of milk. A typical diet includes meat or eggs about twice a week and oranges, melons, dates, and bananas whenever available. *Lassi*, a drink made from buttermilk and spices, is a popular beverage. Almost any cooked food is prepared with *ghee*, clarified butter, which adds to its richness; *halwa*, made from wheat, butter, and sugar, is a favorite sweet dish; and *pilau*, consisting of rice mixed with vegetables, meat, or nuts, is served throughout Pakistan. Corn is sometimes substituted for wheat in the northwest where ground corn meal is used to make unleavened bread. Lamb, beef, chicken, and goat are the principal meats, a popular dish being the familiar *kabob*, pieces of lamb intermixed with onion and roasted on a skewer.

The staple food in East Pakistan is rice, usually eaten with curry and preferably served with fish, goat meat, chicken, or beef but often with only potatoes or eggplant. The average person consumes about a pound of rice every day—mostly milled rice. Pickled mango is a common relish; pilau and dal are both popular. Tea is more common in the cities and village marketplaces than in the rural home, where plain water is the common beverage. The food in East Pakistan is prepared with mustard oil rather than ghee, which makes it spicier but less nutritious than the food of West Pakistan. The heaviest meal is taken in the evening after sunset. Bananas and pineapples are relatively abundant in the East.

The excessive reliance on rice in East Pakistan has been criticized as detrimental to the health of its population. In addition, the rice is usually milled before purchase and washed and cooked in water before consumption, processes that cause the loss of most of the mineral and vitamin content. The situation is aggravated by the fact that less meat and milk are consumed in East Pakistan than in the West and is only partially offset by the greater consumption of fish.

335

Sanitation

Although statistics are not available, it is undoubtedly true that in Pakistan only the better-educated persons—a minute fraction of the population—understand that most disease is caused by germs. Their recognition of this fact has very little practical effect as most of the educated people in Pakistan employ servants to do the cooking and household chores, and their servants, though able to distinguish between something that is clean and something that is dirty, have no understanding whatsoever of the nature of disease.

The roadside, or any vacant land, serves as a public toilet even in the most crowded towns. The more affluent families have private toilet facilities in their homes, but the cleaning of those facilities is invariably delegated to the lowest of all menial specialists, the "sweeper," usually a Hindu of an "untouchable" caste. Flies abound and cockroaches invariably invade the larder.

In matters of personal hygiene, the Pakistani is, except in the most backward areas, as meticulous as the supply of water will permit. A devout Moslem prays several times a day and his religion enjoins him to wash hands and feet before prayer. The orthodox Hindu also has certain rituals and customs which promote cleanliness, although he may prefer polluted river water to a pure supply of well water if the latter has had contact with leather or is poured by an untouchable or non-Hindu. Incongruously, both Hindu and Moslem of the poorer classes may mold by hand the dung of the water buffalo, or cow dung, which is a common cooking fuel throughout most of the subcontinent.

Except in those villages where the government-trained worker has successfully managed to indoctrinate the local citizens in the essential techniques of public health, no one in the rural areas has any concept of environmental sanitation. There is no planned system of drainage; rainwater and sewage stagnate in some low-lying pond. Flies and mosquitoes have ample opportunity to multiply. Adults use the surrounding fields as latrines while the children use any convenient spot. Raw meat and other food supplies in the local market are speckled with flies. Typhoid and the dysenteries are, therefore, easily transmitted.

In the rural areas the water supply is taken from tubular wells, uncovered dug wells, artificial ponds, canals, and rivers. Dug wells are rarely protected from surface drainage and foreign matter. Water may be drawn by hand, or by wheels fitted with buckets and turned by bullocks. Very few water supplies are safe for drinking purposes.

Throughout most of West Pakistan wells 20 to 50 feet deep will reach fresh water though in the hilly areas wells several hundred feet may be required. In some of the larger towns in East Pakistan, tubular wells 200 to 600 feet deep are used to obtain fresh water, which rises to within 10 feet of the surface in such wells so that shallow pumps can be used. The water taken from shallow wells in East Pakistan is frequently saline.

Refugees from India have tended to settle in the urban areas, partly in anticipation of government assistance and partly because of the lack of unused agricultural land. The result, notably in Karachi, has been extreme overcrowding in those areas where the refugees have been permitted to construct rudimentary shelters. Because of the congestion, the sanitation in such areas is even worse than in the villages. In the larger cities, however, there is usually a public water supply which is superior to that found in the villages. On the other hand, there are typically too few water taps in the slum areas so that it may be necessary to wait in line for long periods in order to get a few jugs of water. In the center of most cities there is some form of public latrine and an underground sewerage system. There is very little litter on the streets, in part because it is seized upon for fuel, but also because the municipalities employ street sweepers. Karachi, Lahore, Peshawar, Dacca, Chittagong, and several other cities have water that is piped from a central source. Although the water is treated in several of the cities, routine bacterial examinations of water samples taken from the supply mains are not common, so there is no assurance that the water is safe.

No city in Pakistan has an adequate system of sewage disposal. Existing systems are overloaded. Sewered cities frequently have sewage farms where raw sewage is used for irrigation. Much sewage is collected by sweepers who deposit it in streams or at the edge of the city with the result that river water below the cities is highly contaminated—an important contributing factor in the high incidence of intestinal disorders in Pakistan.

Disease

The individual hospital and medical care which would be required to cure all those who are sick in Pakistan would entail a prohibitive expenditure and a supply of medical personnel that does not exist in the country. Fortunately, many of the most widespread diseases—malaria, tuberculosis, typhoid fever, cholera, and the dysenteries—are amenable to mass preventive medical techniques.

About three out of four Pakistanis live in areas where malaria is prevalent. Of these, about 40 per cent have malaria each year. As many as 150,000 die annually from malaria, and millions are weakened and made more susceptible to other diseases. Malaria control measures through spraying with DDT have been carried on over a number of years and were supplemented in 1961 by a comprehensive program to eradicate malaria within fourteen years. The program is conducted by the Malaria Eradication Board and its two provincial centers. The staff required for the program is trained at the Malaria Institute of Pakistan located in Dacca, with a branch office in Karachi and at the Institute of Hygiene and Preventive Medicine at Lahore. Plants now producing DDT have sufficient capacity to meet all the requirements of the program.

The number of active cases of tuberculosis in Pakistan has been estimated at 750,000, and fatalities from pulmonary tuberculosis probably approach 150,000 a year. Tuberculosis control and training centers in Karachi and Dacca provide medical care and conduct training programs for medical personnel in tuberculosis control methods. To check the spread of the disease, a country-wide campaign of tuberculin testing and of immunization by BCG vaccination is being carried out by sixty-two local teams. By the end of 1960 about 13.5 million had been inoculated. A BCG Vaccine Production Laboratory in Karachi supplies vaccine to all teams. The isolation and treatment of existing tuberculosis cases is difficult and expensive. Only about 2,500 hospital beds are available for tuberculosis patients and the cost of treating an average case has been estimated at 3,000 rupees. The situation is aggravated by the fact that most cases come to the attention of the authorities at a well-advanced stage. The Second Five Year Plan allots 28.4 million rupees specifically for the prevention and treatment of tuberculosis.

During the past century epidemics of cholera, smallpox, and plague have killed many millions. However, in recent years the number of deaths from these diseases has been declining. The incidence of smallpox has been drastically reduced in the last century by vaccination programs to a current average annual rate of 9,000 deaths a year. In 1961 the government initiated a two-year program for the eradication of smallpox. The battle against plague has been largely won in the last forty years on the Indian subcontinent by inoculations, modern drugs, and campaigns to eliminate or control infected fleas and rats. Cholera, on the other hand, has been much more difficult to control. The disease is spread by impure water, and the general lack of any sewage disposal system makes its control difficult. Cholera is much more common in East Pakistan than it is in the West, and in the country as a whole there have been about 10,000 deaths annually. Cholera vaccination is only effective for about a year, so that the authorities perform about forty million inoculations each year. Measures to control typhus are carried out in West Pakistan where it is prevalent.

Typhoid fever is believed to be widespread among infants in Pakistan, but no statistics are available and most cases go undiagnosed. Since it is spread by the contamination of food and water supplies by human excreta, its prevention will necessarily await a considerable improvement in the standards of sanitation in Pakistan. Apparently most adults have developed an immunity to the disease and treatment on any wide scale is not contemplated.

Similarly, dysentery is common and is presumed to be a major cause of the high infant mortality rate. Most adults are believed to develop an immunity to the common bacillary dysentery. Amoebic dysentery is difficult to diagnose but is undoubtedly widespread. Its early symptoms may be relatively mild, but it is insidious in that it later may cause cirrhosis of the liver and other serious complications. Preventive techniques are similar to those required for typhoid fever.

Most cases of *kala azar* are fatal if untreated. The disease is caused by a parasite which attacks the liver, spleen, or bone marrow, causing emaciation and anemia. It is transmitted by the sand fly and is most common in the low-lying regions of East Pakistan. Recovery is rapid after treatment by modern drugs, but there is always the threat of an epidemic. Modern insecticides are effective in destroying the carrier, but it is difficult to eliminate the disease completely because supposedly "cured" individuals may carry the infection in their skin.

There are various indications that the following diseases are also common in Pakistan: trachoma (especially in West Pakistan), poliomyelitis, yaws (in the Chittagong Hill Tracts), leprosy (especially in East Pakistan), the venereal diseases, tetanus, hookworm, roundworm, and dengue. Surprisingly, yellow fever is absent in

Pakistan in spite of the presence of the mosquito which customarily carries the disease. The Pakistan health authorities spray all incoming planes and take other measures to prevent the introduction of the infected mosquitoes.

Medical Care

Most of the medical practitioners in Pakistan are not "doctors" in the occidental sense: there are only 9,200 persons who have medical degrees. Furthermore, treatment by these professionally trained doctors may not be readily available, or may be too expensive or mistrusted. An ailing Moslem villager seeking a cure is more likely to visit a *hakim;* a Hindu may prefer to rely on the *vaid.*

The hakim is a practitioner of the *unani* system of medicine which was introduced to India during the Moslem conquests and is derived from the Greek science of Hippocrates and Galen. Hakims catered to the Moslem nobility of the subcontinent centuries ago and today minister to a large proportion of the population. A Unani Research Center has been operating in Karachi since 1952 dispensing free medical aid.

Vaids, or *kavirajs,* practice the *ayurvedic* (from Ayur-Veda) system of medicine which is even more ancient in its origins, being already well developed by 250 B.C. It is based on a voluminous literature and is regarded by the Hindus as being of divine origin. Its pharmacy made great advances up to 750 A.D. and had a considerable influence on the development of medicine in Europe.

Both the unani and the ayurvedic systems are recognized by the government. In 1957 an act was passed by the National Assembly providing for the registration of the estimated 15,000 practitioners of the unani and ayurvedic systems in an attempt to eliminate quackery. Both systems of medicine emphasize diet; indigenous roots, herbs, and plants are the basic ingredients in most of the medicines prescribed. Pakistan has many plants of interest to the pharmacologist; their products include strychnine, atropine, castor oil, and reserpine. Increasingly, the hakim and vaid are also prescribing some of the synthetic drugs, including sulfa and penicillin, and using stethoscopes and some other tools common in Western medical practice.

The villager who feels indisposed may first approach the local mullah or maulvi, who will usually oblige him by giving him an amulet or some holy water. If the villager gets worse, he will consult the hakim or vaid, knowing that his charges will not be high. If he becomes very miserable, he may seek out an allopathic doctor. In all probability, however, such a doctor is in a town many miles away and will not come to the village. The sick person must seek the doctor, and the cost of transportation alone may give him pause. The villager may be in the last stages of the disease before his troubles come to the attention of a person qualified in modern medical practice. Since many villagers still believe that epidemics and mental derangements are caused by evil spirits, various charms and incantations are looked on favorably, but there is also a general willingness to try modern medicines and techniques when they are readily available.

At partition, Pakistan was faced with many medical problems. Most of the medical personnel, being Hindu, had left the country. Four years after partition, over half of the posts in government health departments in several of the provinces were still vacant. Added to this, the major prepartition medical and public health institutes and four of the five medical store depots were in India. Meanwhile, the influx of refugees created a growing health problem.

Fortunately, medical facilities developed rapidly. For example, Pakistan had only one medical college in 1947 but by 1959 there were nine, and the number of government and registered doctors increased from about 3,500 at partition to 9,200 by 1959, with a 1965 target of 13,000 (see Table 15). In spite of these advances, the shortage of trained personnel, particularly in such categories as nursing, midwifery, and sanitation, remains the principal obstacle to an expanded health program. Perhaps equally important, the standards of those who have received training are not very high and there is a marked reluctance among trained personnel to work in the rural areas where they are most needed.

At present about 500 doctors graduate each year from the nine medical colleges. During the First Five Year Plan period, which ended in 1960, colleges in Peshawar, Hyderabad, and Multan produced their first medical graduates and the medical school at Chittagong became a college. Dacca Medical College and the Institute of Basic Sciences at Karachi, which prepares doctors to teach basic subjects in medical colleges, were slated for improvements. The Institute of Hygiene and Public Health at Lahore expanded its advanced training and research activities in public health. The Institute has a course leading to a diploma in public health which is open to postgraduate medical students with at least one year of experience and lasts eleven months. Ten to twenty doctors are admitted annually. Newest of the medical colleges is the one in Rajshahi. The Fatimah Jinnah Medical College is reserved exclusively for women. Women doctors are in great demand because a large proportion of the women in the country refuse to be treated by a male doctor or even to expose their faces to receive needed dental treatment.

All nine medical colleges are affiliated with universities (see Table 16), most of which award the degree of MBBS (Bachelor of Medicine and Bachelor of Surgery) after the successful completion of a course of study lasting five years. In order to be admitted to one of these colleges, a student must have an Intermediate in Science (twelve years of education) or an equivalent qualification. King Edward Medical College also provides postgraduate work in such special areas as tuberculosis, physiology, and pharmacology.

Specialized institutions operated by the government or the universities include the Institute of Public Health at Dacca, the Institute of Radiology at Lahore, the Institute of Hygiene and Public Health at Lahore, the Cholera Research Laboratory at Dacca, and the Bureau of Laboratories at Karachi. Plans have been completed for the construction of a National Health Research Center at Islamabad.

Several institutions train pharmacists. The King Edward Medical College awards a Bachelor of Pharmacy degree after a three-year course, and the Dow Medical College offers a two-year diploma course. The University of the Punjab has a three-year course and the privately managed Institute of Pharmacy at Lahore offers several types of training. Many doctors compound their own medicines and derive a substantial income from their sale.

Lahore is the site of the DeMontmorency College of Dentistry and there is a College of Dentistry attached to the University of Dacca.

The urgent problem of increasing the number of nurses is a particularly difficult one as women in Pakistan have long lived in relative seclusion and the vocation of nursing requires them to live in a way and to perform tasks that have always been considered improper and contrary to the teachings of Islam. The real difficulty is to find a way to persuade young women to take up this profession and enroll in the institutions which already exist. In 1959 there were eighteen training centers for nurses in the country, with facilities for about 1,000 students; the drop-out rate of the student nurses has been very high, probably a reflection of the fact that many are found to lack a sufficiently high level of prior education.

This confusion with Islamic injunctions does not exist in mid-wifery and the number of trained midwives in the country has been roughly estimated at 1,000. Training for this work is given by maternity hospitals or hospitals with maternity sections, there being such centers at Karachi, Lahore, Peshawar, and Dacca, all equipped and staffed with the assistance of UNICEF and WHO. Either qualified nurses or girls with four to six years of general schooling are eligible for the twenty-seven months of training required.

Pakistan has over 450 hospitals—less than a dozen maintained by foreign religious missions—and roughly 2,000 dispensaries with a 1959 total of approximately 28,000 beds. The typical district (about 4,000 square miles) has a hospital with 50 to 200 beds and several dispensaries, but these hospitals are apt to be overcrowded, in-adequately staffed, and improperly equipped. Present plans en-visage an increase of about 8,000 beds and the expansion of local (district and subdivisional) hospitals, the improvement of surgical and X-ray facilities, and the construction of the first mental hospitals. Dispensaries will also be improved. One interest-ing local adaptation in hospital care stems directly from the shortage of attendants which makes it essential in many cases for the patient to arrange for his own food and his own washing and cleaning facilities. As a result, it has become customary in many hospitals for a servant or close relative of the sick person to ac-company him to the hospital and remain there in order to care for the patient's wants. Increasingly, hospitals are being designed to facilitate this kind of arrangement.

Another important concern is the improvement of maternity and child health services. Although down considerably since 1946, the infant mortality rate is estimated at 120 per thousand live births and the number of mothers who die in childbirth may be 440 to 680 per 100,000 births—five times the rate in more developed countries. By the end of 1959 some 375 maternity and child welfare centers were in operation, as compared to 200 in 1955, with much of this expansion due to the guidance, equipment, and supplies received from UNICEF.

An impressive number of auxiliary health services have been developed in recent years. By 1962 there were ten rural health centers in each wing, each center with three subcenters, and several "health visitors" training schools in operation. A major goal is to give regular medical examinations to all school children and to treat all minor ailments in school clinics. Toward this end a number of experimental school health clinics are in operation and more than a score of mobile dispensaries now roam the country. To help alleviate the shortage of nurses a program of recruiting nursing assistants, called NAIDS, is under way.

About 400 sanitary inspectors are already performing various technical functions in the public health field and more are being trained at centers in Lahore, Dacca, and other towns. The various public health schemes will require large numbers of these technicians, however, and the force is eventually to be expanded to 1,500.

Pakistan produces large quantities of many drugs and vaccines used in the country and enough to meet all needs, under normal conditions, of the following: the typhoid vaccines, cholera vaccine, antirabies vaccine, smallpox vaccine, antiplague vaccine, diphtheria antitoxin and toxoid, BCG (tuberculosis) vaccine, and antivenom serum for use against the venom of the cobra and Russell's viper. An estimated thousand tons of ephedrine is produced annually in Quetta Pishin from the locally grown herb ephedra, and large quantities of santonin are produced in Rawalpindi from the artemisia plant which grows in the Kurram valley and near Gilgit. There is also a penicillin laboratory, set up with the assistance of an international organization affiliated with the United Nations.

Public health and medical relief have been recognized as matters of governmental concern and responsibility on the Indian subcontinent for more than a century: in 1850 a royal commission recommended that health measures be taken to protect both the army and the civilian population; in 1919 health administration became a provincial responsibility in India; and in 1945 a health department was established at the center to coordinate and assist the provincial governments. In continuation of this policy, public health was made a provincial responsibility in the Pakistan constitution. According to a reorganization of the Ministry of Health, Labor and Social Welfare effected in 1961, its Health Division formulates policies relating to medical facilities, public health, medical education, and research, while a so-called Attached Offices handles executive functions under the suboffices of the Health Division. This so-called Health Division gives grants-in-aid to the provinces, coordinates medical education programs for Pakistanis in foreign countries, sets standards, works with international agencies, stimulates research, and assists the local government by lending specialists as need dictates. Quarantine work and health inspections at the airport and seaports also come under the jurisdiction of the Health Division as does supervision of the four Campaign Directorates which have been set up to carry out country-wide campaigns for malaria eradication, family planning, vaccination against tuberculosis, and nutritional research.

In West Pakistan, the minister of health is assisted by a lay civil servant called the secretary of health. The medical director of the department, or director of health services, is assisted by a staff of officers specializing in such functional areas as nursing, drug control, stores and supplies, malaria, tuberculosis, epidemiology, industrial hygiene, food and nutrition, maternal and child health, statistics, and education and research. There is an extensive field organization covering three regions—Khairpur, Bahawalpur, and Peshawar—each of which has a branch, headed by a deputy director, and three subdivisions. Most of the personnel in the subdivisions are appointed by the provincial director of health services. In the rural areas and villages health services are provided directly by the province.

The organization in East Pakistan is considerably more complicated. Instead of a director of health services, there are three technical heads: a chief engineer in charge of water supplies and the disposal of wastes, a director of public health who supervises the campaigns against tuberculosis and malaria, and a surgeon general in charge of medical training and medical stores.

Public health regulations in effect in both provinces govern such matters as food adulteration, drugs, birth and death registration, maternity benefits, and factory sanitation. But enforcement is lax because of the shortage of properly trained personnel and the inadequacy of funds. In a supplemental approach to the country's health problems the central health ministry, functioning since 1952, produces and distributes a variety of educational material.

Public Welfare

Speaking as the prime minister of Pakistan in 1949, Liaquat 'Ali Khan told a large group of his followers that "every person in this land has equal rights to be provided with food, shelter, clothing, education and medical facilities" and "countries which cannot ensure these for their people can never progress." This, he added, is the meaning "in a nutshell" of Islamic socialism.

True to this ideal, the constitution directs that the state shall endeavor to institute free and compulsory education, provide humane conditions of work, discourage prostitution and gambling, raise the standard of living of the common man, provide social security, and, for those citizens permanently or temporarily unable to earn their livelihood, provide the basic necessities of life such as food, clothing, housing, education, and medical treatment. It would be difficult to exaggerate the immensity of the task the state has thus declared its responsibility. The indigent are no small minority group: the overwhelming proportion of Pakistan's citizens do not earn a satisfactory livelihood. Until such time as the food supplies are adequate, all else seems relatively unimportant. Yet because of the government's limited financial resources any large-scale welfare projects must depend primarily on voluntary effort.

Although estimates vary, a typical Pakistan family of five to six persons is believed to have an income of about two rupees per day or, at the present rate of exchange, a little more than forty cents. Assuming conservatively that an adult consumes up to a pound of grain daily at a cost of approximately four annas, half of the family income goes for cereals, the rice or wheat that provides the necessary calories for sustenance. As much as another fourth of the income may also be used to buy food: pulses, meat, eggs, milk, fish, fruit, and spices. Four of the remaining eight annas may be spent on shelter and the rest on clothing and miscellaneous items.

There are, of course, important regional differences, e.g. the urban worker may have to spend an appreciable amount on transportation and the West Pakistani spends a lesser proportion of his food budget on cereals than the East Pakistani. (An indication of the distribution of family expenditures has been given in Table 14.) As might be expected, educational level and income also affect spending. Government clerks earning from 100 to 200 rupees per month spend about one rupee per day on fish, meat, eggs, and milk for their families. With this rupee, on the average, they can buy a half pound of fish and a little more than a pint of milk per day with enough left over for a pound of beef every week, a pound of mutton every two weeks, a dozen eggs per month, and an occasional chicken. About two rupees per month is spent on fruit, an equal amount on potatoes, and about five rupees per month for other vegetables. As income rises to over 300 rupees, more than

50 per cent continues to be spent on food but it also becomes possible to spend more proportionately on milk, fruits, and vegetables. But one should note that in the sample survey from which these data are taken interviewers found that the higher income families had almost twice as many members and were thus not a great deal better off than the lower income families on a per capita basis.

The problems created by the generally inadequate level of income are compounded by the fact that one person out of every ten in Pakistan today is a refugee from India. The migration of Moslems to Pakistan began as soon as the decision to partition India was announced, with literally millions moving across the newly defined borders during 1947 and 1948. A substantial migration continued for nearly ten years. The typical refugee left much of his property behind him, confident that the government of Pakistan would, in some way, compensate him for his loss. No single problem has harassed the government more than this one. Furthermore, the massive population shifts disrupted economic patterns, producing a surplus of agriculturalists, weavers, shoemakers, and other skilled and semiskilled artisans in the western Punjab, for example, but a great scarcity everywhere of bankers, accountants, traders, and sweepers—the jobs traditionally held by Hindus. In their confusion, large numbers of the refugees clustered around Karachi, creating extensive slum areas.

To reinforce and coordinate provincial government efforts to cope with the situation, a Central Ministry of Refugees and Rehabilitation was set up in Karachi and procedures were initiated to give those who had left property in India first claim on the Hindu and Sikh properties abandoned in Pakistan. At the same time, large numbers of agriculturalists were resettled on land in West Pakistan and special relief measures were adopted for widows, orphans, and the aged.

In the urban areas, the main problem continues to be one of housing. Both provincial governments are constructing "satellite towns" for the refugees, a typical housing scheme being the Korangi "township" on the outskirts of Karachi. The Korangi "township" already had 15,000 families of a planned half million settled in new homes by the end of 1962. Similar townships are under construction, also near Karachi.

As to long-range welfare planning, the overwhelmingly rural character of Pakistan's population means that the most effective governmental program is the one aimed primarily at the villager.

Any nationwide program to provide doctors for the sick, houses for the displaced, and rations for the hungry involves an expenditure that is far beyond the economic resources of the country. The few attempts in these areas have been limited, and benefits have accrued primarily to the cities and towns, to the district headquarters, and to a few of the more conspicuous villages. Most of the people have remained ignorant of and unaffected by such endeavors.

A pioneer effort at rural improvement was the Village-AID (Agricultural and Industrial Development) Program, founded on the assumption that the average villager, if properly informed and assisted by a competent government worker in whom he had confidence, would work with his neighbors in a cooperative fashion to raise the living standards of his community—essentially relying on resources already existing in the village. Earlier experience had shown clearly that no annual visit from a specialist in the provincial government or from the deputy commissioner (district officer) would achieve this result on any lasting basis. The specific objectives of the Village-AID Program were: (1) to raise the productive output and real income of the villager by bringing to him the help of modern techniques of farming, sanitation and health, cooperatives, cottage industries, and so on; (2) to multiply the community services available in rural areas such as schools, dispensaries, health centers, hospitals, and sources of pure water supply; (3) to create a spirit of self-help, initiative, leadership, and cooperation among the villagers; (4) to create conditions for a richer and better life through social activities, including recreational facilities for both men and women; (5) to coordinate the working of the different departments of the government and to extend their activities into the villages by extension service techniques; and (6) to give a welfare bias to the entire administrative structure of the government.

The key figure in the program was the Village-AID worker who, at the end of a carefully planned training program, was assigned to a small circle of villages. To win acceptance as teacher, friend, and guide, the Village-AID worker of necessity lived among the villagers and normally was himself originally from a village. There were good reasons for these precautions. For centuries the villager had associated the occasional visits of government officials with problems of tax collection or the maintenance of law and order. If the visitor was a local patwari responsible for keeping detailed land and crop records, an unguarded remark by the villager might result in an increase in taxes. If the visitor was the district officer, the villager would either be awed into silence or use this rare opportunity to voice some long-standing grievance. In either case there would be deference shown to the outsider and the need for an expression of hospitality from the villagers. Real communication would be lacking. The Village-AID worker, on the other hand, tried to gain the confidence of the villagers, understand their fears and feelings, and in this context show them how improvements could be made. The villagers' primary interest being food, the village workers, with the cooperation of the provincial department of agriculture, made improved seed available and in some cases cultivated demonstration plots. Drainage ditches and access roads were built on a cooperative basis and there was some construction of primary schools.

The Village-AID Program was jointly administered by the central and provincial governments, the central government providing overall policy guidance and advisory assistance to the provinces and the provincial authorities assuming responsibility for organization, training, and operation. Each province had a Village-AID administrator and, possibly, several regional directors. The principal operating unit, however, headed by a development officer, was the development area, which included approximately 150 villages with a population of about 100,000 people. The plan covered 640 development areas in the whole of Pakistan.

Recurring expenditures were shared equally by the two levels of government and the central government bore 75 per cent of nonrecurring expenditures. Considerable financial assistance was provided by the Ford Foundation and the International Cooperation Administration (United States) and, to a lesser extent, by UNESCO, the Asia Foundation, CARE, and the Church World Service. The Ministry of Economic Affairs, which coordinates all foreign aid and development plans, was responsible for the program at the central level.

After the Basic Democracies were brought into being in October 1959, the Village-AID organization lost its separate identity. Its workers and its training facilities were used for the instruction of the 80,000 Basic Democrats, and its agricultural extension services were transferred to the newly created agricultural development corporations. However, under the Basic Democracies the program remains essentially the same, the biggest difference being an increased emphasis on local self-help projects.

349

Realization that the population growth of the country is now over 2 per cent annually has brought an interest in family planning. The government assumed the initiative, meeting with no strong opposition from any local groups, and by 1962 there were 800 family planning centers scattered over the country.

Apart from the welfare problems inherent in the low standard of living and backward nature of the villages and the welfare problems of the less fortunate refugees from India, there are a number of problems which neither the government nor the more conscientious and well-placed private citizens can entirely ignore. Notable among these are the care of orphans and juvenile delinquents; the care and rehabilitation of the physically handicapped —including the deaf, dumb, and blind; the protection of widows and indigent women; and the welfare of the sick. Aware of the sporadic and disorganized efforts of both public and private groups in dealing with problems of this type, the central government, by resolution, formed the National Council of Social Welfare early in 1956. This council is responsible for assessing Pakistan's social welfare needs, giving financial and other assistance to deserving organizations engaged in social welfare work, coordinating the assistance extended to social welfare activities by various ministries of the central and provincial governments, and promoting the setting up of new voluntary organizations where needed. Over one million rupees a year are put at the disposal of 150 voluntary social welfare agencies. In addition, both West Pakistan and East Pakistan have established separate provincial social welfare councils.

Begging is widespread in Pakistan and giving alms directly to beggars is very common, almsgiving being considered an act of religious merit. Many of those who resort to begging are, no doubt, destitute and deserving. Others, however, take it up as a profession and, with a proficiency based on long experience, are able to put on a most pitiful appearance. Efforts are under way to reduce beggary by the provision of special facilities such as welfare homes for beggars and homes for destitute and underprivileged women.

In response to the need for trained social workers, the government, with UN assistance, has established short-term training programs in the urban centers. A Department of Social Work, established at the University of Punjab in 1954, provides a two-year program of training leading to the master's degree and a short training course for leaders of voluntary social welfare organizations.

At the private level there is the All-Pakistan Women's Association (APWA), organized in 1949, which works to improve the education and general welfare of the women of Pakistan. The membership of APWA consists largely of the wives of prominent civil servants, politicians, and professional men. Its activities, so far confined primarily to urban areas, include the promotion of cottage industries, the establishment of schools, nursing-aide programs, and voluntary social welfare and health work, as well as the successful campaign for the establishment of the College of Home Economics and the Arts and Science College for Girls, both at Karachi. Other activities, too many to mention here, focus on educating the women of the country to their role in a modern society.

CHAPTER 17

National Economic Goals

THE TWO AREAS WHICH NOW FORM PAKISTAN were the subcontinent's most underdeveloped before partition—producing raw materials for the ports and factories of Calcutta and Bombay but possessing practically no industry. In West Pakistan the little trade, industry, and banking that did exist were almost entirely in the hands of the Hindus and Sikhs, whose departure at the time of partition brought trade and industry almost to a standstill. Fewer non-Moslems left East Pakistan, but greater concentration of economic control there by non-Moslems up to partition meant that the fewer departures had an equally severe effect.

The scope and complexity of the new nation's economic and administrative problems were all but matched by the inadequacy of the new government's resources for effective action in the situation. There was no central bank. The central government in West Pakistan had to work from improvised headquarters in Karachi, with inadequate buildings, poor communications, and no government press. The East Pakistan government faced like handicaps at the new capital in Dacca. Few would have argued with Finance Minister Ghulam Muhammad's claim, made in presenting the first budget in February 1948, that from its inception Pakistan had had "to face unprecedented difficulties—difficulties which would have overwhelmed many an old and well-established government, and shattered the economy of any well-organized country." Ironically, it was because Pakistan was not a "well-organized country" that it was able to bear the strain at all, since the very underdeveloped state of the country's economy gave it considerable resiliency.

The basis of the Pakistan economy is agriculture, which is devoted largely to the production of food for subsistence. Food crops account for nearly 85 per cent of the land under cultivation;

the balance is planted in cash crops—chiefly jute in East Pakistan and cotton in West Pakistan. The rest of the economy depends heavily on the processing, sale, and consumption of agricultural products. Over half the production of large-scale industry in 1959-60 derived from the manufacture of food, textiles, and leather goods from agricultural sources; the movement of agricultural produce to the ports and the distribution of manufactured goods bought in return constitute the bulk of domestic and foreign trade activity; and about 60 per cent of the country's export income is from the sale of jute, cotton, wool, hides, skins, and tea—45 per cent from the sale of jute and cotton alone.

But in the period since partition there has also been a very great rise in the output of some of the organized sectors of the economy. The output of large-scale manufacturing increased more than six and a half times by 1962 and is now more important for the national income than small-scale industry. Manufacturing as a whole more than doubled its output. Mining increased by two and a half times, and the contribution of banking and insurance services increased by 129 per cent. Agriculture nevertheless remains overwhelmingly important, its share of the national income having dropped during this period by only 5 per cent, from 61 per cent to 56 per cent. The "unorganized" nature of the country's economy makes any statistical description of the national income peculiarly difficult (see Table 17). Because most agricultural produce does not leave the villages of origin, there is no easy way to check estimates of agriculture output, leaving most figures for agricultural income open to doubt. The figures for other items in Table 17 are also subject to a considerable margin of error.

In the development of Pakistan's economy the government has played a pre-eminent role, due in part to the fact that Pakistan inherited a system of wartime controls from the former British government, in part to a general belief in planning with the associated hope for a welfare state generally prevalent in the immediate postwar world, and in part to the fact that private business could not handle all the new requirements. A major difficulty facing private business was the departure of the Hindu and Sikh businessmen, which left a great gap in the organized sector of the economy. Of the remaining businessmen very few could claim any experience in large ventures, though the private sectors of trade and industry moved ahead and in relative efficiency often surpassed the public sector. But where the imminent failure of a private industry threatened other sectors of the economy the Pakistan government displayed no hesitation in taking over. The same concern for the common good has usually led the state to relinquish control as soon as private enterprise appeared ready to do its job effectively. An example of this was the establishment by the government in 1954, during the slump following the Korean truce, of the Pakistan Industrial Development Corporation (PIDC) to build and operate industrial plants. With the recent growth of a class of industrial entrepreneurs the PIDC has begun selling some of these plants to private persons and companies. A different situation grew out of the 1949 decision by Pakistan not to follow the United Kingdom, India, and the rest of the sterling area in devaluing its money. The consequent trade war with India caused a major financial crisis. The commercial banks were unwilling to make loans which would support the price of jute and cotton, and the formation of the National Bank of Pakistan, already decided upon, was hurried forward to meet the emergency. The very great rise in raw material prices during the Korean war boom relieved the situation, but for fear of a recurrence the government continues to control the National Bank of Pakistan.

A relaxation of government control in the field of transport and communications is also unlikely. The Pakistan government inherited from the British a department of posts and telegraphs, which had organized as well the very limited telephone service. Inherited too were the government-controlled railways. Since partition the provincial governments have taken over varying amounts of road transport, which together with the railways has proved an important source of government revenue, and in 1951 the privately owned Orient Airways was absorbed by the government-controlled Pakistan International Airlines Corporation.

Until 1958 the government enforced a series of import, industrial, and price controls, although many of these controls were far too ambitious to be enforced by the very limited administrative machinery. The existence of these controls, however, made possible the government operation of industrial plants and transport. In addition, public investment through PIDC was introduced in those fields not attracting private capital because of low profitability and large investment or because other facilities of the nature of infrastructure were lacking.

A revulsion of feeling against controls in early 1958 was followed by abandonment of price control over a wide variety of items. More recently, the growth of a powerful class of private industrialists and businessmen has brought increasing resistance to government operations in the economic field.

Planning in Pakistan started with the six-year development plan of 1950, scheduled to become effective in mid-1951. But this was essentially an outline plan, put together in a hurry to meet the need at that time for a program to be embodied in the Colombo Plan for Co-operative Economic Development in South and South-East Asia. The end of the Korean war boom brought an end to the optimistic assumptions on which the six-year plan had been based. A good start toward a more realistic survey and plan for the Pakistan economy was made by the Economic Appraisal Committee, whose reports were submitted to the government of Pakistan in November 1952 and March 1953. These were necessarily concerned, however, with the country's immediate financial and foreign exchange crises rather than long-range requirements.

The first comprehensive attempt at planning came in 1953 when the Planning Board of the Government of Pakistan was set up. This board, now called the Planning Commission, was aided by Pakistani economists and by foreign experts, mostly American, who had been selected by the Harvard University School of Graduate Studies and financed by the Ford Foundation. The plan was to run from April 1, 1955 to March 31, 1960, but the program of the plan was not presented until May 10, 1956 and by the time it was released a year of the plan had passed. A final version was not adopted until there were less than two years left of the plan period.

The First Five Year Plan was designed to prepare the ground for rapid growth by building up the infrastructure and productive potential of the economy. National income was to be increased by 15 per cent and per capita income by 7 per cent through substantial increases in agricultural and industrial production and through the provision of irrigation, power, transport, and other facilities required for production. The determinants in assigning priorities to various fields of development were: regional food deficiencies; the impact of a development scheme on the balance of payments; the time factor; and the contribution of a development scheme to national income, the capital-output ratio, and the capital-employment ratio. On the basis of the above and of the overall requirements of a balanced economy, the plan gave first priority to agriculture, which along with irrigation, Village-AID, reclamation, and drainage formed about one-third of the total expenditure planned for the public sector. Industry, including power, came next with about 27 per cent of the public expenditure on development. Transport and communications facilities, neglected for twenty years prior to independence, were allocated about one-fifth of the total public expenditure. Another fifth of the total public expenditure, the maximum that could be spared in view of the claims of the productive sectors, went to the social services—education, health, housing, and social welfare.

In allocation of financial resources to specific sectors of the economy, the plan was generally midway between the first and second five-year plans of India. However, proportionately more was allotted to water and power development in Pakistan than in India and relatively less to transport and communications.

The finances of the First Five Year Plan of Pakistan were modest. Total expenditure was projected at Rs. 10,800 million—7,500 in the public sector and 3,300 in the private sector—with the sources of financing estimated as 9 per cent public saving, 52 per cent private saving, and 39 per cent foreign loans and grants. The low figure for foreign aid probably represented an overly optimistic prediction of the growth of private savings during the period.

The Second Five Year Plan, covering the period July 1960 to June 1965 and approved by the Economic Council on June 21, 1960, envisaged a development expenditure of Rs. 19,000 million—9,750 in the public sector, 3,250 in the semipublic sector, and 6,000 in the private sector. The plan was to be financed to the extent of Rs. 11,000 million from domestic savings and Rs. 8,000 million from foreign sources both governmental and private.

Following a more intensive review of certain plan targets and costs, the Planning Commission in April 1961 announced an upward revision of the financial requirements to Rs. 23,000 million, an increase of 21 per cent over the original cost. The estimate of foreign exchange investment was raised by 30 per cent, from Rs. 6,500 million to Rs. 8,450 million; the "maintenance support" required to balance the current foreign exchange account was increased from Rs. 1,500 million to Rs. 2,500 million; and the local currency component registered an increase of about 10 per cent to Rs. 12,050 million. The Economic Council accorded its general approval to the revised plan on June 19, 1961, pronouncing the Rs. 23,000 million figure firm and final.

The increased costs of the revised plan were attributed to a rise in internal and external prices (43 per cent), underestimation of costs for several projects in the original plan, as revealed by later engineering reports and surveys (31 per cent), and some expansion of the physical size of the plan after re-evaluation of requirements in certain sectors of the economy (26 per cent). The higher total for expenditures was therefore mainly from re-costing rather than from any significant expansion of the plan's physical size. Of the Rs. 23,000 million, Rs. 12,400 million were allocated to the public sector, Rs. 3,800 million to the semipublic sector, and Rs. 6,800 million to the private sector (see Table 18).

The principal goals of the Second Five Year Plan were to increase gross national income by 24 per cent and per capita income by 13 per cent, to expand foodgrain production by 21 per cent, to increase industrial production by about 50 per cent and exports by 15 per cent, to achieve substantial progress toward the target of three million new job opportunities, and to raise domestic savings from 6 per cent to 9 per cent. Other important objectives included bringing about a better distribution of income among various income groups of the country and the acceleration of economic growth in the relatively less developed areas of Pakistan.

Total allocations in the revised plan were substantially higher (73 per cent) than actual expenditure under the First Five Year Plan, but the increase in various sectors reflected the changing needs of the country. The share of agriculture increased from 11 to 15 per cent, of water and power from 17 to 19 per cent, and of education and training from 3 to 5 per cent. On the other hand, the industry sector, including fuels and minerals, was reduced from 31 to 27 per cent of total expenditure, and the housing and settlement sector from 19 to 15 per cent. The relative shares of other sectors remained more or less the same as in the First Plan.

There has been gratifying progress during the first two years (1960-62) of the Second Five Year Plan. National income has gone up, in real terms, by about 11 per cent. The plan target for foodgrains production has been virtually achieved three years ahead of schedule, though this is to a large extent due to favorable weather. Industrial production has jumped by about 23 per cent— a rate of increase that, if it continues, could mean exceeding the target of 60 per cent for the plan period. The installed power-generating capacity in 1961-62 was 20 per cent greater than in 1959-60, while the volume of electricity actually generated was 54 per cent larger. In the program of railways development, approximately one-third of the plan's target has already been achieved, with similar progress in road, water, and air transportation as well as in the communications sector. About 42,000 displaced families were settled in the first two years against the plan target of 300,000. A considerable increase in employment has been provided in all fields of economic activity, but the problem of partial and total unemployment remains acute.

In the field of education, almost 700,000 new students have been enrolled in the primary schools, though nearly twenty million children are still deprived of the opportunity to get education and vocational training. An analysis of the results in various economic activities during the mid-plan period showed that the main shortcomings stemmed from the inadequacy of human technical skills and organization. It is becoming obvious that, in a country whose principal asset is its manpower, even more effort will have to be directed toward the raising of skills.

External aid and foreign private investment financed about 30 per cent of total developmental monetary expenditure during the first two years of the plan. The country's own contribution has been significant, rising with the growth of domestic savings, which went from approximately 6.6 per cent in 1959-60 to an estimated 8.1 per cent of the gross national product in 1961-62. If the propensity to save and invest continues, domestic savings could in time take over from foreign financing as the mainstay of Pakistan's economic development—a much-desired goal.

CHAPTER 18

Agriculture

PAKISTAN IS OVERWHELMINGLY DEPENDENT upon agriculture for its livelihood but agricultural productivity, measured either per acre or per man, is low. Methods are traditional: tillage is by ox-drawn plow or harrow, the use of fertilizer or improved seed is rare. The fields are usually fragmented into tiny plots—often smaller than a quarter acre—and separated from each other by raised earthen walls (bunds) which serve to contain the flow of irrigation water but which also reduce the cultivable area. In East Pakistan almost all available land is under cultivation; much of West Pakistan is by contrast a desert where irrigation and agricultural activity must go hand in hand.

In both wings of Pakistan the chief topic of conversation among farmers is water. Irrigation for double and triple cropping is as important in East Pakistan as in West Pakistan but flood regulation problems differ and the navigation benefits from water development schemes in East Pakistan are of much greater significance. The contrast is apparent from the air: East Pakistan looks lush, green, and watery; West Pakistan seems dry and dusty, even the bulk of the irrigated areas looking dry and khaki-colored. East Pakistan has extremely heavy rainfall and is subject to extensive inundation during the monsoon. In West Pakistan, outside a few fringe areas, it is only through irrigation drawn from the river systems that agriculture is possible at all.

In both wings of Pakistan, the runoff from the melting snows of the Himalayas swells the rivers just as the summer monsoon strikes, while there may be too little water during the rest of the year. These floods can only be effectively controlled from outside Pakistan. The Ganges and the Brahmaputra flow through hills in India on their way from Tibet to East Pakistan; and in West

Pakistan four of the five rivers of the Punjab ("the five rivers") flow through hills in Indian territory, or Indian-held Kashmir, on their way to the plains of Pakistan.

Major Crops of East Pakistan

In June most of the province is flooded, but the depth and the duration of the floods vary a great deal from place to place. In many places there is not enough water during the winter months for the farmers to grow major crops, although there is far more double cropping in East Pakistan than in West Pakistan. Rice and jute, which grow best in flood plains, are of overwhelming importance, though rice, the food crop, receives a higher priority than jute, the cash crop. Although East Pakistan devotes over 87 per cent of its area to producing rice, it still must import 150,000 tons in a normal year; and in the all too common years of crop failure the province may have to import as much as two or three hundred thousand tons of rice (see Table 19).

Rice is grown in three crops in East Pakistan. Of these the *aman*, the winter rice crop, is by far the most important, occupying on the average as much as 71 per cent of the total rice area of East Pakistan. This crop may be sown broadcast from the middle of February to the end of April; it may also be raised from seedlings transplanted between July and September. It is harvested between November and January. *Aus*, the autumn rice crop, is next in importance to aman and covers about 25 per cent of the total rice area. Aus rice is also sown broadcast or may be raised from transplanted seedlings. It is harvested from July to September. Aus grows to a height of only four or five feet and therefore cannot be grown in areas which are deeply inundated, but the aus crop, maturing just before the main aman crop when supplies are lowest, is very important. The last crop, the *boro* or summer rice, has the heaviest yield but is grown in the period of low water and can only be cultivated around *bils* (marshlike ponds). Seedlings are planted in October and November and are harvested before the floods begin in May.

Jute is mainly grown in the inundated lowlands where silt deposits act as a natural fertilizer. Because this lowland variety of jute usually dies if water covers more than half the plant, sowing must take place sufficiently early to allow the plants to mature and to be ready for harvesting before the water level becomes too high.

360

Planting starts in February in the lowlands and continues up to May in the highlands, with harvesting taking place between June and October. When the plants reach a height of three to four inches, thinning, weeding, and loosening of the earth begins—a process that must be repeated about four times. After harvest the cut jute plants are steeped in water in the nearest *khal* (pool) for about fourteen days for retting (decomposition of the bark by partial rotting); this stage is very important in determining the quality of the jute. After retting, the jute strands have to be extracted by a worker who stands waist-deep in the water and beats the stalks with a wooden mallet until the fiber is bared. He then strips off the strands, washes and rinses them, and hangs them on lines to dry. The cultivation of jute, particularly its harvesting, is an extremely arduous undertaking that requires considerable skill and judgment. The value per acre is usually considerably above that of rice but relative prices vary a good deal and almost all farmers prefer to be assured of at least a minimum food supply before planting jute.

Mustard, rape, and gram are winter crops sown as the ground dries out in November and harvested in February. They are usually grown in rotation with aus rice or jute. *Sarisha* (mustard) and *rai* (rape) seeds provide the oil so essential to Bengali cooking but not enough is produced in East Pakistan, making it necessary to import oil from West Pakistan where it is little used. Gram, on the other hand, is very important to the diet of West Pakistanis and unimportant to East Pakistanis.

Sugar cane brings high yields per acre but requires much labor and heavy fertilization. Formerly most of the sugar cane was converted into gur, a dark brown mixture of molasses and sugar made by boiling the cane juice but not removing the molasses. Nowadays a high percentage of the crop goes to the modern sugar refineries.

Tobacco, about half of which comes from the Rangpur district, consists largely of the hookah type. The growing plants are irrigated three or four times and harvesting takes place between February and April.

Most of the tea plantations of East Pakistan are located in the Sylhet district hills, which are a geographical extension of the Assam tea growing district of India; a few estates are also situated in the Chittagong Hill Tracts, which have a similar climate. Tea grows best on tropical hillsides, but the Pakistan estates are not situated at an altitude conducive to the production of the best

361

grades of tea. The tea is planted in November and transplanted when the plants are six months to a year old. The leaves are plucked from mature one- or two-year-old plants from March to September.

Major Crops of West Pakistan

Cultivated land makes up only 20 per cent of the total area of West Pakistan, compared to 63 per cent in East Pakistan. Of the 24 million acres under cultivation in West Pakistan some 65 per cent is irrigated. Wheat, the staple food, is generally grown in the autumn and harvested in the spring (see Table 20). This limits the land suitable for the growing of wheat to areas where there is sufficient water in the generally dry winter months. The area under wheat is also limited by the need for a fairly heavy soil but wheat can be planted in rotation with summer crops, such as cotton or maize.

Rice is unsuited to a desert climate but can be grown in the areas subject to periodic floods, such as parts of the former Sind, Gujranwala, and Shekhupura districts near Lahore and the valley bottoms of the Hazara hills in the north of West Pakistan.

Like rice, bajra is a summer crop, but its importance arises from the fact that it needs very little water and can be grown successfully in unirrigated and near-desert areas. It is sown before the monsoons in June or July and harvested after the rains are over in October and November. Jowar and maize also require little water and can be grown in the hot summer season in areas in the north and northwest of West Pakistan.

Barley is a very marginal crop in terms of production but as it has a shorter growing season can be used as a stopgap if floods delay the planting of wheat or gram. Gram, second in importance only to wheat, can be grown in a lighter soil than wheat but, like wheat, is a winter crop sown in September and October and harvested in February to May.

Rape, sesamum, and linseed are oilseed crops, which are of very little importance in West Pakistan except for linseed oil, used in the manufacture of paint.

Cotton is the chief cash crop of West Pakistan and occupies 12 per cent of the cultivated area or almost twice as much area as is devoted to jute in East Pakistan. Both the relatively lighter pressure on land in West Pakistan and the fact that cotton, unlike jute, does not require much more labor than other crops contribute to this difference. On the other hand, the growing of cotton is limited by climatic conditions in West Pakistan. Cotton requires good soil and ample moisture during the growing season, while the period immediately preceding the harvest must be dry. As a result its cultivation is limited to the irrigated areas of the former Punjab and Sind provinces.

Sugar cane and tobacco are mainly grown in the Mardan and Peshawar districts and in the adjoining districts of the Punjab, where there are heavy clay soils and ample irrigation water. Sugar cane can be grown by a process which allows the plants to remain in the soil for two years, but usually the crop is resown each year in March and April and harvested from October to the middle of March. Both tobacco and sugar cane are cash crops, and both can be processed either by indigenous methods or in modern factories. The tobacco is either used for hookah and snuff tobaccos or sold for manufacture into cigarettes.

Land Tenure

In East Pakistan more than 70 per cent of the arable land is actually under cultivation, the remainder being marginal land by any definition. In West Pakistan there is a large amount of land currently classified as "uncultivated" but this is somewhat misleading as the greater part could be brought under cultivation only through the construction of great irrigation projects (see Table 21).

The average farm holding, calculated on the basis of an estimated five persons in the typical Pakistani family, is only a little over 2 acres in East Pakistan and about 5.5 acres in West Pakistan. These figures imply that West Pakistan is more than twice as well off agriculturally as East Pakistan but in fact the yields on the water-hungry desert lands of West Pakistan are much lower than those in East Pakistan, as is the production of major crops. Most farms are badly fragmented and in East Pakistan the typical farmer has to manage an average of more than eight small parcels, nearly 70 per cent of which are one-third of an acre or less, the rest one-sixth or less. In West Pakistan farms are a little larger on average but the degree of fragmentation is about the same. In either wing it is very difficult for the individual farmer to improve his techniques and, in particular, the quality of his seed.

The subdivision of holdings on inheritance, once of only minor importance in the total agricultural picture, has with the rise in population and the near exhaustion of the supply of available uncultivated land just about precluded any increase in farm production through rationalization of agriculture. Moreover, the scarcity of farmland has brought about a sharp increase in landless labor and sharecroppers. Sharecropping was relatively rare in the last century but by partition more than 50 per cent of the cultivated land of Pakistan was being worked by peasants who possessed no permanent ownership or tenancy rights to the land.

In the last century tenant farmers were able to obtain land from landlords on relatively easy terms but more recently, before enactment of new legislation, the rising population pressure had led to fierce competition among prospective tenants and to higher and higher exactions by their landlords. Not only was it customary for the tenant to turn over half of the harvest to the landlord but he might also be called upon to defray the cost of collecting it and to present gifts to the landlord's family on the occasion of weddings, funerals, and births. In addition to these payments of goods, the tenant might have to provide services for the landlord. *Begar* (unpaid labor) has been declared illegal throughout Pakistan but in fact it continues to be practiced on occasion. For example, it was also common for landlords to recruit their servants from among their tenants' families, paying them little or no salary.

Land tenures in Pakistan can be grouped into four major categories:

1. Outright ownership of large estates by individual landlords. This system, under which the village population consists largely of tenants who cultivate the land, prevailed in West Pakistan and over large areas of East Pakistan until the enactment of the East Bengal Estate Acquisition and Tenancy Act of 1950 and, in West Pakistan, the Land Reforms Bill of 1959.

2. Peasant proprietorship of comparatively small areas cultivated by the peasant himself with the help of members of his family or hired workers. The land itself may be held by several owners, in which case the system is known as *bhaichara* where the members are descended from the same ancestor and *pattidari* in other cases. These joint holdings are found in the Punjab and the northwest of West Pakistan.

3. The holding of state-owned land on a direct tenancy basis with security fully guaranteed in practice. Under this system, known as *raiyatwari*, the occupant enjoys heritable and transferable

rights, which places him practically on the same footing as an owner, as well as the freedom to give up any land at will to avoid liability for land revenue. This system prevails in the former Sind and will prevail in East Pakistan with the take-over of land by the government under the East Bengal Estate Acquisition and Tenancy Act.

4. Ownership of *jagir* land by so-called *jagirdars*, who had been granted by the state the right to collect a share of the revenue of the land or to acquire the land itself in lieu of such revenues. The jagirs came into being in the Moghul period; much later the British in India made extensive grants to jagirdars in the hope of promoting loyalty to the crown.

In East Pakistan, prior to 1950, revenue collection from more than 90 per cent of the cultivated lands in the province was regulated by the Permanent Settlement Act of 1793, as amended through the years. This act had conferred proprietory and hereditary rights in land on those who had until then been the revenue collectors and required the new group of landowners, or zamindars, to pay a land revenue fixed in perpetuity by the government at a figure equivalent to nine-tenths of the amount regularly collected from their tenants before 1793. Subsequent increases in the value and yield of the land and in the general price level had brought a corresponding tenfold increase in the rental income of the zamindars so that by 1950 the fixed money payment to the state was only about one-tenth of their total revenue. Furthermore, the direct tenants of the zamindars, themselves rarely cultivators, were often wealthy men who in turn sublet the lands. This process of subletting, technically called subinfeudation, continued until there were often five or ten or sometimes as many as fifty tenants between the actual cultivator and the owner of the land, i.e. the state. Although some of these intermediary "tenants" had been given security in their tenure by a legal decision or a special law, only about half of the land in East Pakistan was actually worked by persons with such security, the rest being farmed by sharecroppers and hired laborers.

The resultant confusion as to rights and the small share of land revenue accruing to the state had long been considered an impediment to any increase in agricultural production. The East Bengal Estate Acquisition and Tenancy Act of 1950 moved to correct this by limiting landholdings to 33 acres per family or 3.3 acres per family member, whichever was larger. In addition, all rent-receiving interests between the cultivator and the state were abolished and provision was made for the consolidation of small holdings with restrictions on future subdivision of the land. The implementation of this bill was made easier by the fact that most of the zamindars and intermediary tenants were Hindus.

The situation in West Pakistan developed in much the same way. By the time the British occupied the area, the defects of the Permanent Settlement Act were becoming clear. A system of temporary settlement was adopted which provided for reassessment of land revenues about every thirty years on the basis of a careful account of the actual yields and the rentals paid, as compiled by a revenue staff operating in all the villages. British policy favored a land-owning peasantry, partly because a growing middle class whose vested interests depended upon continuation of British rule was the best insurance for the permanence of that rule. In addition a large number of chieftains were confirmed in control of their lands, sometimes as jagirdars. The result was that by the time of partition land in West Pakistan was almost equally divided between landlords and peasants who owned the land that they worked. In a few areas of the former North-West Frontier province there were also important groups of tenants with occupancy rights similar to those in Bengal, but these were changed under legislation passed in 1951 to ownership.

In West Pakistan the problem of landownership was complicated by both the expulsion of large numbers of Hindu and Sikh landlords and the influx of Moslem refugees and tenants from India. The landlords among the refugees were compensated for the lands they lost in India by lands in West Pakistan. Often, however, compensation was made only after a considerable amount of time during which the erstwhile tenants of the departed Sikh and Hindu landlords had come to think of the land as their own. Attempts to collect rents and, even more, to expel tenants for the nonpayment of rent resulted in a great deal of tension and sometimes riots.

The Land Reforms Bill of 1959 effected major changes in the patterns of land ownership and control in West Pakistan: occupancy tenants were granted legal ownership and all jagir rights were abolished; individual holdings were limited to 500 acres of irrigated land or 1,000 acres of unirrigated land; and excess holdings were taken over by the state in exchange for compensation bonds yielding 4 per cent interest and maturing in twenty-five years. The 2.3 million acres acquired by the state were sold to the farmers with the purchase price to be paid in twenty-five annual installments. At the same time, efforts were made to create subsistence holdings. Such holdings varied from 13 to 64 acres, depending upon the relative fertility of the land.

Productivity and Marketing

Crop yields in Pakistan are among the lowest in the world. There are a number of reasons for this, a major one being the abovementioned fragmentation of landholdings into plots too small to be economically cultivated or scientifically managed. Another is the fact that the large proportion of nonlandowning cultivators has reduced the incentive to improve the land and employ new methods. Very little use is made of improved seed and plant varieties nor are plant protection and pest control carried out on a large scale.

Greater use of chemical fertilizers and manures would contribute to substantial increases in yields but high cost or unavailability very seriously restrict their usage. Large fertilizer plants are operating in both wings but it is estimated that the government will have to absorb approximately 50 per cent of the sale price in order to achieve maximum utilization. Organic manures are either in short supply because of alternative uses or because prevailing practices do not recognize their usefulness. Much cattle dung is dried and used for fuel but fish meal, bone meal, and oil cakes are for the most part exported.

In the extensive irrigated areas of West Pakistan, unlined canals and poor drainage facilities have contributed to a rising water table in many areas. Often this has resulted in waterlogging or the formation of salts at the surface. Both conditions either markedly reduce yields or make the land completely unproductive.

Market intelligence relating to agricultural prices is generally not available to the cultivator, who is, therefore, not likely to realize the best price for his produce. An adequate system for storage of food grains does not exist and consequently most cultivators are obliged to sell their crop as soon as it is harvested. Moreover, the lack of adequate storage facilities prevents the stocking of food reserves which can be made available in years of acute foodgrain shortages. The transport system, most notably the road network, is also inadequate, limiting the cultivator's access to market places.

Livestock

Livestock plays an important role in the economy, providing motive power, meat, milk, hides and skins, wool, and dried cattle manure, the last serving as an important source of fuel in the rural areas. At the time of the most recent livestock census, in 1948, it was estimated that there were 24 million head of cattle in the country, over 60 per cent in East Pakistan. Water buffalo are raised in both wings primarily for their milk and secondarily for meat and hides and draft purposes. Their use in the latter capacity is much less common than in other parts of Asia. Oddly enough nearly 90 per cent of the estimated 5 million buffalo are in West Pakistan. Their greater bulk and consequently greater feed requirements appear to be the chief cause of this discrepancy. Otherwise the paddy culture of East Pakistan would seem to be much more suitable for the breed. Lack of feed is a major factor limiting livestock production and the cattle in the eastern wing have been described as "skeletons wrapped in hide."

Sheep are raised primarily for their wool, though mutton and hides are also important. Of the estimated 6 million head in 1948, over half were concentrated in the former Punjab with the remainder in the former Bahawalpur and Baluchistan. Only 5 per cent of the total were located in the eastern wing. In the case of goats, milk, meat, and hides are the most important products of some 10 million animals. About 42 per cent of the goat population were to be found in East Pakistan.

Camels and horses each were estimated to number half a million head, and donkeys, one million head. All of these are important pack and draft animals, though they are not widely used for plowing or harrowing or other activities of the cultivators.

Both the quantity and quality of livestock products are adversely affected by poor stock and widespread disease, and government projects have been established to develop more suitable stock and reduce the incidence of disease.

While meat forms a very small fraction of the average diet because of high cost and low per capita income, milk is widely used and ghee (clarified butter) is an important cooking adjunct. The other by-products—skins, hides, wool, and bone meal—are not only valuable raw materials for local manufacture but important sources of foreign exchange earnings.

Forests

Fuel and timber are in short supply throughout Pakistan, with the area under forest management only about 8.7 million acres. Of these, 3.2 million are located in East Pakistan. The Chittagong Hill Tracts and the Sundarbans of East Pakistan, both possessing the humid tropical climate for intensive forest growth, are the principal sources of timber and firewood in the country. These forests include both hard and soft woods and are capable of sustained yields at levels above current production rates.

The Khulna newsprint mill in East Pakistan produces paper from the *gewa* tree, a hard wood. Annual output of over 25,000 tons of newsprint satisfies national requirements and provides a surplus for export. The Karnaphuli paper mill, near Chittagong, turns out 30,000 tons of a variety of papers each year, all made from bamboo.

Fisheries

The fisheries of Pakistan represent a source of food and an important source of by-products whose potential has not yet been fully realized. The actual size of the annual catch from fresh water and marine fisheries is not accurately known but an estimate made in 1959-60 placed the figure at 290,000 tons. Of this amount 223,000 tons came from East Pakistan waters. In East Pakistan nearly three-quarters of the catch comes from inland waters while in West Pakistan the bulk is from marine waters. Even on the basis of preliminary surveys experts have estimated that the country's inland and marine waters are capable of considerably greater yields. Most of the marine fishing in both provinces is carried out fairly close inshore, rarely including areas more than ten miles from the coast. In some districts of East Pakistan fish farming is carried out in the flooded rice fields, and in many areas fish are raised in ponds and other enclosed bodies of water.

There appears to be a large domestic market and an even larger export market for fish and fish products, but the present catch is not fully utilized because of inadequate storage, processing, and marketing facilities. An estimated 90 per cent of the fresh-water and 20 per cent of the marine catch are sold fresh in the domestic and export trade of the eastern province; a large part of the balance is dried, or dried and salted, for human consumption; the remainder is made into fish meal for livestock feed or organic manure.

CHAPTER 19

Resources and Industry

PAKISTAN, AT PARTITION for the most part a producer of raw materials and a consumer of finished products, has since 1947 had a spectacular rate of industrialization comparing favorably with the highest rate achieved in the industrialization of any country. The beginning of this development from so small an industrial base has meant, however, that despite its high rate of growth large- and small-scale manufacturing provided only 13 per cent of the national income in 1960-61.

Ultimately the industrial potential of the country will be determined by the available domestic supplies of fuel and raw materials and the skill and effectiveness of its labor force. Known mineral resources are limited and domestic fuel supplies, such as coal and natural gas, contribute only about one-third of the energy consumed in the country. Agricultural raw materials must compete with food crops for the available arable land and, with food production already marginal to the needs of the population, marked expansion of nonfood crop production seems rather unlikely. Despite these obvious limitations present resources are by no means fully utilized and geological exploration of the country is far from complete. With the government and the articulate minority in the population both dedicated to industrialization there seems no reason to doubt that present resources are capable of supporting a continued expansion of industry. In fact, industrial progress since partition has been impressive, revealing a degree of managerial and entrepreneurial ability which was wholly unsuspected. Production in large-scale manufacturing industries increased fivefold from 1950 to 1959. However, thus far industrial development has been dominated by the growth of consumer goods industries. A beginning for heavy industries is being made in the Second Five

Year Plan with steel mills, machine tool plants, and oil refineries, and it is anticipated that the Third Five Year Plan will place even more emphasis upon heavy industries.

Of immediate concern in the achievement of maximum utilization of available resources is the shortage of technically trained personnel. Skilled machinists, foremen, accountants, salesmen, and managers are in short supply. Assuming that this shortage of skilled technical personnel can gradually be overcome, still another and fundamentally important element in the country's industrial development and political future must be considered—the fact that industrialization means not only an economic but a social revolution. The migration of workers from agriculture to industry means new urban concentrations with all the consequent problems of housing, sanitation, family disruption, and new ways of life. The government has begun to cope with these problems through such measures as the construction of public housing in urban areas, insistence that the larger industrial enterprises provide modern living quarters for employees, and the tailoring of education to correspond to the changing times.

Cottage Industries

Probably about ten times as many people are engaged in cottage industries as in large-scale industry, with a disproportionately larger number of these in the eastern wing. The greater importance of cottage industries in East Pakistan is traceable in part to greater population pressure, which produces a willingness to work for lower wages, and in part to the far poorer communications. The latter tend to increase the isolation of the villages which in turn emphasizes self-sufficiency among the agriculturalists while raising the cost of nonindigenous goods to a point where village products can compete in price.

The single most important cottage industry is handloom weaving. This alone occupies about half a million people and might be a significant source of revenue except that estimates indicate only one-tenth of the handlooms currently in operation are turning out good quality cloth. Most are being used to produce *khadi*, a coarse handwoven cotton cloth usually worn only by the poorest of peasants, which is inferior to almost all factory cloth. Working on the traditional loom, the weaver can produce only five or six yards a day, as opposed to the thirty yards which can be produced

371

on each of the three or four looms tended by a factory weaver. Originally the handloom worker was dependent upon homespun yarn but home spinning is even less economical than hand weaving and has practically died out. Furthermore, homespun yarn was almost always uneven and weaker than factory yarn, making homespun the worst kind of khadi. The handloom weaver now depends upon "excess" production of yarn by the mills, the supply of which is uncertain since the factories prefer to weave such yarn themselves. The weavers also need actual cash to buy the yarn, and this has disrupted the traditional village barter system of trade.

Most of the other persons reported as working in cottage industries make goods for consumption in nearby villages. There are, however, a number of centers whose handicrafts have a wider market. Thus in East Pakistan silkworm production and silk weaving is carried on in Rajshahi; Dacca specializes in muslin cloth and silver work; and other areas in the production of coir matting, cane articles, conch shell bangles, and mother-of-pearl buttons. In West Pakistan very attractive multicolored blankets and curtains are made in Swat; fine embroidery work of different types is done in Peshawar and Baluchistan; lacquerwork furniture and toys are produced in Dera Ismail Khan; carpets, glazed pottery, and silk fabrics at Multan; and wonderfully keyed padlocks in Gujranwala.

Tribal manufacture of guns at factories at Durra in the Kohat Pass represents a particularly interesting form of cottage industry. Copies of foreign pistols, rifles, sten guns, and shotguns are turned out here by crude mass production methods, often bearing the die cut markings of famous arms manufacturing firms in America and Britain. Very good sports equipment, ranging from polo mallets to badminton rackets, surgical instruments, bagpipes (which even have a market in Scotland), as well as electroplated tableware are made in Sialkot.

Most cottage industries, however, produce crude and simple products which cannot compete with the much cheaper factory products. The existence of such industries, which probably account for about nine-tenths of the employment in this sector, is seriously threatened, but government protection would be warranted only as a means for promoting village self-sufficiency. There is little support for this idea in Pakistan and it seems likely that, as more factories are built and transportation facilities improve, East Pakistan will see a decline in cottage industry similar to the earlier decline in West Pakistan.

The case of the cottage industries producing better quality products is different. Though the better quality products are as a rule too high-priced for the domestic market in Pakistan, where low per capita income remains a real deterrent to the growth of manufacturing, a hopeful solution to survival of these industries lies in the possible expansion of export trade. Unfortunately the goods in this category are still unstandardized, extremely expensive to handle, and poorly adapted to competition with the similar products of India and Japan.

Modern Industries

Under British rule relatively little industrialization occurred in what is now India and Pakistan, due in part to the pressure of British manufacturing interests on the government in India against the protection of infant industries. But perhaps more important was the fact of foreign rule itself which reduced initiative and motivation among potential local industrialists. The subcontinent could be compared to a sea of subsistence agriculture with only little islands of industry joined by the lines of railways. Although Lahore was an important rail junction, the railways centered on Bombay and Calcutta, which are closer to the heart of the subcontinent than Karachi and Chittagong.

Most of the industrialization that took place in the Indian subcontinent before partition was outside the area that became Pakistan. While Pakistan's share of the total area and population of undivided India was 23 per cent and 18 per cent respectively, Pakistan obtained only about 10 per cent of the total number of industrial establishments, i.e. 1,406 out of 14,569. With a few exceptions the only industries already in Pakistan were those that had had to be close to sources of raw material, such as jute baling in East Pakistan and cotton ginning in West Pakistan. Even so, the spinning and weaving of jute and cotton was concentrated at Calcutta and Bombay, both within Inda.

The area that became West Pakistan was not much less industrialized than the Indian part of the subcontinent, but East Pakistan, with a majority of the new state's population, could claim only 9 per cent of the installed capacity of electrical energy and 6 per cent of kilowatt hours generated.

The movement for the establishment of Pakistan by the middle and upper Moslem classes was to some degree a movement to claim for the Moslems and the Moslem-majority areas their share of industrial and commercial incomes. Jinnah's advocacy of commercial education was symptomatic of the community's need for modern ideas and techniques. As if to illustrate this need, partition brought a near collapse of the industrial output of Pakistan due to the emigration of the non-Moslem clerks, managers, and skilled workmen, and the most strenuous efforts were required just to keep the existing industrial and commercial framework functioning.

The situation was eased by large foreign exchange earnings in 1950-51 during the Korean boom, but with the end of the boom the situation reverted to the earlier stalemate. The rapid drain on foreign exchange reserves led to restrictions on almost all imports of consumer goods to permit necessary imports of industrial equipment. With such government encouragement, there was rapid industrial growth in Pakistan after 1951. Under the First Five Year Plan, investment in industry almost doubled by 1960 and output rose almost as much. The proportionate rate of increase from 1951 to 1955 compares favorably with any ever achieved in more advanced countries. The Second Five Year Plan envisages an even greater advance in the local industries.

The very rapid rate of increase from a very limited base has meant that industry has faced peculiar problems. Thus, factories have been plagued by a lack of power, particularly in East Pakistan. Managing directors have often traveled from factory to factory in search of a single skilled laborer, such as a pipefitter, needed to keep their factories in operation. That these factories came into production resulted from the energy and initiative of a comparatively few persons. Profits of over 100 per cent rewarded those whose textile factories first relieved the shortage in 1954, and by 1957 Pakistan had become a net exporter of textiles.

A less encouraging aspect is the one-sidedness of the industrialization so far. In 1954 agricultural processing still accounted for about 75 per cent of the value of national production. The First Five Year Plan envisioned a shift in emphasis toward heavy industries such as cement, chemicals, natural gas transmission, iron, steel, and shipbuilding and by 1960 the picture had in fact changed (see Table 22). Though cotton, jute, and sugar cane processing remained paramount, the natural gas transmission, cement, fertilizer, and shipbuilding industries had moved ahead to significantly larger shares of national production.

As a result of the First and Second Five Year Plans it is expected that the processing of agricultural products will drop to a little over half. For example, the value of the output of large-scale industry increased from Rs. 3,400 million in 1954 to Rs. 6,400 million in 1960—about Rs. 800 million of this increase being attributable to greater utilization of existing capacity, the balance to investment in additional capacity. The gross value added by manufactures rose from about Rs. 1,190 million in 1954 to roughly Rs. 2,140 million in 1960. This gain is also a gross measure of the increase in national income resulting from the large-scale industry program.

This shift from dependence on agricultural production, however healthy in the long run, indicates that the first and perhaps the easiest stage of Pakistan's industrialization is drawing to a close. Partition placed a barrier between the raw jute and cotton of Pakistan and the mills in which they had been manufactured. A very large part of the industrialization to date has been concerned with replacing factories now located in Indian territory. The Pakistan government can, and does, assure the continued profitability of these industries even in export markets by assuring them of supplies of raw materials at less than world prices. Thus, export duties are levied on raw cotton and jute but not on manufactures. However, substantial proportions of both the cotton and jute crops are already processed internally and more processing is planned. Further extension of such industry will be possible only with the production of more agricultural produce.

Mineral Resources

Pakistan's proven mineral resources are not only limited but very unequally distributed, though it should be noted that less than 30 per cent of the country has been adequately surveyed geologically. Discoveries of new resources have been made and production of previously exploited minerals has been expanded since independence, but with minor exceptions mineral production is inadequate to meet the current requirements of domestic consumption or to provide the basis of any substantial export trade. In the important area of fuels, there are some locally available supplies of coal, petroleum, and natural gas.

Though petroleum production has increased more than fourfold since partition indigenous supplies are able to meet only one quarter of domestic requirements. All the producing wells are located in

West Pakistan but structures favorable to the concentration of petroleum have been recorded in both wings. While exploration for new oil fields continues under an agreement concluded in 1961 with the USSR, gas fields have been discovered in both wings. In West Pakistan the field at Sui is one of the largest in the world: pipelines run from the field to Karachi and to Multan. Other fields of natural gas are located to the west of the Indus river, while in East Pakistan a field in Sylhet is under exploitation. These fields supply both fuel and the primary material used in fertilizer plants.

Coal production and known reserves in Pakistan are confined to the western wing. The coal measures are young geologically, occurring for the most part in narrow seams which are steeply inclined and often at considerable depths. The coal has a high ash and sulphur content, tends to crumble easily, has a rather low caloric value, and cannot be used for coking. These qualities, added to fragmented mining operations and little mechanization, result in relatively high pithead prices. The production in 1961 was less than the import of 1.3 million tons, but the bulk of these imports went to East Pakistan.

Other proven or exploited minerals include at least three deposits of iron ore of varying iron content and accessibility. The ores with the highest iron content are reported in the Chitral valley in the northern mountains of West Pakistan. Plans have been made to erect steel mills at Karachi and Chittagong, with these mills processing local ores and imported pig iron and steel scrap. One mineral, chromite, is being exported on a small scale. Rock salt, pottery clays, gypsum, limestone, and graphite are abundant and being produced in quantity.

With few exceptions, the mineral resources of the country are found in West Pakistan since only a relatively small portion of the eastern province lies outside the area of alluvium. Excepting the major gas field in Sylhet, extensive deposits of peat, adequate sand and clay resources, and some salt manufactured by evaporation, East Pakistan has no economically exploitable mineral resources. All coal and petroleum requirements in East Pakistan are currently imported. Even aggregate for construction purposes is in such short supply that a large proportion of gravel and stone requirements must be imported. A common construction practice when mixing concrete is to substitute bits of broken brick for the normal gravel filler. Brick chips are also the only locally available ballast for road foundations in most of the province.

The fuel and mineral resources of the two wings are not economically interchangeable because of high transportation costs or short supply. Such a resource disparity means that the western wing enjoys a considerable advantage for potential industrial development. To the detriment of East Pakistan, alternative trade arrangements with India have not been fully exploited due to continuing differences between the two governments. Coal, stone, cement, gypsum, salt, and even petroleum could be exchanged across the Indian-West Pakistan border for Indian goods in quantities necessary to balance an exchange of coal, oil, and limestone for jute and fish products across East Pakistan's borders. The economic geography of the subcontinent is such that an exchange of this nature represents both a more economic use of resources and the only hope the eastern wing has for partially overcoming its mineral resource deficiency.

Electric Power

A comparison of the development of electric generating capacity in the two wings of Pakistan reveals that the total generating capacity is still relatively small and that very considerable differences exist between the two parts of the country. As Table 23 indicates, installed capacity in West Pakistan at the time of partition was considerably greater than in the eastern wing eight years later. Comparison on the basis of per capita figures reveals an even greater discrepancy. Other differences between the two wings exist in their respective hydroelectric development and potential. On the basis of current data it is estimated that the hydroelectric potential in East Pakistan is about 200,000 kilowatts, in West Pakistan several million kilowatts. In 1955 the only electricity generated by water power came from an installed capacity of 83,000 kilowatts in West Pakistan. The First Five Year Plan anticipated adding 169,471 kilowatts of generating capacity in East Pakistan by 1960 of which 120,000 kilowatts were from one hydroelectric installation on the Karnaphuli river. In West Pakistan 427,000 kilowatts of generating capacity was added of which 164,000 kilowatts was from water power.

Partition brought about a disruption of the transport system in Bengal and Assam, and congestion at the port of Chittagong caused further delays and difficulties for the industrialization of East Pakistan. However, in West Pakistan the port of Karachi had a

377

much greater capacity at the time of partition, and problems of congestion arose only with increased emphasis on industrialization. The western railway system is almost entirely broad gauge and at partition inherited well-equipped workshops at Lahore which helped to keep it running. The differences in the transportation systems of the two wings arise largely out of difficulties in construction of roads and railways in the deltaic region of East Pakistan. However, the very rivers that make the construction of land communications in East Pakistan so difficult can be developed even further as a cheap means of transport.

Industrial Management

Pakistan is very meagerly provided with the skilled persons needed to manage modern plants. In many, but not all, of the new plants, one will find that at least the resident engineer is a foreigner. In some cases these technicians are former displaced persons from Europe, but more often they are British personnel employed on a contract basis. Foreign technicians, while often worth the higher cost when setting up new industries, are very expensive, as they must be paid additional allowances over and above the rate of pay prevailing in their home countries to be induced to work in Pakistan. Experience suggests that there is no insurmountable difficulty in training Pakistanis to take the place of foreigners in all posts. Indeed industrialization itself removes one of the difficulties confronting such a change—that of giving practical instruction to new technicians.

Until recently, a more serious difficulty had been the lack of industrial experience among the business community. There were very few Moslems among the business communities before partition and it was partly to compensate for this lack that the government started the Pakistan Industrial Development Corporation (PIDC). The industrial growth which has already occurred means, of course, that there are now a number of businessmen who have successfully started textile mills and other light industries though there continues to be a comparative scarcity of such persons in East Pakistan, where one of the greatest difficulties in the way of economic development is the lack of technically trained persons in all grades who can speak Bengali. The employment of non-Bengalis in East Pakistan has been one of the major causes of political disturbances and even riots, and such conditions do not encourage either West

Pakistan or foreign private capital to invest in East Pakistan. Pressures from East Pakistan political leaders will probably assure it of more industries in the future. However, new industries can be set up only under license from the government, and the import of machinery is subject to government controls.

Any remaining shortage of managerial skill should be overcome through the institution of the managing agency. Inherited from the British rule in India, this is essentially an adaptation of the holding company concept to conditions in the subcontinent. In theory, the managing agents operate plants in return for a fee (usually based upon a share of the profits together with a percentage of sales) for owners who lack the necessary industrial experience. In practice, the managing agents usually have complete control, own most of the equity capital, and increase their personal security and profits by charging high fees to client firms before allowing any dividends to be paid to minority shareholders. The device has become so embodied in Pakistan economic life that almost all firms are run by managing agents. This is partly because of tax and other legal advantages. The device is best suited to a situation like that in Pakistan today, where the rapid expansion of industry is based on the enterprise of a very limited group of businessmen. Very often in Pakistan industry the firm of managing agents is made up of erstwhile wholesale merchants who had to raise part of the money from landowners who understood little of such matters. The managing agency provided the perfect instrument to do this—particularly as the system was given respectability by also being used by the government through the PIDC.

The Pakistan Industrial Development Corporation (PIDC) was set up largely because of the feeling of frustration at the low rate of progress in industrialization from 1947 to 1950. However, by January 1952, when the corporation actually began operations, this situation had already changed. Nevertheless, the PIDC has been very important in the fields where private enterprise has not ventured, or has not ventured enough. Structurally, the PIDC is a corporation whose common stock is wholly owned by the government. It builds industrial plants and runs them. The declared policy of the PIDC is that such plants should be sold to private individuals when this can be done on advantageous terms. This has been done partly by the setting up of separate operating companies for the management of the plants, some of whose stock is sold to the general public, and partly by selling plants as going concerns to the public. Nearly one-half of the total investment in large-scale industry during the First Five Year Plan was made by the PIDC on behalf of the government and a politically dictated balancing of investment in East and West Pakistan was obvious (see Table 24).

In practice, the PIDC investments are usually the sole investments in the particular field entered—because the project is either too big or too risky for private enterprise to be interested. However, this does mean that monopoly power over the production of such things as paper, chemicals, ships, and, possibly in the future, iron and steel will remain in the hands of the government. While the PIDC is the instrument of the government in most industrial enterprises, the ordnance factories are directly under the Department of Defense and the telephone equipment factory under the control of the Department of Posts and Telegraphs. These exceptions were started before the PIDC was originated, and the factories concerned sell all their production to the parent government departments.

During the period of the Second Five Year Plan comparable investments will be made in industry through the PIDC, and again emphasis will be placed upon the development of East Pakistan (see Table 25). Apart from Rs. 1,064 million of government investment in industry, the expected investment from PIDC's own resources, private investments, loans, etc., is estimated at Rs. 575 million during the Second Plan period. In 1962 in order to streamline PIDC operations, it was divided into the West Pakistan PIDC and the East Pakistan PIDC.

CHAPTER *20*

Public and Private Finances

THE LARGEST SINGLE SOURCE OF GOVERNMENT REVENUE on the Indian subcontinent was the land tax, and its collection one of the most important functions of the British administration. Although land and irrigation revenues continued to be important after partition, far more productive sources of income became available to the government. Today customs duties, income and corporation taxes, and excise and sales taxes account for approximately half of the total government receipts (see Table 26).

The constitution specifies the various sources of tax revenue of the central government, these being for the most part the new and more remunerative sources, including customs and income taxes. The provincial governments retain taxes on land, revenues from irrigation charges, and certain other established taxes. As the country's development proceeds, the tax revenues of the central government have tended to outstrip those of the provinces, so that the central government now collects about two-thirds of the total government revenues of the country. Looking at this another way, since partition the central government revenues have risen 100 per cent, those of the provinces about 70 per cent. At the same time the central government has assumed the increasingly heavy financial burden imposed by the armed services and the development programs. These two obligations alone take well over half of the country's total revenues. Total government expenditures trebled between the fiscal years 1948-49 and 1961-62. The expenditure on development increased almost fourfold during this period and is now almost as great as the amount allocated to the armed services, which increased only 30 per cent during the same period.

381

Sources of Revenue

Pakistan government budgets are divided into capital and revenue accounts, the theoretical basis for the division having been stated by Chaudhri Muhammad 'Ali, then the central finance minister, in presenting the budget for 1954-55:

> The Capital section [of the budget] accommodates expenditure intended to create assets of lasting character. It is the policy of the Government that while normal administrative expenditure should be kept within the limits of revenue receipts the economic development of the country should not be allowed to be circumscribed by our ordinary resources, which are in themselves an index of our underdeveloped economy. The division of the budget into Revenue and Capital is designed to be in conformity with this policy.

The revenue budgets of all levels of government in Pakistan have been kept in approximate balance ever since partition (see Table 27), sometimes by means of judicious shifting of items between the two accounts. Thus in the years 1950-51 and 1951-52, when there were very high returns from taxation due to the effects of the Korean war on the demand for Pakistan exports, surpluses amounting to about Rs. 500 million were placed in funds allocated for social welfare, economic development, and so on, which were spent in the following years of lower export proceeds. On the other hand, there may have been some minor shifting of items the other way to keep the revenue budget in balance, especially in the defense department.

The estimated national income in 1960-61 was Rs. 22.6 billion. Expressed as a percentage of national income, therefore, revenue was just under 10 per cent and total expenditure was about 10 per cent. These percentages of estimated national income flowing through the government sector are quite high for an underdeveloped country, although very low compared with the more developed areas of the world.

The government has faced great problems in raising revenue. Partly these problems are economic: the real burden of taxes is much greater in Pakistan than it is in more advanced countries. In part the problems are also administrative: it is extremely difficult to raise taxes from subsistence agriculture. Indirectly, of course, a great deal of the burden of export duties on agricultural produce

382

is borne by the agriculturists, but collection takes place at the ports, not the villages.

As pointed out in the First Five Year Plan, one of the best ways to finance rural development would be to raise land revenue rates. In East Pakistan the program of land reform is already slowly raising the net income of the government. Until the new record of rights is complete, however, there will be many technical difficulties in raising the taxation rates. In West Pakistan the record of rights is complete, but the rates of revenue were set at various dates and are often inequitable. Land revenue, the main source of revenue for pre-twentieth-century British governments, was fixed in money terms and has, because of generally rising prices and real incomes, become gradually less important. Revenue administration is very important, however, as a means of registering and confirming rights in land and has been strongly recommended by the Planning Commission.

Charges for irrigation are often considerably higher than land revenue, but here too the rates were fixed initially in relation to the costs of the irrigation works supplying the water and the rise in price levels during and after World War II makes these rates comparatively light today. In most cases irrigation fees are collected by the revenue department at the same time the land revenue is collected. Since water meters would be prohibitively expensive, the system of charges is on a per acre basis but with heavier charges for some crops than for others. As a result it is probable that the acreage of crops bearing high rates is usually understated.

While provincial and central government revenue averages about 10 per cent of the total national income, it was nearly a quarter of the nonagricultural income in 1954-55 and increased to 34 per cent in 1961-62. Customs duties accounted for 23 per cent of the total revenue in 1954-55 and 20 per cent in 1961-62. Some of these duties were collected on exports, some imports and exports are duty free, but rates of more than 100 per cent ad valorem are common in the Pakistan customs tariff. The latter produce a great temptation to avoid the payment of customs duties. This may be attempted either by bribing officials or by outright smuggling. The fact that there are only three major seaports has made it reasonably easy to exercise sufficient supervision at ports, so that smuggling across land frontiers has been more important. In East Pakistan the border is long and frequently crossed by navigable waterways and attempts to stop smuggling have been very costly. In West Pakistan the border is largely desert and the costs of transport discourage smuggling, though appreciable quantities of gold and such small items as watches, fountain pens, and, from time to time, cloth are believed to be smuggled by fishermen and Pathan and Baluchi tribesmen.

With the exception of a few large firms, most of which engage in manufacturing, business operations in Pakistan are family affairs. Accounts are kept largely in the head of the owner of the business, and in the absence of a well-developed banking system a very large proportion of all transactions are in cash. This makes it far easier than in Western countries to prepare two sets of books—one for the tax collectors and another for one's own use. If the business is not a family concern a third set of books may be prepared for inspection by the minority shareholders.

Under these conditions it is not surprising that income and corporation duties amounted to only 10 per cent of total revenues in 1954-55 and again in 1961-62. They have risen to an estimated Rs. 306 million in the 1961-62 budget, but this is still little over one per cent of the total national income. It has been suggested that at least half of the legally liable income was not being assessed.

One result of the difficulty in collecting direct taxes has been the attempt to concentrate taxation in those fields where there is likelihood of enforcing compliance, e.g. customs duties at seaports. Another has been the practice of collecting both excise and sales duties: both are single-point taxes payable on imports by the importer, on manufactured goods by the manufacturer, on goods sold by a licensed wholesaler, and on exports by the exporter in the case of a few specified goods. Corresponding to the sales taxes with which we are familiar are the octroi duties, or terminal duties, payable on most goods when they enter cities and towns for sale. The octrois form a major part of local urban government revenues.

Under the constitution the central government has exclusive powers to raise money from duties of customs, including export duties; duties of excise, including duties on salt, but excluding alcoholic liquor, opium, and other narcotics; corporation taxes and taxes on income other than agricultural income; estate and succession duties; taxes on the capital value of assets, not including taxes on capital gains on immovable property; taxes on sales and purchases; terminal taxes on goods or passengers carried by sea or air, and taxes on their fares and freights; and taxes on mineral oil, natural gas, and minerals for use in the generation of nuclear energy.

These include practically all the main sources of taxation in any modern state and allow far more exclusive jurisdiction to the central government than is usually allowed in a federal state. There is, however, one exception: the constitution states that all matters affecting agriculture come under the exclusive jurisdicion of the provincial governments, including all agricultural taxation. This division of powers, based on the fact that the administration of agricultural affairs had been the responsibility of local governments before partition, represented a victory by the politically powerful West Pakistani landlords.

Both provincial and central taxes are progressive taxes but do not take account of each other. This means that a rich man with the same total income will pay less tax if his income is drawn from both agricultural and nonagricultural sources than if it all comes from one or the other source. The exclusion of agriculture from federal taxation has also led to difficulties in deciding what income is properly taxable on large estates or plantations where agricultural produce is at least partly processed.

At the time of partition there was considerable doubt about the financial stability of the new central government of Pakistan. About half of the revenue of the central government of undivided India had come from income and corporation taxes drawn predominantly from the industrial areas outside Pakistan's share of the subcontinent. Yet the very exclusion of these industrial areas meant that the jute and cotton of Pakistan were now exported in a raw state, with manufactured goods imported in exchange, and the resulting revenue from customs duties, particularly during the postwar and Korean booms, led to large budget surpluses. Since 1952 the lower demand for exports, combined with the growth of Pakistan industry, commerce, and banking, has led to a reduction in the relative place of revenue from customs but has been accompanied by a rise in the revenue from income, corporation, and sales taxes and from central excise. Industrialization has also meant a rising trend in the income of the central government from its ownership of the railways, the post office, the State Bank, and the mint. Income has also started to flow from the government-sponsored financial and investment institutions and, in particular, from the Pakistan Industrial Development Corporation.

There has been considerable change in the balance of functions between the central and provincial governments. For a time the tendency was centralizing but this has been reversed in more recent years. It now appears that the trend is toward limiting central government operations. At least four-fifths of the army and practically all the navy and air force troops and installations are located in West Pakistan, and practically all the central governmental bureaucracy is located in Karachi and Rawalpindi. As a result, most central government expenditure takes place in West Pakistan. More important in recent years than the revenue expenditures of the central government have been the capital disbursements (refer to Table 27). No geographical breakdown is available for capital expenditure but most of the expenditure is for development projects which are located in both wings, with the pressure of Bengali opinion ensuring an equitable share of the expenditure in East Pakistan.

The constitution does not specify the types of taxes that may be levied by provincial governments. However, these include taxes on agricultural income and the capital value of agricultural land; estate and succession duties on agricultural land; taxes on land and buildings; stamp duty; excises on alcohol and drugs; taxes on electricity, vehicles, boats, advertisements, animals, luxuries, professions and trades, amusements, entertainments, betting and gambling; capitation taxes; and tolls, terminal taxes, and taxes on goods and passengers carried by road or waterways. While this is a long list, all these taxes appear to be very difficult to collect and, with the possible exception of the various taxes on land and agriculture, seem to earn little revenue. The provincial governments have to depend largely upon the income from taxes levied by the central government, by grants-in-aid, and by development loans (see Table 28).

The financial difficulties of the provincial governments are recurrent. East Pakistan's position is particularly bad, considering that it has more than half the population. However, the comparatively larger income of West Pakistan is due largely to the taxes on water in irrigation projects, while heavy expenditure is required to keep them in operation. Since a large part of the civil administration is concerned with police and justice and is, in fact, occupied with the raising of revenue, relatively little is left for productive purposes.

Until the present constitution was adopted the provincial governments were usually dominated by the central government in fiscal as in other matters. Although the political initiative now seems to be more equally divided between the two, the central government still has a dominant position in the fiscal field. In 1961-62 central revenues were Rs. 2,993.6 million. The combined revenues of the provincial governments were only Rs. 1,440 million or less than half as much. The position of the provinces in relation to the central government is made worse by the fact that their revenues have been slower to increase than those of the central government.

The provinces did receive some revenue collected by the central government. Then, the improved position of the central government during the Korean war boom, contrasted with provincial needs, caused a reconsideration of the relationship. Accordingly, in June 1951 the leaders of the central and provincial governments requested Sir Jeremy Raisman, an Englishman who had at one time been in charge of the finances of the government of undivided India, to investigate the situation and make an award. Under his award half the proceeds of the income tax and the central excises on tea and tobacco were divided between East and West Pakistan in the ratio 45:55. Each province retained half the net proceeds of the sales tax collected in its area. West Pakistan also received 50 per cent of the collections in the former federal capital area of Karachi. East Pakistan received 62.5 per cent of the export duty on jute, this accounting for about 20 per cent of its total revenue. In addition, the subvention for the former North-West Frontier province was increased from Rs. 10 million to Rs. 12.5 million.

Since the Raisman Award nearly a decade ago the national economy and revenue structure have undergone considerable change. Some sources of revenue, such as the sales tax, which were relatively unimportant have expanded greatly, while export duties on raw cotton have fallen drastically. Moreover, the increasingly important role of planning and development requires that internal and external resources be so distributed as to facilitate development in the country as a whole. Since the provincial governments are mainly responsible for the economic development in their regions, greater resources should be placed at their disposal.

To meet this situation, the cabinet in May 1961 appointed a committee with Zahiruddin Ahmed, joint secretary in the Ministry of Finance, as convener, and with the two provincial finance secretaries and two other officials as members, to review the workings of the existing arrangements for apportionment of revenues between the central and provincial governments and to suggest changes where necessary. The committee presented its report in August

387

1961, recommending the establishment of a finance commission after the promulgation of the new constitution.

The government accepted the recommendation but decided to act immediately. A high-powered finance commission of ten members headed by H. A. Majid, the finance secretary, was named on December 19, 1961 and on the basis of its report, submitted in January 1962, the president issued the "Distribution of Revenues and Consolidation and Payment of Loans Order 1962" to take effect July 1, 1962, with these main provisions:

i) The Provinces shall be assigned in each year beginning on and after the first day of July 1962 a share of the net proceeds of the following taxes and duties levied and collected by the Central Government in that year calculated according to the percentage specified hereunder:

a) Taxes on income — 50 per cent

b) Sales tax — 60 per cent

c) Federal excise duties on tea, betel nuts, and tobacco (manufactured and unmanufactured) — 60 per cent

d) Export duties on jute and cotton — 100 per cent

ii) The sums assigned to the Provinces above shall not form part of the Federal Consolidated Fund and shall be distributed between the Provinces in the following manner, namely:

a) Sales tax

(1) Of the 30 per cent of the sum assigned in each year, each Province shall receive an amount bearing to the said 30 per cent the same proportion as the collections in that Province in that year bear to the total collections.

(2) Of the balance of 70 per cent of the sum so assigned in each year, East Pakistan shall receive 54 per cent and West Pakistan 46 per cent.

b) Estate and succession duties in respect of agricultural lands

c) Other taxes and duties
Of the sum so assigned in each year, East Pakistan shall receive 54.25 per cent and West Pakistan 45.75 per cent.

iii) 'Taxes on income' include corporation tax but do not include taxes payable in respect of Federal emoluments and any surcharge levied and collected by the Central Government for

Federal purposes. These shall be charged upon the Federal Consolidated Fund and paid in each year to the Province of West Pakistan to the sum of Rs. 22.7 million as a grant-in-aid.

iv) All loans made by the Central Government to the Provinces after the fourteenth day of August 1947 (other than foreign loans including rupees) and outstanding on the thirtieth day of June 1961 shall be written down by 50 per cent and converted into two loans, each of which shall be repayable by the Province concerned to the Central Government over a period of twenty-five years commencing on the first day of July 1961.

v) For the purposes of the preceding paragraph 'loans' excludes such loans which the Central Government obtained from foreign agencies for the Provinces.

Local government powers vary widely from area to area: in some of the units integrated into West Pakistan all education and practically all health and road programs were and still are administered directly by the provincial government; in the former Punjab and in East Pakistan they are more often administered by local government organizations, although often with financial aid from, and subject to inspection by, the provincial government.

Local governments depend upon surcharges on the land revenue, while urban governments depend for much of their revenue upon the proceeds of octroi taxes levied upon goods brought into the town for selling purposes. Besides octrois and surcharges on the land revenue, local governments collect house taxes, fees for the use of space, and license fees for traders and various professions. The Second Five Year Plan estimates resources of Rs. 200 million from the local level for financing public development programs.

Banking and Currency System

Though it had developed as an integral part of the general Indian system, the currency and banking system in what is now Pakistan was hit particularly hard by partition. It was at least in part because of the expectation of very grave difficulties that it was decided before partition that the Reserve Bank of India should continue to function in Pakistan for an interim period. Its work was soon taken over, however, by the State Bank of Pakistan, which opened on July 1, 1948. The State Bank of Pakistan had to recruit an almost entirely new staff—few of whom had experience in any kind of banking, let alone central banking—but since 1948 the State Bank and the Pakistan mint have replaced Indian currency by new Pakistani currency and a new banking structure has been developed. In the wake of partition, banking operations had virtually come to a halt with the exodus of the non-Moslem banking community. Out of thirteen scheduled banks with head offices in areas comprising Pakistan, twelve owned and run by non-Moslems transferred their head offices to India. Only one Moslem-owned scheduled bank moved its head office from India to Pakistan. Overnight the number of bank offices fell from 631 to 213. The situation in West Pakistan was even worse than figures for the country as a whole would indicate for only 69 bank offices remained of the previous 487 offices. But under the guidance of the State Bank of Pakistan there was a steady development toward the banking system—powerful, cohesive, and national in character—that exists today. The number of scheduled banks stood at 33 by the end of March 1962 with a total of 674 scheduled bank offices as compared to 636 a year earlier and 473 two years earlier.

In theory *riba* should be outlawed in an Islamic state and the constitution of 1956 stated that the aim was "to eliminate riba as early as possible." The constitution of 1962 declared flatly that "riba should be eliminated." Elements within the state continue to insist upon its elimination, but given the fact that the feature of paying interest on money pervades the entire banking structure it seems extremely unlikely that any such change will be made.

There has been a continuing increase in the money supply in Pakistan, but with the exception of years of crop failure the cost of living index, which mainly reflects the prices of the cheapest foods and textiles, has been remarkably steady (see Table 29). There is no apparent immediate connection between the volume of money in circulation and the cost of living index.

The basic unit of currency in Pakistan is the rupee, which is worth 21 American cents at the official rate of exchange. The coinage and the one rupee note are issued by the government of Pakistan, while higher denomination notes of 5 rupees, 10 rupees, 50 rupees, and 100 rupees are issued by the State Bank of Pakistan. On January 1, 1961 the government introduced a system of decimal coinage. The existing rupee was retained as the main unit and for the smallest unit a new coin equal to 1/100th of the rupee and termed a paisa was introduced. It is expected that the withdrawal of the old coins will be completed in a few years. So far only 1 paisa, 5 paisa, and 10 paisa pieces have been introduced. The currency reform is to be followed by the introduction of the metric system of weights and measures, which will be phased out over a much longer period of time.

The State Bank of Pakistan maintains its accounts in the form adopted by the Bank of England, with separate balance sheets for the issue and banking departments. The liabilities of the issue department are the State Bank note issue. By law at least 30 per cent of the assets of the issue department must consist of gold coin, gold bullion, silver bullion, or approved foreign exchange, while the remainder may consist of rupee coins, rupee securities, and certain types of bills of exchange and promissory notes. Pakistani currency is not freely convertible into gold and the reserves held in the issue department of the State Bank of Pakistan are in fact the foreign currency reserves of the government of Pakistan.

The currency system works well. The banking system, on the other hand, is inadequate for it does not exist at all outside the bigger towns. The rural economy is only partly monetized and complete monetization is bound to be a slow process. Money can be transferred by telegram and by money order—the Pakistani postal money order contains a space for a receipt which is returned to the sender, thus making it more useful for business purposes than its American equivalent. The Post Office Bank also takes deposits of money but does not provide credit facilities. Before partition the "indigenous bankers"—who often were partly merchants and engaged in money lending—provided means of transferring money, but these *shroffs, chetties,* and *mahajans* were almost all non-Moslem and have practically disappeared. Some few *arthias* (commission agents) who sell rural produce to processors and retailers in the larger towns do provide credit to the farmers for whom they act, but apparently only to their better customers and at a high cost. The village shopkeeper often provides small amounts of credit at a very high price to his fellow villagers, but even this is difficult to do. Usually the village shopkeeper cannot obtain credit from his suppliers and the lack of banking institutions means that there is no other source of credit. Peasants who own land can sometimes obtain money on a usufructuary mortgage, and a few may be able to borrow from sympathetic landlords. But the general lack of credit has a crippling effect upon the economic development of Pakistan.

The very shortage of banking institutions has made the operations of those which do exist in some ways more difficult. The fact that so much business is done by cash means that the banks are liable at any moment to face sudden and unexpected demands for actual cash, and this has kept the balances in the tills large and led to a great desire on the part of the bankers to keep a large part of their assets in a form which can be discounted or pledged with the State Bank of Pakistan whenever additional cash is needed. Against this background it is easy to understand the big differences between the 3 to 4 per cent interest which Pakistan government bonds yield and the 12 per cent at which some bank loans are made. Following British practice, many bank loans are made in the form of overdrafts on bank balances and interest is paid only on the actual day to day debit balances. This form of bank loan is legal in Pakistan, although illegal in America, but obviously it is difficult for the banks to pledge such loans with the State Bank of Pakistan. It is believed that the far lower rates of interest which the banks are prepared to offer upon loans made in the form of bills rediscountable with the State Bank of Pakistan has led to an increase in their use, but no details are available. For most borrowers the fact that interest is paid only on the actual debit balance of an overdraft is more than enough to counteract higher rates of interest. Since January 1959 the State Bank has kept its bank rate stable at 4 per cent, and the interest on government bonds was kept steady at between 3 and 4 per cent.

Though the State Bank of Pakistan is the central banking institution of Pakistan, the general public is more aware of the "scheduled" banks, so called because they are "scheduled" by the State Bank of Pakistan. To be "scheduled" a bank must have a paid up capital and reserves amounting to at least half a million rupees, and also must be approved by the State Bank of Pakistan. Besides the scheduled banks there are a small and decreasing number of smaller unscheduled banks. Some of these are survivors of the indigenous banking institutions and some are apex banks of the cooperative banking structure. Finally there are a number of specialized institutions to finance industry, agriculture, and house-building.

The capital of the State Bank of Pakistan is partly owned by the government and partly by private persons resident in Pakistan. The private ownership of part of the capital is not, however, an indication of private control over the bank. On the contrary the

392

government appoints the governor, the deputy governor, and a majority of the members of the board of directors, retains a power of issuing directions to the bank, and sets the rate of return upon bank shares. Under the circumstances, the only purpose served by having some private shareholding is to provide a convenient method of associating the mercantile and industrial community with the affairs of the State Bank of Pakistan, both so that business leaders may be informed of the intentions of the State Bank and so that the State Bank can obtain their views. At the time of its annual meeting the bank publishes a very valuable review of the financial situation of the country.

Like all central banks the State Bank acts as banker to the central government and the other banks and controls the note issue. It also acts as banker to the provincial governments, acts as agent of the central Ministry of Finance in controlling foreign exchange, and provides facilities for the large amounts of money. Besides its head office in Karachi, the State Bank of Pakistan has branches in the provincial capitals of Dacca and Lahore, the former provincial capitals of Peshawar and Quetta, the ports of Chittagong and Khulna, and the textile center of Lyallpur. All of these branches—except Quetta—operate as clearing houses. The system of branches enables the State Bank to keep in touch with smaller unscheduled banks and to be well informed about economic conditions in Pakistan.

The State Bank has broad responsibilities for developing banking and has been instrumental in founding the National Bank of Pakistan, the Agricultural Bank, and the Pakistan Industrial Credit and Investment Corporation. It also has encouraged the formation of the Karachi, Dacca, and Lahore stock exchanges, has tried to encourage agricultural credit operations, and in cooperation with the scheduled banks has started the Institute of Bankers in Pakistan, which acts as the bankers' professional organization and conducts training courses, administers examinations, and produces a journal.

The scheduled banks are divided into three groups: the foreign non-Indian banks, formerly called exchange banks and now called "foreign banks"; the Indian banks; and the Pakistani banks. The origins and nature of present business of the three groups differ widely, and banking statistics are available to differentiate them.

The earliest banks in the modern sense in Pakistan were the British "exchange banks," with head offices in London. These were of various origins and at the time of partition were practically the only scheduled banks which effectively conducted business. As late as 1951 they were believed to have 40 per cent of the demand deposits in Pakistan. While their deposits have increased, the rapid expansion of the Pakistani banks—particularly the National Bank of Pakistan and the Habib Bank—have lessened their share of a rapidly increasing total business. The State Bank of Pakistan, as a matter of policy, does not allow foreign banks to open new branches outside major port towns or other places with a major interest in foreign trade. Most government and semigovernment institutions have shifted their accounts to Pakistani banks, especially the National Bank of Pakistan. It seems likely, however, that the foreign banks will continue to dominate foreign trade since to undertake this type of work a bank needs large capital funds, substantial deposits at the important financial centers of the world, extensive financial resources to allow a large turnover of funds, and a trained staff. In as much as the Pakistani banks do not have substantial assets or access to foreign reserves, they find it very difficult to compete, for foreign exchange business, with the foreign banks. Besides the several British banks, there are now branches of the American Express Co., the National City Bank of New York, the Bank of America, the Bank of China (incorporated in Peking), the Bank of Tokyo, and the Netherlands Trading Society.

Before partition many of the scheduled banks had their head offices in what is now Pakistan—particularly in Lahore. For a time after partition some Indian banks remained in nonactive operation in Pakistan, but these have now suspended operations. The remaining Indian banks in Pakistan are expected to stay and gradually to become concerned solely with the financing of Indo-Pakistan trade. The Indian banks are far more important in East Pakistan than in West Pakistan. This is probably due to the fact that many of the Hindus have stayed in East Pakistan, and still help to operate the banks, and to the far closer trading and cultural connections of East Pakistan with Calcutta than of West Pakistan with any Indian city.

By 1962 there were thirteen Pakistani banks on the schedule of the State Bank of Pakistan. The largest was believed to be the National Bank of Pakistan, followed fairly closely by the Habib Bank and the Moslem Commercial Bank, the founders of which migrated to Pakistan at the time of partition. The Habib Bank was founded by the Habib family which also owns textile mills and other factories and is a member of the Khoja community, a Moslem trading group. The Habib Bank is reportedly largely staffed and run by Khojas and, in a sense, represents a modern adaptation of the shroff tradition. Largely in order to serve this same Khoja community, the Habib Bank (Overseas) has been founded, with branches at Bombay, Colombo, Rangoon, and Mombasa (East Africa). The Moslem Commercial Bank was founded by M. A. H. Ispahani, whose family owned a jute mill in Calcutta before partition and now controls extensive tea trading, shipping, and jute and other industrial firms, particularly in East Pakistan.

The remaining Pakistani scheduled banks are much smaller and local in character. The Australasia Bank is so called because its Punjabi founder made his fortune in Australia and wished to commemorate the fact. The Bank of Bahawalpur, as its name suggests, was originally founded to serve the State of Bahawalpur but since Bahawalpur has been absorbed into the Province of West Pakistan the bank has opened branches in Lahore and elsewhere in West Pakistan. The Punjab Co-operative Bank has only two branches, but it is the apex of the Punjab cooperative banking structure. As will be obvious from the above most Pakistani banks form part of large business interests. It is believed that it was in order to avoid banking with their competitors' banks that a number of businessmen, almost all from Karachi, started the new National Commercial Bank toward the end of 1957.

It was partly, at least, to have a more neutral vehicle for its agency operations that the State Bank started the National Bank of Pakistan but it was also to have an agent for government policy. The government of Pakistan has provided 25 per cent of the capital and the governor of the State Bank of Pakistan is ex officio the president of the National Bank of Pakistan. The National Bank of Pakistan acts as agent of the State Bank of Pakistan in places where the latter does not have branches and is paid a commission by the State Bank for doing so. The National Bank of Pakistan has been consciously used as an instrument of government policy. At first, contrary to all normal banking practice, loans to individuals were made directly by the State Bank of Pakistan. The National Bank of Pakistan was hurriedly opened in East Pakistan to perform such functions. Similarly, the National Bank of Pakistan has given loans for new industries when some of the other banks were chary of entering this field.

Largely in order to provide competition with the extremely high rates of interest charged by the village banias and mahajans the central and provincial governments have tried to stimulate the cooperative credit movement, but with very limited success. The movement has always been under the strict control of the government, which has set interest rates and rules. In general the government has insisted that the primary unit be a small society of about ten persons, with unlimited liability, who would be allowed to borrow from higher "centrals" at low rates of interest, but with repayment on a strict schedule. As the rates of interest that the central could offer on deposits were very low—at a time when the moneylender often received 100 per cent a year—practically all the money lent came direct from government funds.

Where there was competition to obtain loans, political favorites often won out and their loans were not always repaid. Where loans had been made without political consideration, an antipathetic government official with no understanding of the local situation could find something wrong with the procedure and order the societies wound up at the most inconvenient time. The combination of red tape and government favoritism meant that loans were largely made to such literate salaried persons as schoolmasters, revenue officials, and the rural notables the government could not afford to offend and were largely used for weddings and other costly ceremonies. The peasant continued to prefer to go to the bania or, since partition, to relatives, friends, landlords, or the village shopkeepers. At present cooperative credit institutions exist in all parts of Pakistan, though many are moribund. One of the problems today is that the cooperative banks, having found that normal banking business is far less troublesome than supplying rural credit, have deserted the function for which they were started.

In the absence of other banking institutions, the post office serves for banking far more than in Western countries. Postal money orders are widely used as the most convenient method of payment for everyone outside the largest centers. It is also possible to send money by insured post and by telegram, but these are relatively more expensive and therefore less popular. The post offices generally provide facilities for the deposit of money as well. In 1959-60 there were some 8,100 offices or more than seventeen times the number of scheduled bank offices. Accounts can be opened with a minimum of two rupees and provide the only effective competition against gold and jewels for the savings of clerks, teachers, and laborers. Many a small shopkeeper will put what surplus cash he has in them. The one big disadvantage compared with banks is that one cannot draw by check, but legislation was passed in December 1957 opening the way to this too. In addition to current accounts, time and fixed accounts at a higher rate of interest are allowed. Deposits rose from Rs. 171.8 million in 1952 to Rs. 330.5 million in 1961. Net investment in savings certificates rose from Rs. 11.8 million in 1952 to Rs. 47.6 million in 1961. Total deposits in scheduled banks as of March 1962 were Rs. 3,377.6 million, of which Pakistani banks held Rs. 2,287.8 million.

The banks in Pakistan have followed the British practice and tried to keep as much of their assets as possible in a liquid, self-liquidating form. Before partition there was very little industry in what is now Pakistan and the British exchange banks—the only ones really functioning during the early years of Pakistan—continued to specialize in the financing of trade, particularly the export of jute and cotton, so that on June 30, 1950, 67.3 per cent of advances were covered by merchandise, pledged or hypothecated, and more than half of this was by goods normally exported, such as jute, cotton, hides, skins, wool, goat hair, and tea.

The very small amount of credit extended to agriculture is easily understandable in view of the urban nature of the banking system and the fact that the typical Pakistani farmer with his holding of five acres in West Pakistan—half that in East Pakistan—has little or no security to offer in return for a loan.

An investigation into the existing audit structure of the country by the Credit Enquiry Commission in 1959 revealed the inadequacy of the institutional arrangements for industrial finance, particularly in the field of long-term finance for the medium- and small-scale industries. As recommended by the commission, the government established the Industrial Development Bank of Pakistan on July 27, 1961. Actually a reorganization of the former PIFCO but with enlarged functions, the bank is primarily concerned with providing long-term credit to medium- and small-scale industries which its predecessor could not do. The present lending limit of the bank is Rs. 1 million in case of limited companies and Rs. 5 lakhs in the case of other concerns except with the approval of the government. The bank finances the establishment of new industries as well as balancing and modernization of existing industries.

In order to meet finance and development needs the government set up a number of "finance corporations" which had 51 per cent of their capital supplied by the government and, like the National Bank of Pakistan, were under effective government control. Thus in 1949 the Pakistan Industrial Finance Corporation was organized, in 1952 the House Building Finance Corporation and the Agricultural Development Finance Corporation, in 1955 the Small Industries Corporation, and in 1957 the Pakistan Industrial Credit and Investment Corporation. The Pakistan Refugee Rehabilitation Finance Corporation is in a class by itself as, unlike the others, it was regarded from the first as a subsidy rather than a commercial undertaking. These finance corporations, unlike the Pakistan Industrial Development Corporation, are not supposed to provide equity capital but are supposed to provide loans for periods of up to twelve years at rates of interest of around 5 per cent. While the Small Industries Corporation was not too active, the Pakistan Refugee Rehabilitation Finance Corporation had by June 1958 extended assistance in the amount of Rs. 39.5 million.

The limited success of these institutions led to the establishment of an Agricultural Development Bank on February 18, 1961 under the Agricultural Development Bank Ordinance of 1961. The new bank represented a merger of the former Agricultural Development Finance Corporation (ADFC) established in 1952 and the Agricultural Bank of Pakistan (ABP) established in 1957 as recommended by the Credit Enquiry Commission. Before this merger, both the ADFC and ABP were providing agricultural credit in areas allocated to them by the government, each functioning in half of the districts of East and West Pakistan. Although both organizations were providing the same kind of credit facilities, the fact of different managements led to important differences in their policies and procedures, e.g. even the rate of interest was not quite uniform. As the functions of both organizations were similar, and both were working with capital provided by the government, it was felt desirable to merge them into one organization in order to have a uniform policy and procedure in the provision of credit facilities to agriculturists all over the country and to reduce overhead expenses.

On February 18, 1961 the paid-up share capital of the former ADFC was Rs. 50 million, all subscribed by the central government, and of the ABP, Rs. 32.5 million of which a sum of Rs. 22.5 million was subscribed by the central government and Rs. 5.0 million each by the governments of East and West Pakistan. The merged organization therefore started with a paid-up share capital of Rs. 82.5 million. A sum of Rs. 17.5 million was subscribed toward the share capital of the bank during 1961-62, thus raising the total to Rs. 100 million.

In order to augment its resources for loan operations, the bank has been authorized to borrow money against the security of its assets or otherwise and also accept money on deposit. The bank provides fixed deposit and savings bank facilities in rural areas on attractive terms and provides credit, both in cash and in kind, for agricultural purposes as well as for cottage industries. The loans are advanced for short, medium, and long terms, with interest at the rate of 7 per cent on loans up to five years and 6 per cent on loans for periods exceeding five years. The bank also charges an additional .5 per cent interest in the case of default in the repayment of loans from the date of default. Loans by the bank have been increasing steadily from 1953-54 to 1961-62, the total rising from Rs. 0.89 million in 1953-54 to Rs. 14.81 million in 1957-58 to Rs. 142.01 million in 1960-61. During 1961-62 (up to March 1962) the loans were Rs. 192.35 million, of which Rs. 98.14 million went to East Pakistan and Rs. 94.21 million to West Pakistan. The overall position of recoveries since inception till the end of March 1962 has been 78 per cent—80 per cent in East Pakistan and 75 per cent in West Pakistan.

Unlike the Agricultural Development Bank, the Pakistan Industrial Credit and Investment Corporation (PICIC) is a new type of organization for Pakistan and indeed for the world. Organized under the joint auspices of the State Bank of Pakistan and the International Bank for Reconstruction and Development, it represents an attempt to secure the cooperation of Pakistani and American, Canadian, British, Japanese, and other capital interests in the industrialization of Pakistan. The corporation is authorized to provide medium- and long-term (seven to twelve years maturity) general loans in foreign and local currency, to participate in direct equity financing, and to arrange local and external financing from private and institutional sources. The rate of interest charged by PICIC is 7½ to 8½ per cent as against 5½ to 6 per cent paid on its own foreign borrowings.

During the period 1958-61, PICIC sanctioned 232 loans totaling Rs. 257.5 million, of which Rs. 224.8 million were in foreign currencies and Rs. 32.7 million in local currency. Annual loan volume during this period went from Rs. 36.8 million in 1958 to Rs. 110.5 million in 1961. These loans together with matching entrepreneurial investment estimated at Rs. 265.2 million have meant an effective capital formation of Rs. 522.7 million. In addition, the corporation has entered into four underwriting commitments for public issue of shares aggregating Rs. 15.1 million.

The demand for PICIC's financial assistance has grown with the tempo of industrial progress in the country. Out of 232 projects which have been financed, 119 involved new units and 113 were for balancing and modernization of existing industrial units. Diversification of the loan operations is evident in the fact that a wide range of 57 different industries have so far used the PICIC facilities. PICIC also investigates the possibilities of investments in new and untapped fields for the convenience of prospective investors. For example it has undertaken a survey of the cement industry in Pakistan. In an effort to broaden the capital market, the corporation has required some larger enterprises to convert from private companies into public joint stock companies. The result has been the formation of seventeen new public limited companies, which are listed on the stock exchange. PICIC has also been given a significant role to play in the implementation of the Second Five Year Plan. Of the industrial investment schedule of Rs. 3,080 million formulated for private sector of industries, PICIC is expected to provide foreign currency loans of Rs. 750 million. This together with matching private investment of an equivalent amount would account for about half of the total. To fulfill its investment target the corporation proposes to raise $157 million from abroad, $45 million of which has already been obtained.

Insurance

As in the case of the banks, the insurance business of Pakistan is conducted by a mixture of Pakistani, Indian, British, and other foreign insurance companies. Partition hit the insurance business probably even harder than the banking business, but statistics are not as readily available. Even more than banking, insurance is concentrated in the towns and among the upper classes and is practically unknown elsewhere.

The relationship of the Pakistan Insurance Corporation, 51 per cent of whose capital is owned by the government, to the insurance business is very similar to that of the State Bank to the banking business. By law, at least 10 per cent of the insurance business written in Pakistan must be reinsured with it, and the Pakistan Insurance Corporation has used the bargaining position thus conferred to secure favorable reinsurance treaties with insurance companies in other countries. It also has the statutory duty of encouraging the growth of insurance in Pakistan and has particularly encouraged the growth of Pakistani insurance companies. Probably because the writing of insurance is largely an urban phenomenon at this time, an estimated four-fifths of the business is done in West Pakistan (including Karachi) and only one-fifth in East Pakistan.

The Postal Life Insurance Fund was constituted over seventy years ago for the benefit of post office employees, but even before partition other government employees were allowed to take out policies. Since 1953 the organization has made steady progress, with a coverage of Rs. 268 million in 92,631 policies by 1961.

CHAPTER *21*

Domestic and Foreign Trade

THE DOMESTIC TRADE OF PAKISTAN is very largely bound up with foreign trade. The rural areas are nearly self-sufficient in both wings, but in order to obtain manufactured goods and pay their taxes the people must sell their cash crops, especially jute and cotton. The new industries, largely centered in West Pakistan, have meant that practically all the textiles and other simple consumer goods needed in Pakistan are now made locally.

Patterns of Domestic Trade

Before partition the trade of both wings of Pakistan was predominantly in the hands of non-Moslems. In East Pakistan many traders stayed after partition but as trade shifted away from Calcutta, where these traders had always maintained most of their connections, the control of trade slowly gravitated into the hands of Moslem groups with connections in West Pakistan. In West Pakistan practically all the Hindu and Sikh trading community emigrated. There was, however, a more than balancing immigration of Moslems from India. Thus, 90 per cent of the cotton gins of West Pakistan were declared to be "evacuee property" and assigned to refugees, many of whom had never operated gins before. For a relatively brief period a great deal of the trade was handled by cooperative organizations, organized in fact by the provincial government, which exercised complete control over the cooperative movement.

The urgent need for traders was partially met by local inhabitants, especially those who had had some experience in handling money, and soon thereafter by the Parsis and such tightly knit groups of trading Moslems from Bombay as the Khojas, Memons, and Ismailis. It is generally believed that these groups monopolize the wholesale trade and reap undue profits from it, though there is no statistical proof. While these relatively small communities of experienced traders do appear to have secured a great degree of control over the trade of Pakistan, with resultant high profits, it is also true that they have shown a great ability to adapt very swiftly to changing market conditions.

Before partition, East Pakistan jute had partly flowed to the mills of the Calcutta industrial area, while almost all the cotton of West Pakistan flowed to the mills of Bombay and Allahabad. In return, a large part of the manufactured goods consumed in Pakistan had come from the same industrial areas of Calcutta, Allahabad, and Bombay. While this pattern of trade continued, haltingly, for a time after partition, Indo-Pakistan trade almost collapsed with the devaluation of the Indian rupee in 1949 and Pakistan was forced to turn to the rest of the world. The Korean war led to a great boom in Pakistan's foreign exchange earnings, which made feasible the import of great quantities of consumer goods, but the prices of raw jute and cotton collapsed with the end of the Korean conflict. The consequent decision to use the limited exchange left to build up Pakistan industry meant an almost complete prohibition on the import of consumer goods and it was only gradually that new supplies were forthcoming from the new industries.

The fact that most of these new industries have been located in West Pakistan has led to a pattern of trade whereby East Pakistan exports of jute earn a very large part of the foreign exchange while West Pakistan takes most of the imports. The balance is maintained partly by the fact that most central government expenditure is in West Pakistan and partly by the flow of manufactured goods, particularly textiles, from West Pakistan to East Pakistan. As the industry is new, it is not surprising that these manufactured goods are often of poor quality and very expensive, but the value of the interwing trade continues its remarkable rise (see Table 30).

The country's merchant fleet rose from 2,000 tons dead weight at the time of partition to 180,000 in 1955, but the ships acquired were assorted craft mostly over thirty years old. Only six ships totaling about 50,000 tons could be regarded as modern. This largely uneconomic fleet, long overdue for scrapping, was costly in foreign exchange expenditure on repairs, fuel, and the insurance of ships and cargo. One objective of the First Five Year Plan was to develop a dependable modern merchant fleet to carry the coastal trade as well as to share in the country's foreign trade. Specific proposals called for the augmentation and renovation of the coastal cargo fleet, a government contribution of Rs. 60 million for the purchase of six or seven modern ships and for working capital, development of passenger service between Karachi and Chittagong, including the purchase of a new passenger ship for this service and another for the pilgrimage traffic, and the formation of a national shipping corporation to participate in both coastal and international traffic. Because Pakistan shipping companies showed readiness to invest in developing the industry, the proposal for a national shipping corporation was dropped. These private companies have since purchased ten comparatively new cargo ships, bringing the fleet as of June 1960 to twenty-six ships—sixteen of which were less than twenty years of age—with a total cargo capacity of 700,000 tons a year between the two provinces. The Second Five Year Plan has provided Rs. 105 million, Rs. 2 million in the public sector and Rs. 103 million in the private sector, for the development of shipping and the acquisition of thirteen more ships. By 1962 the merchant fleet stood at forty-two ships—three passenger ships, one cargo-passenger ship, two tankers, and the rest cargo ships. Nor have other aspects of the overall problem been neglected: a merchant navy academy, to train personnel for the merchant fleet, has started functioning at Chittagong and the administration of ports and shipping was streamlined with the appointment of a director-general of ports and shipping beginning in 1961-62.

The Pakistan International Airlines (PIA) has grown enormously since its inauguration in March 1955. Capacity is now four times and revenues over five times the 1955-56 figures, and total operating revenues for the year 1960-61 were Rs. 114.3 million (40.5 per cent higher than the previous year) for an operating profit of Rs. 9.23 million. PIA's foreign operations are now earning and saving 80 per cent of all the foreign exchange used by PIA on its internal, interwing, and foreign routes.

The Role of the Government in Domestic Trade

Though exceptions are fairly common, the various levels of government in Pakistan have generally professed a doctrinaire line that domestic trade should be left in the hands of private enterprise except for the provision of transport facilities and some attempt to control weights and measures. Trade in both wings is complicated by the great variety of weights and measures employed. The standard maund (82⅖ lbs.) of 40 seers and the seer of 80 tolas are the most widely used by trade and industry and government institutions, including the post office—and particularly for railway and road freight, transactions in the regulated markets, and business among industrial concerns, especially in the former Punjab and Sind. But local markets often use other measures such as the *katcha* (unripe) seer of Peshawar, equal to only half the standard or *pukka* (ripe) seer. It is an all too common practice among merchants to buy produce from peasants by the pukka seer but sell to them by the katcha seer. In East Pakistan the customary weights of the maund range from 30 through 40, 40½, 41, 42, to 60 seers; and the seer is 60, 75, 80, 90, or 96 tolas dependent on the local custom in different tracts. It is difficult to enforce a standard system of weights as most petty tradesmen do not possess proper weights, using instead rocks, stones, or bits of metal of about the right weight.

During World War II the central and provincial governments of undivided India gradually built up a network of price controls and rationing of many essential commodities. Only in 1958 did Pakistan abolish central government price controls on medicines and other items in a wide range of commodities, though at the same time retaining controls on such basic products as cement, iron and steel, newsprint, coal, and mechanically propelled vehicles (together with the tires, tubes, and other spare parts used in them). The retention of controls over these was defended on the dual grounds that it would be useful in directing essential raw materials to development projects and that controls over these few items could be kept reasonably effective. A variety of controls are also imposed by the provincial governments over foodstuffs, especially sugar and the primary foodstuffs—namely, rice in East Pakistan and the wheat and other grains transformed into *atta* (coarse flour) in West Pakistan.

Beginning with the Second Five Year Plan the government has adopted a policy of progressive relaxation of price and distribution controls, the first commodities being wheat, cotton textiles, cotton yarn, and twenty-nine other items decontrolled in 1960-61. The country, as a whole, has gained considerably from the policy of decontrol, which has brought a noticeable improvement in the supply of goods and free market prices well under the former black market levels. The effect that the abolition of price controls will have on domestic trade is extremely uncertain in the absence of repeal of controls over imports. As long as import controls are maintained, attention of most traders will continue to be focused upon the securing of import licenses, ownership of which is a source of great profit.

Under the earlier system, pressures were exercised upon the civil servants and ministers in a position to grant such licenses with firms located in Karachi having the best chance, those located elsewhere in West Pakistan reasonably close to Karachi the next best, and Bengalis the least. Of course, almost any system in the allocation of licenses inevitably favors established firms by basing the issue of licenses upon the firm's share in trade in some earlier base period or, more rarely, upon some measure of the capacity and resources of the firms under consideration. But in pursuance of a presidential directive issued in 1959 a completely new system of licensing through the banks was introduced. The categories of various imports were carefully scrutinized and uneconomic amounts were merged to give individual importers a sizable category in items representing their main line of business. Once the categories had been amalgamated and codified, the importers applied for a license through their own banks. Special licensing counters were established in Karachi, Lahore, Chittagong, and Rawalpindi which functioned as commercial banks where the license forms presented on behalf of the importers by the banks were verified, authenticated, and returned to the banks within twenty-four hours. The trading in licenses was reduced considerably as the exchange control copy of each license remained in the hands of the commercial bank and the importer received only a customs copy for the clearance of goods.

Patterns of Rural Trade in East Pakistan

The rural trade patterns are quite different in the two wings of the country. The villages of East Pakistan were traditionally self-sufficient, and the picture has hardly changed. Indeed, in recent years the growth of population and the growing pressure on the land appear to have pushed the peasants back toward self-sufficiency as they find it more and more difficult to feed themselves, let alone to provide enough to trade for other goods. This is suggested by the census estimate that the percentage of the labor force in trade and commerce dropped from 6.0 to 2.0 from 1931 to 1959, although the rise in the total labor force from 7.8 millions to 26.9 millions meant that there was a slight rise in absolute numbers.

In East Pakistan the absence of nucleated village settlements, and therefore of village shops, fostered development of the traditional system of *hats* (weekly markets) and bazaars. Excluding Sylhet and the Chittagong Hill Tracts, there are today 4,434 market places in 44,252 square miles, or just about one for each ten square miles. For the most part these consist of open places with only the most rudimentary kind of shelter to which the surrounding peasantry and cottage craftsmen bring their produce on the market days. The very few people who live solely by trade are likely to move their goods on a regular circuit of these weekly markets, though some hats have a small number of more permanent stalls forming a permanent bazaar. But even at the stalls the great bulk of business comes on the market days.

While hats and bazaars work well enough for the great majority of the goods sold in them, it is obvious that dealers selling heavy or bulky goods cannot move their entire stocks from one hat to another five times a week, nor afford to be idle a large part of the time. As a result, when a villager wants to buy corrugated iron for roofing, timber, hardware, or better kinds of cotton goods, he has to go to the bigger bazaar of one of the very small number of sizable towns. This may involve several days' journey by country boat or oxcart, and considerable expense.

Besides the weekly hats there are a number of annual *melas* (fairs) held in various parts of East Pakistan, usually in connection with some religious occasion such as the *ur* of a Moslem or Hindu holy man, at which a good deal of trading takes place. Though most of these are purely local, they do provide an occasion for a day out for large numbers of the rural population and may also be used to buy a luxury or two. A few melas of wider scope are held and at least until recently were a very vital link in the wholesale trade of the province, drawing local traders from other sections of the province who come to replenish their stocks of goods. It is clear, however, that better transportation is gradually increasing the importance of the bigger cities as wholesale centers in competition with these melas.

The best estimates are that around three-fourths of the rice produced in East Pakistan is consumed by the producers directly, that a considerable amount of the rice sold goes to nearby neighbors at the local hats and bazaars, and that very little leaves the district of origin. Most of the paddy is apparently now parboiled and husked at local rice-husking mills very widely scattered through the province, with the mill owner normally being paid in a share of the finished product. Tobacco is manufactured into cigarettes and their local counterpart called *bidis*, but the only important cash crops in East Pakistan are jute and tea.

Jute is essentially a cash crop. After it has been retted, the jute is sold to small dealers called *farias*, who make house to house purchases in small country boats. When the faria has collected about a ton of jute he will take it to some hat to sell it there to a *beopari*, or middleman, who in turn sells it to a baler or his agent. Some of the baling firms in the larger jute centers advance money to beoparis who advance money in turn to farias, but this practice is believed to have declined. Baling presses may be either *pukka* (powered), producing very tightly packed bales suitable for export, or crude *katcha* local presses. Formerly, most baling in East Pakistan was katcha, for dispatch to the mills of Calcutta, but the establishment of pukka presses and jute mills has now stopped this dependence upon Calcutta.

The variation from one year to the next in receipts at individual baling centers is very striking. There is reportedly a good deal of cheating and sharp practice in the selling of jute, and a very big margin between the price that the farmer receives and the price paid at the baling center. However, as jute is a very bulky commodity in proportion to value it is not certain that this margin is bigger than would be reasonable.

At partition there was no jute manufacturing in Pakistan, but by 1957 about 200,000 tons or about a fifth of the jute crop was consumed by the Pakistani jute industry with around 7,800 looms in operation. Under the First Five Year Plan it was expected that there would be about 12,000 looms in 1960, which would, by then, be processing about 40 per cent of the jute grown in Pakistan. However, there has been a heavy shortfall: only three additional mills with a total capacity of 1,500 looms were installed, bringing the total number of looms in 1960 to 8,040 in fourteen jute mills. Production rose from 53,000 tons in 1954 to an estimated production of 250,000 tons in 1959-60. The target of 12,000 looms is expected to be reached by the end of the Second Five Year Plan. Present performance indicates that a production of at least 380,000 tons may be reached by 1964-65, of which up to 270,000 tons should be available for export. At present the industry is heavily concentrated in the Dacca-Narayanganj area (which is also the largest baling center) and the two major export points, Chittagong and Chalna, although a limited dispersal of the jute industry is taking place.

Pakistan tea is graded on the plantations on which it is grown, then packed in wooden tea chests for transport. In 1961-62 some 58.8 million pounds of tea were produced, and the export quota was fixed at 12.5 million pounds.

In return for the sale of these cash crops, the rural areas of East Pakistan receive a very limited supply of manufactured goods. For the most part these are imported into East Pakistan, as they have always been, but increasingly in recent years they have been imported from West Pakistan rather than the industrial areas around Calcutta, as before partition, or the rest of the world, as for a few years after partition. They are imported predominantly through the port of Chittagong, and their distribution is alleged to be in the hands of a monopolistic ring of West Pakistanis and refugees from India who reportedly extract very high profits from the trade through their possession of the right contacts.

Patterns of Rural Trade in West Pakistan

The internal trade of West Pakistan is different in importance, kind, and method from that of East Pakistan. According to the 1951 census the labor force employed in "trade and commerce" in West Pakistan was almost double that of East Pakistan and the discrepancy is believed to have grown since then. As in East Pakistan, the agriculturists of West Pakistan grow most of the food they consume but, in contrast to the Bengalis, the rural people of the former Punjab and the North-West Frontier province live predominantly in sizable nucleated villages and have a completely different pattern of rural trade. In the larger villages there are village shops, which typically sell foodstuffs, cloth, and the few other things that the villagers consume. The cloth is mostly of poor quality but will as a rule be brilliantly patterned and red-colored. There may also be simple sewing requisites, some coarse soap, and even hurricane lamps. As a touch of frivolity there are likely to be long black cotton strings with tasseled ends for use in lengthening and beautifying the braids of the women.

It is to these shops that the farmer often sells most of what he himself does not consume, and the shopkeeper in return may extend some very small amounts of credit, generally not more than 30 rupees. The trifling size of the credit is not surprising because the shopkeeper is usually as poor or poorer than his fellow villagers and is rarely able to obtain much credit himself.

Whether through the sale of cash crops or through some other means, a village as a whole must somehow obtain the rupees to pay its taxes and to buy the things it needs. The poorest areas of West Pakistan are those which have no easily sold cash crops, although they may be better fed than other areas. It is from these poorer areas, such as the more remote areas of the former North-West Frontier province, that most immigrants to the towns come.

The marketing of products varies very widely. Cotton is apparently often sold to the gins directly by the growers but may also be sold through a series of middlemen essentially similar to those handling jute in East Pakistan. Sugar cane is usually sold direct to the collecting stations of sugar factories but this is because most sugar cane in factory areas is grown by large landowners. In other areas it may be sold in much smaller amounts to a fellow villager for manufacture into the crude semirefined substitute called *gur*. Virginia tobacco is ordinarily sold by the growers direct to the collecting stations of the tobacco factories, while the growers of tobacco used in hookahs sell their crop to one of a number of shopkeepers who resell through *arthias* (commission agents) and *dallals* (brokers) situated in the larger towns, whence it is redistributed to small shopkeepers. The smaller fruit-growers of the Peshawar region sell their fruit on-the-tree to a merchant who probably owns orchards of his own. This merchant-farmer employs pickers and packers for the fruit and arranges for the transport of the fruit by truck or rail to the larger markets of Lahore or Karachi and for their sale through an arthia. As he has good reason to doubt the honesty of such arthias, the farmer-merchant often transports the fruit himself, and indeed the fruit merchants as far away as Calcutta and Burma in many cases started as Pathan farmers who found trading more congenial and profitable.

In so far as one can discern a pattern it is that the newer agricultural processing industries try to buy direct from the producers in an attempt to control the quality and quantity of their raw material. For agricultural products where production has become more routine, or processing is negligible, it is more likely that there will be a long chain of middlemen between the primary producer and the final user. But this pattern is extremely weak and is affected by crosscurrents. Thus the Baluchi or Pathan tribesman from the desert and mountainous areas usually brings his product to market himself, partly because of the lack of other transport and partly because a large part of his living is from his herds of animals, who have to move seasonally in any case.

In the north, the Peshawar bazaars are still a meeting place for hillmen from an area stretching from Waziristan in the south to the Chinese-Tibetan border in the north and into Afghanistan. But the development of roads, railways, and air traffic has come to mean that more and more of the trading of these people is done at the edges of the settled areas, such as the railhead of Tank, or the sugar town of Mardan, or the markets near the airport of Gilgit. Some of the eastern areas of Baluchistan similarly depend on Hyderabad and other Indus valley centers, but Quetta has preserved its pre-eminence far more than Peshawar.

Foreign Trade Relations

Pakistan's foreign economic relations are still undergoing adjustment to the new nation's foreign and domestic policies, but the basic lineaments of these relations are determined by geography and historical associations as well as the structure of the domestic economy and the vagaries of contemporary power politics. The basic ingredient of these relations, foreign trade, consists primarily of exports of agricultural raw materials and of imports of manufactured items and fuel whose volume is largely determined by the foreign exchange earnings of the exports. In part export earnings have been augmented by foreign aid in various forms, though not until recent years has such aid become relatively important. Membership in the British Commonwealth and the sterling area have been other important influences in Pakistan's economic relations. Common membership in the Commonwealth and unifying factors of geography and history notwithstanding, economic relations with India have steadily deteriorated since 1947.

Before partition the trade between the areas now in Pakistan and the industrial areas of Bombay and Calcutta was domestic. The areas which became Pakistan were essentially sources of raw materials for the industries located in what is now the Republic of India. In return the Pakistan areas obtained most of the manufactured goods, especially textiles, which they consumed from these same Indian industrial areas.

The same trading became international with partition, and this change produced an immediate effect on the economy. An agreement at the time of partition allowing free movement of goods across frontiers soon broke down in a welter of disagreements on interpretation and an atmosphere of general mistrust. In 1949 India followed the United Kingdom in devaluating its currency, but Pakistan did not. India refused to recognize the new Indo-Pakistan exchange rate and there was a complete breakdown in legal trade until the trade agreement of April 1950, which circumvented the exchange rate difficulty by a strictly barter agreement. It was not until February 26, 1951 that India officially accepted the new Indo-Pakistan rupee exchange ratio.

To reduce dependence on the port of Calcutta, Pakistan was forced to develop the East Pakistan ports of Chittagong and Chalna. India pushed the growing of raw jute to ensure a supply for its mills; Pakistan developed a textile industry to avoid dependence upon Indian mills. India and Pakistan were rapidly moving from a basically complementary economic relationship to a largely competitive one. In 1957 only about 6 per cent of Pakistan's total international payments involved India, and India was considerably less important than the United Kingdom, the United States, or Japan in Pakistan's foreign economic relations.

Pakistan's relations with the United Kingdom were not weakened, at least at first, by partition. In fact the departure of non-Moslem bankers, traders, and skilled managerial personnel left a gap which was initially filled by the British. There are no longer British provincial governors and the remaining British in the civil service are fast disappearing, but economic relations have remained very close. The managers of new jute mills are largely from Scotland, and British-owned exchange banks still hold about a quarter of total demand deposits.

In 1955-56 almost half of Pakistan's international payments for imports and services went to the United Kingdom, though possibly some of these represent imports from other countries financed through London. In more recent years trade with the United Kingdom has been nearly as important (see Table 31). Trade and payment relationships are made easier by the fact that most of the countries trading with Pakistan settle their mutual accounts through payment in pounds sterling in London. Pakistan is a member of the sterling area, which also includes the other members of the Commonwealth and their mandated territories, protectorates, and protected states, as well as Burma, Iceland, Iraq, the Irish Republic, Jordan, and Libya. Thus there are practically no exchange restrictions on the movement of funds from the United Kingdom or most other countries of the sterling area to Pakistan, but Pakistan does apply some restrictions to payments to the other members, as do other members of the sterling area.

There is one other tie with the United Kingdom and the Commonwealth. In 1932 the members of the British Empire and Commonwealth agreed at Ottawa to award each other preferential treatment in trade, including in many cases freedom from customs duties and tariffs. Pakistan, as a successor state to the Empire of India, accepted these generally lower rates of tariff on Commonwealth goods and in turn benefits from having lower rates of tariff applied to its products by most of the other Commonwealth countries.

Pakistan is also a member of the General Agreement on Tariffs and Trade (GATT), which includes practically all non-Communist countries. GATT members agree to apply favored treatment in trade with fellow members on a reciprocal basis. Through this membership Pakistan has been able to secure the renewal of a number of tariff concessions and obtain additional ones from the European Economic Community and other members on the export of processed goods from Pakistan.

The most important restraint on Pakistan's foreign trade is exercised through exchange and import controls, first imposed by the British at the outbreak of World War II and inherited by Pakistan in 1947. Until the end of the Korean boom in 1951 controls were gradually being relaxed, but with the collapse in receipts from exports in 1952 controls were reapplied with ever increasing intensity. Combined with the expansion of the 1950s, controls led to a situation in which the key to success in many lines was the possession of a license, which enabled the licensee to take advantage of the often big difference between the cost of an imported product, including duties, and the internal price. However, as noted earlier, Pakistan has made great headway in liberalizing the import and export trade, especially since 1959, and has evolved methods to stop the trading in licenses.

Pakistan's foreign trade consists essentially of the export of raw materials in exchange for imported manufactured goods (see Table 32). All agricultural products exported by Pakistan are essentially raw materials for industry, and its imports are overwhelmingly the products of the industrial areas of the world. Pakistan is very dependent upon the terms upon which it can sell its exports for industrial goods, and these have proved variable. The best available index is that of the terms of trade, i.e. the volume of imports purchasable per unit of exports (see Table 33). With relatively few exceptions, this volume was high until the end of the Korean war boom in 1951, but since then it has been low and the same volume of exports will now purchase less than half the volume of imports purchasable during the boom year of 1950.

As can be seen from Table 32, raw and manufactured jute now accounts for about 65 per cent of the value of Pakistan exports. More than half the world's production of jute fiber and virtually all the raw jute that enter into international trade channels come from Pakistan. India accounts for very nearly all the balance of the production of jute fiber but this is consumed entirely in Indian mills. The virtual monopoly of India and Pakistan in jute supplies means that some consideration of the market for jute is necessary for an understanding of the patterns of Pakistan's foreign trade. Pakistan's other exports contribute a small fraction to the world supply of these products, and while any price changes bearing indirectly on these raw materials are important to Pakistan they are not as vital as changes in the price of jute. Over three-quarters of the mill-manufactured jute is used—in the form of bags, sacks, baling material, or twine—for packaging, principally of agricultural produce. Despite the marked increase in global agricultural production, the volume of jute goods used in the mid-1950s was smaller than in the late prewar years. This decline is due mainly to the fact that in the more advanced countries, and particularly the United States, most agricultural produce now is moved in bulk, obviously reducing the need for jute containers. The increase in agricultural production in places like America therefore has not led to a concomitant rise in the demand for jute. It is uncertain whether the production of agricultural produce in the less-developed areas of the world will continue to rise and, if so, whether bulk handling will spread so rapidly as to cut into the potential new market for jute in these countries.

The market for jute in the more economically developed countries has also declined due to changing methods of retail trade.

Twenty years ago many products were supplied in bulk in sacks made of jute to the small retailer, who then made up individual packages as required. This is now unthinkable in the more modern shops throughout the world and jute has as a consequence lost a large market to the makers of paper and cellophane wrapping materials.

At best there is only limited optimism for the future world market for jute. The one encouraging sign is increased use of jute as a backing for floor coverings, such as carpets and linoleum, but even here there is strong competition and the future is most uncertain. Since jute accounts for more than half of Pakistan's foreign exchange earnings, this raises considerable doubt about its long-run balance of payments position. Pakistan's jute industry has grown up under the very considerable protection afforded by the export duty levied on raw jute but not manufactured jute. Any expansion beyond that envisaged in the First Five Year Plan would appear difficult in view of the desire of many other countries to protect their own jute industries. For the time being, Pakistan's jute industry has the great advantage of possessing the latest machinery and, despite the present high cost and shortages of fuel, power, and skilled labor in East Pakistan, the industry has been competing successfully with the Indian jute mills in world markets. About two-thirds of Pakistan's raw jute exports are to Europe, North America, and Japan (see Table 34).

In contrast to its large share of the world jute market, Pakistan produces only about 3 per cent of the world's cotton. As a consequence the short-run market situation is very different. In the long run the market for cotton probably depends upon somewhat similar considerations to those of jute—in particular there is the common problem of competition from modern substitutes. But of far more immediate concern to Pakistan is the day-to-day level of world prices for cotton, which are influenced in large part by United States policy regarding its surplus cotton stocks.

Pakistani cotton faces other problems as well. Before partition Punjabi cotton had a very good reputation as being generally of high quality and well prepared. The departure of the Hindu and Sikh farmers and especially of the owners and skilled operators of the cotton gins has resulted in a heavy fall in the quality of ginning. The gins were initially allocated to unskilled refugees who for the most part had no interest in maintaining the property or the quality of the product, even if they knew how.

415

A large part of Pakistan's cotton has been sold to the Far Eastern countries, with Japan taking large quantities (see Table 35). Communist China has been an important though very erratic buyer, but sales of cotton provide a strong economic link with China and a material motive for the continued recognition of the Peking government.

Most of the other exports of Pakistan—wool, tea, hides, and skins being most important—go to industrialized countries for further processing. Pakistan wool is coarse, tough, and short, and is generally used for carpet making. In fact the domestic textile industry depends heavily upon imported Australian wool. The tea, of the black and coarser varieties, is used as a base for higher quality varieties in various commercial blends. The hides and skins are of variable quality but seem to be of generally poor quality, largely because of poor flaying and tanning. Several million rupees worth of sports goods are exported annually, chiefly to Commonwealth countries where they are given preferential tariff treatment (Pakistan sells bagpipes to Scotland!), but they only amount to about one-half of one per cent of total exports. There are even smaller exports of surgical instruments and machinery. All these come from the cottage industries of Sialkot, Gujranwala, and neighboring areas of the Punjab.

Pakistan's importing is partly in private hands and partly in the hands of government agencies (see Table 36). A large percentage of the government's imports are defense stores and, as a security measure, very little information is released about imports. Since 1954 there have also been large and growing imports financed by foreign aid; these too are not usually included in the figures for imports.

At the time of partition, most of Pakistan's imports consisted of consumer goods and fuels or of raw materials, most of which were in fact transformed into consumer goods through the most simple of manufacturing processes or through use as fuel. The large decrease in receipts from exports after 1951 (see Table 36) necessitated a great restriction of imports. As an act of deliberate policy, a practical prohibition was placed on the import of cotton cloth and other kinds of consumer goods while at the same time the limited supplies of foreign exchange were diverted to the build up of Pakistani industries (see Table 37).

It was this shift in the kind of imports that was an additional factor in the decline in the relative importance of India as a supplier of imports, from the top of the list to nearly the bottom (see Table 38). Since imports by land (almost entirely from India) were not always included in 1948-49, the relative shift has almost certainly been understated in the table, even after making an allowance in the other direction for smuggling and purchases by short-term visitors to India. The decline in imports of simple manufactured goods as Pakistani industry developed was also instrumental in the decline in similar imports from mainland China and Hong Kong. The great importance of the United Kingdom can be largely explained by the traditional relationship with the United Kingdom, which has resulted in a marked consumer preference for British goods and continued reliance on the established channels of trade for their distribution. These same established channels of trade, and the absence of a language barrier, are believed to have given the British an edge in the construction of new industries.

Foreign Aid

Of negligible proportions before 1954-55, foreign aid has since that date become increasingly important in Pakistan's economic affairs, accounting for almost half of all international payments during the trade year 1960-61. This rapid rise in foreign aid is accounted for by both a growing need on Pakistan's part and a changing climate in world opinion, particularly as reflected in American aid (see Table 39). After 1951 Pakistan's balance of payments was under great stress because of several circumstances. The fall in the prices of its exports, and a concomitant worsening in the terms of trade, meant that the same quantity of exports in 1956 and 1957 would purchase only half as much as they would in 1950. If the terms of trade had been the same in 1956-57 as in 1950, Pakistan's exports would have earned not Rs. 1,700.5 million but approximately Rs. 3,400 million. Even without foreign aid its imports could have been some Rs. 600 million higher than they actually were.

America's reasons for giving aid to Pakistan are quite as diverse as Pakistan's reasons for requesting aid: a military desire to secure a friend in Asia, a belief that the best way to combat Communism was to help the development of the less-developed areas, and a desire to alleviate the suffering of the poverty stricken people of Pakistan. While at times the military aspect has appeared to conflict with other aspects, it has been generally realized that no

417

firmly founded military alliance can be constructed without economic development. The result has been an almost exclusive emphasis, until recently, on technical assistance.

American technical assistance falls into two categories—the provision of experts for aid projects in Pakistan and the training of Pakistani students in the United States. Over 300 foreign experts (mostly Americans) had been sent to Pakistan by June 1961 and 1,197 Pakistanis had received training in the United States or at the American University in Beirut, Lebanon. A good deal of contact between Pakistanis and Americans at the middle and higher levels of administration and society has grown out of this program, providing a great influence on the attitudes of educated Pakistanis toward the United States. There is also, of course, a fair sprinkling of Pakistanis among the officer corps of the armed services and among equivalent groups in government, educational institutions, and industry who have received training in the United States.

Technical assistance seems to hold forth the most hope for helping Pakistan's economic development in the long run, especially as it opens the minds and eyes of many young Pakistanis to new and better ways of doing things. The work of the American-financed Institute of Public and Business Administration at the University of Karachi, the Fulbright scholars at all of Pakistan's universities, and American advisers in the former Village-AID program have been especially useful.

Direct economic assistance is channeled to major development projects such as the Karnaphuli hydroelectric project—a project for producing electricity and controlling the Karnaphuli river near Chittagong—which received $4.5 million in 1957-58 for equipment and an additional $20.25 million from the Development Loan Fund in 1961. Another example is the $10 million made available for a fertilizer plant near Daud Khel in West Pakistan. Essentially such assistance means supplying the needed foreign exchange for building up new development projects in Pakistan. Thus, in most cases, the Pakistan government bears the local rupee cost (which is often several times as much as the foreign exchange needed for equipment and technicians) and the projects are usually built by a joint Pakistani-American group of engineers. These projects are all essential to the future economic development of Pakistan, but for the most part Pakistan does not have the technical knowledge to build them herself.

The Commodity Assistance and Surplus Agricultural Products

418

Program provides for the import of commodities for which the Pakistan government does not have the necessary foreign exchange. The commodities are then sold by the government to private parties who pay for them in rupees which are subsequently placed in a counterpart fund which can only be used for projects agreed upon between the American and Pakistan governments, e.g. the development projects discussed above or those of the Pakistan Industrial Credit and Investment Corporation.

Well over three-quarters of the foreign aid reaching Pakistan in recent years has been American (see Table 40). Thus, out of the total of $1,728.95 million received by the end of 1961, the United States supplied $1,525.83 million or almost 88 per cent. This total excludes foreign loans and credits by various governments and agencies like the World Bank, AID, and the Export-Import Bank.

Other aid offered was for projects similar to those supported by American aid. Thus the bulk of Canada's aid has gone into the Warsak irrigation and power project on the Kabul river near Peshawar and most of the Australian aid has gone into tube wells and canal links in the former Punjab, though both have also granted technical assistance and funds for the development of social welfare projects. British and German aid, on the other hand, goes almost entirely into scholarships for further study in their respective countries.

The United Nations and specialized agencies have usually given grants for technical assistance, although UNICEF did give the machinery for the DDT factory at Nowshera. The Ford Foundation has extended large grants to the Village-AID program and financed the foreign experts advising the government's Planning Commission. There are a number of other private agencies giving aid to Pakistan, such as the Asia Foundation of San Francisco and the schools, colleges, and hospitals sponsored by the various Christian missions, but no figures are available. Perhaps the smallest in dollar amount, but potentially very important, has been the aid given by the Japanese government, which sent two groups of three Japanese farmers each—one to East Pakistan and one to the former province of Sind in West Pakistan—to demonstrate the growing of rice by Japanese methods. These two groups have successfully demonstrated that a 60 per cent increase in yield can be obtained with Japanese methods of cultivation. Adoption of the Japanese technique throughout Pakistan might bring a complete change in Pakistan's economic prospects.

Tables

Table 1. POPULATION OF PAKISTAN, 1951 and 1961

Region	Area in thousand sq. mi.	Population in thousands		Population density	
		1951	1961	1951	1961
East Pakistan	55,126	42,062	50,853	763	922
West Pakistan	310,403	33,780	42,978	108	138
Karachi	8,405	1,126	2,139	1,339	
Kalat	72,944		534		
Quetta	53,115		658		
Hyderabad	39,821		3,292		
Multan	24,828		6,615		
Khairpur	20,293		3,134		
Bahawalpur	17,508		2,575		
Sargodha	17,095		5,987		
Dera Ismail Khan	11,130		1,217		
Lahore	8,907		6,452		
Rawalpindi	11,206		3,986		
Peshawar	28,153		6,382		
Pakistan	365,529	75,842	93,831	207	256

Source: *Census of Pakistan 1951; Census of Pakistan 1961.*

Table 2. MAJOR CITIES OF PAKISTAN, 1961

City	Population in thousands
Karachi	1,916
Lahore	1,297
Dacca[a]	558
Chittagong	363
Hyderabad	434
Rawalpindi	343
Multan	358
Lyallpur	426
Sialkot	168
Peshawar	213
Gujranwala	197
Narayanganj[a]	

(a) East Pakistan.

Source: *Census of Pakistan 1961.*

Table 3. LANGUAGES COMMONLY SPOKEN IN PAKISTAN

(*percentage of the total population*[a])

	Bengali	Punjabi	Urdu	Pushtu	Sindhi	English
East Pakistan	98.0	...	1.1	...	...	1.3
West Pakistan	...	64.0	15.0	16.0	13.0	2.5
Pakistan	56.0	28.0	7.2	7.1	5.8	1.8

(a) Because some people speak more than one language the sum of the percentages does not equal 100.

Source: *Census of Pakistan 1951*, v. 1, pt. II, table 7-A.

Table 4. EXPANSION OF EDUCATION, 1948-49 TO 1959-60

Type of institution	Number of schools			Number of students		
	1948-49	1953-54	1959-60	1948-49	1953-54	1959-60
Primary schools	38,122	41,651	44,200	3,643,000	4,962,000	4,706,000
Secondary schools	6,275	5,551	6,000	916,000	1,171,000	1,099,000
Nonprofessional colleges	90	132	209	36,000	60,000	116,442
Universities	3	6	6	....	....	8,935
Primary teachers training institutions	125	99	75	6,145	7,500	7,410
Teachers training colleges	11	22	23	785	1,500	1,841

Source: *First Five Year Plan 1955-1960; Second Five Year Plan 1960-1965.*

Table 5. NUMBER OF TECHNICAL AND PROFESSIONAL SCHOOLS

Type of institution	1948-49	1953-54	1959-60
Technical high schools	0	1	8
Polytechnic institutes	0	2	..
Agricultural colleges	3	4	4
Animal husbandry colleges	1	2	2
College of forestry	0	1	1
Medical colleges	3	6	9
Medical schools	6	7	3
Nurses training institutes	..	..	18
Engineering colleges	3	4	4
Law colleges	..	8	14

Source: *First Five Year Plan 1955-1960; Second Five Year Plan 1960-1965.*

424

Table 6. CENTRAL GOVERNMENT OF PAKISTAN, 1947-58

Dates	Governor general or president	Prime minister	Political make-up of cabinet
Aug. 1947-Sep. 1948	Mahomed 'Ali Jinnah	Liaquat 'Ali Khan	Moslem League
Sep. 1948-Oct. 1951	Khwaja Nazimuddin	Liaquat 'Ali Khan	Moslem League
Oct. 1951-Apr. 1953	Ghulam Muhammad	Khwaja Nazimuddin	Moslem League
Apr. 1953-Oct. 1954	Ghulam Muhammad	Muhammad 'Ali Bogra	Moslem League
Oct. 1954-Aug. 1955	Ghulam Muhammad	Muhammad 'Ali Bogra	Emergency (nonpolitical)
Aug. 1955-Sep. 1956	Iskandar Mirza	Chaudhri Muhammad 'Ali	Moslem League United Front
Sep. 1956-Oct. 1957	Iskandar Mirza	Husayn Shaheed Suhrawardy	Republican Party Awami League
Oct. 1957-Dec. 1957	Iskandar Mirza	I. I. Chundrigar	Moslem League Republican Party Krishak Sramik Party Nizam-i-Islam Party
Dec. 1957-Oct. 1958	Iskandar Mirza	Malik Firuz Khan Noon	Republican Party Krishak Sramik Party

Table 7. CONSTITUENT ASSEMBLY INITIAL MEMBERSHIP, AUGUST 1947

Province	Hindu, etc.	Sikh	Moslem	Total
Punjab	3	2	12	17
North-West Frontier Province	..	..	3	3
Sind	1	..	3	4
Baluchistan	..	..	1	1
East Bengal	13	..	31	44
Total	17	2	50	69

Source: Adapted from Government of Great Britain, India Office, India (Cabinet Mission) Statement of May 16, 1946, Cmd. 6821, par. 19; and ibid., Indian Policy Statement of June 3, 1947, Cmd. 7136, par. 14.

Table 8. COMPOSITION OF CONSTITUENT ASSEMBLY OF 1955

Province	Non-Moslem	Total
East Bengal	9	40
Punjab	1	21
North-West Frontier Province	..	4
Sind	1	5
Baluchistan	..	1
Karachi	..	1
Bahawalpur	..	2
Khairpur	..	1
Frontier States	..	1
Baluchistan States Union	..	1
Tribal Areas	..	3
Total	11	80

Source: *Dawn*, May 29, 1955.

Table 9. LANGUAGE DISTRIBUTION OF PAKISTANI PUBLICATIONS, 1958

Publications	English	Urdu	Gujarati	Sindhi	Bengali	Pushtu	Persian	Arabic	Punjabi	Total
Dailies	12	71	3	7	10	..	..	..	..	103
Biweeklies	2	2	1	3	3	..	..	..	..	11
Weeklies	29	29	1	65	67	1	..	..	..	192
Fortnightlies	16	16	2	7	11	12	1	..	..	65
Monthlies	71	315	1	13	27	3	..	1	1	432
Quarterlies	24	12	..	1	2	..	1	..	..	40
Annuals, etc.	11	11	..	..	2	..	..	..	..	24
Total	165	456	8	96	122	16	2	1	1	867

Source: *General List of Newspapers Published in Pakistan*, Press Information Department, Karachi, 1958.

Table 10. POPULATION OF KASHMIR STATE BY RELIGIOUS GROUP AND PROVINCE

Province	Area in square miles	Moslems	Hindus	Other	Total population
Jammu province	12,378	1,215,676	722,835	42,922	1,981,433
Kashmir province	8,539	1,615,478	85,580	27,647	1,728,705
Frontier districts	63,554	270,093	750	40,635	311,478
Kashmir State (Total)	84,471	3,101,247	809,165	111,204	4,021,616

Source: *Census of India 1941: Jammu and Kashmir State* (vol. XXII), table XIII, pp. 341-43.

Table 11. CIVILIAN LABOR FORCE OF PAKISTAN

	Pakistan	East Pakistan	West Pakistan
Male	21,382,000	11,887,000	9,495,000
Female	1,316,000	999,000	317,000
Total	22,698,000	12,886,000	9,812,000

Source: *Census of Pakistan 1951.*

Table 12. DISTRIBUTION OF LABOR FORCE BY OCCUPATIONAL GROUPS

(*in thousands*)

	Large towns (over 50,000)	Small towns (less than 50,000)	Villages (less than 5,000)	Total
Professional and technical	100	200	600	900
Managerial, administrative, and clerical	200	100	300	600
Sales and related	300	300	1,200	1,800
Agricultural	(a)	1,000	17,100	18,100
Mining	(a)	(a)	(a)	(a)
Transport operation	(a)	(a)	200	200
Manufacturing and crafts	500	500	2,700	3,700
Services	200	300	1,100	1,600
Totals	1,300	2,400	23,200	26,900

(a) Less than 100,000.

Source: Department of Manpower and Employment, *Pakistan: 1959-1960.*

Table 13. FREQUENCY DISTRIBUTION OF PRESENT FACTORY WORKERS, BASED ON A SURVEY IN EAST PAKISTAN

Occupation	Respondent's previous occupation	Occupation of respondent's father or grandfather	Occupation which respondent prefers
Farming	117	244	88
Cottage industry	19	12	6
Landless labor	53	42	2
Trade	53	48	187
Factory work	156	38	145
Other occupation	73	85	37
No response	0	2	6
Totals	471	471	471

Source: Adapted from A.F.A. Husain, *Human and Social Impact of Technological Change in Pakistan.*

Table 14. DISTRIBUTION OF FAMILY EXPENDITURES (MONTHLY) IN SELECTED CITIES OF PAKISTAN BY OCCUPATIONAL GROUP, 1956-57

	Income (in rupees)	Total	Percentage Distribution			
			Food	Apparel	Housing	Other
Industrial workers						
Karachi	154	100	60	11	11	18
Dacca	137	100	69	9	12	10
Chittagong	120	100	77	5	9	9
Narayanganj	108	100	73	10	9	8
Lahore	110	100	63	7	15	15
Peshawar	142	100	67	5	13	15
Hyderabad	125	100	66	7	13	14
Quetta	126	100	62	13	14	11
Government employees						
Karachi	280	100	49	12	14	25
Chittagong	223	100	58	10	15	17
Lahore	180	100	57	8	17	18
Commercial employees						
Karachi	333	100	47	13	12	28
Chittagong	327	100	56	11	14	19
Lahore	218	100	56	6	16	22

Source: *National Family Expenditure Survey, 1956-1957,* adapted from pages 71 and 72 in *Statistical Bulletin,* January-February 1958.

Table 15. MEDICAL FACILITIES AND PERSONNEL IN PAKISTAN

	1955	1959	1965 target
Medical colleges	5	5	9
Nurses training institutes	14	18	22
Doctors	6,000	9,200	13,000
Nurses	1,414	2,000	3,500
Hospital beds	23,000	28,000	36,000
Maternity centers	200	375	. . . . .

Source: Adapted from information included in *Second Five Year Plan 1960-1965*.

Table 16. MEDICAL COLLEGES IN PAKISTAN, 1962

College	Location	Enrollment (approximate)
Dow Medical College	Karachi	884
King Edward Medical College	Lahore	746
Nishtar Medical College	Multan	113
Liaquat Medical College	Hyderabad	411
Fatimah Jinnah Medical College for Women	Lahore	532
Khyber Medical College	Peshawar	339
Dacca Medical College	Dacca	957
Rajshahi Medical College	Rajshahi	. . .
Chittagong Medical College	Chittagong	. . .

Table 17. NATIONAL INCOME AT CONSTANT PRICES BY INDUSTRIAL ORIGIN, 1950-51 TO 1962-63

(at factor cost of 1949-50 to 1952-53: in million rupees)

Sector	1950-51	1952-53	1954-55	1956-57	1958-59	1959-60	1960-61	1961-62	1962-63
Agriculture	11,317	11,062	11,591	11,820	11,438	11,980	12,303	13,040	12,735
Major crops	6,465	6,012	6,434	6,860	6,611	7,121	7,453	7,981	7,583
Minor crops	1,753	1,882	1,833	1,707	1,552	1,575	1,654	1,679	1,705
Livestock	2,478	2,452	2,535	2,561	2,587	2,583	2,475	2,638	2,681
Fishing	606	699	771	675	671	685	704	725	749
Forestry	15	17	18	17	17	16	17	17	17
Mining and quarrying	27	31	33	40	48	52	61	65	73
Manufacturing	1,399	1,707	2,200	2,575	2,866	3,040	3,197	3,444	3,649
Large-scale	382	626	1,061	1,373	1,599	1,738	1,860	2,069	2,238
Small-scale	1,017	1,081	1,139	1,202	1,267	1,302	1,337	1,375	1,411
Construction	260	332	278	340	425	486	563	661	748
Electricity, gas, water, and sanitary services	29	30	41	44	49	52	56	68	77
Transportation, storage, and communications	606	635	673	721	796	808	838	863	887
Wholesale and retail trade	1,741	1,748	1,888	1,972	1,960	2,059	2,126	2,261	2,258
Banking and insurance	58	58	77	91	106	113	133	150	170

(continued on next page)

Table 17. NATIONAL INCOME AT CONSTANT PRICES BY INDUSTRIAL ORIGIN,
1950-51 TO 1962-63 (continued)

(*at factor cost of 1949-50 to 1952-53: in million rupees*)

Sector	1950-51	1952-53	1954-55	1956-57	1958-59	1959-60	1960-61	1961-62	1962-63
Ownership of dwellings	911	960	1,014	1,074	1,142	1,178	1,216	1,257	1,301
Public administration, health, education, and defense	917	997	1,116	1,056	1,130	1,022	1,083	1,111	1,214
Services	1,367	1,477	1,441	1,654	1,908	1,966	2,002	2,049	2,140
Net domestic product at factor cost	18,623	19,037	20,352	21,387	21,868	22,756	23,578	24,969	25,252
Net factor income from rest of the world	—9	—14	—9	—12	—10	—18	—19	—13	—21
National income	18,623	19,023	20,343	21,375	21,858	22,738	23,559	24,965	25,231
Population, in millions	76,450	80,830	83,790	86,770	90,130	91,900	93,720	95,610	97,570
Per capita income, in rupees	244	235	243	246	243	247	251	261	259

Source: Adapted from *Economic Survey of Pakistan 1963-64*, Statistical Section, table 6.

432

Table 18. SECTORAL ALLOCATION OF EXPENDITURE, SECOND FIVE-YEAR PLAN

Million rupees

Sectors	Allocation	Percentage of total allocation
Agriculture	3,420	14.9
Water and power	4,390	19.1
Industry	5,120	22.3
Fuels and minerals	1,000	4.3
Transport and communications	4,050	17.6
Housing and settlements	3,410	14.8
Education and training	1,055	4.6
Health	420	1.8
Social services	100	0.4
Manpower and employment	35	0.2
Total	23,000	100.0

Source: Adapted from *Second Five Year Plan 1960-1965*, table 1.

Table 19. ACREAGE AND PRODUCTION OF PRINCIPAL CROPS IN EAST PAKISTAN

(average of 1957-58 to 1961-62)

Crop	Acreage (in 1,000 acres)	Percentage of total area	Production (in 1,000 tons)	Average yield per acre (in tons)
Rice	20,776	87.42	8,397	.27
Jute	1,609	6.77	1,042	.41
Rape and mustard seed	536	2.24	91	.11
Sugar cane	269	1.13	3,917	9.90
Gram	140	.59	35	.27
Tobacco	108	.45	32	.20
Tea	77	.32	23	.20
Other crops	255	1.08	51	.19
Total	23,770	100.00	13,588	

Source: *Economic Survey of Pakistan 1962-63*, Statistical Section, tables 12 and 13.

Table 20. ACREAGE AND PRODUCTION OF PRINCIPAL CROPS IN WEST PAKISTAN

(*average of 1957-58 to 1961-62*)

Crops	Acreage (in 1,000 acres)	Percentage of total area	Production (in 1,000 tons)	Yield per acre (in tons)
Food grains				
Wheat	11,709	41.93	3,772	.32
Rice	2,878	10.31	988	.35
Bajara	1,947	6.98	314	.16
Jowar	1,124	4.03	217	.19
Maize	1,148	4.12	462	.40
Barley	489	1.76	138	.28
Other food crops				
Gram	2,842	10.18	604	.21
Sugar cane	996	3.50	11,683	11.72
Rape and mustard seed	1,340	4.80	231	.17
Commercial crops				
Cotton (lint)	3,365	12.05	296	.09
Tobacco	93	.34	58	.63
Total	27,931	100.00	18,763	

Source: *Economic Survey of Pakistan 1961-62*, Statistical Section, pp. 22-26.

Table 21. TOTAL AREA AND AREA UNDER CULTIVATION

(*in million acres*)

	East Pakistan[a]	West Pakistan[b]	Total
Net area sown	21.00	31.00	52.00
Current fallow	1.20	9.20	10.40
Total cultivated area	22.20	40.20	62.40
Other uncultivated land, excluding current fallow	2.00	21.60	23.60
Forests	5.50[c]	3.20[d]	8.70
Not available for cultivation	5.00	51.00	56.00
Total area	34.70	116.00	150.70
Area unreported	.70	82.40	83.10

(a) Data for East Pakistan are for the year 1954.

(b) Data for West Pakistan are for the year 1957, except for Hyderabad, Jacobabad, Quetta, and Kalat regions for which data for 1956 have been used.

(c) Includes an area of 2.3 million acres classified as "scrub forests."

(d) Only wooded area.

Source: Ministry of Food and Agriculture (as reproduced in the Second Five Year Plan).

Table 22. INVESTMENT AND CAPACITY INCREASE, 1955-60

(for industries in which capital investment exceeded Rs. 50 million by 1960)

Industry	Capital investment (Rs. million) 1955	Capital investment (Rs. million) 1960	Rank in groups 1955	Rank in groups 1960
Cotton textiles	530	912	1	1
Jute goods	186	286	2	3
Sugar	87	369	7	4
Natural gas transmission	84	298	8	5
Cotton ginning	134	151	3	6
Cement	66	145	9	8
Medium and light engineering	104	151	5	7
Fertilizer	56	388	11	2
Edible vegetable oils	105	116	4	10
Shipyards	35	145	14	9
Total	1,387	2,961		

Source: *First Five Year Plan 1955-1960*, pp. 424-25.

Table 23. ELECTRIC POWER RESOURCES OF PAKISTAN[a]

Year	East Pakistan	West Pakistan
1947	22,000	92,000
1955	67,000	212,000
1960	175,000	731,000
1965 (planned)	298,000	974,000

(a) Installed capacity in kilowatts.

Source: *First Five Year Plan 1955-1960*, pp. 346, 355, 369; *Second Five Year Plan*, p. 412.

435

Table 24. INVESTMENT PROGRAM OF THE PAKISTAN INDUSTRIAL DEVELOPMENT CORPORATION, 1955-60

(in million rupees)

Industry	East Pakistan	West Pakistan	Total
Sugar	176.4	6.0	182.4
Newsprint	115.0	nil	115.0
Jute goods	150.0	nil	150.0
Fertilizers	180.0	152.0	332.0
Shipyards	27.4	82.1	109.5
Cement	nil	54.4	54.4
Iron and steel and re-rolling	100.0	30.0	130.0
Cardboard and strawboard	46.0	3.8	49.8
Natural gas transmission	54.0	106.0	160.0
Caustic soda	3.5	nil	3.5
Hardboard	19.2	nil	19.2
Natural gas distribution	nil	18.0	18.0
Animal feed	nil	5.0	5.0
Rosin and turpentine	nil	1.0	1.0
Power alcohol	nil	2.0	2.0
Asbestos cement sheets	nil	0.6	0.6
Other (pharmaceuticals, penicillin, dyes, D.D.T., etc.)	34.5	16.2	50.7
Total	906.0	477.1	1,383.1

Source: *First Five Year Plan 1955-1960*, table 2, p. 435.

Table 25. INVESTMENT PROGRAM OF THE PAKISTAN INDUSTRIAL DEVELOPMENT CORPORATION, 1960-65

(in million rupees)

Industry	East Pakistan	West Pakistan	Total
Sugar	58.00	nil	58.00
Jute manufactures	115.00	nil	115.00
Paper	50.00	nil	50.00
Chemical industries	244.40	203.17	447.57
Non-metallic mineral products	23.00	23.10	46.10
Basic metal industries	106.40	127.13	233.53
Metal products (excluding machinery)	3.45	2.30	5.75
Machinery (excluding electric machinery)	4.60	nil	4.60
Transport equipment	17.25	32.00	49.25
Miscellaneous industries	11.90	nil	11.90
Petro-chemicals	nil	40.00	40.00
Machinery (machine tools)	nil	2.30	2.30
Total	634.00	430.00	1,064.00

Source: "Revised List of Schemes," *Second Five Year Plan 1960-1965*, pp. 146-49.

Table 26. SOURCES OF CENTRAL GOVERNMENT REVENUE IN SELECTED YEARS

(in million rupees)

Revenue head	1950-51	1954-55	1955-56	1956-57	1957-58	1958-59(a)	1959-60	Revised estimates 1960-61	Budget estimates 1961-62
Customs	776.2	416.1	557.9	469.6	420.5	493.6	509.3	534.5	590.8
Income and corporation tax	132.4	194.1	214.2	211.4	240.4	334.4	304.8	306.3	306.0
Central excise	67.2	115.5	135.0	144.9	193.7	264.1	287.4	323.3	343.5
Sales tax	71.1	106.0	137.2	132.3	142.7	170.2	164.2	242.2	247.3
Other tax heads	45.9	67.7	68.9	63.6	51.0	127.9	60.5	66.4	68.5
Nontax heads(b)	180.4	273.3	322.6	309.6	476.7	568.5	561.5	494.7	588.0
Total	1273.2	1172.7	1435.8	1331.4	1525.0	1958.7	1887.7	1967.4	2144.1

(a) Accounts for the year 1958-59 cover fifteen-month period from April 1958 to June 1959.

(b) Includes railways, post and telegraph, debt services, civil administration, defense services, and others.

Source: *Economic Survey of Pakistan 1961-62*, Statistical Section, p. 131.

Table 27. BUDGET OF THE CENTRAL GOVERNMENT

(in million rupees)

Year	REVENUE		CAPITAL Development expenditure				Nondevelopment expenditure	CAPITAL Financed by resources	
	Receipts	Expenditure	Direct	Loans to local bodies	Provincial governments	Total[a]		Internal[b]	External
1947-48	198.9	236.0	8.1	3.3	86.7	98.1	22.4	120.5	.....
1948-49	667.6	647.0	49.6	6.7	144.0	200.3	298.2	498.5	.....
1949-50	885.4	856.0	100.9	16.8	208.1	325.8	738.3	1064.1	.....
1950-51	1273.2	1266.2	70.6	8.4	139.6	218.6	280.9	499.5	.....
1951-52	1448.4	1442.3	206.6	17.3	145.8	369.7	536.5	903.9	2.3
1952-53	1334.4	1320.1	250.4	19.1	119.0	388.5	475.6	790.7	73.4
1953-54	1110.5	1108.7	255.3	46.7	439.1	741.1	172.1	893.5	19.7
1954-55	1172.7	1172.6	258.2	49.8	268.4	576.4	87.9	625.5	38.8
1955-56	1435.8	1433.4	379.3	38.2	377.1	794.6	—88.0	692.1	14.5
1956-57	1331.4	1330.7	405.3	34.4	340.1	779.7	173.8	914.4	39.1
1957-58	1525.0	1521.8	643.6	82.9	628.2	1354.7	120.4	1410.4	64.7
1958-59	2070.2	2067.7	804.3	95.1	546.1	1445.5	15.4	580.8	880.1
1959-60	1887.7	1733.8	908.5	105.5	563.9	1577.9	189.8	1076.6	691.1
1960-61	2094.7	1775.7	738.0	84.4	1009.9	1882.9	250.7	1108.6	930.0
1961-62	2198.5	1885.9	1030.9	84.2	1212.5	2327.6	86.1	829.6	1469.8
1962-63	2099.9	1927.2	2431.6	35.3	2192.9	2647.9	169.2	737.4	1910.5
1963-64	2240.4	2077.5	3370.4	317.0	2679.8	3738.9	218.5	924.6	2814.3

(a) Includes contingency items.

(b) Includes ad hoc treasury bills and cash balance utilization.

Source: *Economic Survey of Pakistan 1961-62*, Statistical Section, table 72; *Economic Survey of Pakistan 1963-64*, tables 80 and 82.

439

Table 28a. REVENUE AND EXPENDITURE: EAST PAKISTAN, 1950-51 TO 1963-64

(*in million rupees*)

Item	1950-51	1954-55	1956-57	1958-59	1959-60	1960-61	1961-62	1962-63	1963-64 (*budget*)
Revenue									
Customs	42.5	39.7	45.1	51.7	47.5	33.0	61.9	50.0	46.7
Central excise	....	....	17.5	26.2	18.0	27.7	26.5	50.9	52.9
Corporation tax	....	....	....	....	....	....	....	29.3	29.8
Taxes on income other than corporation tax	7.8	25.0	29.8	57.6	36.9	39.1	44.0	108.2	112.9
Sales tax	16.5	20.3	25.2	36.2	33.7	52.1	62.2	136.6	149.4
Land revenue	22.4	50.2	51.5	130.5	93.5	108.3	145.5	80.0	145.0
Stamps	20.3	21.5	27.5	40.2	43.5	46.0	45.8	42.5	43.4
Rehabilitation taxes	....	....	.2	2.0	1.9	3.2	2.5	3.7	3.7
Other heads	46.0	41.8	37.1	65.4	55.3	58.1	69.6	65.4	66.5
Irrigation works, etc.	—.5	—2.1	.6	.9	—.1	....	....	....	....
Debt services	1.7	2.0	1.5	5.9	4.1	6.2	28.7	55.0	101.4
Civil administration	11.8	24.7	20.1	53.8	29.8	26.1	25.8	18.4	27.2
Civil works	3.6	8.3	8.5	21.9	14.7	10.5	12.2	7.7	6.4
Miscellaneous	9.9	10.7	34.6	19.4	5.9	33.0	21.2	15.4	14.0
Grants-in-aid from central government	....	.6	4.6	11.1	13.2	4.4	2.0	25.7	45.3
Foreign aid and grants from central government	....	....	....	....	....	....	158.2	....	158.9
Extraordinary items	....	1.5	....	....	....	....	.1	....	....
Total[a]	182.0	244.2	303.8	522.7	397.9	447.7	706.1	688.8	1,003.5

Expenditures									
Direct demands on revenue	12.8	25.4	44.7	62.9	57.0	60.0	60.7	78.6	100.9
Revenue and capital account of irrigation works, etc.	2.5	4.2	6.6	18.1	2.1	...	...	...	...
Debt services	1.0	30.0	22.0	108.1	23.6	4.6	7.6	114.2	188.1
General administration	21.8	22.1	23.5	30.9	25.1	27.9	29.9	24.5	34.9
Police	38.1	47.0	52.5	74.5	58.5	53.0	60.5	64.9	65.9
Education	20.9	23.1	22.5	34.4	25.2	62.5	67.2	77.1	93.2
Medical and public health	8.3	8.9	11.9	19.6	20.0	28.1	30.5	37.2	38.0
Agriculture	9.0	9.5	8.2	10.8	9.6	10.5	11.1	12.2	12.5
Industries	1.7	1.8	2.3	3.4	2.9	3.0	2.8	3.3	3.3
Other departments	20.9	21.0	21.4	36.2	29.2	31.0	31.9	37.1	36.2
Civil works	2.1	31.2	—.2	12.8	14.4	29.9	50.1	21.1	30.5
Miscellaneous	26.5	25.6	85.1	40.4	36.7	50.0	37.2	49.2	42.6
Extraordinary charges	6.1	.5	.5	.5	.5	.6	.6	.7	.3
Development expenditure	18.6	34.4	37.5	68.3	74.1	109.8	169.4	114.3	280.7
Total	190.3	284.7	338.5	521.0	378.9	470.9	559.5	644.4	917.1
Surplus/Deficit	—8.3	—40.5	—34.7	1.8	19.0	—23.2	146.6	44.4	86.4

(a) Totals here and below have been rounded separately and so may appear at variance.

Source: Adapted from *Economic Survey of Pakistan 1963-64*, Statistical Section, table 74.

441

Table 28b. REVENUE AND EXPENDITURE: WEST PAKISTAN, 1950-51 TO 1963-64

(*in million rupees*)

Item	1950-51	1954-55	1956-57	1958-59	1959-60	1960-61	1961-62	1962-63	1963-64 (budget)
Revenue									
Customs	.6	....	....	....	....	....	....	40.9	40.9
Central excise	....	14.5	20.3	31.2	23.1	31.0	25.4	43.9	44.0
Corporation tax	....	....	....	....	....	....	....	24.9	26.1
Taxes on income other than corporation tax	.1	20.4	26.6	36.4	29.4	34.6	42.9	84.6	89.4
Sales tax	59.2	60.7	101.0	127.5	111.1	168.5	175.3	164.9	175.6
Land revenue	32.8	44.0	117.5	178.5	138.6	133.6	116.0	68.0	74.5
Stamps	6.4	10.3	15.4	21.7	20.7	26.0	27.6	33.7	34.3
Other heads	47.9	55.6	63.3	127.4	102.2	108.6	114.0	148.5	171.5
Irrigation works, etc.	78.1	72.0	48.4	50.7	85.6	108.0	100.4	169.0	144.0
Debt services	5.6	12.3	6.4	14.0	33.5	19.5	47.2	130.9	158.6
Civil administration	6.4	8.0	10.2	25.9	24.8	15.5	13.8	14.2	29.7
Civil works	9.1	13.9	10.5	21.7	29.5	16.5	9.0	9.0	10.3
Beneficent departments	19.0	27.5	33.7	88.8	77.3	46.2	45.2	37.8	46.0
Receipts from electricity schemes	3.6	16.7	26.6	18.2	....	....	.2	.4	.1
Miscellaneous	42.6	63.3	21.1	37.2	33.7	38.7	28.4	26.9	26.8
Grants-in-aid from central government	10.1	13.3	67.2	49.0	31.2	23.7	131.2	219.5	147.7
Extraordinary items	38.3	42.7	44.9	52.7	64.2	52.8	56.6	70.6	125.8
Total	359.9	475.2	613.1	880.9	804.9	823.2	933.2	1,287.8	1,345.3

Expenditures									
Direct demands on revenue	48.1	53.7	38.6	56.2	48.5	45.7	50.7	55.8	56.6
Irrigation	6.6	9.3	28.0	41.0	27.9	16.5	22.2	8.0	7.7
Debt services	20.8	44.5	70.2	84.2	22.8	29.3	30.3	151.6	192.2
General administration	21.6	28.6	34.3	43.6	34.6	41.0	46.8	56.5	59.3
Police	54.1	60.1	70.9	93.6	72.0	85.3	90.9	102.7	108.0
Frontier regions	....	....	8.0	45.6	39.9	10.3	11.2	12.0	17.4
Other heads	16.6	20.5	23.5	35.6	27.6	30.7	32.3	35.9	39.8
Education	42.9	74.8	100.6	136.6	115.7	121.9	144.1	206.4	233.9
Health services	11.6	14.7	30.5	47.5	42.4	43.4	48.3	66.0	70.6
Agriculture	8.3	9.6	14.4	99.9	80.0	47.1	33.3	30.8	30.3
Veterinary	2.6	3.4	6.4	8.6	8.0	10.5	10.6	9.0	10.7
Industries	4.6	7.8	11.0	12.2	9.9	9.1	8.9	9.0	9.4
Development expenditure	....	....	....	....	....	82.2	110.3	194.1	256.4
Civil works	36.3	51.7	47.9	93.8	49.2	44.8	61.3	46.9	58.4
Other heads	8.6	10.0	6.8	7.2	6.4	9.3	8.2	9.2	12.1
Miscellaneous	46.3	37.4	56.9	72.6	69.1	59.5	72.5	68.7	64.1
Extraordinary items	.7	9.2	.1	.1	.3	....	....	....	....
Total	329.7	435.3	548.1	878.3	654.3	686.6	781.9	1,062.1	1,226.9
Surplus/Deficit	30.1	39.9	65.0	2.6	150.6	136.6	151.3	225.1	118.4

Source: Adapted from *Economic Survey of Pakistan 1963-64*, Statistical Section, table 76.

Table 29. VOLUME OF MONEY AND COST OF LIVING INDEX FOR PAKISTAN, 1948-63[a]

Year	Currency in circulation	Demand deposits (general)	Other deposits with State Bank of Pakistan	Total supply money	Cost of living index (general)
1948	1707.9	891.7	35.3	2634.9	. . .
1949	1739.4	886.3	44.5	2670.2	
1950	1991.9	907.2	33.4	2932.5	96
1951	2467.4	1190.3	40.1	3697.8	92
1952	2147.7	1022.7	34.9	3205.3	103
1953	2368.7	1151.4	21.0	3541.1	105
1954	2571.4	1170.4	58.7	3800.5	105
1955	2986.4	1326.3	53.5	4366.2	97
1956	3463.0	1429.7	26.9	4919.6	102
1957	3579.9	1562.1	88.5	5230.5	108
1958	3739.0	1708.6	51.4	5499.0	117
1959	3841.2	1871.3	46.2	5758.7	113
1960	4179.3	1932.8	47.0	6159.1	120
1961	4057.2	2100.0	51.2	6208.4	123
1962	4103.3	2358.6	50.2	6512.1	129
1963	4537.2	2881.5	50.8	7469.5	129

(a) Volume of money is given in million rupees and the year for money supply is the calendar year. For the cost-of-living index the financial year of 1st July to 30th June has been used; base, 1948-49 = 100.

Source: *Economic Survey of Pakistan 1961-62*, Statistical Section, pp. 69, 107-08; *Economic Survey of Pakistan 1963-64*, table 60.

Table 30. INTERWING TRADE[a]

(*in million rupees*)

Year[b]	Imports into East Pakistan from West Pakistan	Imports into West Pakistan from East Pakistan
1948-49	137.6	18.8
1949-50	229.2	32.3
1950-51	210.8	46.0
1951-52	161.2	36.4
1952-53	177.0	101.1
1953-54	370.0	130.7
1954-55	293.0	180.7
1955-56	318.9	220.7
1956-57	510.1	235.1
1957-58	690.2	264.0
1958-59	660.7	277.6
1959-60	542.6	361.0
1960-61	798.7	361.0
1961-62	829.7	392.5
1962-63	917.6	466.9

(a) These data do not include airborne trade between the two wings and are derived on the basis of imports into Karachi, Chittagong, and Chalna ports confined to Pakistan merchandise; the movement of foreign merchandise has been excluded because it is not possible to identify it properly from the point of view of origin and destination. Hence this information should be regarded as indicating the trend of interwing trade only.

(b) Figures up to 1956 relate to private accounts only, thereafter to both private and government accounts.

Source: Central Statistical Office, *Bulletin No. 12, 10* (December 1962), 2288; *Economic Survey of Pakistan 1963-64*, Statistical Section, table 34.

Table 31. GEOGRAPHICAL DISTRIBUTION OF PAKISTAN'S PAYMENTS ON CURRENT ACCOUNT FOR THE YEAR 1961-62

(in million rupees)

	Receipts (exports, etc.)	Payments (imports, etc.)	Balance Surplus	Deficit
United Kingdom	1065.7	1021.7	43.9	....
United States	1027.5	1076.9	...	49.4
Japan	100.2	201.4	...	101.4
India	171.5	117.9	53.6	....
Canada	66.4	71.2	...	4.8
Western Europe (O.E.E.C.)	281.0	527.3	...	246.1
Middle East (sterling and non-sterling areas)	113.7	48.4	65.3	....
Far East (sterling and nonsterling areas)	125.3	122.6	2.7	....
Other sterling areas	152.4	34.1	118.2	....
Latin America	8.7	8.0	0.6	....
Eastern Europe	59.6	51.4	8.2	....
Rest of the world	45.9	37.4	8.4	....
Total[a]	3214.2	3315.5	...	101.3

(a) As the figures are rounded off separately, the subtotals and totals may exhibit minor differences.

Source: State Bank of Pakistan, *Pakistan's Balance of Payments, July 1961-June 1962*, pp. 4-37.

Table 32. EXPORTS OF PAKISTAN, 1954-61

(in million rupees)

Items	1954	1955	1956	1957	1958	1959	1960	1961
Raw jute	545.5	696.8	750.9	781.9	835.9	680.1	806.3	895.2
Jute manufactures	17.3	67.2	93.5	92.6	108.4	212.6	245.5	347.6
Raw cotton	348.7	402.9	363.8	331.7	240.5	120.7	211.2	103.7
Cotton manufactures	....	7.5	60.9	86.4	15.4	148.4	190.5	67.9
Hides and skins	33.8	31.5	39.9	40.7	40.9	64.1	67.9	58.8
Raw wool	42.5	67.4	71.1	103.4	45.8	61.5	77.4	79.5
Tea	47.0	34.2	54.3	23.5	33.0	29.1	9.6	11.1
Miscellaneous	152.7	197.5	185.6	143.7	97.0	210.7	264.8	341.2
Total	1187.5	1505.0	1620.0	1603.9	1416.9	1527.2	1873.2	1905.0

Source: *Economic Survey of Pakistan 1961-62*, Statistical Section, tables 33 and 34, pp. 50-52.

Table 33. PRICES PER UNIT OF THE CHIEF PAKISTAN EXPORTS, INDICES OF EXPORT-IMPORT PRICES, AND TERMS OF TRADE FOR THE FIRST QUARTER OF THE YEARS 1950 TO 1962

Average prices in rupees	1950	1951	1952	1953	1954	1955	1956(a)	1957	1958	1959	1960	1961	1962
Jute (bale)	193.40	171.30	202.40	111.50	116.70	123.50	152.60	182.10	177.90	163.50	142.20	357.00	213.60
Cotton (bale)	475.10	854.90	717.50	410.00	443.20	423.90	487.00	544.60	497.70	406.10	425.40	484.30	461.50
Wool (pound)	1.29	3.48	1.65	2.01	2.90	1.96	2.70	2.72	2.47	2.15	2.36	2.41	2.39
Tea (pound)	1.62	1.55	1.30	1.22	1.39	2.64	2.18	2.63	2.37	2.62	2.37	2.75	1.87
Hides and skins (piece)	3.07	6.35	3.92	4.16	4.22	3.34	4.17	3.74	4.48	4.92	7.24	6.76	10.37
Indices of unit prices(b)													
Exports	93.20	109.00	108.50	64.20	67.90	70.20	83.80	96.70	93.00	83.90	79.60	153.80	106.80
Imports	73.90	88.00	93.20	82.70	90.80	82.10	127.70	152.30	158.60	150.00	156.60	168.10	158.50
Terms of trade(c)	126.10	123.70	116.80	77.60	74.80	85.50	65.60	63.50	58.60	56.00	51.00	91.50	67.50

(a) The devaluation of the Pakistan rupee on July 31, 1955 accounts for most of the rise in rupee prices in subsequent years.

(b) Base: April 1948–March 1949 = 100.

(c) Volume of imports purchasable per unit of exports.

Source: *Economic Survey of Pakistan 1961-62*, Statistical Section, tables 38 and 39, pp. 57-58, 59-60; *Economic Survey of Pakistan 1963-64*, Statistical Section, tables 40 and 41.

Table 34. EXPORTS OF RAW JUTE FROM PAKISTAN BY AREA

(in thousand bales)

Country	1952-53	1953-54	1954-55	1955-56	1956-57	1957-58	1958-59	1959-60	1960-61	1961-62
India	1,491	1,361	1,231	1,354	614	641	172	619	358	382
United Kingdom	842	702	791	692	667	929	798	767	466	681
Belgium, Luxembourg	408	426	470	591	454	367	404	393	230	446
Germany	392	512	544	536	436	615	388	389	229	247
France	343	469	438	476	347	438	376	415	205	...
Italy	347	274	285	294	296	214	259	266	133	167
United States	520	307	317	390	231	492	284	318	93	244
Japan	158	150	165	185	170	182	180	263	165	200
Argentina	17	77	114	34	82	53	53	51	18	34
Union of South Africa	54	95	115	110	80	89	130	155	132	160
Netherlands	82	67	102	99	77	56	80	79	66	77
Mainland China	...	...	65	238	37	23	40	95	52	9
All other countries	620	692	502	682	576	781	922	1,004	800	1,381
Total	5,274	5,132	5,139	5,681	4,067	4,880	4,086	4,814	2,950	4,028

Source: State Bank of Pakistan, *Report on Currency and Finance 1956-1957*, p. 168; ibid. *1961-1962*, table 62.

449

Table 35. EXPORTS OF RAW COTTON FROM PAKISTAN BY AREA

(in thousand bales)

Country	1952-53	1953-54	1954-55	1955-56	1956-57	1957-58	1958-59	1959-60	1960-61	1961-62
Japan	577	378	268	322	350	219	250	202	117	91
France	84	91	62	101	112	102	7	16	8	13
Mainland China	174	188	60	211	66	24	66	51	103	13
Hong Kong	106	129	89	64	43	41	44	60	45	43
Germany	112	41	27	42	20	9	5	5	...	5
United Kingdom	118	105	79	71	15	17	20	18	5	11
Italy	56	84	38	39	3	(a)	1	...	...	4
All other countries	280	155	100	98	55	35	67	96	15	93
Total	1,507	1,171	723	948	664	447	460	448	293	273

(a) Below 500 bales.

Source: State Bank of Pakistan, *Report on Currency and Finance 1956-1957*, table 50; ibid. *1961-1962*, table 62.

Table 36. IMPORTS AND OTHER PAYMENTS ON CURRENT ACCOUNT, 1952-53 TO 1960-61

(in million rupees)

	1952-53	1953-54	1954-55	1955-56	1956-57	1957-58	1958-59	1959-60	1960-61
Imports on private account	1,214.1	734.5	738.2	834.5	869.5	909.5	755.8	912.8	1,186.3
Imports and other payments on government account	480.6	488.8	388.2	535.9	915.7	790.8	728.3	675.1	660.9
Other payments	233.2	226.0	208.3	360.8	391.1	361.3	299.3	435.3	528.8
Total payments	1,927.9	1,449.3	1,328.7	1,731.2	2,176.3	2,061.7	1,783.5	2,023.2	2,376.0
Imports and other payments under foreign aid	...(a)	...(a)	34.3	412.3	643.1	1,312.5	569.8	976.5	1,270.3
Total payments including foreign aid	1,927.9	1,449.3	1,363.0	2,143.5	2,819.4	3,374.2	2,353.3	2,999.7	3,646.3

(a) Not adjusted and presumed negligible.

Source: State Bank of Pakistan, *Report on Currency and Finance 1955-1956*, pp. 158-59; ibid. *1956-1957*, pp. 174-75; ibid. *1958-1959*, pp. 200-01; and ibid. *1960-1961*, pp. 218-19.

Table 37. VALUE OF IMPORTS ON PRIVATE ACCOUNT, 1951-61

(in million rupees)

	1951	1952	1953	1954	1955	1956	1957(a)	1958	1959	1960	1961
Consumer goods	991.8	1032.7	330.6	409.2	458.0	521.3	1318.8	1080.8	960.8	1797.3	1207.7
(cotton cloth only)	(333.3)	(273.6)	(14.3)	(29.7)	(26.1)	(51.3)	(8.6)	(1.4)	(1.7)	(3.4)	(4.1)
Raw materials and fuels	436.0	527.4	178.4	223.3	229.7	279.1	1459.5	493.0	382.3	680.3	1217.6
(cotton yarn only)(b)	(215.6)	(195.6)	(48.5)	(48.4)	(10.7)	(13.0)	(9.5)	(4.3)	(2.6)	(18.4)	(16.6)
Investment goods	140.8	173.0	119.4	274.5	250.1	182.9	318.2	314.0	337.9	634.4	631.0
Percentage distribution											
Consumer goods	63.22	59.59	52.61	45.12	48.84	53.02	62.90	57.25	57.16	57.75	39.52
Raw materials and fuels	27.80	30.43	28.39	24.62	24.49	28.38	21.92	26.12	22.74	21.86	39.83
Investment goods	8.98	9.98	19.00	30.26	26.67	18.60	15.18	16.63	20.10	20.39	20.65
Total	100.00	100.00	100.00	100.00	100.00	100.00	100.00	100.00	100.00	100.00	100.00

(a) Data up to December 1956 relate to private account only for figures in parenthesis, from 1957 to both government and private accounts.

(b) The figures for cotton yarn also include cotton thread since July 1960.

Source: *Economic Survey of Pakistan 1961-62*, Statistical Section, pp. 53-54, 56.

Table 38. PERCENTAGE OF IMPORTS ON PRIVATE ACCOUNT BY COUNTRY OF ORIGIN, 1948-49 TO 1962-63

	1948-49	1949-50	1950-51	1951-52	1952-53	1953-54	1954-55	1955-56
India	31.8	24.3	15.1	17.7	13.5	5.3	4.0	1.4
United Kingdom	28.1	25.4	26.4	20.4	28.8	31.8	32.2	26.3
Belgium, France, West Germany, Italy, and Luxembourg	6.4	8.6	11.7	12.6	13.5	20.8	16.4	21.3
Japan	1.2	11.0	16.2	23.8	15.4	8.7	16.3	16.9
United States	8.0	9.8	6.6	6.1	8.7	7.0	9.2	10.8
Mainland China	7.3	3.2	6.1	1.2	0.7	1.4	0.2	...
Hong Kong	0.5	0.5	3.3	2.2	0.7	0.9	0.1	...
Other countries	16.3	17.2	14.6	16.0	18.5	23.9	21.3	23.3
Totals	100.00	100.00	100.00	100.00	100.00	100.00	100.00	100.00

	1956-57[a]	1957-58	1958-59	1959-60	1960-61	1961-62	1962-63
India	1.3	0.8	0.7	0.7	1.1	3.1	2.7
United Kingdom	30.0	29.1	22.1	18.6	22.8	20.3	15.2
Belgium, France, West Germany, Italy, and Luxembourg	24.4	28.4	26.9	19.4	24.5	17.7	15.2
Japan	4.7	6.9	7.2	10.8	10.2	7.9	6.7
United States	14.7	13.1	13.3	14.2	12.1	30.8	40.0
Mainland China	...	...	...	...	...	...	...
Hong Kong	...	...	...	...	...	...	...
Other countries	24.9	21.7	29.8	36.3	29.3	20.2	20.2
Totals	100.00	100.00	100.00	100.00	100.00	100.00	100.00

(a) Imports on government account have been included since January 1957. Previously these figures included imports on private account only.
Source: *Report on Currency and Finance 1959-1960*, pp. 195-96; ibid. *1960-1961*, pp. 212-15; and *Economic Survey of Pakistan 1963-64*, table 36.

Table 39. AID TO PAKISTAN CONSORTIUM: COMMITMENTS FROM OCTOBER 1960 THROUGH MAY 1963

(in million dollars)

Belgium	10.0
Canada	76.8
France	35.0
Germany	145.0
Italy	10.0
Japan	95.0
Netherlands	8.8
United Kingdom	93.2
United States	842.1
IBRD and IDA	289.4
Total	1,605.3

Source: *Economic Survey of Pakistan 1963-64.*

Table 40. FOREIGN AID TO PAKISTAN: COMMITMENTS FROM JULY 1960 THROUGH MARCH 1964

(in million dollars)

Country/agency	Grant	Loan	Total
Australia	6	. . .	6
Canada	68	12	80
France	. . .	7	7
Germany	3	182	185
Italy	. . .	6	6
Japan	. . .	108	108
New Zealand	1	. . .	1
Sweden	3	. . .	3
United Kingdom	3	93	96
United States[a]			
1. DLF	. . .	30	30
2. AID	194	470[b]	664
3. Eximbank	. . .	48[c]	48
4. Suppliers credit	. . .	8	8
U.S.S.R.	. . .	30	30
Yugoslavia	. . .	15	15
IBRD/IDA	. . .	163	163
IFC	. . .	4	4
Ford Foundation	13	. . .	13
United Nations Agencies	4	. . .	4
United Nations Special Fund	11	. . . .	11
Total[d]	305	1,175	1,480

(a) Does not include Public Law 480 allocations which totaled $621.55 million from 1961 through 1964, nor grants under Public Law 665/138 (Defense Support) for which figures are not available.

(b) Includes $130 million loans authorized but not concluded by the end of March 1964.

(c) Includes $7 million loans authorized but not concluded by the end of March 1964.

(d) Totals may exhibit small differences due to rounding off figures.

Source: Adapted from *Economic Survey of Pakistan 1963-64,* table 97.

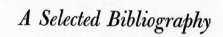

A Selected Bibliography

A Selected Bibliography

Section I.   Sociological

ABBAS, ZAINAB GHULAM, *Folk Tales of Pakistan,* Karachi, Pakistan Publications, 1957.

ABERNETHY, GEORGE L., *Pakistan: A Selected, Annotated Bibliography,* New York, American Institute of Pacific Relations, 1960.

AHMAD, NAFIS, "The Pattern of Rural Settlement in East Pakistan," *Geographical Review, 46* (1956), 388-98.

AKBAR, MUHAMMAD, *The Punjab under the Mughals,* Lahore, Ripon, 1948.

ALI, S. AMJAD, "The Role of the Press in Pakistan," *Pakistan Quarterly, 11,* (1963), 2-16.

An Analysis of the Working of Basic Democracy Institutions in East Pakistan, Dacca, Bureau of National Reconstruction, 1961 (mimeographed).

AZIZ BEG, ed., *Grass Roots Government,* Rawalpindi, Pakistan Patriotic Publications, 1962.

BARTH, FREDERICK, *Political Leadership among the Swat Pathans,* New York, Humanities Press, 1959.

BARY, WILLIAM T. DE, *Sources of Indian Tradition,* New York, Columbia University Press, 1958.

BESSAIGNET, PIERRE, *Tribesmen of the Chittagong Hill Tracts,* Dacca, Asiatic Society of Pakistan, 1958.

————, *Social Research in East Pakistan,* Dacca, University of Dacca, 1960.

Biographical Encyclopedia of Pakistan: Edition 1955-56, Lahore, International Publishers (Pakistan), n.d.

BREMBECK, COLE S. and EDWARD W. WIEDNER, *Education and Development in India and Pakistan: A Select and Annotated Bibliography,* East Lansing, Michigan State University, n.d. (1962?).

BROHI, A. K., *Fundamental Law of Pakistan,* Karachi, Din Muhammadi, 1958.

BROWN, PERCY, *Indian Architecture,* 2 vols. Bombay, Taraporevala, 1942.

BRYANS, ROBIN, *Gateway to the Khyber Pass,* London, Robert Hale, 1959.

CAROE, OLAF, *The Pathans,* London, Macmillan, 1958.

CHATTERJI, SUNITI K., *Languages and the Linguistic Problem,* Oxford

459

Pamphlets on Indian Affairs, No. 11, London, Oxford University Press, 1943.

————, *The Origins and Development of the Bengali Language,* Calcutta, Calcutta University Press, 1926.

CLARK, JOHN, *Hunza: Lost Kingdom of the Himalayas,* London, Hutchinson, 1957.

COUPLAND, R., *The Indian Problem,* 3 vols. New York, Oxford University Press, 1943.

Crescent and Green: A Miscellany of Writings on Pakistan, London, Cassell, 1955.

The Cultural Scene in Pakistan 1960-61: Literature, Karachi, Pakistan Publications, 1961.

DANI, A. H., *Muslim Architecture in Bengal,* Dacca, Asiatic Society of Pakistan, 1961.

DAS GUPTA, T. C., *Aspects of Bengali Society from Old Bengali Literature,* Calcutta, University of Calcutta, 1935.

DAVIS, KINGSLEY, *The Population of India and Pakistan,* Princeton, Princeton University Press, 1951.

Dawn of a New Era: Basic Democracies in Pakistan, Karachi, Bureau of National Reconstruction, n.d.

DUPREE, LOUIS, *Peshawar University,* American Universities Field Staff Report, South Asia Series, Vol. 7, No. 6, 1963.

EGLAR, ZEKIYE, *A Punjabi Village in Pakistan,* New York, Columbia University Press, 1960.

ELAHI, KHWAJA NUR, et al., *A Guide to Works of Reference Published in Pakistan,* Karachi, Educational Press, 1953.

FARRAR, CURTIS, "Education and Research in Pakistan," *Asia Foundation Program Bulletin* (1963), pp. 1-4.

FEROZE, S. M. A., *Press in Pakistan,* Lahore, National Publications, 1957.

Film Catalogue, Karachi, Department of Films and Publications, 1962.

GIBB, H. A. R., *Mohammedanism,* 2d ed. New York, New American Library of World Literature, 1955.

GUHA, B. S., *Racial Elements in the Population,* Oxford Pamphlets on Indian Affairs, No. 22, London, Oxford University Press, 1944.

A Guide to Pakistan Libraries, Learned and Scientific Societies and Educational Institutions, Biographies of Librarians in Pakistan, Karachi, Printers Combine, 1960.

Handbook to the Universities of Pakistan, Karachi, Inter-University Board of Pakistan, 1963.

HIMES, MILO, *Reflections on Workers' Education in Pakistan,* Ithaca, Cornell University Press, 1962.

HUNTER, WILLIAM W., *The Indian Musalmans,* Edinburgh, Comrade Publishers, 1945.

HUQ, MUHAMMAD SHAMSUL, *Compulsory Education in Pakistan,* UNESCO Studies on Compulsory Education, Vol. *12,* Paris, 1956.

HUSAIN, A. F. A., *Human and Social Impact of Technological Change in Pakistan*, 2 vols. Dacca, Oxford University Press, 1956.

HUSAIN, MUHAMMAD, *East Pakistan: A Cultural Survey*, Karachi, Ferozsons, 1955.

HUTTON, J. H., *Caste in India*, 2d ed. Bombay, Oxford University Press, 1951.

IKRAM, S. M., *Muslim Civilization in India*, New York, Columbia University Press, 1963.

IKRAM, S. M. and P. SPEAR, eds., *The Cultural Heritage of Pakistan*, London, Oxford University Press, 1955.

INAYATULLAH, ed., *Bureaucracy and Development in Pakistan*, Peshawar, Pakistan Academy for Rural Development, 1963.

INAYATULLAH, *Study of Union Councils in Nowshera Tehsil*, Peshawar, West Pakistan Academy for Village Development, 1961.

India, *Census of India 1931*, Provincial Volumes, Delhi, Government of India Press, n.d.

IQBAL, MUHAMMAD, *The Reconstruction of Religious Thought in Islam*, London, Oxford University Press, 1934.

"Islamabad," *Engineering Forum*, Vol. 3, No. 6, 1961.

KABIR, HUMAYUN, ed., *Green and Gold: Stories and Poems from Bengal*, Bombay, Leaders Press, 1958.

KARIM, NAZMUL, *Changing Society in India and Pakistan: A Study in Social Change and Social Stratification*, Dacca, Oxford University Press, 1956.

KIERNAN, V. G., trans., *Poems from Iqbal*, London, John Murray, 1955.

MAJUMDAR, S. C., H. C. RAYCHAUDHURI, and K. DATTA, *An Advanced History of India*, London, Macmillan, 1953.

MARON, STANLEY, ed., *Pakistan: Society and Culture*, Behavior Science Monographs, New Haven, Human Relations Area Files, 1957.

MAYNE, PETER, *The Narrow Smile*, London, John Murray, 1955.

Minorities in Pakistan, Karachi, Pakistan Publications, n.d.

MOON, PENDEREL, *Divide and Quit*, London, Chatto and Windus, 1961.

MORELAND, W. H. and A. C. CHATTERJEE, *A Short History of India*, 2d ed. New York, Longmans, Green, 1945.

MUNIRUZZAMAN, A. N. M., *The Living and Working Conditions of the Students of the Universities and Colleges of Dacca, 1957*, Dacca, Department of Statistics, University of Dacca, 1961.

NETELAND, E. and LEE H. STONER, *Teacher Education in Pakistan*, Bloomington, University of Indiana, 1962.

NIZAMI, MAJID, *The Press in Pakistan*, Lahore, Department of Political Science, University of the Punjab, 1958.

NOORANI, *The Muslim Family Laws Ordinance*, Karachi, Pakistan Publishing House, 1962.

NORTH, LT. COL. R., *Literature of the North-West Frontier of India:*

A Select Bibliography, Peshawar, Superintendent of Government Printing, 1945.

Notification, January 31, 1961 (Decision of the Wage Board for Working Journalists and Schedule of Wages . . .), Ministry of Health, Labour and Social Welfare, Karachi, Government of Pakistan Press, 1961.

Pakistan, *Census of Pakistan 1951*, Vols. 1-8, and *Census Bulletin No. 2 (Population According to Religion)*, Karachi, Government of Pakistan Press, 1951.

————, Ministry of Education, *Report of the Commission on National Education*, Karachi, Government of Pakistan Press, 1961.

————, Ministry of Finance, *Report on Socio-Economic Survey of Korangi, December 1960-January 1961*, Karachi, Government of Pakistan Press, 1961.

————, Ministry of Health and Social Welfare, *Basic Democracy: NDO-BD Integration and Training Programs*, Karachi, West Pakistan Government Press, n.d.

————, Ministry of Home Affairs, *Population Census of Pakistan 1961; Census Bulletin 2: Sex, Urban-Rural, Religion; Census Bulletin 3: Age, Sex and Marital Status; Census Bulletin 4: Literacy and Education*, Karachi, Manager of Publications, 1961-62.

————, Ministry of Law, *Report of the Law Reform Commission 1958-59*, Karachi, Government of Pakistan Press, 1959.

————, Ministry of Law, *The Basic Democracies Order, 1959*, Rawalpindi, Government of Pakistan Press, 1959.

————, Ministry of National Reconstruction and Information, *Municipal Ordinance, 1960*, Karachi, Government of Pakistan Press, 1960.

————, Ministry of National Reconstruction and Information, *Scope and Functions of Basic Democracies and Their Contribution to Development*, Karachi, Government of Pakistan Press, 1961.

The Press and Publications Ordinance, 1960, Ministry of National Reconstruction and Information, Karachi, Government of Pakistan Press, 1960.

Qureshi, Ishtiaq Husain, *The Muslim Community of the Indo-Pakistan Subcontinent*, The Hague, Mouton, 1962.

————, *The Pakistan Way of Life*, New York, Praeger, 1956.

Rawlinson, H. G., *India: A Short Cultural History*, New York, Praeger, 1952.

Report of the Press Commission, March 1959, Karachi, Government of Pakistan Press, 1959.

Sajjad, Husain S., *East Pakistan: A Profile*, Dacca, Orient Longmans, 1962.

Sassani, Abdul Hassan K., *Education in Pakistan*, Washington, U. S.

Department of Health, Education and Welfare, Office of Education, 1954.

A *Select Pakistan Bibliography*, Karachi, Department of Advertising, Films and Publications, 1958.

SHARMA, S. R., *The Crescent in India: A Study in Medieval History*, Bombay, Hind Kitabs, 1954.

SIDDIQI, MUHAMMAD MAZHERUDDIN, *Women in Islam*, Lahore, Institute of Islamic Culture, 1952.

SINGH, IQBAL, *The Ardent Pilgrim: An Introduction to the Life and Work of Mohammed Iqbal*, Calcutta, Orient Longmans, 1951.

SMITH, MARIAN W., "The Misal: A Structural Village Group of India and Pakistan," *American Anthropologist*, 54 (1952), 41-56.

SMITH, WILFRED C., *Islam in Modern History*, New York, New American Library of World Literature, 1959.

—————, *Modern Islam in India and Pakistan*, Lahore, Ripon Printing Press, 1947.

SPAIN, JAMES W., *The Pathan Borderland*, The Hague, Mouton, 1963.

—————, *People of the Khyber: The Pathans of Pakistan*, New York, Praeger, 1963.

SPATE, OSCAR H. K., *India and Pakistan: A General and Regional Geography*, New York, E. P. Dutton, 1954.

SPEAR, PERCIVAL, *India, Pakistan and the West*, New York, Oxford University Press, 1952.

STEPHENS, IAN, *Horned Moon: An Account of a Journey through Pakistan, Kashmir and Afghanistan*, London, Chatto and Windus, 1953.

A *Study of Knowledge of and Attitudes towards Basic Democracies*, Lahore, Government Printing, West Pakistan, 1960.

SUFRIN, SIDNEY C. and SYED A. SARWAR, *The Status of Trade Unions in Pakistan*, Syracuse, Syracuse University Press, 1962.

TITUS, MURRAY T., *Indian Islam*, Bombay, Oxford University Press, 1930.

University of Peshawar, Peshawar, Ferozsons, 1962.

VAHID, S. A., *Introduction to Iqbal*, Karachi, Pakistan Publications, n.d.

WHEELER, ROBERT E. M., *Five Thousand Years of Pakistan*, London, C. Johnson, 1950.

WILLIAMS, L. F. RUSHBROOK, ed., *A Handbook for Travellers in India, Pakistan, Burma and Ceylon*, 1962.

YASIN, MUHAMMAD, *A Social History of Islamic India, 1605-1748*, Lucknow, Upper India Publishing House, 1958.

Section II. Political

ABBOTT, FREELAND K., "The Jama'at-i-Islami of Pakistan," *Middle East Journal*, 11 (1957), 37-51.

AHMAD, COL. MOHAMMAD, *My Chief*, Lahore, Longmans, Green, 1960.

AHMAD, MUSHTAQ, *Government and Politics in Pakistan*, New York, Praeger, 1963.

————, *The United Nations and Pakistan*, Karachi, Pakistan Institute of International Affairs, 1955.

AHMED, N., "China's Himalayan Frontiers: Pakistan's Attitude," *International Affairs, 38* (1962), 478-84.

ALBIRUNI, A. H., *Makers of Pakistan and Modern Muslim India*, Lahore, Ashraf, 1950.

AYUB KHAN, MOHAMMAD, "Essentials of Pakistan's Foreign Policy," *Pakistan Horizon*, Fourth Quarter, 1961.

————, "The Pakistan-American Alliance: Stresses and Strains," *Foreign Affairs, 42* (1964), 195-209.

————, "Pakistan Perspective," *Foreign Affairs, 38* (1960), 548-56.

————, "Strategic Problems of the Middle East," *Asian Review, 54* (1958), 220-28.

Azad Kashmir News, Rawalpindi.

AZIZ, K. K., *Britain and Muslim India: A Study of British Public Opinion vis-à-vis the Development of Muslim Nationalism in India, 1857-1947*, London, Heinemann, 1963.

"The Basic Democracies Order, 1959," *Gazette of Pakistan*, Karachi, October 27, 1959.

BINDER, LEONARD, "Pakistan and Modern Islamic-Nationalist Theory," *Middle East Journal, 11* (1957), 382-96; *12* (1958), 45-56.

————, *Religion and Politics in Pakistan*, Berkeley, University of California Press, 1961.

BIRDWOOD, LORD (CHRISTOPHER B. B.), *A Continent Decides*, London, Robert Hale, 1953.

————, *Two Nations and Kashmir*, London, Robert Hale, 1956.

BLUNT, EDWARD, *The I.C.S.: The Indian Civil Service*, London, Faber and Faber, 1937.

BOLITHO, HECTOR, *Jinnah: Creator of Pakistan*, New York, Macmillan, 1955.

BRAIBANTI, RALPH, *The Civil Service of Pakistan*, Durham, Duke University Press, 1959.

BRECHER, MICHAEL, *The Struggle for Kashmir*, New York, Oxford University Press, 1953.

BROHI, A. K., *An Adventure in Self-Expression*, 2d ed. Karachi, Din Muhammadi Press, 1955.

BROWN, W. NORMAN, *The United States and India and Pakistan*, 2d ed. Cambridge, Harvard University Press, 1963.

CALLARD, KEITH, *Pakistan: A Political Study*, London, Allen and Unwin, 1957.

————, *Pakistan's Foreign Policy: An Interpretation*, 2d ed. New York, Institute of Pacific Relations, 1959.

————, *Political Forces in Pakistan, 1947-1959*, New York, Institute of Pacific Relations, 1959.

CAMPBELL, ROBERT D., *Pakistan: Emerging Democracy*, Princeton, Van Nostrand, 1963.

CHAUDHRI, MOHAMMED ASAN, *Pakistan and the Regional Pacts*, Karachi, East Publications, 1959.

CHOUDHURY, G. W., *Constitutional Development in Pakistan*, New York, Institute of Pacific Relations, 1960.

————, *Democracy in Pakistan*, Dacca, Green Book Company, 1964.

————, "Democracy on Trial in Pakistan," *Middle East Journal*, 17 (1963), 1-13.

———— and PARVEZ HASAN, *Pakistan's External Relations*, Karachi, Pakistan Institute of International Affairs, 1958.

CHOWDHURY, H. H., *Pakistan's Foreign Policy*, Karachi, Ministry of Foreign Affairs, 1956.

The Constitution of the Republic of Pakistan, Karachi, Government of Pakistan Press, 1962.

The Constitution: A Study, Karachi, Bureau of National Reconstruction, n.d. (1962).

DAS GUPTA, JYOTI BHUSAN, *Indo-Pakistan Relations, 1947-1955*, Amsterdam Djambatan, 1958.

FARUQI, ZIYA-UL-HASAN, *The Deoband School and the Demand for Pakistan*, London, Asia Publishing House, 1963.

FELDMAN, HERBERT, *A Constitution for Pakistan*, Karachi, Oxford University Press, 1955.

————, *Pakistan: An Introduction*, London, Oxford University Press, 1960.

FRANCK, DOROTHEA SEELYE, "Pakhtunistan: Disputed Disposition of a Tribal Land," *Middle East Journal*, 6 (1952), 49-68.

GOODNOW, HENRY F., *The Civil Service of Pakistan: Bureaucracy in a New Nation*, New Haven and London, Yale University Press, 1964.

GRIFFITHS, PERCIVAL, *The British Impact on India*, London, Macdonald, 1952.

GUPTA, SISIR K., "Islam as a Factor in Pakistani Foreign Relations," *India Quarterly*, 18 (1962), 230-53.

HARDING, SIR JOHN, "The India and Pakistan Armies of Today," *Asian Review*, 51 (1955), 175-87.

HASAN, K. S., *Pakistan and the United Nations*, New York, Manhattan Publishing Company, 1960.

IQBAL, MUHAMMAD, *Letters of Iqbal to Jinnah*, Lahore, Ashraf, n.d.

————, *Presidential Address: Allahabad Session, Dec. 1930*, Delhi, Muslim League Printing Press, 1945.

JENNINGS, SIR IVOR, *Constitutional Problems in Pakistan*, London, Cambridge University Press, 1957.

Kashmir in Maps, no publisher, n.d.

KHAN, MAJOR-GENERAL FAZAL MUQEEM, *The Story of the Pakistan Army,* Karachi, Oxford University Press, 1963.

KORBEL, JOSEF, *Danger in Kashmir,* Princeton, Princeton University Press, 1954.

LAMBERT, RICHARD D., "Religion, Economics, and Violence in Bengal," *Middle East Journal,* 4 (1950), 307-28.

LEVI, WERNER, "Pakistan, the Soviet Union and China," *Pacific Affairs,* 35 (1962), 211-22.

LUMBY, E. W. R., *The Transfer of Power in India,* London, Allen and Unwin, 1954.

MALIK, HAFEEZ, *Moslem Nationalism in India and Pakistan,* Washington, D.C., Public Affairs Press, 1963.

MARON, STANLEY, "The Problems of East Pakistan," *Pacific Affairs,* 28 (1955), 132-44.

MAUDUDI, ABUL 'ALA, *Islamic Law and Constitution,* ed. and trans. Khurshid Ahmad, Lahore, Islamic Publications, 1960.

MENON, V. P., *The Transfer of Power in India,* Princeton, Princeton University Press, 1957.

NEWMAN, K. J., "The Dyarchic Pattern of Government and Pakistan's Problems," *Political Science Quarterly,* 75 (1960), 94-108.

Pakistan, Ministry of Law, *The Constitution of the Islamic Republic of Pakistan,* Karachi, Government of Pakistan Press, 1956.

"Pakistan and Its Neighbour—Burma," *Pakistan Horizon* (1961), pp. 301-19.

"Pakistan's Relations with the People's Republic of China," *Pakistan Horizon,* No. 3 (1961), pp. 212-32.

PALMER, NORMAN D., "New Directions for Pakistan," *Current History,* 46 (1964), 71-77.

PHILIPS, CYRIL H., *The Evolution of India and Pakistan, 1858 to 1947,* New York, Oxford University Press, 1962.

RAJPUT, A. B., *Muslim League Yesterday and Today,* Lahore, Ashraf, 1948.

Report of the Basic Principles Committee, Karachi, Government of Pakistan Press, 1952.

Report of the Court of Enquiry Constituted under Punjab Act II of 1954 to Enquire into the Punjab Disturbances of 1953, Lahore, Punjab Government Press, 1954.

SAIYID, M. H., *Mohammad Ali Jinnah,* Lahore, Ashraf, 1953.

SARWAR, HASAN K., *Pakistan and the Commonwealth,* Karachi, Pakistan Institute of International Affairs, 1950.

————, *Pakistan and the United Nations,* New York, Manhattan Publishing Company, 1960.

————, *The Strategic Interests of Pakistan,* Karachi, Pakistan Institute of International Affairs, 1954.

SAYEED, KHALID BIN, "Collapse of Parliamentary Democracy in Pakistan," *Middle East Journal, 13* (1959), 389-406.

————, *Pakistan: The Formative Phase,* New York, Institute of Pacific Relations, 1960.

————, "Pakistan's Basic Democracy," *Middle East Journal, 15* (1961), 249-63.

————, "Pakistan's Constitutional Autocracy," *Pacific Affairs, 36* (1963-64), 365-77.

————, "Pakistan's Foreign Policy: An Analysis of Pakistani Fears and Interests," *Asian Survey, 4* (1964), 746-56.

————, "Religion and Nation Building in Pakistan," *Middle East Journal, 17* (1963), 279-91.

"Shamloo," *Speeches and Statements of Iqbal,* Lahore, Pakistan Printing Press, 1948.

SIDDIQI, ASLAM, *Pakistan Seeks Security,* Lahore, Longmans, Green, 1960.

SPAIN, JAMES W., "Pakistan's North West Frontier," *Middle East Journal, 8* (1954), 27-40.

STEPHENS, IAN, *Pakistan,* London, Ernest Benn, 1963.

STREIFF, ERIC, "Pakistan's Border Agreement with Peking," *Swiss Review of World Affairs, 13* (1963), 12-13.

SYMONDS, RICHARD, *The Making of Pakistan,* London, Faber and Faber, 1951.

Ten Years of Pakistan, 1947-1957, Karachi, Pakistan Publications, 1957.

TINKER, HUGH, *India and Pakistan: A Political Analysis,* New York, Praeger, 1962.

Verdict on Kashmir: Being an Account of the Security Council Debate from 21st February to 2nd April 1951, New York, Pakistan Delegation to the Security Council, 1951.

WELTY, PAUL S., "Islam and the Constitution of Pakistan," *World Affairs, 125* (1962), 92-94.

WILCOX, WAYNE A., *Pakistan: The Consolidation of a Nation,* New York, Columbia University Press, 1963.

WILLIAMS, L. F. RUSHBROOK, *The State of Pakistan,* London, Faber and Faber, 1962.

WINT, GUY, *The 1958 Revolution in Pakistan,* St. Anthony's Papers, No. 8, London, Chatto and Windus, 1960.

Section III. Economic

ABBAS, S. A., *An Appraisal of Pakistan's First Five Year Plan,* Rotterdam, Netherlands Economic Institute, 1956.

Agricultural and Animal Resources of East Bengal, 1955, Dacca, Government of East Bengal Press, 1956.

AHMAD, NAFIS, *An Economic Geography of East Pakistan,* London, Oxford University Press, 1958.

AKHTAR, S. M., *Economics of Pakistan*, 2d ed. 2 vols. Lahore, Publishers United, 1955.

ANDRUS, J. RUSSELL and AZIZALI F. MOHAMMED, *The Economy of Pakistan*, Stanford, Stanford University Press, 1958.

Annual Report(s), Karachi, State Bank of Pakistan.

BAKHSH, MALIK KHUDA, *Land Reforms in West Pakistan*, Vol. 1, Lahore, Lion Art Printers, 1960.

DARLING, MALCOLM, *The Punjab Peasant*, London, Oxford University Press, 1946.

DORFMAN, ROBERT, "An Economic Strategy for West Pakistan," *Asian Survey*, 3 (1963), 217-23.

East Pakistan: Visiting the PIDC, Karachi, PIDC Press, n.d. (1962).

Economic Developments in Pakistan 1961, Washington, U.S. Department of Commerce, 1961.

Employees' Welfare in Pakistan, Karachi, Pakistan Institute of Personnel Administration, 1955.

FEI, JOHN C. H., *An Analysis of the Long-Run Prospect of Economic Development in Pakistan*, Karachi, Institute of Development Economics, 1962.

————, et al., *A Study of Planning Methodology with Special Reference to Pakistan's Second Five Year Plan*, Karachi, Institute of Development Economics, 1960.

HUSAIN, A. F. A., et al., *Problems of Economic Reform and Development in Pakistan*, Karachi, Pakistan Institute of International Affairs, 1950.

Investment Climate in Pakistan: Report of the U.S. Department of Commerce, U.S. Investment Development Mission to Pakistan November 6–December 15, 1961, Washington, U.S. Department of Commerce, n.d. (1962?).

ISLAM, DR. NURUL, "Private and Public Enterprises in the Economic Development of Pakistan," *Asian Survey*, Vol. 3, 1963.

JACK, J. C., *The Economic Life of a Bengal District*, Oxford, Oxford University Press, 1916.

KEDDIE, NIKKI R., "Labor in Pakistan," *Journal of Asian Studies, 16* (1954), 575-89.

MEENAI, S. A., *Banking System of Pakistan*, Karachi, State Bank of Pakistan Press, 1964.

Pakistan, Ministry of Economic Affairs, *The First Five Year Plan 1955-60 (Draft)*, Vols. 1 and 2, Karachi, Government of Pakistan Press, 1956.

————, Ministry of Economic Affairs, *Report of the Economic Appraisal Committee*, Vol. 2, Karachi, Government of Pakistan Press, 1953.

————, Ministry of Finance, *Budget of the Central Government for 1962-63*, Karachi, Government of Pakistan Press, 1962.

————, Ministry of Finance, *Economic Survey of Pakistan 1961-62,* Karachi, Government of Pakistan Press, 1962.

————, Ministry of Finance, *Foreign Economic Aid: A Review of Foreign Economic Aid to Pakistan,* Karachi, Government of Pakistan Press, 1962.

————, Ministry of Finance, *Government Sponsored Corporations,* Karachi, Government of Pakistan Press, n.d.

————, Ministry of Finance, *High-Lights of Pakistan's Second Five Year Plan 1960-65,* Karachi, Department of Films and Publications, 1962.

————, Ministry of Finance, *Major Commodities of Pakistan: A Review,* Karachi, Government of Pakistan Press, 1960.

————, Ministry of Finance, *Report on Currency and Finance* (Annual), Karachi, State Bank of Pakistan.

————, Ministry of Finance, *Statistical Pocket-Book of Pakistan 1962,* Karachi, Manager of Publications, 1961.

————, Ministry of Food and Agriculture, *Crop Wealth of Pakistan,* Karachi, Government of Pakistan Press, 1952.

————, Ministry of Food and Agriculture, *Report of the Food and Agriculture Commission,* Karachi, Manager of Publications, 1960.

————, Ministry of Labour, *Report by Sir Malcolm Darling on Labour Conditions in Agriculture in Pakistan,* Karachi, Government of Pakistan Press, n.d. (1955).

————, Planning Commission, *Mid-Plan Review of Progress in 1960/ 61-1961/62 under the Second Five Year Plan,* Karachi, Government of Pakistan Press, 1962.

————, Planning Commission, *The Second Five Year Plan (1960-65), Including Revised Estimates—November 1961,* Karachi, Government of Pakistan Press, n.d.

Pakistan—1959-1960, Karachi, Pakistan Publications, 1960.

Pakistan—1960-1961, Karachi, Pakistan Publications, 1961.

Pakistan Development Review (Quarterly), Karachi, Institute of Development Economics.

Pakistan Statistical Yearbook(s), Karachi, Economic Affairs Division, Central Statistical Office.

PEACH, W. N., M. UZAIR, and G. W. RUCKER, *Basic Data of the Economy of Pakistan,* Karachi, Oxford University Press, 1959.

PITHAWALLA, MANECK B., *The Problem of Baluchistan,* Karachi, Government of Pakistan Press, 1953.

Prosperity through Industry: PIDC in West Pakistan, Karachi, PIDC Press, n.d. (1962).

QURESHI, M. L., ed., *Population Growth and Economic Development with Special Reference to Pakistan,* Karachi, Institute of Development Economics, 1960.

————, *Report on the Seminar on Industrialization and Labour*

Management Relations, Held in Karachi in January 1959, Karachi, Institute of Development Economics, 1959.

RAB, ABDUR, *Acreage, Production and Prices of Major Agricultural Crops of West Pakistan (Punjab): 1931-59*, Karachi, Institute of Development Economics, 1960.

RANIS, GUSTAV, *Industrial Efficiency and Economic Growth: A Case Study of Karachi*, Karachi, Institute of Development Economics, 1961.

Report of the Committee of Experts on the National Accounts of Pakistan, Karachi, Institute of Development Economics, 1962.

Report of the Land Reforms Commission for West Pakistan, January, 1959, Lahore, Government Press, West Pakistan, 1961.

"Report of the Scientific Commission of Pakistan," *Minerva*, 1 (1962), 75-86.

SAHA, K. B., *Economics of Rural Bengal*, Calcutta, Chuckvertty, Chatterjee, 1930.

SHAFI, M., *Labour Policy of the Pakistan Government*, Karachi, Bureau of Labour Publications, 1961.

SIDDIQUI, AKHTAR H., *The Economy of Pakistan: A Select Bibliography, 1947-1962*, Karachi, Institute of Development Economics, 1963.

Statistical Bulletin (Monthly), Karachi, Economic Affairs Division, Central Statistical Office.

VAKIL, C. N., *Economic Consequences of Divided India*, Bombay, Vora, 1950.

WATERSTON, ALBERT, *Planning in Pakistan, Organization and Implementation*, Economic Development Institute, International Bank for Reconstruction and Development, Baltimore, Johns Hopkins Press, 1963.

Index

Index